The Myth of the Imperial Judiciary

The Myth of the Imperial Judiciary

Why the Right Is Wrong about the Courts

Mark Kozlowski

Foreword by Anthony Lewis

A BRENNAN CENTER FOR JUSTICE BOOK

NEW YORK UNIVERSITY PRESS
New York and London

NEW YORK UNIVERSITY PRESS
New York and London

Library of Congress Cataloging-in-Publication Data
Kozlowski, Mark, 1958-
The myth of the imperial judiciary : why the right is wrong
about the courts / Mark Kozlowski.
p. cm.
Includes bibliographical references and index.
ISBN 0-8147-4775-2 (cloth : alk. paper)
1. Justice, Administration of—United States.   2. Courts—
United States.   3. Political questions and judicial power—
United States.   4. Conservatism—United States.
5. United States—Politics and government—1989.   I. Title.
KF8700   .K69   2002
347.73—dc21   2002012771

New York University Press books are printed on acid-free paper,
and their binding materials are chosen for strength and durability.

Manufactured in the United States of America
10 9 8 7 6 5 4 3 2 1

For Janet Kozlowski

With all thy gifts America . . .

. . .

What if one gift thou lackest?

. . .

The gift of perfect women fit for thee—what if that gift
       of gifts thou lackest?

. . .

The mothers fit for thee?

                         —Walt Whitman

Contents

Foreword   ix
Anthony Lewis

Acknowledgments   xv

Introduction: The Ballad of Alexander and Alexis   1

1   The Imperial Judiciary and Its Malcontents   11

2   The Constitution and the Judiciary   51

3   The Judiciary in History   86

4   The Judiciary and the Extent of Rights   117

5   The Judiciary and the Politics of Rights   150

6   The Judiciary and the Polity   177

     Conclusion: Why the Courts   217

     Notes   221

     Index   285

     About the Author   293

Foreword

Anthony Lewis

Political criticism of judges in this country goes back at least as far as Thomas Jefferson, who called federal judges "sappers and miners" working to undermine the constitutional system. (He did not like Chief Justice John Marshall's expansive view of federal power.) From time to time ever since, judges have been political targets. In the 1930s, there was President Franklin Roosevelt's struggle with the "nine old men," as critics called them, who had held some of his New Deal legislation unconstitutional. In the 1950s and 1960s, billboards in the South said "Impeach Earl Warren" because of the Warren Court's decision against racial segregation in public schools.

But I doubt that we have ever had as sustained, as broad, or as intensely ideological an assault on the courts as we have today. The targets include judges at all levels, state and federal. Some of the attacks challenge courts as an institution, their independence, and their function. The assault includes verbal brickbats of all kinds and more than words: restrictive legislation, threats of impeachment, and refusal to confirm judicial nominees.

The tone of the attacks is strident. Judges are denounced as "totalitarians" who "threaten to undermine our nation's moral fabric." That last phrase came from Steve Forbes, the sometime candidate for the Republican presidential nomination, who used it in condemning an abortion decision of the Arizona Supreme Court. The theme of judicially imposed moral decay is often sounded. It is central in the denunciatory works of Robert Bork, former law professor, judge, and failed Supreme Court nominee. "American courts," Judge Bork wrote, "enforcing liberal relativism, are leading the parade to Gomorrah."

The assault on the courts comes mainly from the ideological right. Its code word for judges it condemns is "activist." That is a slippery word, hard to define with any firm content. It suggests judges who disregard precedent and read their own predilections into the law. Conservative judges may have those characteristics; the series of 5-4 decisions by the Supreme Court that gave the states sovereign immunity from lawsuits seeking to enforce federal statutes were breaks from precedent with little or no basis in the text of the Constitution. Then there was the 5-4 decision in *Bush v. Gore*, which awarded the presidency to George W. Bush in the teeth of the Constitution's explicit designation of Congress as the body to resolve presidential election disputes. But the right-wing critics do not denounce those decisions as "activist." They use the word for judges, and decisions, that expand the rights of individuals under the Constitution: the protections of criminal suspects, for example, and the right to be free of state-imposed religious expression.

The attackers sound as if only today's judges were, in their view, unduly bold; in the past, judges meekly ratified whatever politicians decided. Mark Kozlowski shows in this book that that proposition is a travesty of history. From the beginning, indeed even before the adoption of the Constitution and the formation of the Union, American judges have acted forcefully to give meaning to constitutional promises.

In 1780, John Adams drafted a constitution for Massachusetts, then a colony in rebellion, and the people adopted it. The case of Quock Walker, a Massachusetts slave, arose three years later. At the age of twenty-eight, he ran away, claiming that he had been promised his freedom at twenty-five. His owner, Nathaniel Jennison, found him, beat him, and brought him back. Jennison was prosecuted for assault and battery. His defense was that slavery was well established in Massachusetts and that he had every right to seize and punish a runaway. But the new constitution, as Chief Justice William Cushing wrote in his notes on the case, "sets off with declaring that all men are born free and equal and that every subject is entitled to liberty."

The constitution's talk of freedom and equality might have been regarded as merely a statement of ideals, not rules to be enforced by judges. But Jennison's lawyers evidently did not make the argument, a sign that constitutionalism had already seized the American imagination, at least in Massachusetts. What the lawyers argued was that, as Chief Justice Cushing noted, "rights to slaves, as property acquired by law, ought not be divested by any construction of the constitution by implication; and that slavery in that instrument is not expressly abolished." But the Chief Justice disagreed.

"Slavery," Cushing wrote, "is in my judgment as effectively abolished as it can be by the granting of rights and privileges wholly incompatible and

repugnant to its existence. . . . Perpetual servitude can no longer be toler-
ated in our government." So, twenty years before Chief Justice Marshall's
decision in *Marbury v. Madison*, the Massachusetts court enforced a constitution as binding law. The court was not deterred by the fact that the
text did not expressly abolish slavery. It did not, as conservatives today insist must be done, examine the intention of the constitution's framers. By
the light of today's conservative judicial critics, Chief Justice Cushing and
his colleagues were "activists"—which shows what an ahistorical position
those critics have.

The framers of the federal Constitution expected judges to enforce its
terms. They were worried about abuse of power by the legislative branch,
which could be effectively constrained, Alexander Hamilton wrote in *The
Federalist*, "in no other way than through the medium of courts of justice."
And the Supreme Court of the United State was not shy, from the earliest
days, about making bold decisions. Think of *Gibbons v. Ogden*, decided in
1824. New York and New Jersey were vying for control of trips by the recently invented steamboat on the Hudson River. The Supreme Court held
that the state laws were invalid because they were in conflict with the Constitution's clause that gave Congress the power to legislate on interstate
commerce—even though Congress had not passed a directly relevant
statute.

The Supreme Court was never shy. Nor were other courts. The history
traced by Mark Kozlowski is utterly compelling. There is nothing new
about judges creatively adapting the language of the Constitution so as to
apply its values to new situations. The Court has never subscribed to the
notion that it should be bound by a narrow, literalist view of the intention
of the framers—if that intention could ever be identified with any certainty. Chief Justice Charles Evans Hughes wrote:

> If by the statement that what the Constitution meant at the time of its
> adoption it means today it is intended to say that the great clauses of the
> Constitution must be confined to the interpretation which the framers,
> with the condition and outlook of their time, would have placed upon
> them, the statement carries its own refutation.

Of course, some judges are readier than others to make bold decisions, to
interpret the Constitution in fresh ways. But that is not a characteristic of
judges with only one outlook. The decisions that are generally regarded as
having strayed too radically from the proper judicial role were the

Supreme Court cases of the first third of the twentieth century that held state and federal economic regulation unconstitutional. That course of decision seemed finally to have ended in 1937, but the recent cases that have held parts of the federal gun statute and the Violence against Women Act unconstitutional as intrusions on state power indicate that reports of the old doctrine's death may have been exaggerated.

In the end, whether a judge has overstepped his or her role into "activism," whatever that is, depends on the onlooker's view of the outcome of the case. If a critic disagrees with the decision, it is "activist"; if he approves, it is a piece of judicial statesmanship.

Nor are judges consistent. Justice Felix Frankfurter, of the Supreme Court, used to preach the values of self-restraint. But when some official offended his deepest values—his "can't helps," as Justice Oliver Wendell Holmes Jr. called them—he did not hesitate to be bold. He was readier than most of his colleagues to find that state action amounted to an establishment of religion in violation of the First Amendment. And, when a New Hampshire investigation of communism demanded that a professor at the University of New Hampshire answer questions, former professor Frankfurter boldly read into the free speech clause of the First Amendment a protection of academic freedom. His opinion in *Sweezy v. New Hampshire* remains a beacon for harried professors and universities.

The earliest use of the word "activist" that I found was in Justice Robert H. Jackson's book *The Supreme Court in the American System of Government*, published posthumously in 1955. Justice Jackson had been quarreling with Justice Hugo L. Black, the boldest modern exponent of such rights as free speech and equal voting weight in legislative districts.

Perhaps that quarrel was in his mind when he wrote, in a book otherwise devoid of such attacks:

> A cult of libertarian/judicial activists now assails the Court almost as bitterly for renouncing power as earlier "liberals" once did for assuming too much power. This cult appears to believe that the Court can find in a 4,000-word eighteenth-century document or its nineteenth-century Amendments, or can plausibly supply, some clear bulwark against all dangers and evils that beset us internally.

Yet the same Justice Jackson had used his rhetorical gifts in one of the Court's groundbreaking free speech decisions. During World War II, public school pupils in some states were required to salute the flag daily. To Jehovah's Witnesses, that involved a forbidden act: bowing to a graven image. When their children in West Virginia refused to carry out the flag salute, they were threatened with expulsion. Justice Jackson, writing for the Supreme Court, found that the children were protected by the First Amendment. "If there is any fixed star in our constitutional constellation," he memorably said, "it is that no official, high or petty, can prescribe what shall be orthodox in politics, nationalism, religion, or other matters of opinion or force citizens to confess by word or act their faith therein."

Those who assail judges nowadays with such adjectives as "imperial" sometimes earnestly ask courts to use their constitutional sword. The New Jersey legislature passed a law forbidding discrimination on account of "sexual orientation." When it was applied to find unlawful the Boy Scouts' dismissal of a gay troop leader and the state supreme court upheld that ruling, a critic denounced the judges as "elite nihilists." What they actually were was judges, performing the judicial duty of deciding whether the state law violated the Boy Scouts' right under the First Amendment to determine their own message. The critics wanted the state court to hold the law unconstitutional—as the Supreme Court of the United States eventually did, by a vote of 5-4. The critic might ordinarily have attacked the use of judicial power to strike down a democratic political decision, but not in this case. What she cared about—what she detested—was protection of gay Americans from discrimination.

The great power of American judges to interpret and enforce the Constitution has certainly been misused on occasion. Think of the *Dred Scott* decision of the Supreme Court in 1857, which held that blacks could not be American citizens; the decision helped to bring on, and was effectively overruled by, the Civil War. Or think of *Plessy v. Ferguson*, the 1896 decision that found racial segregation constitutional.

But, over history, the constitutional role of our courts has surely been beneficent. Without the Supreme Court's increasingly enlightened interpretation of "the freedom of speech" promised by the First Amendment, for example, we would surely not be the kind of country we are today: open, disputational, and free. Since World War II, many democratic countries have copied the American model of constitutionalism, giving their courts the power to protect individual rights against political abuse. Among them are France, Germany, South Africa, Israel, Canada, India, and, now, Britain. The reason was pungently stated by the president of the Supreme Court of Israel, Aharon Barak. "One of the lessons of the Second World War and the Holocaust," Justice Barak said, "is that it is vital to place formal limits in the power of the majority. The concept that 'It is not done' needs to receive the formal expression, 'It is forbidden.'"

It would be a distressing irony if this country were to weaken the protective power of judges just as other countries are copying the American model. That is why the current assault on the courts is so dangerous. Congress has already stripped the courts of power to review certain decisions that profoundly affect individuals—immigrants, for one. Far-right leaders have called for impeachment of judges whose decisions they dislike. A Senate under Republican control blocked many of President Clinton's judicial nominations at the behest of conservative groups. (Democrats, in payback mood, then delayed action on some Bush nominees.) In states where judges are elected—which includes most states—powerful conservative interests are giving huge sums to judicial campaigns.

The assault on the courts has proceeded under a cloak of history: the assertion that judges have historically played only a submissive part in our political structure and that anything more than that is illegitimate. It is false history, designed to weaken an institutional that the founders of this country intended to be one of three coequal branches of government. That is why this is an important book.

Acknowledgments

I would not have had the opportunity to undertake this project were it not for the support of three institutions. The Brennan Center for Justice at New York University School of Law provided me with a supportive environment in which to write the book and indulgently allowed me to expend a great deal of time in order to complete it. Two foundations—The Open Society Institute and the Deer Creek Foundation—graciously funded the Center's Judicial Independence Project so that the book could be written.

All current and former staff members of the Brennan Center have contributed in some way to this project. But I must single out Deborah Goldberg, Deputy Director of the Democracy Program, under whose supervision I worked while I wrote the book. I am extremely grateful for her encouragement, insight, and patience. In addition, several of the Brennan Center's Research Associates—Tatiana Martins, Praveen Krishna, Daniel Seltz, and Luke McLoughlin—were constantly helpful. All of them are now attending law school, and I confidently predict that each of them will be a credit to the profession.

My book agent, Joe Spieler, and my editor at NYU Press, Jennifer Hammer, both deserve great thanks, as do a number of readers of the manuscript, especially my friend Robert Amdur.

But my greatest debt is to my family—my late father Arthur Kozlowski, David, Jackie, Michael, Peter, Jia Hui, Mei Jie, Thomas, Steven, Barbara, David, Daniel, William, and Robert—which has supported me in ways beyond counting. This list does not include my mother, Janet Kozlowski. She must be set apart on account of her decades of sacrifice and labor on behalf of all her children. This book is dedicated to her with love and gratitude.

Introduction

The Ballad of Alexander and Alexis

The aftermath of the 2000 presidential election was extraordinary by any measure. In the wake of the inability of Florida's electoral technology to record or count votes accurately, the nation was subjected to several weeks' worth of courtroom and public relations combat conducted at a fever pitch. Any number of commentators began using terms, such as "putsch" and "coup d'etat," that are not often introduced in American political discourse.

One subgenus of all the postelection commentary was particularly striking. Even as they hewed to the primary task of elevating the Texas governor to the Oval Office, a number of conservatives took the time to direct fire at a longstanding enemy, the American judiciary. Specifically, the role played by the courts in resolving the election conflict brought forth a wave of right-wing revulsion. While praising the U.S. Supreme Court for the substance of its actions reversing the prorecount rulings of the Supreme Court of Florida, conservative writers expressed real alarm that courts were deciding the conflict at all.

Especially insistent here was William Kristol, the editor of the *Weekly Standard*. Writing in the *New York Times* three weeks after Election Day, Kristol set forth the basic lament:

> So, four decades of judicial activism, at both the state and federal levels, mostly unchallenged by the other branches of government, culminates in this: judges may now select the next president of the United States. . . .
>
> Commentators, liberal and conservative, have both largely agreed with the politicians. In their view, only the courts, especially the United States Supreme Court, have the political legitimacy to resolve the struggle over the presidency.

They are wrong. Now is the time to rethink decades of judicial activism, which has undermined the rule of law and enfeebled self-government.[1]

Two weeks later, in the *Washington Post,* Kristol announced what would be the reaction of "some of us" to a Gore victory based upon vote recounts ordered by the Florida Supreme Court:

> Some of us will not believe that Gore has acceded to the presidency legitimately. Still, if he does, he will receive our best wishes upon assuming the burdens of office. We will support his policies when we think they are right for the country. We will pay proper respect to the office of the presidency. We will hope (some will pray) that Al Gore's presidency proves a success, and that it leaves the United States of America a stronger and better nation.
>
> But the action of the Florida court is not constitutionally defensible, and some of us will therefore continue to insist that he gained office through an act of judicial usurpation. We will not "move on." Indeed, we will work for the next four years to correct this affront to our constitutional order. This does not mean simply—indeed it does not mean primarily—defeating Al Gore in 2004. It means defeating the understanding of the rule of law, the role of the courts, and the meaning of the Constitution that are embodied by this decision.[2]

In sum, as Kristol and a coauthor put it in the *Weekly Standard,* "the way in which Al Gore is trying to steal the election is exactly the way modern liberalism has tried to hijack the American people's ability to govern themselves."[3] In this view, to criticize the decisions of the Florida Supreme Court and to stop at that is to miss a vast forest for a single tree, albeit a redwood. This is precisely the point of Ramesh Ponnuru, writing in the *National Review:*

> Few court rulings have been denounced as swiftly or as harshly as the Florida supreme court's decision on the night of November 21....
>
> These criticisms were correct: the Florida court did exceed its lawful powers, with astonishing inventiveness, in a case where the political stakes could hardly be higher. But the court's many defenders had a good point, too, when they said that the justices had not departed from widely accepted legal norms. The difference between their activism and the every-

day activism of the courts is one of degree only. Yes, the decision is a scandal. But so is the legal culture of which it is a piece. If the decision has any salutary effect, it will be to draw attention to that culture's pathologies.[4]

Similarly, George F. Will wrote that the postelection debacle "will be partly redeemed if it brings to a roiling boil a new chapter in America's political argument":

> Until now, the central question in that argument has been: How much government do we want? For some while—at least since the New Deal—the basic answer has been clear: lots of it. But now that question about the quantity of government should be supplanted at the center of political discourse by this question: What should be the principal source of government—the judiciary or the political branches?

Court-bashing conservatives faced a bit of a dilemma when the U.S. Supreme Court finally put an end to the matter by declaring George W. Bush the winner in Florida. How was one to celebrate this marvelous result issuing from the wrong quarter? A number of commentators decided to savor the delicious irony of liberals tearing into the Court for its decision. Here is Paul Gigot, of the *Wall Street Journal*:

> How remarkable to have liberals join the judge-bashing club. For years conservatives have wailed as courts jumped into political disputes to create law out of "penumbras" and "emanations."
> But having turned the Supreme Court into a superlegislature, the left is now horrified to see what it's created. The same folks who invited the courts to settle this year's presidential election are now stumped that the Supreme Court took them up on the offer.[5]

The syndicated columnist Maggie Gallagher took an even more acid tack:

> Liberals aren't used to this. For the last fifty years, the courts have been their personal secret weapon. Again and again, conservatives arduously use the democratic process to gain legislative victories—only to see the Supreme Court rummage around in that black bag they call our constitutional values and pull out a trump card for the liberal view. . . .
> If Democrats want to threaten the moral authority of the Supreme Court—the very authority they depend on for forcing the rest of us to

accept abortion on demand, gay marriage and a rewriting of our backward (read: Judeo-Christian) ideas of sexual virtue—I say let 'em.[6]

Soon after George W. Bush had settled into the White House, the aim of conservative commentators was not to bring any new chapter of America's political argument to a boil but to ensure that the new president's federal judicial nominees received Senate confirmation. But success in this task was viewed as being of the greatest importance to the republic because, it was argued, the only hope of countering unchecked judicial power was to staff the federal bench with as many judges as possible who eschew the exercise of such power. As the *Wall Street Journal*'s Tunku Varadarajan put it shortly after Bush announced his first batch of judicial nominees, "[b]ig government vs. small government pales in comparison with big courts vs. small courts" because in the wake of "the ascent of courts . . . the rule of law has died an ugly death."[7] Some months later, the Cato Institute's Roger Pilon issued almost the same warning with respect to winning judicial confirmation battles: "Do we want to restore limited constitutional government and, let's be clear, the rule of law? Those are the stakes in the current debate."[8] Finally, after a year during which conservatives protested endlessly about the purportedly slow pace at which Bush's judicial nominees were being confirmed by the Democratic-controlled Senate, Robert Bork declared that "[t]he political struggle for control of the courts has become open and savage precisely because it is a major part of the war in our culture, a battle for dominance between opposed moral visions of our future."[9]

The criticism leveled at the American judiciary by conservatives over the course of the past three decades, of which the grenades lobbed at the Florida Supreme Court are only the latest expression, is of a qualitatively different sort than the typical liberal objection to a case, or class of cases, decided by the Rehnquist Court.

The conservative attack on the Florida Supreme Court, for example, went well beyond the assertion that the judges involved reached mistaken results, or even that the judges were personally incompetent. Rather, the tenor of these critiques was that the particular decisions at issue are indicative of the state of the contemporary American judiciary as a whole. They were taken to be illustrative of a judiciary whose self-aggrandizing tendencies have resulted in courts that now possess powers far beyond those that they should properly wield in a democratic polity. Indeed, their powers are asserted to have grown so great that they may perhaps have become unrestrainable and may therefore threaten the very existence of democracy itself. Thus, Max Boot, of the *Wall Street Journal*, in a passage that is wholly typical of this line of argument, asserted, in his 1998 book devoted to court-bashing, that this is what we have come to:

> America used to be a democracy, a government of, by, and for the people. Now it has all the earmarks of a *juristocracy*, a government of, by, and for people who have attended law school. Judges have assumed unprecedented authority over our lives, usurping the powers once delegated to elected lawmakers, based on no solid grounding in the text of either a statute or the Constitution itself.[10]

Under this analysis, even the act of petitioning courts for relief becomes an affront to democracy. Thus, David Frum excoriates lawyers who conduct death penalty appeals for "regard[ing their] tactics as legitimate" in the face of majoritarian support for death penalty legislation. Such alleged arrogance has resulted in "[t]he spectacle of lawyers and judges tying up capital cases in never-ending procedural review" in utter disregard of popular will.[11] Or, as put more succinctly by the conservative columnist Don Feder, the purported alliance between the "judicial activists and liberal litigators" leads inescapably to the conclusion that "liberals hate democracy."[12]

It is now routinely argued on the right that judges are willfully writing their policy preferences into law, that, as Robert Bork has asserted darkly with respect to the U.S. Supreme Court, "[t]he Justices know full well what they are doing. . . . [They] have decided to rule us without any warrant in law."[13] Specifically, the judiciary is said to be engaged in the imposition by fiat of a comprehensive vision of a social order that judges prefer. In the words of University of Texas law professor Lino Graglia, the courts for decades now "have almost uniformly served to advance the political agenda of those on the far left of the American political spectrum."[14]

The purpose of this book is to explore the American right's attack upon the courts, which I shall henceforth refer to as "the Imperial Judiciary thesis." I believe this term expresses perfectly the essence of the argument being made by right-wing critics of judicial power. The American judiciary is said to have strayed so far from its intended powers and functions that it has become unmoored from the values of a democratic order. It may therefore be said to have become "imperial"—that is, monarchical—and to have also become imperialist in the sense that its self-aggrandizing tendencies have resulted in its having usurped powers and functions that are properly exercised by other political institutions, especially legislatures peopled with elected representatives.

By way of introduction, it may be helpful to consider briefly what right-wing commentators believe the power of the American judiciary was intended to be. Conveniently, this too may be summed up effectively in a phrase, which is taken from Alexander Hamilton's discussion, in number 78 of *The Federalist*, of the relative strengths of the three branches of republican government—the legislative, the executive, and the judicial:

> Whoever attentively considers the different departments of power must perceive that, in a government in which they are separated from each other, the judiciary, from the nature of its functions, will always be the least dangerous to the political rights of the Constitution; because it will be least in a capacity to annoy or injure them. The executive not only dispenses the honors but holds the sword of the community. The legislature not only commands the purse but prescribes the rules by which the duties and rights of every citizen are to be regulated. The judiciary, on the contrary, has no influence over either the sword or the purse; no direction either of the strength or of the wealth of the society, and can take no active resolution whatever. It may truly be said to have neither FORCE nor WILL but merely judgment; and must ultimately depend upon the aid of the executive arm even for the efficacy of its judgment.[15]

Spend any amount of time among the writings of contemporary right-wing critics of judicial power, and you are virtually assured of seeing repeated application of the phrase "least dangerous branch," or some close variant, to the judiciary.[16] The phrase has come to be taken as the definitive statement of the original intent of the Founding Fathers with respect to judicial power. In short, it is taken to mean that they wanted judicial power to be slight, intermittent, and peripheral to the main arena of democratic politics. The phrase is therefore invoked ubiquitously by conservative commentators in order to establish how far the contemporary judiciary has corrupted that vision.

Consider some examples. Here is the historian Forrest McDonald in his influential study of the making of the U.S. Constitution:

Hamilton observed, in *Federalist* number 78, that of the three branches, the "judiciary, from the nature of its functions, will always be the least dangerous to the political rights of the Constitution." This was true in the eighteenth century; and it was true of the Constitution as it was written. The framers could not have foreseen the development of judicial activism a century later.[17]

A variation on this theme, one that expresses nicely the conservative conviction that liberal academics have vast influence in our politics, is asserted by George F. Will. Although offering no factual support for his perspective on judicial illegitimacy, Will writes with complete assuredness as follows:

Alexander Hamilton considered [the judiciary] the "least dangerous" branch because it supposedly is the least responsive to opinion. But it has become the most dangerous, in part because it is the most susceptible to gusts of opinion. . . .

But the judiciary is even more blown about by opinion that is more volatile, and often less sober, than the opinion of the public—that of the intelligentsia. Change the academic culture of six law schools—Harvard, Yale, Columbia, Michigan, Chicago, Stanford—and the intellectual content of the judiciary will follow, quickly.[18]

Conservative politicians display no trace of doubt when proclaiming how far the judiciary has come from its intended function. Here is an excerpt from a speech delivered in March 1997 by then Republican Senator John Ashcroft of Missouri—now Attorney General of the United States—to the Conservative Political Action Committee:

Over the last half-century, the federal courts have usurped from school boards the power to determine what a child can learn, and removed from the legislatures the ability to establish equality under the law. The courts have made liars of Hamilton and Madison, confirming our forefathers' worst fears—for what the framers intended to be the weakest branch of government has become the most powerful.[19]

Not surprisingly, calls by conservative politicians to rein in a supposedly imperial judiciary are invariably presented as effecting a *restoration* of the proper balance of forces among the branches of government, that is, putting the judiciary back in its place as the least dangerous branch. Curiously, these plans tend to involve undermining the institutional characteristics that made the judiciary a distinct branch of government in the first place. Here, for example, are the views of Representative Bob Barr, of Georgia, expressed in hearings on judicial misconduct and discipline held in 1997 by the House Judiciary Committee:

> It is time to begin exploring how and in what way we might take steps to "re-balance" and restore integrity to our federal judicial system. . . . There are, as with other problems confronting our institutions, a number of ways that the problems of judicial activism, or overreaching, can be addressed: defining "good behavior"; limiting tenure of judges; limitations on the jurisdiction of judges; and impeachment.[20]

The phrase "least dangerous branch" has now achieved a talismanic power among right-wing critics of the judiciary. But these critics rarely, if ever, refer to another declaration about judicial power in the American polity that has also achieved a kind of canonical status. It comes from Alexis de Tocqueville's *Democracy in America*. Surveying the polity of Jacksonian America, Tocqueville made the following observation about its ubiquitously legalistic character: "There is hardly a political question in the United States which does not sooner or later turn into a judicial one."[21]

Thus, even as he noted that the American federal and state constitutions uniformly established substantial formal limits upon judicial power, such as the rule that judges cannot enact laws but must limit themselves to deciding lawsuits that arise from laws enacted by the popular branches of government, Tocqueville declared that judges in America were "invested with immense political power."[22] It was therefore his view, as the late Judith Shklar has written, that "American political culture is radically legalistic and focused on the courts."[23]

Here we encounter a paradox of our own. For the perspectives of Hamilton and Tocqueville to which we have alluded appear to contradict each other. How can the judiciary be thought of as the "least dangerous" branch of government if there "is hardly a political question" that does not make its way to the courts, where judges wield "immense political power"? Can it be that judicial power had grown so vast by the time Tocqueville was writing *Democracy in America*, some fifty years after Hamilton collaborated in the composition of *The Federalist,* that Hamilton's supposed vision of a marginal judiciary was already obsolete? After all, as the Yale law professor Grant Gilmore has asserted, "[f]rom the beginning our courts, both state and federal, seem to have been willing to answer any conceivable question which any conceivable litigant might choose to ask."[24] And it remains the case today that "[t]here is almost no legal or political issue that is unlikely to come before a judge of an American court, state or federal, of general jurisdiction."[25]

I argue in this book that, properly understood, the declarations of Hamilton and Tocqueville regarding judicial power in America are not really in contradiction. Here is what I hope to do in the six chapters that follow:

- Investigate the claims of the Imperial Judiciary thesis; the nature of the evils that are said to flow from a judiciary whose power has become illegitimately vast and the proposed cures for reining it in;
- Consider the intent of Hamilton and his fellow framers with respect to the judiciary established by the Constitution, with the hope of demonstrating that "least dangerous" was not meant to be synonymous with "insignificant" or "marginal";
- Establish not only that Tocqueville was correct at the time he wrote but also that there has never been a time in our nation's politics when judicial power has in fact been insignificant or marginal with respect to many of the most pressing issues of the day;
- Argue that the Imperial Judiciary thesis, which rails against the judicial expansion of rights, largely fails to appreciate that the boldest judicial expansions of rights in recent decades have not favored liberals but have enhanced the quality of the polity at large and that the judicial expansion of the rights of groups liberals are thought to believe are within their special care—the poor and criminal defendants—was not so expansive as is generally believed and has been subject to substantial contraction;
- Consider the efficacy of the Imperial Judiciary thesis as it applies to (1) *Roe v. Wade,* the decision that the thesis most deplores and (2) the judicial treatment of the role of money in politics, which conservatives generally applaud; and
- Detail the quite vast powers that have been conferred upon American courts in recent decades by the elected representatives of the people, who yet maintain a range of means to contract judicial power.

I should also say a word about what I do not intend to do. I will generally avoid stating my opinions regarding the correctness of particular judicial decisions (although there will be times when I will be unable to restrain myself in this regard). I do not intend to advocate that American courts pursue any particular jurisprudential course. Most especially, even as I attack the Imperial Judiciary thesis, I am not engaged in an effort to rouse liberal support for the defense of an independent judiciary by proving that the courts have been "good" for liberals. Rather, I will attempt to make a *realistic* appraisal of the power of the American judiciary as a means of showing that conservatives have a highly *unrealistic* conception of this power. In the end, I hope that I will have done something to convince Americans who, regardless of their other ideological commitments, are committed to the well-being of our democratic polity that, even as they disagree with particular judicial decisions, the institution of an independent judiciary is something to be defended from unwarranted attack.[26]

1

The Imperial Judiciary
and Its Malcontents

Prologue: Strange Bedfellows

Mark Tushnet is a well-known professor of constitutional law at Georgetown University. In 1998, he published an article in the venerable democratic socialist quarterly *Dissent* entitled "Is Judicial Review Good for the Left?" He began by expressing puzzlement that "[m]any liberals have warm and fuzzy feelings about judicial review," the power according to which courts may declare statutes to be unconstitutional and void.[1] Such feelings, he asserted, were quite unwarranted:

> Looking at judicial review over the course of U.S. history, we see that the courts have regularly been more or less in line with what the dominant national political coalition wants. Sometimes the courts deviate a bit, occasionally leading to better political outcomes and occasionally leading to worse ones. Adapting a metaphor from electrical engineering, we can say that judicial review amounts to noise around zero. It offers essentially random changes, sometimes good and sometimes bad, to what the political system produces.[2]

This is a conclusion guaranteed to dampen warm and fuzzy feelings: the courts follow the election returns, and the election returns certainly do not always follow the liberals. Yet, Tushnet ends his article with this intriguing speculation:

> Things would be different, of course, if we had better judges. But we'll get better judges only if we have better politics. And if we have better politics, we might not need better judges.[3]

Tushnet then spent some time pondering how to construct a "better politics." In 1999, he published the fruit of his ruminations, the title of which sets forth his program: *Taking the Constitution Away from the Courts*. Why does Tushnet wish to take the Constitution away from the courts? Because if we replace conventional judicial review with "populist constitutional law," which will "distribute responsibility for constitutional law broadly" throughout the polity, great bounty for the left will ensue.[4]

Tushnet has warm feelings for populist constitutional law, but he is more than a little fuzzy as to what exactly it is and how it will operate. It will, he says, allow "the public" to "participate in shaping constitutional law more directly and openly."[5] How? By employing "discussions among the people in the ordinary political forums."[6] This will be "a self-creating activity in which the people of the United States daily decide whether to continue to pursue the course we have been pursuing."[7] As Oscar Wilde said of socialism, populist constitutional law is clearly going to take a lot of evenings.

To put it mildly, this is something less than a comprehensive operational plan. But I'm not sure that the details matter all that much to Tushnet. What clearly does matter is that populist constitutional law holds forth the prospect of ending the agony of the American left. Specifically, "[f]reed of concerns about judicial review, we [may] be able to develop a more robust understanding of constitutional welfare rights, which are recognized in many constitutions throughout the world."[8] Thus, the result may be to remedy "[o]ur economy's failure to satisfy the basic needs of many people."[9] In other words, populist constitutional law may bring European social democracy to our shores.

Lino Graglia is a law professor at the University of Texas. I am quite sure he would not quarrel with being characterized as one of the most conservative legal academics in the United States. One would think he wouldn't have a good word to say about the likes of Professor Tushnet, a man whom he describes in a 1999 letter to the journal *Commentary* as "a self-described Marxist."[10]

But, in the same letter, Graglia goes on to laud Tushnet as "an exceptionally able, independent, and original thinker." And, even as he realizes that Tushnet's book is rooted in dissatisfaction with the fact that the Supreme Court "can no longer be relied on to enact a left-liberal agenda," Graglia contends that *Taking the Constitution Away from the Courts* is "an extremely valuable contribution to the cause of limiting judicial power." And that cause, says Graglia, is a noble one. It is the Supreme Court, after all, "that has deprived the states of the power to restrict abortion, provide for prayer in schools, aid religious schools, limit the distribution of pornography, assign students to neighborhood schools, maintain an effective criminal procedure, prohibit flag-burning, and so on endlessly." Thus, in the spirit that posits that the enemy of my enemy is my friend, Graglia concludes that something like Tushnet's populist constitutional law might be just what the doctor ordered for the right: "The abolition of judicial review, returning decision making on basic social policy issues to the people of each state, would be the single most important step we could take to return the country to political and social health."[11]

It is not every day that one sees such jurisprudential concord between Thurgood Marshall's admiring biographer and a man who in 1979 urged public officials in Texas to declare that federal court orders mandating busing for the purpose of school desegregation should not be enforced.[12] But their detente is not an occasion for celebration. For starters, the framers of the U.S. Constitution would likely have looked upon a scheme like populist constitutional law with some unease. In *The Federalist*, James Madison spoke of "[t]he danger of disturbing the public tranquillity" that would be occasioned by "a frequent reference of constitutional questions to the decision of the whole society."[13] One senses that Madison would not rush to embrace Tushnet's daily "self-creating activity."

This aside, however, it is clear that the Tushnet-Graglia accord is indicative of a deep antipathy to the judiciary, one that is not exclusive to one side of the political spectrum. Nevertheless I think that, if one excludes members of the hard left, to whom the entire American constitutional order is without legitimacy, the percentage of the left that would share Tushnet's views with any enthusiasm is not high. It would at least not be high after the implications of "populist constitutional law" were considered soberly and the dissonance between populism and the constitutional imperative to protect the rights of minorities came to mind. On the other hand, as I have tried to establish in the Introduction, Graglia-like views are a fixture of the contemporary American right. Why is this?

"Something Was Supposed to Happen, and Didn't"

The Chief Justiceship of Earl Warren lasted from 1953 until 1969. There is near-universal agreement that the Supreme Court under Warren's leadership effected a jurisprudential revolution in American political life. It is therefore entirely appropriate that Lucas Powe begins his history of the Court under Chief Justice Warren with the following declaration: "The Warren Court created the image of the Supreme Court as a revolutionary body, a powerful force for social change."[14] One of the Warren Court's admirers has summarized the nature of its revolution:

> The Warren Court was the first and, so far, the only Court in American history that empathized with the outsider. . . . The Warren Court was the first Court in American history that really identified with those who are down and out—the people who received a raw deal, those who are outsiders, the marginal, the stigmatized. It was the first sympathetic treatment that blacks received from the Supreme Court. . . . Moreover, not only blacks but other minorities—religious minorities, political dissenters, illegitimates, poor people, prisoners and accused criminals—received sympathetic treatment.[15]

As revolutions tend to do, however, the Warren Court generated no shortage of critics and enemies. It, of course, won the hatred of segregationists because of *Brown v. Board of Education* and subsequent decisions that sought to eliminate de jure racial discrimination. The Court's (less than consistent) defense of the civil liberties of American Communists caused Senator McCarthy himself to charge that Justice William Brennan "harbors an underlying hostility to congressional attempts to investigate and expose the Communist conspiracy."[16] Richard Nixon, capitalizing on public fears regarding rising crime and social unrest, made opposition to the Warren Court a centerpiece of his successful 1968 presidential campaign. In a typical blast at the Court, one we now read with grim irony in light of the record of the Nixon White House, he accused it of going "too far in weakening the peace forces as against the criminal forces in this country."[17]

The Warren Court was also not exempt from the vigorous criticism of legal academics. One of the Court's most powerful conservative critics was the late Philip Kurland, a constitutional law scholar at the University of Chicago. In a series of lectures delivered in 1969, Kurland decried the sheer number of precedents that had been overruled by the Court under Warren. As a result, he argued, "a very large number of constitutional landmarks that once were the law of the land were made into artifacts for the study of historians."[18] This disregard for stare decisis—the rule of adherence to precedent—plus what Kurland saw as the Court's casual attitude toward explaining the constitutional reasoning for its decisions, had wrought a serious diminution of public respect for the Court:

> The Warren Court accepted with a vengeance the task of protector of the individual against government and of minorities against the tyranny of majorities. But it has failed abysmally to persuade the people that its judgments have been made for sound reasons. . . . [It has exercised] a judicial arrogance that has refused to believe that the public should be told the truth instead of being fed on slogans and platitudes.[19]

Still, in marked contrast to the tenor of today's court-bashing conservatism, Kurland did not proclaim the death or even the terminal illness of democracy in America due to what he viewed as unwise judicial activism. On the contrary, in a quite wonderful passage, he celebrated the Court's function as a check upon purely majoritarian democracy:

> [T]he Court is not a democratic institution, either in makeup or in function. . . . It is politically irresponsible and must remain so, if it would perform its primary function in today's harried society. That function, evolving at least since the days of Charles Evans Hughes, is to protect the individual against the Leviathan of government and to protect minorities against oppression by majorities.[20]

And, contrary to the conventional belief that the Warren Court met with a universal chorus of approval from liberal precincts, it faced no small amount of criticism from liberals for its boldness. The most prominent voice here was perhaps that of Archibald Cox, who, as Lyndon Johnson's solicitor general, had encouraged the Court's progress in certain realms of the law, especially in race discrimination cases. In a series of lectures he delivered in 1967, shortly after he left government service, Cox forthrightly endorsed many of the results reached by the Court. But these results, which Cox thought would win "general and enthusiastic praise . . . if laid down by a bevy of Platonic guardians instead of a court," were too often reached with scant attention to interpretive rigor.[21] The Court had therefore brought about "major institutional changes whose long-range consequences are difficult to measure and which the present Court seems to brush aside without careful consideration for immediate progress."[22] Cox saw a Court that, instead of adhering to any settled method of constitutional interpretation, too often issued decisions that "seem to turn on intuitive judgments of right and wrong rather than the impartial application of principle."[23] Indeed, Cox argued, "some opinions of the Court seem to slide off into sentimentality or run libertarian dogma into the ground at the expense of the substance of liberty."[24] But, like Kurland, Cox did not advocate any radical reaction to the Court's waywardness. Instead, he simply admonished the Justices to pay "more attention to professional method."[25]

Kurland and Cox both made their criticisms in the final years of the Warren Court. After the Warren Court's successor Court, under the Chief Justiceship of Warren Burger, had established itself, conservative criticism of the Court and of the judiciary in general began to take on a more worried—and eventually alarmist—cast. In short, the transition was made from criticism of judicial unwisdom to strident denunciations of supposed judicial power madness.

In 1973, the historian Arthur Schlesinger, Jr. published *The Imperial Presidency*, in which he argued that the executive branch of the federal government had come to accumulate powers dangerously beyond those granted it by the Constitution. In 1975, however, another scholar, the Harvard sociologist Nathan Glazer, adopted Schlesinger's title to argue that the *judiciary* was in fact the branch of government that had broken the boundaries of its legitimate powers. Glazer's article "Towards an Imperial Judiciary?" was published in the fall 1975 issue of *The Public Interest* and later appeared as part of what would become a highly influential symposium of neoconservative writings.[26]

Glazer begins with a sweeping declaration: "The courts have truly changed their role in American life. . . . [They] are now far more powerful than ever before. . . . [They] now reach into the lives of the people, against the will of the people, deeper than they ever have in American history."[27] But this is not his central thesis. Rather, Glazer is most concerned to establish the proposition that the expansion of judicial power may have become *irreversible*. As he says, "we must at least consider the possibility that there has been a permanent change in the character of the courts and their role in the commonwealth, rather than simply a somewhat extended activist cycle."[28]

Thus, Glazer wonders whether the character of the judiciary has now *permanently* altered so that it has become "imperial," that is, incompatible with the functioning of a vigorous democratic order. The chief contention here is that courts have been occasionally "activist" in the course of American history but that, from the Warren Court on, the assertion of judicial power has been fundamentally different in kind. For Glazer, the difference is easily stated: before the Warren Court, courts asserted their power by reining in the powers of the other branches of government, but "[t]he distinctive characteristic of more recent activist courts has been to *extend* the role of what the government could do, even when the government did not want to do it."[29] What is more, Glazer fears that this new type of judicial assertiveness may have become inexorable: "[I]t appears that the controls on [Supreme] Court power have become obsolescent and that the role of the Court—and courts generally—-has changed significantly, such that the most powerful Court and Judiciary in the world have become even more powerful, raising questions of some gravity for the Commonwealth."[30]

Glazer's analysis as to *why* judicial power is likely to expand without hindrance does not bear much attention today for the simple reason that so much of it has proven wrong. His particular focus upon judicial assertiveness in school busing and welfare rights cases has a decided air of quaintness about it in a time that has seen the virtual abandonment of school integration as a social goal to be promoted by government and "the end of welfare as we know it." (It is also striking, given the future course of denunciation of the judiciary by the right, that Glazer makes only the merest mention of *Roe v. Wade*, which was issued in 1973.) His further contention that "[t]he courts will not be allowed to withdraw from the broadened positions they have seized, or have been forced to move into, because of the creation of new and powerful interests, chief among them the public advocacy law centers" is the sentiment of an age before the sustained campaign to diminish, if not eliminate, the power of legal services organizations.[31]

But what is particularly arresting is the tone of Glazer's polemic. The sense is palpable that he is surprised, even shocked, that he should be making such an argument in 1975. It is a tone that is clearly born of dashed hope, for "in 1969 something was supposed to happen, and didn't."[32] What did not happen, of course, is that the Burger Court did not answer the fondest hopes of conservatives by overruling Warren Court precedents, one after another. On the contrary, says Glazer, to the disappointment and bewilderment of conservatives, "the Burger Court has been surprisingly like the Warren Court."[33] In sum, as the title of a 1986 collection of essays put it, the Burger Court was *The Counter-Revolution That Wasn't.*[34]

It has thus become an obsessive theme of conservative commentary that the right has never won back the courts in the thirty years since the end of the Warren Court. Conservatives wanted nothing less than a comprehensive rollback of Warren Court precedents in as many areas as possible, probably most of all in matters of criminal procedure. What they got instead was a Court that "not only maintained its commitment to most of the major Warren Court constitutional innovations, it continued to extend the range of its scrutiny of majoritarian legislation, venturing into areas where the Warren Court's review posture had been cautious. Two major examples were gender discrimination and a species of 'liberties' in the due process clauses that the Court associated with privacy, personhood, or family relations."[35]

These setbacks were at first explainable by the fact that the Court that handed down *Roe v. Wade* in 1973 was staffed by a combination of Warren Court survivors and Nixon appointees. But this explanation was no longer available after the twelve years of the Reagan and the George H. W. Bush administrations, a period that included six years in which there was a Republican majority in the U.S. Senate. These administrations placed five Justices on the Supreme Court and named a majority of judges on the lower federal bench.[36] Still, as G. Edward White has recorded, the deepest jurisprudential desires of conservatives were again not met:

> William Rehnquist's succession to the Chief Justiceship on Warren Burger's retirement in 1986 brought forth predictions that the Court would now make a decisive turn to the right end of the political spectrum. But in four areas where Warren and early Burger Court decisions had generally been identified as "liberal" and had drawn opposition from right-wing groups—abortion, school prayer, gender discrimination, and First Amendment protection for flag desecration—the Rehnquist Court reaffirmed and extended those decisions.[37]

Conservative anticipation regarding the consignment of the Warren Court to the dust bin of history was particularly great during the early years of Ronald Reagan's tenure in the White House. Bruce Fein, an official of the Reagan Justice Department, predicted in 1984 that a host of Warren Court landmark decisions were "going to go out the window."[38] Hence the unbridled conservative anger over the subsequent failure of numerous Warren Court precedents—to say nothing of *Roe v. Wade*—to be squarely overruled. The prevailing conservative mood was stated flatly in 1997 by Terry

Eastland, another Reagan Justice Department veteran: "[H]ere we are in 1997, and judicial appointments have not fixed the problem of judicial activism. In fact, some of the opinions drawing the sharpest criticism from conservatives were written or joined by Reagan and Bush appointees."[39] Three years later, Don Feder summed up: "We've had Republican presidents for twelve of the last twenty years. They gave us exactly two reality-based justices—Scalia and Clarence Thomas."[40]

Much of this anger finds an outlet in personal attacks upon those considered apostates. In this regard, nothing comes close to the conservative loathing for the supposed renegade tendencies of Justices Sandra Day O'-Connor, Anthony Kennedy, and David Souter. The excoriation of this trio has never stopped since they joined the 5-4 majority that upheld *Roe v. Wade* in the 1992 *Casey* decision, a result that prompted Justice Antonin Scalia to howl in dissent, "The Imperial Judiciary lives."[41] In a typical blast, Bruce Fein labeled the three Justices "vanilla-styled conservatives who do not have strong convictions" and referred to Justice Souter specifically as "a judicial nothing whose opinion is up for grabs in every case."[42] Because he was appointed to the Court by President George H. W. Bush, who is himself seen as something of an apostate on the right, it is Justice Souter who is despised most among all others. Here is the *Wall Street Journal*'s editorial board on his supposed faithlessness:

> Justice Souter has . . . become a reliable member of the court's four-person liberal bloc. He told his interviewers in the Reagan years that he was a conservative. But once safely confirmed, he turned out to want media respectability, bowing to what federal Judge Laurence Silberman has called "the Greenhouse effect," after Linda Greenhouse, the *New York Times* reporter and alpha female of the Supreme Court press pack.[43]

Imperial Judiciary theorists, however, see the failure of subsequent courts to undo Warren Court precedents and related outrages as more than the result of poor personnel choices. Rather, they have come to see the problem as one of institutional transformation. That is, courts are no longer truly judicial institutions. Rather, they have become unaccountable and, consequently, arrogant policy-making entities that are incompatible with the functioning of democracy.

The Judicial Usurpation of Politics

In her 1991 book *Rights Talk*, the Harvard Law School professor Mary Ann Glendon considered the political condition of an America that "is undoubtedly one of the most law-ridden societies that has ever existed on the face of the earth."[44] A central attribute of this condition is our "increasing tendency to speak of what is most important to us in terms of rights, and to frame nearly every social controversy as a clash of rights."[45] What is particularly striking about a politics dominated by "rights-based claims," says Glendon, is not that anyone's life has been made better for it but "the transformations" that such claims "have produced in the roles of courts and judges."[46]

In America, argues Glendon, "rights claims" are often absolutist. They are assertions of an entitlement to say whatever one wants, to do whatever one wants with one's property, especially one's body, and so on. The problem with a politics saturated with such "rights talk" is that it is really no politics at all. According to the deathless cliche, politics is the art of compromise, but "the language of rights is the language of no compromise. The winner takes all and the loser has to get out of town. The conversation is over."[47]

Glendon expands upon this theme in her 1994 book *A Nation under Lawyers*. This time, however, she is explicit that the heightened role of courts in our polity is not the result of "the rights revolution." Rather, it is an aggrandizing judiciary itself that has "discovered new rights" and thus made our society one dominated by rights claims. Glendon has stated here a central tenet of the Imperial Judiciary thesis: that the courts have made themselves the central arena of our politics at the expense of legislatures, through which popular will is expressed directly.

True to the genre, and with an approving citation to Glazer, Glendon's principal culprit is the Warren Court. But she is not without some praise for the latter's record. She asserts specifically that *Brown v. Board of Education* and the "one person-one vote" decisions mandating equality of representation in state legislatures were a proper "response to insufficiently representative political processes."[48] Beyond these, however, Glendon broadly claims that a host of decisions promoting individual and minority rights have subverted the democratic process to such an extent that they may be termed "antagonistic to democratic decision making as such."[49] Considered cumulatively, these decisions have administered "a beating" to "[t]he right of local self-determination within constitutional limits."[50] More comprehensively, Glendon asserts that "Warren and Burger Court majorities"

> wreaked havoc with grass-roots politics. The dismal failures of many local authorities in dealing with racial issues became pretexts for depriving citizens everywhere of the power to experiment with new approaches to a wide range of problems that often take different forms in different parts of the country. Constitutional provisions designed to protect individuals and minorities against majoritarian excesses were increasingly used to block the normal processes through which citizens build coalitions, develop consensus, hammer out compromises, try out new ideas, learn from mistakes, and try again.[51]

This was a decidedly odd claim to be making in 1994, because the 1990s were unquestionably a time of great state and local experimentation in such realms of public policy as the administration of welfare programs, the provision of health care and education, and, perhaps most of all, the punishment of criminals, as seen in the implementation of a wide range of sentencing experiments, such as "three-strikes" laws and mandatory minimum sentencing. Further, Glendon's uncritical advocacy of "local trial and error," as opposed to "[j]udicially ordained, top-down regulations," stands in unexamined contradiction to her approval of *Brown* and the decisions that mandated that state legislative seats be apportioned fairly.[52] The regimes of brutal segregation and disproportionate election districts that were invalidated by judicial intervention were each, of course, maintained for decades by the "grass-roots politics" that Glendon romanticizes.

What is more, as we shall see in chapter 6, Glendon commits an error that is common among Imperial Judiciary theorists when she implies that the expansion of rights over the past several decades has been an exclusively judicial enterprise. In fact, a great amount of the rights enforcement litigation that conservatives decry constantly is brought pursuant to *statute*—one need only think of Title VII of the Civil Rights Act of 1964 and the Americans with Disabilities Act—not under any judicially created cause of action. Curiously, in *Rights Talk*, Glendon calls the Civil Rights Act a "momentous social achievement" without mentioning the fact that the Act directs individuals to go to court to seek relief—that is, make "rights claims"—for alleged acts of discrimination.[53]

Regardless of these facts, Glendon contends that the expansion of judicial power has, to a great extent, *stopped* democratic politics in America. There is actually, she argues, an inverse relationship between the two:

> [E]ach time a court sets aside an action of the political branches through freewheeling interpretation, the American experience in self-government suffers a setback. Political skills atrophy. Men and women cease to take citizenship seriously. Citizens with diverse points of view lose the habit of cooperating to set conditions under which all can flourish. Tolerance suffers as communication declines. Adversarial legalism supplants the sober legalistic spirit that Tocqueville admired.[54]

The Imperial Judiciary thesis holds that there is no better illustration of this phenomenon than the results of *Roe v. Wade.* Justice Scalia makes such a contention in his dissenting opinion in *Casey.* Before *Roe,* Scalia contends, local democratic politics was working quite effectively with regard to abortion:

> Profound disagreement existed among our citizens over the issue . . . but that disagreement was being worked out at the state level. . . [T]he division of sentiment within each State was not as closely balanced as it was among the population of the Nation as a whole, meaning not only that more people would be satisfied with the results of state-by-state resolution, but also that those results would be more stable. Pre-*Roe,* moreover, political compromise was possible.[55]

Scalia's conclusion is characteristically blunt:

> We should get out of this area, where we have no right to be, and where we do neither ourselves nor the country any good by remaining.[56]

The abortion issue also drives the most notorious statement regarding the alleged hijacking of democratic politics by the courts, the symposium in the November 1996 issue of the journal *First Things* entitled "The End of Democracy? The Judicial Usurpation of Politics." Responding to "an entrenched pattern of government by judges," the "proposition" of the symposium is explained as follows by the journal's editors: "[W]hether we have reached or are reaching the point where conscientious citizens can no longer give moral assent to the existing regime."[57] This is said to be the situation at hand:

> The government of the United States of America no longer governs by the consent of the governed. With respect to the American people, the judiciary has in effect declared that the most important questions about how we ought to order our life together are outside the purview of "things of their knowledge." Not that judges necessarily claim greater knowledge; they simply claim, and exercise, the power to decide. The citizens of this democratic republic are deemed to lack the competence for self-government. . . . The courts have not, and perhaps cannot, restrain themselves, and it may be that in the present regime no other effective restraints are available. If so, we are witnessing the end of democracy.[58]

The symposium is most famous for its allusion to the Third Reich—"America is not and, please God, will never become Nazi Germany, but it is only blind hubris that denies it can happen here and, in peculiarly American ways, may be happening here"—and for its contemplation of "possible responses to laws that cannot be obeyed by conscientious citizens—ranging from noncompliance to resistance to civil disobedience to morally justified revolution."[59]

This extremist rhetoric caused some members of the editorial board of *First Things*, to their great credit, to resign in protest.[60] And the rhetoric was clearly too much for Glendon, who, although she remains on the *First Things* board, was not prepared to contemplate abandoning the weapon of criticism in favor of criticism by means of weapons. In her response to "The End of Democracy?," Glendon bespeaks caution in a manner quite at odds with her argument in *A Nation under Lawyers*, where, but for the bygone days of segregation and unjust legislative apportionment, all "pathology" was judicial:

> There is a good case to be made that we are already living in a de facto oligarchy. It is less clear, however, that the courts are principally to blame. To be sure, the judiciary has steadily usurped power over matters that the Constitution wisely left to ordinary political processes. But the courts could never have carried off that power grab were it not for pathology in other parts of the body politic.[61]

As of this writing, no revolution, violent or otherwise, against judicial tyranny has broken out. But neither have Imperial Judiciary adherents given up playing the totalitarianism card. Early in 2001, for example, Thomas Sowell, in his syndicated column, invoked Hitler, Stalin, and Mao and asserted that "we need to take a look back at the twentieth century, to see what lessons it offers that we should remember in the future." This is certainly a wise directive. But consider the demagogic use to which it is immediately put:

> At the heart of totalitarian dictatorship is the idea that there is no rule of law superior to the will of those who hold power or the ideology they are promoting. Though defeated on the stage of world history, such ideas are gaining a foothold in the society that played the biggest role in defeating them—the United States of America.
>
> American courts have increasingly moved away from their role as defenders of the constitutional framework of the rule of law to deciding many substantive policy issues directly—from abortion to affirmative action—and even ordering taxes imposed to carry out some judge's notions of what ought to be done in schools or in prisons. Far from restraining the lawlessness of those in power, judges have themselves become one of the lawless powers.[62]

"The Religion of Radical Selfism"

If, as Sowell contends, the "lawless powers" exercised by the courts are exercised in pursuit of "liberal causes," what does the Imperial Judiciary thesis consider the imperatives of contemporary liberalism to be? Consider *Romer v. Evans*, a 1996 decision in which the Supreme Court struck down an amendment to Colorado's constitution, Amendment 2, that prohibited state and local government entities from enacting any statute or regulation that would grant homosexuals "any minority status, quota preferences, protected status or claim of discrimination." Writing in dissent, Justice Scalia accused the Court's majority of imposing an alien system of mores upon the supporters of Amendment 2:

> The Court has mistaken a Kulturkramf for a fit of spite. The constitutional amendment before us here is not the manifestation of a "'bare . . . desire to harm'" homosexuals, but is rather a modest attempt by seem-

ingly tolerant Coloradans to preserve traditional sexual mores against the efforts of a politically powerful minority to revise those mores through use of the laws.

This Court has no business imposing upon all Americans the resolution favored by the elite class from which the Members of this institution are selected, pronouncing that "animosity" toward homosexuality is evil.[63]

Justice Scalia is quite wrong to assert that the Court characterized animosity toward homosexuals as evil. Rather, the Court declared that no legitimate government interest was served by enacting such animosity into law in the manner of Amendment 2, which effectively denies to homosexuals the ability to press their collective interests in the normal course of democratic politics. An amendment that forbids the passage of measures barring discrimination against Communists would likely be struck down for the same reason, but this would in no sense amount to a declaration that opposition to Communism is evil. Nevertheless, Scalia concludes rancorously:

When the Court takes sides in the culture wars, it tends to . . . reflect[ ] the views and values of the lawyer class from which the Court's Members are drawn. How that class feels about homosexuality will be evident to anyone who wishes to interview job applicants at virtually any of the Nation's law schools. . . . [I]f the interviewer should wish not to be an associate or partner of an applicant because he disapproves of the applicant's homosexuality, then he will have violated the pledge which the Association of American Law Schools requires all its member-schools to exact from job interviewers: "assurance of the employer's willingness" to hire homosexuals. . . . This law-school view of what "prejudices" must be stamped out may be contrasted with the more plebeian attitudes that apparently still prevail in the United States Congress, which has been unresponsive to repeated attempts to extend to homosexuals the protections of federal civil rights laws.[64]

The first thing that strikes one about these passages is the dissonance between Justice Scalia's characterization of homosexuals as "a politically powerful minority" and his acknowledgment that they have not only been unable to win the most minimal protections under the federal civil rights laws but were also unable to prevent the passage of Amendment 2 in Colorado. More to the point, Scalia here applies a central tenet of the Imperial

Judiciary thesis: that not only is the judiciary in the midst of "the culture wars" but also it has quite blatantly allied itself with one of the contenders. And, as Thomas Sowell wrote in reaction to *Casey*, the judiciary has enlisted on the side that's winning:

> Even so-called conservative Supreme Court justices such as Sandra Day O'Connor, David Souter, and Anthony Kennedy have bent the knee to these cultural elites by referring . . . to how "the thoughtful portion of the nation" would view their ruling. That the Supreme Court of the United States would play to this gallery while using these elite "evolving standards" instead of the Constitution they were sworn to uphold is one sign of where we are in the culture wars.[65]

For perhaps the most comprehensive statement of judges as cultural warriors, we return to Professor Graglia. For the past several years, he has made numerous speeches to law school audiences in which he has pounded away at a single theme. Indeed, a review of the published versions of his talks reveals that, but for slight variations of invective, he has been making the *same* speech. One of the titles of these pretty much sums up his argument regarding the ideological bent of the contemporary judiciary: "Constitutional Law: A Ruse for Government by an Intellectual Elite."[66]

For Graglia, the past forty years has seen the judiciary transform judicial review into an ideological cudgel. Thus, "the Supreme Court's rulings of unconstitutionality have not been random in terms of their political impact. On the contrary, they have almost uniformly served to advance the political agenda of those on the far left of the American political spectrum."[67] How did this "extraordinary uniformity of result" come about? Graglia explains:

> The answer, very briefly, is that government by the Supreme Court in present-day America is government by and for an educational and cultural elite. Academics, particularly at our leading law schools, are—along with other members of the "knowledge class"—overwhelmingly to the left of the majority of the American people. The justices are almost always graduates of these schools and members of this class. Free from electoral accountability, they are much more subject than other public officials to the influence of academics. The legitimacy their policymaking lacks in democratic theory they must seek, instead, in academic approval.[68]

Graglia immediately follows up by setting forth this dark symbiotic relationship:

> The nightmare of the American academic intellectual is that public policymaking should fall into the hands of the American people. The American people, after all, actually favor such policies as capital punishment, suppression of pornography, prayer in the schools, effective criminal law, and neighborhood schools. It is only the Supreme Court that can keep their views from prevailing. Academics, and specifically professors of constitutional law, see it as their function, in turn, to defend Supreme Court policymaking by arguing that the Justices are uniquely trustworthy, nonpartisan public servants and that their revolutionary decisions are unavoidable mandates of the Constitution.[69]

Statements like this are legion among conservative commentators. Thus, Gary McDowell has opined that "[u]nder the tutelage of scholars like [the NYU and Oxford law professor Ronald] Dworkin, [the Harvard law professor Laurence] Tribe and [the Stanford historian Jack] Rakove, a generation or more of jurists [has] been taught to see the Constitution as nothing more than what judicial opinion interprets it to be."[70] The conservative philosopher John Kekes has recently revealed that judges "across the land hang on every word [Dworkin] utters."[71] Similarly, David Frum argues that this nefarious influence has now taken on an international dimension. The courts of Canada, Frum declares, have themselves become imperial, and "the authorities Canadian courts cite when they embark on their radical projects are almost always the gurus of American legal liberalism: Ronald Dworkin, Laurence Tribe, and [the University of Michigan law professor] Catharine MacKinnon."[72] John Leo has concluded as follows:

> Why have ten Republican nominees made so little headway against [judicial activism]? One reason is the legal world is dominated by the activist left. Enormous pressure is brought to bear on dissenters. Opinion at the law schools, which are increasingly devoted to freewheeling judicial activism, matters a lot to members of the judiciary. . . . As a result of this pressure, the system is set up to produce converts, ostensibly conservative judges who "grow" on the bench.[73]

What can one possibly make of this bluster, which is summed up nicely in Jeremy Rabkin's declaration that "there is no doubt that only one side

derives direct assistance from the Supreme Court, while the other is reduced almost exclusively to politics?"[74] Graglia and company are a little
light on supporting evidence. Neither they nor, to my knowledge, other
Imperial Judiciary adherents have ever attempted to actually document
the supposed constant interchange between left-wing academic opinion
and the work of the Supreme Court, or any other court for that matter.
But you don't have to document a phenomenon whose existence you simply assume. Thus, in the course of a rant against leftist judicial activism,
the conservative columnist Maggie Gallagher breaks the following news:

> Recently, I read two distinguished legal scholars have published an essay
> arguing that abstinence education in public schools violates religious free-
> dom because it is based on Christian values. Only moral values unaccept-
> able to the Judeo-Christian majority can, under this new legal theory, be
> taught in public schools.[75]

The clear implication is that, some day soon, some court is going to adopt
this reasoning. I wouldn't hold my breath on this.[76]

Consider any number of examples that call into question the reality of
the judicial/left-wing legal academic axis. How, for instance, has the interchange manifested itself in Supreme Court decisions of recent years that
have allowed states to impose prison sentences of virtually any length, no
matter how trivial the crime;[77] that have severely restricted the ability of
elected officials to enact affirmative action programs[78] and to draw election
districts in a manner conducive to the election of minority candidates (expressing no regret about thereby having "wreaked havoc with grass-roots
politics");[79] that have allowed the National Endowment for the Arts to
evaluate artists' grant applications on the basis of criteria of "decency and
respect for the diverse beliefs and values of the American public" (so much
for the supposed omnipotence of the cultural elite!);[80] and that have unanimously refused to constitutionalize a right to die, even though the "creation of new rights" is purportedly the quintessential project of liberal judicial activism?[81] Or what are we to make of Graglia's thesis in light of the
welter of recent decisions from the Rehnquist Court that have all but eliminated the capacity of federal law to regulate the operations of state governments, a development that flies in the face of the liberal judiciary's supposed drive to aggrandize federal power at the expense of local politics?[82]

For adherents of the Imperial Judiciary thesis, it is as if none of this has
happened. Thus, consider that a prominent liberal law professor, Cass

Sunstein of the University of Chicago, in his 1999 book *One Case at a Time*, described the Supreme Court of recent years as exhibiting "judicial minimalism," an adjudicative stance undertaken by "judges who seek to avoid broad rules and abstract theories, and attempt to focus their attention only on what is necessary to solve particular disputes."[83] In other words, the current Court is not by a long shot staffed with effete leftists. In his review of *One Case at a Time*, however, Gary McDowell makes no effort to disprove its thesis regarding the Court's moderation. Rather, he is concerned only to opine that "[i]t is increasingly unlikely" that "the Constitution of the United States can survive the flood of constitutional theorizing that now passes for legal scholarship."[84]

It is striking how closely musings such as these resemble what Richard Hofstadter described famously almost forty years ago as "the paranoid style in American politics." Indeed, we may borrow from Hofstadter directly to describe the sense in which the Imperial Judiciary adherent "feels dispossessed: America has been largely taken away from them and their kind. . . . The old American virtues have already been eaten away by cosmopolitans and intellectuals."[85]

The Hofstadter reference seems particularly applicable to the argument set forth in Robert Bork's 1996 book *Slouching toward Gomorrah*. While Mary Ann Glendon wishes to establish that the judiciary has wounded America's political culture, Bork is concerned to establish that the judiciary is subversive of all that is healthy in American culture as a whole. Indeed, says Bork, "[i]t is arguable that the American judiciary—the American Supreme Court, abetted by the lower federal courts and many state courts—is the single most powerful force shaping our culture."[86]

Bork does not pause to offer any support for this polemical thunderbolt. Rather, he proceeds directly to the assertion that culture is now "made by fiat" by the judiciary, which is said to have embraced "radical liberalism" as a guiding set of values.[87] The tenets of this supposed doctrine are "radical egalitarianism (the equality of outcomes rather than opportunities) and radical individualism (the drastic reduction of limits to personal gratification)."[88] Following Bork, a writer in *First Things* has conveniently termed the doctrine "the religion of radical selfism," the establishment of which by the judiciary is "something the Constitution explicitly condemns."[89]

Bork's criticisms of individual decisions handed down by a judicial regime in the thrall of radical individualism are relentlessly condemnatory. No surprise there. The point to be emphasized, however, is that Bork in fact believes without reservation that the contemporary judiciary is a *regime*, in the pejorative sense, one that now rules with unabashed self-consciousness of its powers and aims. Thus, says Bork, "[w]e are no longer free to make our own fundamental moral and cultural decisions because the Court oversees all such matters, when and as it chooses."[90] Or, as he has put the matter in his contribution to "The End of Democracy?," "[t]he Justices know full well what they are doing, . . . a majority of Justices have decided to rule us without any warrant in law."[91] The result, he concludes, is that "[t]he judicial adoption of modern liberalism has produced a crisis of legitimacy."[92]

From "We the People" to "I the Judge"

As already noted, when Richard Nixon ran for president in 1968, one of his major campaign themes was his attack on the Warren Court, particularly with respect to its rulings in favor of the rights of criminal defendants. Thus, "Nixon promised to name 'strict constructionists' [to the Supreme Court] and implied that he would use the power of judicial selection to change the balance on the [federal] courts from liberal activism to conservative law and order."[93] For several years afterward, "strict constructionist" became a conservative buzz phrase for the sort of judicial style with which conservatives were comfortable.

Although still encountered, "strict constructionism" was largely replaced in the 1980s by "originalism," that is, a jurisprudence that claims to employ the specific intent of the framers in the interpretation of constitutional provisions. It is now something of a commonplace among conservatives that, as Robert Bork says, a jurisprudence informed by original intent is the only legitimate method of constitutional adjudication because "only the approach of original understanding meets the criteria that any theory of constitutional adjudication must meet in order to possess democratic legitimacy."[94] The alternative, in the words of the Reagan administration grandee Edwin Meese, is "seeing the Constitution as an empty vessel into which each generation may pour its passion and prejudice."[95]

It was Meese who did yeoman's service during the 1980s for the cause of popularizing originalism. In a series of speeches, Meese announced and defended the principle that "[t]hose who framed these [constitutional] principles meant something by them. And the meaning can be found, understood, and applied."[96] Always finding its way into these addresses was a broad-based attack on the alleged judicial activism that had, in Meese's view, dispensed with the Constitution altogether:

> In recent decades many have come to view the Constitution . . . as a char-
> ter for judicial activism on behalf of various constituencies. Those who
> hold this view often have lacked demonstrable textual or historical sup-
> port for their conclusions. Instead they have "grounded" their rulings in
> appeals to social theories, to moral philosophies or personal notions of
> human dignity, or to "penumbras," somehow emanating ghostlike from
> various provisions—identified and not identified—in the Bill of Rights.[97]

The late Raoul Berger's *Government by Judiciary: The Transformation of the Fourteenth Amendment*, published in 1977, became a central text of the originalist movement and, in the judgment of Gary McDowell, elevated Berger to the status of "one of the great intellectual heroes of American conservatism."[98] The book is written in two parts. The first is an attack on the legitimacy of all modern Fourteenth Amendment jurisprudence. That jurisprudence is based upon the premise that most of the provisions of the Bill of Rights, which were originally held to restrain only the actions of the federal government, were made applicable to the state governments by the passage of the Fourteenth Amendment in 1868. Supreme Court majorities began to accept this premise in the 1920s. Beginning at that time, through a process known among constitutional lawyers as "incorporation," the Supreme Court began to strike down state statutes on the basis of particular provisions of the Bill of Rights, with the result that most provisions of the first ten amendments to the Constitution are now held to be applicable to the states.[99]

Berger's argument is that incorporation is all a mistake or, more properly, a delusion. It is his contention that the framers of the Fourteenth Amendment had no intention whatever of nationalizing the Bill of Rights, or any part of it. On the contrary, the Fourteenth Amendment's framers had only the most modest goals in mind. In spite of the sweeping phrases they used—"equal protection," "due process," "privileges and immunities"—Berger argues that their intention was no greater than to constitutionalize the provisions of the Civil Rights Act of 1866, which guaranteed the rights of freed slaves to own property and make contracts. What it did not guarantee was an end to racial segregation generally, which leads Berger to the conclusion that, upon an originalist reading of the Fourteenth Amendment, *Brown v. Board of Education*, the foundation of modern civil rights law, was wrongly decided. It is this stance that has made Berger's book controversial, to say the least.

Berger's arguments from history regarding incorporation and the scope of the Fourteenth Amendment have been comprehensively questioned by numerous scholars, most effectively in recent years by Akhil Amar, who relies heavily upon the work of Michael Kent Curtis.[100] Amar has argued persuasively that Berger's work is in the thrall of a long-discredited Reconstruction historiography. Written in the decades surrounding the turn of the twentieth century and dominated by Southern scholars, this historical school viewed Reconstruction as tragic in that it sought a dangerous expansion of federal power and an imposition of equality between races greatly unequal in terms of intellectual and social capacity. But Amar sees a kind of tragedy in the fact that work such as Berger's "continues to exert such influence in legal circles long after many of its intellectual foundations have been undermined by decades of serious and sustained scholarship of professional historians."[101]

More important for our purposes is the second part of *Government by Judiciary*. Here Berger attempts to demonstrate the intent of the framers of the original Constitution with respect to the proper scope of judicial review. Not surprisingly, he contends that "judicial review was conceived in quite narrow terms—as a means of policing the constitutional boundaries, the 'limits' of a given power."[102] What is more, judicial review was meant to be used solely as a vehicle by which the specific intentions of the framers would be applied to legislative acts. Thus, Berger argues that the framers "drew a line between the judicial reviewing function, that is, *policing* grants of power to insure that there were no encroachments beyond the grants, and legislative policymaking *within* those bounds."[103] Since this "policing function" is to be undertaken solely by means of the application of the specific intent of the framers, any departure from their intent is nothing but an exercise of arbitrary judicial discretion.

Given his arguments regarding the judicial misapprehension or disregard of the intentions of the framers of the Fourteenth Amendment, Berger sees virtually *all* modern civil rights and civil liberties jurisprudence as an exercise of arbitrary judicial discretion. This is a central tenet of the Imperial Judiciary thesis. As Walter Berns puts it, "[t]hanks in large part to the Court's Fourteenth Amendment jurisprudence, the Constitution came to be seen not as the embodiment of fundamental and clearly articulated principles of government but as a collection of hopelessly vague and essentially meaningless words and phrases inviting judicial construction."[104] This is said to have resulted in disaster, a perversion of democracy from which Berger takes his title, *Government by Judiciary*. Or, as stated more recently by Paul Craig Roberts, another former official of the Reagan administration, "The Constitution begins, 'We the People,' but we the people have been shoved aside by judges who have illegally rewritten the Constitution to read, 'I the Judge.'"[105]

This is harsh rhetoric, but it is no harsher than that employed by Berger himself to describe judging that has become untethered from original intent. Liberals idolize the Warren Court, says Berger, but "how short is the memory of man. . . . Do we need Hitler or Indira Gandhi to remind us that the lesson of history is: put not your trust in saviors?"[106] The usurpations of the judiciary are met with this warning:

> How long can public respect for the Court, on which its power ultimately depends, survive if the people become aware that the tribunal which condemns the acts of others as unconstitutional is itself acting unconstitutionally? Respect for the limits on power are the essence of a democratic society; without it the entire democratic structure is undermined and the way is paved from Weimar to Hitler.[107]

Finally, we are told that judging based on personal preferences "perilously resembles the subordination of 'law' to the attainment of ends desired by a ruling power which was the hallmark of Hitlerism and Stalinism."[108]

In terms of impact upon conservatives generally, Berger's book has been surpassed by Robert Bork's 1990 book, *The Tempting of America*. Bork has of course attained martyr status on the right because of the defeat of his 1987 nomination to the Supreme Court, a defeat he terms "the revenge of the Warren Court."[109] Not surprisingly, therefore, the encomiums on the cover of the paperback edition are more inflated than is usual even for the genre. George Will says it "belongs among the few masterpieces of American political reflection," while Irving Kristol terms it "the most powerful, most readable—and wisest—book on constitutional law to have been published in this century." In sum, in the words of Henry Jaffa, who stands almost alone as a conservative critic of Bork, "[i]t is difficult to remember when conservatives have been so nearly unanimous in according a book something approaching a neo-scriptural status."[110]

But, on many occasions, *The Tempting of America* is simply at war with sense. Thus, as already noted, Bork announces dogmatically that "only the approach of original understanding meets the criteria that any theory of constitutional adjudication must meet in order to possess democratic legitimacy."[111] Yet, even though he views the entire body of cases "validating certain New Deal and Great Society programs" as wrongly decided on originalist grounds, these decisions should not now be overturned because to do so "would be to overturn most of modern government and plunge us into chaos."[112] In other words, although originalism is the "only" method of constitutional adjudication compatible with democracy, to apply it to the body of law on which "modern government" is based would be to destroy our democracy. I also note the curiosity that same man who has contemplated "the end of democracy" because of judicial imperialism has also declared the unconstitutionality of the legislative program of the New Deal, which was arguably the greatest democratic upsurge in our history.

Bork similarly falls into incoherence when he attempts to define what materials may properly be consulted in the search for original intent. He declares that the "subjective intention" of individual framers is irrelevant to a determination of original intent and that therefore statements in private letters are not relevant to the task. Instead, original understanding is to be gleaned "in the words used and in secondary materials, such as debates at the [ratification] conventions, public discussion, newspaper articles, dictionaries in use at the time, and the like."[113] But aren't statements made by individuals in convention debates, in public discussion, and in newspaper articles often expressions of subjective intent? Are we to assume, for example, that when James Madison wrote his quite extraordinary letters to Thomas Jefferson in hopes of winning the latter's support for the ratification of the Constitution, he was speaking wholly subjectively but that when he contributed to the series of newspaper articles that became *The Federalist* he was somehow channeling the nation's collective consciousness?

All of this establishes Bork's personal limits as an originalist. But the limitations of originalism itself are implicated when we compare Bork's readings of the text of the Constitution with those of other originalists. Take Raoul Berger, who, as we have said, writes that the doctrine of Fourteenth Amendment incorporation is wholly mistaken. By contrast, Bork writes that "[t]he controversy over the legitimacy of incorporation continues to this day, although as a matter of judicial practice the issue is settled."[114] This is a weirdly agnostic statement to encounter in a book devoted to excoriating settled judicial practice with perfect assurance.

Or consider *McCulloch v. Maryland*, a landmark 1819 case that upheld the constitutionality of a congressionally chartered national bank.[115] Bork, with no explanation, proclaims John Marshall's opinion "a magnificent example of reasoning from the text and structure of the Constitution."[116] Berger, however, believes that the case was wrongly decided because the Philadelphia Convention "had specifically rejected a proposal for incorporation of banks."[117]

But the fullest appreciation of the gulf that separates Berger and Bork is to be found in Berger's review of *The Tempting of America*. It's an odd piece. Berger begins by declaring that he can well understand why "[e]minent conservatives have showered [Bork] with praise."[118] He himself is more than willing to "join in the course as a deep-dyed liberal and lifelong Democrat."[119] Indeed, says Berger, the book "might well have been entitled *The Intelligent Person's Guide to Judicial Review*."[120]

But the review soon takes a wrenching turn. Berger declares that "an odd aspect of Bork's commentary on original intention [is] that he rarely summons the historical materials that reveal it."[121] Indeed, this inattention to what should be the focus of any originalist's attention leads Bork into certain "mistaken glosses" on the Constitutional text.[122] Berger then proceeds to contend that Bork has reached the wrong originalist conclusion on a number of the most important constitutional questions of the past century and a half. The only conclusion that can be drawn by an intelligent person is that Berger's unstated assessment must be that Bork is a thorough failure as a practicing originalist.

Berger himself has been the subject of similar treatment. In his review of the second edition of *Government by Judiciary*, Robert George reports that he found it "a pleasure to reread Berger's masterwork."[123] But George concludes his review by stating that recently performed "careful and exhaustive historical research gives us reason to subject to renewed scrutiny Berger's claim that the outcome in *Brown* is unsupported by, and indeed incompatible with, the original understanding of the Fourteenth Amendment."[124] The reader is left to wonder how a book can be called a "masterwork" if its central argument may be flatly incorrect.

The "careful and exhaustive historical research" to which George refers is a 1995 article published in the *Virginia Law Review* by the originalist scholar Michael McConnell.[125] It is McConnell's contention that originalist support for *Brown* can be found in the efforts of Republicans in Congress to add a provision barring segregated public schools to the legislation that became the Civil Rights Act of 1875. Whether or not one is an originalist, the article is a fascinating account of debates about the scope of the newly enacted Fourteenth Amendment. But it is also intriguing that

McConnell himself is less than thoroughly convinced by his own argument. He forthrightly admits that evidence drawn from legislative debates taking place *after* the passage of the Fourteenth Amendment "might be inferior in principle to information directly bearing on the opinions and expectations of the framers and ratifiers during deliberations over the Amendment itself."[126] However, says McConnell, there is no alternative because *"there is no significant body of evidence concerning the latter."*[127]

More crucially, McConnell must also deal with the fact that efforts to add school desegregation to the 1875 Civil Rights Act were *unsuccessful*. As McConnell details, *simple* majorities of both houses of Congress supported desegregation, but they were unable to carry the day on numerous procedural votes that blocked further consideration of desegregation because these votes required *super*majorities for passage. Thus, McConnell arrives at the less than resounding conclusion that, "[a]t a minimum," the result in *Brown* "is within the legitimate range of interpretations of the [Fourteenth] Amendment on originalist grounds."[128]

But other originalists have been unwilling to go this far. Thus, the legal historian Earl Maltz has written recently that, even after McConnell's article, "*Brown* cannot be defended by reference to the original understanding" of the Fourteenth Amendment.[129] For his part, Raoul Berger has judged McConnell's argument to be the product of "exuberant fancy."[130]

To return to Bork, his treatment of *Brown v. Board of Education* deserves special mention. He argues that the proper result was reached in *Brown* but excoriates Chief Justice Warren's opinion because it is not based on the intent of the framers of the equal protection clause of the Fourteenth Amendment. This latter assertion is certainly correct, and Warren made no pretense to the contrary. Rather, he stated forthrightly that the evidence regarding the intent of the Fourteenth Amendment's framers with respect to segregated schools was "inconclusive."[131] However, because of the psychological and educational consequences for African Americans subjected to segregation, Warren concluded that "[s]eparate educational facilities are *inherently* unequal," whatever the intent of the framers.[132]

But Bork contends that "the result in *Brown* is consistent with, indeed is compelled by, the original understanding of the Fourteenth Amendment's equal protection clause."[133] The reader is arrested by this declaration because, a few paragraphs earlier, Bork has declared that "[t]he inescapable fact is that those who ratified the [Fourteenth] Amendment did not think that it outlawed segregated education or segregation in any aspect of life."[134] Bork is not daunted, however. The framers, he argues, *also* wanted to establish equal justice under law. When *Brown* was decided, the time had come to opt for the latter principle:

> By 1954, when *Brown* came up for decision, it had been apparent for some time that segregation rarely if ever produced equality. . . . The Supreme Court was faced with a situation in which the courts would have to go on forever entertaining litigation about primary schools, secondary schools, colleges, washrooms, golf courses, swimming pools, drinking fountains, and the endless variety of facilities that were segregated, or else the separate-but-equal doctrine would have to be abandoned. Endless litigation, aside from the burden on the courts, also would never produce the equality the Constitution promised. The Court's realistic choice, therefore, was either to abandon the quest for equality by allowing segregation or to forbid segregation in order to achieve equality. There was no third choice. Either choice would violate one aspect of the original understanding, but there was no possibility of avoiding that.[135]

This is simply untenable. According to Bork, originalism can justify both a scheme of comprehensive racial apartheid and court-ordered integration in the entire range of public facilities. More than sixty years of the former, enshrined in the separate-but-equal doctrine, set forth in the 1896 case of *Plessy v. Ferguson*,[136] was not wrong as a matter of constitutional principle, untold multitudes of stunted African American lives notwithstanding. But, by 1954, it appears to have failed as *policy*.[137] This, plus the fact that maintaining the policy would put a terrific strain upon judicial resources, meant it was time to opt for the end of segregation. It is no wonder that Michael McConnell asserts that Bork's treatment of *Brown* "is more typical of the constitutionalist methodology Bork criticizes than it is of his own professed originalist methodology."[138]

Bork's treatment of the "privileges or immunities" clause of the Fourteenth Amendment is a good example of how he is at odds with originalists other than Berger. Without discussion, Bork declares that the intention of the framers with respect to the clause is "largely unknown." Now the question of what criteria one should use in deciding that the meaning of a constitutional clause is "unknown" is surely a very absorbing one. But it is clear that Bork has no doubts as to how a judge should treat such a clause: "that the ratifiers of the amendment presumably meant something is no reason for a judge, who does not have any idea what that something is, to make up and enforce a meaning that is something else."[139] In other words, the clause is to be written out of the Constitution. This would seem to be a pretty naked exercise of judicial power.

However, Justice Clarence Thomas, who is, of course, an outspoken proponent of the jurisprudence of original intent, has not heeded Bork's ukase. In *Saenz v. Roe*, a 1998 case, the Supreme Court held unconstitutional a California statute that denied full benefits to welfare recipients until they had resided in the state for a year.[140] Justice Thomas based his dissenting opinion on the privileges or immunities clause, which is acknowledged on all hands to be a much neglected part of the Fourteenth Amendment. He avers that scholars, including Bork, in deep disagreement as to the meaning of the clause.[141] To break the deadlock, Justice Thomas concludes that the reading of the analogous privileges *and* immunities clause in Article IV, Section 2, of the original Constitution contained in *Corfield v. Coryell*, an 1825 federal circuit court decision written by Justice Bushrod Washington while he was sitting as a federal circuit judge, is definitive. The reason is that "*Corfield* indisputably influenced the Members of Congress who enacted the Fourteenth Amendment."[142] Taking *Corfield* to mean that the privileges and immunities clause protects only "fundamental rights, rather than every public benefit established by positive law," Justice Thomas concludes that "the majority's conclusion—that a State violates the privileges or immunities clause when it 'discriminates' against citizens who have been domiciled in the State for less than a year in the distribution of welfare benefit appears contrary to the original understanding and is dubious at best."[143]

While it is correct that *Corfield* influenced the framers of the Fourteenth Amendment, it is doubtful that they read the case as Justice Thomas does. *Corfield* does not even purport to be an exhaustive declaration of the scope of rights protected by the privileges and immunities clause. On the contrary, Justice Washington set forth certain rights he believed to be within the purview of the clause—including the rights of travel, voting, and habeas corpus—and concluded as follows: "These, *and many others which might be mentioned*, are, strictly speaking, privileges and immunities."[144] Justice Thomas quotes this passage in his *Saenz* dissent but makes nothing of it.

But the framers of the Fourteenth Amendment made much of the passage. During the debates on the Amendment, one senator quoted *Corfield* at length and then explained that "these privileges and immunities . . . *are not and cannot be fully defined in their entire extent and precise nature.*"[145]

Similarly, a congressman had earlier asserted that *Corfield* set forth "*some of the particular privileges and immunities of citizens*" of the United States.[146]

What is most interesting here, however, is that, in utter contrast to Bork's reading the privileges or immunities clause out of the Constitution because of its purported opacity, Justice Thomas wants very much to see the clause become a central focus of Fourteenth Amendment jurisprudence precisely because he believes its original meaning is discernable. "Because I believe that the demise of the privileges or immunities clause has contributed in no small part to the current disarray of our Fourteenth Amendment jurisprudence," Justice Thomas declares, "I would be open to reevaluating its meaning in an appropriate case."[147]

The other vocal adherent of originalism on the current Court is, of course, Justice Antonin Scalia. Scalia, however, emphasizes that he gives the unadorned constitutional text primacy over the intent of the framers expressed elsewhere. "The text," he has said, "is the law, and it is the text that must be observed":

> I will consult the writings of some men who happened to be delegates to the Constitutional Convention. . . . I do so, however, not because they were framers and therefore their intent is authoritative and must be the law; but rather because their writings, like those of other intelligent and informed people of the time, display how the text of the Constitution was originally understood. . . . What I look for in the Constitution is precisely what I look for in a statute: the original meaning of the text, not what the original draftsmen intended.[148]

Interestingly, however, Justice Scalia joined the majority opinion in *Saenz v. Roe* against which Justice Thomas dissented so vigorously. And, although it is often noted that they are in agreement more than any other pair of Justices on the Court, there are other examples that illustrate that originalism, at least as practiced by Justices Scalia and Thomas, does not always lead to certain results.

Take *Troxel v. Granville*, a case decided in 2000.[149] Here the Court struck down a so-called grandparents' rights law enacted by the State of Washington. In order to ensure that grandparents retained visitation rights with respect to their grandchildren, especially in the case of divorce, the Washington law allowed a court to authorize visitation privileges for "any person" at "any time." Given the stunning breadth of the statute, the Court ruled it unconstitutional on the ground that the due process clause of the Fourteenth Amendment "does not permit a State to infringe on the fundamental right of parents to make child-rearing decisions simply because a state judge believes a 'better' decision could be made."[150]

Justice Thomas concurred in the judgment. Pointing out that no party in the case had questioned that the Constitution protected the right of parents to make child-rearing decisions, Justice Thomas noted that he would accept its existence for the purposes of the present case only and would "leave the resolution of that issue for another day."[151]

But, without any apparent hesitation, Justice Scalia dissented in *Troxel* with his signature disdain for those who disagree with him. He declared emphatically that the judicial recognition of parents' rights of any sort is an affront to the constitutional text:

> In my view, a right of parents to direct the upbringing of their children is among the "unalienable Rights" with which the Declaration of Independence proclaims "all Men . . . are endowed by their Creator." And in my view that right is also among the "othe[r] [rights] retained by the people" which the Ninth Amendment says the Constitution's enumeration of rights "shall not be construed to deny or disparage." The Declaration of Independence, however, is not a legal prescription conferring powers upon the courts; and the Constitution's refusal to "deny or disparage" other rights is far removed from affirming any one of them, and even farther removed from authorizing judges to identify what they might be, and to enforce the judge's list against the laws duly enacted by the people. . . .
>
> If we embrace this unenumerated right . . . we will be ushering in a new regime of judicially prescribed, and federally prescribed, family law. I have no reason to believe that federal judges will be better at this than state legislatures; and state legislatures have the great advantages of doing harm in a more circumscribed area, of being able to correct their mistakes in a flash, and of being removable by the people.[152]

This is surely a problematic reading because it reduces the Ninth Amendment to a practical nullity. The amendment reads as follows: "The enumeration in the Constitution of certain rights shall not be construed to deny or disparage others retained by the people." The Constitution thus explicitly recognizes the existence of rights other than those set forth in its text. Justice Scalia's argument is that, whatever these rights are, judges may not recognize or protect them. But neither can legislatures. Legislatures can create rights of a sort through statute, such as when Congress gave individuals a judicially enforceable right against employment discrimination in the Civil Rights Act of 1964. But these cannot be rights contemplated by the Ninth Amendment, because any legislative act may be altered or repealed by a future legislative act. (Indeed, says Justice Scalia, this may be done "in a flash," an assessment that I think almost no American legislator now living would agree with.) That is, any rights created by statute may be denied or disparaged by the subsequent passage of another statute.

So what rights does the Ninth Amendment protect? On Justice Scalia's reasoning, this simply cannot be determined. Since the amendment is "far removed" from affirming any particular right, there can be no convincing argument that a right protected by the Amendment is being denied or disparaged. Scalia himself demonstrates this in his *Troxel* dissent when he states both that *he* believes parental rights are protected by the Ninth Amendment and that such rights have no constitutional protection against "laws duly enacted by the people." The temptation is strong, therefore, to conclude that he has effectively negated a constitutional provision that has been known to give conservatives fits.

Still, conservatives are generally very much in favor of parental rights, which is why *Troxel* was applauded widely on the right. Writing in the *Wall Street Journal* on the day after the decision was issued, the Notre Dame law professor Richard Garnett called *Troxel* "a much-needed reaffirmation of family privacy, parents' rights, and limits on government." To contend that government has broad discretion to trump parents' rights to determine with whom their children will associate would be "nothing short of revolutionary: that after centuries at the center of Anglo-American legal tradition, the right of nonabusive parents to raise their own children as they see fit should yield to ad hoc judicial intervention at third parties' request. . . . Sometimes states must intervene in family life to protect children from abuse and neglect—but only in extreme cases."[153]

George Will nicely captures—without attempting to resolve—the conservative dilemma here. The Washington state court opinion that allowed grandparent visitation rights over the objections of the Troxels, says Will, was "an appalling justification for judicial usurpation of parental rights. However, Justice Scalia, dissenting, said there also was judicial presumptuousness in the Supreme Court's affirmation of parental liberty." Will concludes: "Most conservatives favor judicial restraint, but parental liberty, too. They immediately applauded the ruling that evoked this dissent from

Scalia. The astringency of his restraint calls the bluff of many conservative advocates of judicial restraint."[154]

Of course, as Bork himself acknowledges, a judge, even a U.S. Supreme Court Justice, should be willing to forgo deciding a case according to the intent of the framers in favor of adhering to the rule of stare decisis. Thus, the fact that Justices Thomas and Scalia disagreed as to whether *Troxel* presented a salutary opportunity to reexamine whether decades of precedent recognizing parental rights were grounded properly in original intent is not troubling in itself. However, beyond the directive to overturn *Roe v. Wade* at any opportunity, I'm not sure that Justices Thomas and Scalia—or any other originalist, for that matter—have articulated convincing objective standards to guide the decision between originalism and stare decisis.

Further, even when Scalia and Thomas both assert outright that they are deciding a case in accordance with original intent, they have arrived at different results. Take *McIntyre v. Ohio Elections Commission*, a 1995 decision.[155] In that case, the Court held that an Ohio statute that prohibited the distribution of anonymous campaign literature violated the First Amendment, at least as the law applied to a lone citizen pamphleteer. The majority based its holding upon the nation's "respected tradition of anonymity in the advocacy of political causes."[156]

Justice Thomas concurred in the judgment, stating, with no small degree of hauteur, that he based his conclusion not upon some supposed tradition that had existed *throughout* U.S. history but upon a determination of whether the First Amendment, "*as originally understood*, protected anonymous political leafletting."[157] He answered the question affirmatively because "the historical evidence indicates that Founding-era Americans opposed attempts to require that anonymous authors reveal their identities on the ground that forced disclosure violated the 'freedom of the press.'"[158]

However, even though he employed the same tone and methodology, Justice Scalia dissented in *McIntyre*. For Scalia, none of the examples of Founding-era literature cited by Justice Thomas is of any consequence because "not a single one involves the context of restrictions imposed in connection with a free, democratic election, which is all that is at issue here."[159] Finding no such examples himself, Justice Scalia concluded that the framers would certainly have believed the Ohio law to be constitutional.

Justices Scalia and Thomas have similarly come to opposite conclusions on matters such as whether Congress may grant the president a line item budget veto[160] and, in the Supreme Court's very first interpretation of the Eighth Amendment's prohibition upon "excessive fines," whether a federal forfeiture statute was unconstitutional.[161] One would think that these cases would be precisely the sort that originalists would be able to answer in unison because they do not involve applying original intent to modern technological or social conditions.

Turning to Justice Scalia alone, there is no small evidence of the inconsistency of his originalism. Consider the issue of drug testing. Justice Scalia wrote for the Court in *Veronia School District 47J v. Acton*, a 1995 decision concerning whether an Oregon public school district could subject students to random drug tests conducted by school officials as a condition of participation in interscholastic sports.[162] The specific constitutional issue was whether such testing violated the Fourth Amendment's mandate that government searches and seizures must be "reasonable."

Justice Scalia began by asserting that originalism had nothing to say on the question because "there was no clear practice, either approving or disapproving the type of search at issue, at the time" the Fourth Amendment was enacted.[163] More specifically, Scalia noted that the framers knew neither compulsory education nor urine tests: "Not until 1852 did Massachusetts, the pioneer in the 'common school' movement, enact a compulsory school attendance law. The drug problem, and the technology of drug testing, are of course even more recent."[164]

In light of this, Scalia declares, the Court has no alternative but to rely upon a judge-made test of reasonableness that balances the "intrusion on the individual's Fourth Amendment interests against [the searches'] promotion of legitimate government interests."[165] Using this test, Justice Scalia found the test to be reasonable.

But compare *Veronia* to Justice Scalia's opinion for the Court in *Kyllo v. U.S.*, a 2001 case.[166] In *Kyllo*, federal drug agents were able to obtain a warrant to search a suspect's home on the basis of the results of a warrantless search that utilized a "thermal imaging device." This device enabled the agents to detect a highly unusual amount of heat emanating from the suspect's home, which indicated that he might be—as he in fact was—using high-intensity lamps within to cultivate marijuana.

The warrantless use of the imager was ruled to be a violation of the Fourth Amendment. In contrast to *Veronia*, however, Justice Scalia finds no obstacle here to "tak[ing] the long view, from the original meaning of the Fourth Amendment forward."[167] But Scalia actually engages in no exposition whatever to explain why the framers would have frowned upon warrantless searches by means of a thermal imaging device. In fact, it is quite clear that Scalia is simply employing the same reasonableness test relied upon in *Veronia*.

Although conservatives profess a reflexive distaste for letting criminals go free on account of "technicalities," Justice Scalia received no small degree of praise from right-wing commentators for his opinion in *Kyllo*. The reason is that the opinion was taken to be a refutation of the charge that originalism cannot be applied legitimately in cases that involve technologies of which the framers could only have dreamed. Thus, George Will saw the case as a rebuke to those who would portray President George W. Bush's federal judicial nominees "as too much like Scalia, and hence too strict in their 'originalist' constitutional construction to understand the applicability of the [Constitution] to modern conditions."[168] But neither Will nor anyone else, so far as I know, has explained why the modern condition of a thermal imaging device is amenable to originalist analysis but the modern condition of urine testing is not.

And there are instances in which Justice Scalia simply avoids the issue of originalism's applicability when the result of applying original intent would be all but universally unacceptable within the context of the modern American polity. The best example here involves questions that concern the scope of free expression protected by the First Amendment. A great deal of scholarly work has been done on the framers' conception of the liberties of free expression. Scholars are in accord that the framers of the First Amendment conceived of its scope as far more constrained than would any American court today. Although differences certainly existed among them, members of the late-eighteenth-century political class tended strongly toward the belief that, beyond spoken or written communication about political affairs, a republican government had wide discretion with respect to restricting expression. Even with respect to political communication itself, the framers believed that the government could legitimately punish purportedly seditious and libelous speech to an extent far beyond what virtually anyone today would argue would be proper.[169]

First Amendment law, in so far as it existed at all, did not venture beyond this narrow scope for more than a century. "To the contrary, throughout the first 150 years of the First Amendment, federal courts regularly enforced severe restrictions on citizens' ability to speak freely."[170] As Michael Kent Curtis has recently written, "the Supreme Court came to its current protective view of free speech only very gradually and only in the twentieth century."[171] As late as 1924, H. L. Mencken could write accurately that the prevailing view of the First Amendment

> permits the state to condition free speech, and even to suspend it altogether, whenever it is deemed desirable. Our statute books are heavy with laws proscribing ideas. I could make a long list of them. Many of them are ideas that thousands of intelligent persons cherish as true, and even voice freely in private; nevertheless, it is forbidden to print them, and whoever attempts it is commonly punished very severely.[172]

The validity of Mencken's point is demonstrated by the fact that, in 1919, the Supreme Court unanimously upheld the ten-year jail sentence imposed upon Eugene V. Debs for speaking in opposition to U.S. participation in World War I.[173] Such a sentence would simply be unthinkable today.

It would be unthinkable because, as Chief Justice Rehnquist has said, in the 1920s the First Amendment began to "come into its own."[174] This is an oblique way of saying that, in the 1920s, American judges began to assert that a vibrant democratic society demanded constitutional protections of expression far greater than those that had prevailed in America since the Founding. They began to recognize, as Justice Cardozo put it in 1937, that "freedom of thought and speech . . . is the matrix, the indispensable condition, of nearly every other form of freedom."[175] Making allowance for more than occasional backtracking, a revolution has occurred. Cass Sunstein has usefully summarized the First Amendment's current scope in the aftermath of this revolution:

> The concrete results have been nothing short of extraordinary. Constitutional protection has been given to commercial speech; to most sexually explicit speech; to many kinds of libel; to publication of the names of rape victims; to the advocacy of crime, even of violent overthrow of the government; to large expenditures on election campaigns; to corporate speech; to flag burning; and to much else besides.[176]

And there is no question that this revolution in First Amendment interpretation was not guided by originalism. On the contrary, as David Strauss has recently written, "the text and the original understanding of the First Amendment are essentially irrelevant to the American system of freedom of expression as it exists today. One could, as a thought experiment, imagine forbidding any reference to the text or the original understandings; as long as the precedents could still be invoked, the operative law of freedom of expression would remain undisturbed."[177]

Consider against this background the case of *Hill v. Colorado*.[178] In this 2000 opinion, the Supreme Court upheld a state law that makes it unlawful for a person acting within one hundred feet of the entrance of a health care facility to "knowingly approach" within eight feet of another person, without the latter's consent, in order to distribute "a leaflet or handbill to, to displa[y] a sign to, or engag[e] in oral protest, education or counseling with that person. . . ."[179] Without any explicit mention of a particular form of protest, the clear intent of the statute is to limit the actions of anti-abortion protesters.

Justice Scalia, joined by Justice Thomas, wrote a long and powerful dissent. But, except for a single desultory assertion to the effect that "the framers surely" would have disagreed with the majority, the dissent is silent about the original intent of the First Amendment.[180] Scalia therefore makes no attempt to demonstrate that James Madison, who lived very much in an age of gentlemen, believed that the First Amendment demands that even a gentleman—to say nothing of a gentlewoman—must submit to being confronted on a public street by a fellow citizen, of whatever social status, for the purpose of being engaged in a political debate.

Rather, Scalia's anger flows from his contention that the majority has betrayed the commitment to free expression developed by *the Court* in the twentieth century. Thus, Scalia argues not that the majority has betrayed the intent of the framers but that it has engaged in "an unabashed repudiation of our"—that is, the Court's—"First Amendment doctrine."[181] He is especially concerned to refute the majority's contention that persons who approach health care facilities possess a right to be free from being confronted with unwelcome expression. If such a right "was part of our infant First Amendment law in 1921, I am shocked to think that it is there today."[182] In conclusion, Scalia laments that "[r]estrictive views of the First Amendment that have been in dissent since the 1930s suddenly find themselves in the majority."[183]

This stirring defense of the judge-made revolution in First Amendment jurisprudence stands in very stark contrast to the tone Scalia takes in other contexts. For example, in his numerous speeches to law school and professional audiences, it is almost guaranteed that Scalia will ridicule the notion of "a living Constitution," that is, the assertion that the Constitution's terms must be understood in light of current social and political conditions, rather than simply according to the intent of the framers. He has labeled the doctrine "absolute madness"[184] and has sarcastically referred to a living Constitution as "that wonderful document that morphs from generation to generation."[185]

Yet, at least in the crucial area of free expression, Justice Scalia is an ardent defender of a constitutional jurisprudence that is based upon the very notion that, whatever the conceptions of an eighteenth-century polity, a modern mass democracy cannot tolerate the granting to the government of a broad power to restrict the ideas and communications of its citizens. Writing three years before *Hill*, Laurence Tribe asserted that, "despite what he says, Justice Scalia has not interpreted the freedom of speech as a mere codification of the memories . . . of [American] colonists about what rights they believed had been secure as of a certain moment in the late eighteenth century."[186]

My purpose in all of this is not to offer anything like a comprehensive critique of the jurisprudence of original intent. This has been done quite effectively by others.[187] Nor is it to suggest that originalism is a useless interpretive method. That is certainly not the case, at least when one is willing to acknowledge, in the words of one of originalism's adherents, that the doctrine "is no walk in the park and, despite our best efforts, may not always yield definitive meanings."[188]

Adherents of the Imperial Judiciary thesis, however, generally resist making any such acknowledgment. Professor Keith Whittington of Princeton recently wrote a very thoughtful defense of originalism that nonetheless admitted the limits of the doctrine:

> There can be substantial disagreements both within originalism and over the nature of the theory. . . . [T]here can be disagreement within a single theory over correct interpretations. In arguing for originalism as a "neutral" mechanism, an "objective" standard, or as pointing to a "fixed and stable" text, originalists should not be misunderstood to mean that there cannot therefore be disagreements among sincere and competent originalist judges.[189]

But this simply will not do for the true believer. In his review of Whittington's book, Gary McDowell chided him because he is "[u]nwilling to be lumped together with the leading figures in the originalist camp like Judge

Bork, Raoul Berger and Lino Graglia" and because "he cannot bring himself to embrace originalism fully. Whenever he draws close, conceding its necessity, he ultimately shies away, arguing its insufficiency."[190] What accounts for this kind of tenacity among Imperial Judiciary theorists, which asserts the "necessity" of originalism, but refuses to concede any of the doctrine's shortcomings?

The answer is not difficult. Calling oneself an adherent of originalism and asserting that the doctrine is the only legitimate method of constitutional interpretation is a marvelous way to *delegitimize* the entire body of constitutional adjudication with which one disagrees. The stance was summed up wonderfully by Justice Clarence Thomas in a speech he gave to a conservative think tank in 1999. When it comes to constitutional adjudication, Justice Thomas opined, "you can either try to figure out what the framers intended, or you can make it up."[191] With trademark snideness, Justice Scalia made much the same point in a 1988 address to a law school audience. He declared there that "originalism is not, and had perhaps never been, the sole method of constitutional exegesis. It would be hard to count on the fingers of both hands and the toes of both feet, yea, even on the hairs of one's youthful head, the opinions that have in fact been rendered not on the basis of what the Constitution originally meant, *but on the basis of what the judges currently thought it desirable for it to mean.*"[192] This is Robert Bork's version: "Either the Constitution and statutes are law, which means that their principles are known and control judges, or they are malleable texts that judges may rewrite to see that particular groups or political causes win."[193]

This is a fundamentally Manichaean view: the judge as passive mouthpiece for the framers versus the judge as untethered visionary. This has the tendency to reduce constitutional interpretation to a morality play. The full perspective is perfectly set forth in the concluding passage of *The Tempting of America:*

> The difference between our historically grounded constitutional freedoms and those the theorists, whether of the academy or of the bench, would replace them with is akin to the difference between the American and French revolutions. The outcome for liberty was much less happy under the regime of the abstract "rights of man" than it has been under the American Constitution. What Burke said of the abstract theorists who produced the calamities of the French Revolution might equally be said of those, judges and professors alike, who would remake our constitution

out of moral philosophy: "This sort of people are so taken up with their theories about the rights of man that they have totally forgotten his nature." Those who made and endorsed our Constitution knew man's nature, and it is to their ideas, rather than to the temptations of utopia, that we must ask that our judges adhere.[194]

This is stirring rhetoric. But it may be that the framers of the Constitution were beyond thinking of constitutional adjudication in terms of facile dichotomies.

Conclusion: "Sacred" Courts Practicing "Moral Intimidation"

Adherents of the Imperial Judiciary thesis see themselves as champions of democracy. But what sort of democracy do they champion? Robert Bork, for example, writes in *Slouching towards Gomorrah* that "[t]here appears to be only one means" by which American democracy can be saved from the usurpations of a rampaging judiciary. (This recalls Hofstadter's observation that "[t]he apocalypticism of the paranoid style runs dangerously near to hopeless pessimism, but usually stops short of it.")[195] This unique means is "a constitutional amendment making any federal or state court decision subject to being overruled by a majority vote of each House of Congress."[196] Failing this, says Bork, "the democratic nation is helpless before an antidemocratic, indeed, a despotic, judiciary."[197]

Bork's proposed amendment would effect majoritarian rule at something approaching its crudest form. We shall later see that, if anything can be discerned about the intent of the Constitution's framers, it is that not much would be more antithetical to it than this. But it is really stunning just how little faith Bork has displayed in popular wisdom and fortitude since announcing what "the democratic nation" needs to survive. Employing the kind of world-weary condescension one usually expects to encounter from a Marxist convinced that the people are possessed of "false consciousness," Bork asserted in 2002 that the American citizenry simply lacks the self-control necessary for the survival of our constitutional order: "The public does seem ready to jettison long-term safeguards and the benefits of process for the short-term satisfaction of desires. That is always and everywhere the human temptation. But it is precisely that temptation that a constitution and its judicial spokesmen are supposed to protect us against."[198]

Indeed, it is because of the people's failings that Bork came to the conclusion, stated in his forward to Max Boot's 1998 book, *Out of Order*, that his proposed amendment would not work. Why not? After declaring the international dimensions of the problem of judicial perfidy—"Judicial usurpation of democratic prerogatives is just about universal wherever judicial independence is an ideal and particularly where there is a written constitution containing a bill of rights"[199]—Bork concludes that Canada's attempt to break free from the thrall of judges seals the case for despair:

> Canada's new constitution provides not only for judicial review of statutes and official acts but for a reciprocal legislative power, both in the Parliament and in the provincial legislatures, to override the acts of the courts. Canada had no long history of judicial supremacy, as we do. . . . If a legislative override would succeed anywhere, it should be in Canada. Legislative efforts to exercise the power given the legislatures by the constitution nonetheless provoked cries of outrage. They are, it is said, impermissible attempts to interfere with judicial independence, and that notwithstanding that the constitutional provision [*sic*] for just such interference. The courts are, apparently, more sacred than the Constitution. The same thing is true of the United States, and it is predictable that a legislative override . . . would rarely be attempted and even more rarely succeed. The power and independence of the courts lies not in historical or textual meaning of the Constitution but in moral intimidation.[200]

Is Bork correct in saying that the American people are even more subject to "moral intimidation" in the face of judicial power?[201] Or is it the case that, while courts are, and have been throughout our history, powerful, we have realized (1) that there is value in respecting the principle of judicial independence and (2) that courts have never become so powerful that democratic politics has stopped. The rest of the book seeks to answer these questions.

2

The Constitution and the Judiciary

The era of the American Revolution saw the greatest concentrated burst of constitution making in history, at least before the implosion of the Eastern Bloc in 1989. In the wake of the outbreak of armed struggle with the British Empire, each of the thirteen American states formed a new constitution, usually after engaging in extensive debate as to the proper form of popular government. This experience of course culminated in the creation of the federal Constitution by the Philadelphia Convention in 1787, its successful ratification by conventions of the several states the following year, and the addition of ten amendments—what we now call the Bill of Rights—in 1791.

The institution of government that underwent the greatest conceptual transformation during the Revolutionary Era was the judiciary. As we shall see presently, out of the debates of the Revolutionary Era, the judiciary was constituted for the first time as a truly independent branch of government, one invested with powers that would ensure its autonomy from the legislative and the executive branches. During this time, according to the historian Gordon Wood, the judiciary "suddenly emerged out of its colonial insignificance to become by 1800 the principal means by which popular legislatures were controlled and limited. The most dramatic institutional transformation in the early Republic was the rise of what was called an 'independent judiciary.'"[1]

This chapter considers this transformation and sets forth the political concerns that motivated the reconception and enhancement of judicial power. The goal is to establish that the idea of the judiciary as a vital presence in our politics is very much consistent with our constitutional order as originally conceived. In short, this chapter presents an investigation into original intent.

The Judiciary in Theory and Practice

As men of the Enlightenment, the leading constitutional thinkers in America during the Revolutionary Era were possessed of a faith in the progressive improvement of the practical sciences, one of which was politics. Alexander Hamilton declared in *The Federalist* that, after centuries of conceptual torpor, the science of politics had recently experienced "great improvement. The efficacy of various principles is now well understood, which were either not known at all, or imperfectly known to the ancients."[2] One of the most important of these advances, said Hamilton, was the employment of "[t]he standard of good behavior for the continuance in office of the judicial magistracy. . . . [I]t is the best expedient which can be devised in any government to secure a steady, upright, and impartial administration of the laws."[3]

If the idea that judges should retain their offices during good behavior was a recent idea at the time Hamilton wrote, so too was the more fundamental notion that the judiciary constituted a distinct branch of government. In his *Second Treatise of Government*, John Locke, whose influence in America was considerable, set forth a theory of the separation of powers among the legislative, executive, and "federative"—the foreign relations function of the state—branches of government, without reference to the judiciary.[4] According to the Locke scholar Peter Laslett, Locke vaguely conceived of the judiciary as "no separate power, it was a general attribute of the state."[5] Montesquieu, who was also widely read in America, similarly had little notion of the judiciary as a coequal branch of government. He did write that "there is no liberty, if the judiciary power be not separated from the legislative and executive."[6] But the reason behind this belief was the concern that the legislative and executive branches might use judges to further their own oppressive designs. Standing by itself, said Montesquieu, the judiciary was "in some measure next to nothing."[7]

Judicial independence received tremendous practical advancement, however, with the English Act of Settlement of 1701, which established life tenure during good behavior for all judges appointed by the Crown. To William Blackstone, whose *Commentaries on the Laws of England* were essential reading for all American lawyers seeking any degree of professional prominence, the imposition of permanent tenure for judges was a salutary reform of the first order. While courts had long been "the grand depository of the fundamental laws of the kingdom, and have gained a known and stated jurisdiction," they were now a depository of real status:

In this distinct and separate existence of the judicial power, in a peculiar body of men, nominated indeed, but not removable at pleasure, by the crown, consists one main preservative of the public liberty; which cannot subsist long in any state, unless the administration of common justice be in some degree separated both from the legislative and also from the executive power. Were it joined with the legislative, the life, liberty, and property, of the subject would be in the hands of arbitrary judges, whose decisions would be then regulated only by their own opinions, and not by any fundamental principles of law. . . . Were it joined with the executive, this union might soon be an overbalance for the legislative.[8]

But the Act of Union was not extended to the American colonies. Before the Revolution, generally speaking, American judges were appointed and removable at will by colonial governors, who themselves held office at the suffrage of the British regime. What is more, colonial governors could generally create courts without seeking legislative approval. In the years immediately before the Revolution, such courts became a primary instrument for the enforcement of hated British commercial taxes and regulations.[9]

These conditions of judicial dependency were frequently decried by American critics of British colonial policy. In one of the most influential pamphlets of the time, *Letters from a Farmer in Pennsylvania*, John Dickinson put the matter as follows:

As to "the administration of justice"—the judges ought, in a well regulated state, to be equally independent of the executive and the legislative powers. Thus in England, judges hold their commissions from the crown "*during good behaviour*," and have salaries, suitable to their dignity, *settled*, on them by parliament. The purity of the courts of law since this establishment, is a proof of the wisdom with which it was made.

But in these colonies, how fruitless has been every attempt to have the judges appointed "*during good behaviour?*" Yet whoever considers the matter will soon perceive, that *such commissions* are beyond all comparison more necessary in these colonies, than they were in England.[10]

In England itself, Edmund Burke recognized that America's revolutionary movement was fueled by the desire for "a fair and unbiased judicature," which could not be had "as judges, at all levels, from justices of the peace to chief justices of the supreme courts, were not only appointed on the nomination of the royal governor, but were dismissible by the governor's fiat."[11] Accordingly, included in the Declaration of Independence's bill of indictment against George III was the charge that he had made "judges dependent on his will alone, for the tenure of their offices, and the amount and payment of their salaries."[12]

Given this background, one would think that the wave of constitution making that took place in the states after the break with England would have advanced the cause of judicial independence. John Adams, in *Thoughts on Government*, a widely read pamphlet written in 1776, urged this course, stating there that judges "should not be dependent upon any man, or body of men. . . . [T]hey should hold estates for life in their offices; or, in other words, their commissions should be during good behavior, and their salaries ascertained and established by law."[13] However, because of their recent experience with governors and courts as arms of hated royal authority, the Revolutionary state constitution makers moved in another direction, toward the aggrandizement of the legislature at the expense of the other branches of government. As the historian M. J. C. Vile puts it, the end of royal authority in the states "was followed by period of government by convention in which the revolutionary legislature absorbed all power into its own hands, carrying out all the tasks of government through the medium of its committees."[14] Or, as James Madison himself observed in *The Federalist*, "the compilers of most of the American constitutions" had ensured that [t]he legislative department is everywhere extending the sphere of its activity and drawing all power into its impetuous vortex."[15]

As an adjunct to diminishing executive power, the Revolutionary state constitutions generally took the power of appointing judges away from the governor, placing it instead with the legislature. And, as David Currie describes, "[s]everal states in which judges served during good behavior subjected them to removal [without cause]. Even those that provided for removal only by impeachment (for such causes as crime, misbehavior, maladministration, absence, or incapacity) tended to do nothing to prevent the legislature from reducing judicial salaries."[16] What is more, in matters of court structure and procedure, the state legislatures exercised almost unchecked powers. Indeed, judicial decisions themselves were frequently overturned by legislative fiat. Gordon Wood has noted that the goal of such constraints upon judicial power was to eliminate judicial discretion to the greatest possible extent:

The aim, as Jefferson put it, was to end "the eccentric impulses of whimsical, capricious designing man" and to make the judge "a mere machine." . . . Once the legislatures had clarified and written down the laws, then judges would presumably no longer have any justification for following their own inclinations and pleasure in interpreting the law. . . . Only then could the people be protected from becoming "slaves to magistrates." Only scientific codification and strict judicial observance of the text of the law would free the people from judicial tyranny.[17]

Note the resemblance between this description of a particular facet of the Spirit of '76 and today's Imperial Judiciary theorists. But this was *not* the vision that was to be embodied in the federal Constitution composed in 1787. On the contrary, it was precisely the aggrandizement of legislative power in the states that alarmed the men who composed that document and managed its ratification. Thus it was that some of the supporters of constitutional reform began, in the words of one, to look upon the judiciary as "the only body of men who will have an effective check upon a numerous Assembly."[18]

Although the Philadelphia Convention was certainly concerned with reforming the practically moribund federal government established by the Articles of Confederation, "the weaknesses of the Articles of Confederation were *not* the most important reasons for the making of the Constitution."[19] As James Madison declared to Thomas Jefferson shortly after the Convention, concerns regarding the state of the American union were decidedly *secondary* to disquiets raised by the practice of politics under the Revolutionary state constitutions. The injustices of state politics, said Madison, had been

so frequent and so flagrant as to alarm the most steadfast friends of republicanism. I am persuaded I do not err in saying that the evils issuing from these sources contributed more to that uneasiness which produced the Convention, and prepared the public mind for a general reform, than those which accrued to our national character and interest from the inadequacy of the [Articles of] Confederation to its immediate objects.[20]

Moreover, as we shall see, the problem of legislative aggrandizement was not seen by Madison and his allies as concerning merely an institution that had grown too powerful for its own good. Rather, the problem was far deeper, to the extent that "many Americans who became Federalists reassessed the promise of American life under republican government."[21]

Rethinking Popular Government

What specifically were the state legislatures doing that alarmed the men who strove for federal constitutional reform? To begin with, these men were deeply concerned about the *quality* of the legislative process that characterized the Revolutionary state legislatures. They believed that the Revolution had brought many individuals into political life who lacked legislative skills. As Alexander Hamilton remarked bluntly, there were "many inconsiderable men in possession of considerable offices under the state governments."[22] These "inconsiderable men" too often wrote laws that were convoluted or unintelligible, and they enacted and repealed statutes with what was perceived to be frightening dispatch.

Madison summarized these complaints in *Vices of the Political System of the United States*, a sort of position paper he wrote for himself shortly before the Philadelphia Convention. America during the Revolutionary Era, he said, had experienced a "luxuriancy of legislation":

> The short period of independency has filled as many pages as the century which preceded it. Every year, almost every session, adds a new volume. . . . A review of the several codes will show that every necessary and useful part of the least voluminous of them might be compressed into one-tenth of the compass, and at the same time be rendered tenfold as perspicuous.
>
> We daily see laws repealed or superceded, before any trial can have been made of their merits, and even before a knowledge of them can have reached the remoter districts within which they were to operate.[23]

More troubling than badly written laws, however, were the objects toward which many of these laws were directed. As has been detailed by many historians, during the Revolution and in the years immediately afterward, state legislatures "often paid little heed to abstract considerations of property rights. They turned instead to debtor-relief laws and the issuance of paper money, measures designed to aid debtors at the expense of creditors. State legislatures repeatedly intervened in debtor-creditor relations with a host of laws staying executions for debts, permitting the payment of obligations in installments, and making depreciated paper currency legal tender."[24]

A survey of the statements of the principal backers of national constitutional reform in these years reveals instance after instance of pejorative references to these legislative initiatives. In *Federalist* 10, Madison characterized the "rage for paper money, for an abolition of debts, for an equal division of property," as "wicked projects."[25] At the Pennsylvania ratification convention, James Wilson stated more generally that, if the politics of the Revolutionary Era had proven anything to him, it was that "to give permanency, stability and security to any government, I conceive it of essential importance, that its legislature should be restrained."[26]

What most troubled the framers was the popularity of what the legislatures were doing. In the republican polities of the thirteen states, legislatures were elected pursuant to the broadest suffrage laws then existing. Indeed, republican theory itself placed great weight upon the idea that a legislature should be a direct embodiment of the will of the people. As Bernard Bailyn explains, the people were not "merely an ultimate check on government, they *were* in some sense the government. Government had no separate existence apart from them; it was *by* the people as well as *for* the people; it gained its authority from their continual consent."[27] Melancton Smith, a leading Anti-Federalist, declared that it was the conventional wisdom of republicanism that representatives should "resemble those they represent; they should be a true picture of the people; possess the knowledge of their circumstances and their wants; sympathize in all their distresses, and be disposed to seek their true interests."[28] Thus, in the eyes of Madison and his allies, whenever a legislature enacted an injustice like paper money into law, it could only be assumed that it was acting at the immediate behest of a majority of the people. Therefore, he said, the problem of a republican legislature is that it has an institutional tendency "to feel all the passions which actuate a multitude."[29]

Shortly after a revolution that had thrown off the oppression of the British monarchy, Madison and his allies were therefore confronting the highly unsettling notion that the people themselves could be as oppressive as a monarch. "Is not history as full of the vices of the people, as it is of the crimes of the kings," asked Benjamin Rush, of Pennsylvania?[30] If that is the case, said James Winthrop, of Massachusetts, "[i]t is therefore as necessary to defend an individual against the majority in a republick, as against the king in a monarchy."[31] Madison made the same point in a speech to the First Congress when that body was considering the constitutional amendments that would become the Bill of Rights:

> In our government it is, perhaps, less necessary to guard against the abuse in the executive department than any other; because it is not the stronger branch of the system, but the weaker: It therefore must be levelled against the legislative for it is the most powerful. . . . But I confess that I do conceive, that in a government modified like this of the United States, the great danger lies rather in *the abuse of the community* rather than in the legislative body. The prescriptions in favor of liberty, ought to be levelled against that quarter where the greatest danger lies, namely, that which possesses the highest prerogative of power: But this is not found in either the executive or legislative departments of government, but in *the body of the people operating by the majority against the minority.*[32]

Madison was particularly distressed by the problem of majority tyranny because, according to his analysis of the future course of development of the American nation, it was likely to become much worse.[33] In the famous tenth number of *The Federalist*, he asserted that "the most common and durable source of factions has been the verious and unequal distribution of property. Those who hold and those who are without property have ever formed distinct interests in society."[34] He did not add here a sentiment that he expressed several times in both private correspondence and public speech during the years surrounding the Philadelphia Convention. For Madison felt strongly that America as it then existed—thirteen states on the Eastern seaboard and some unsettled territory across the Appalachians with very uncertain prospects for development—would rapidly become, as he termed it, "fully peopled." The situation was this, he told the Virginia ratification convention:

> The period cannot be very far distant when the unsettled parts of America will be inhabited. At the expiration of twenty-five years hence, I conceive that in every part of the United States, there will be as great a population as there is now in the settled parts. We see already, that the most populous parts of the union, and where there is but a medium, manufactures are beginning to be established.[35]

In Madison's eyes, there were decidedly painful political consequences to be expected from this demographic movement. At the Philadelphia Convention, he spoke with complete candor regarding these. It was true, Madison admitted, that there was no hereditary aristocracy in the United States, nor was there yet the sort of extreme inequalities of wealth that typified European nations. At this point, however, the good news ended. "Even at this time," he said, it would be wrong to believe that American society can be likened to "one homogenous mass in which everything that affects a part will affect in the same manner the whole." Further, the only safe assumption one could make about the future was that American society would become even *less* homogeneous:

> In framing a system which we wish to last for ages, we shd. not lose sight of the changes which ages will produce. An increase of population will of necessity increase the proportion of those who will labour under all the hardships of life, and secretly sigh for a more equal distribution of its blessings. These may in time outnumber those who are placed above the feelings of indigence. According to the equal law of suffrage, the power will slide into the hands of the former.... [S]ymptoms of a leveling spirit ... have sufficiently appeared in certain quarters to give notice of the future danger. How is this danger to be guarded agst. on republican principles?[36]

Thus, power in the American republic would increasingly come to be exercised by what Madison called in *Federalist* 10 "the superior force of an interested and overbearing majority."[37] Hence the dilemma: what sort of institutional mechanisms would preserve republican government while at the same time providing the best hope of alleviating the increasing capacity of popular majorities to invade the rights of the propertied minority? The historian Drew McCoy is thus starkly correct when he declares that "Madison's republic was in a race against time."[38]

For our purposes, the most important point here is that at the very heart of the movement for federal constitutional reform was a reexamination of the central tenet of popular government: majority rule. In Gordon Wood's assessment, "Americans thus experienced in the 1780s not merely a crisis of authority—licentiousness leading to anarchy—which was a comprehensible abuse of republican liberty, but also a serious shattering of older ways of examining politics and a fundamental questioning of majority rule that threatened to shake the foundations of their republican experiments."[39]

Expressions of unease with respect to the moral authority of majorities were ubiquitous among the leading framers. Madison stated the problem as follows in a 1786 letter to James Monroe:

> [In a republic] the interest of the majority is the political standard of right and wrong. Taking the interest as synonymous with "ultimate happiness," in which sense it is qualified with every necessary moral ingredient, the proposition is no doubt true. But taking it in the popular sense, as referring to the immediate augmentation of property and wealth, nothing can be more false. In the latter sense it would be the interest of the majority in every community to despoil and enslave the minority.[40]

But it was not merely in private correspondence that such concerns were expressed. At the Philadelphia Convention, Hamilton spoke forthrightly about the potential for majorities to commit injustice:

> The voice of the people has been said to be the voice of God; and however generally this maxim has been quoted and believed, it is not true in fact. The people are turbulent and changing; they seldom judge or determine right.[41]

Hamilton was only slightly less candid on the matter in *The Federalist*:

> It is a just observation that the people commonly *intend* the PUBLIC GOOD. This often applies to their very errors. But their good sense would despise the adulator who should pretend that they always *reason right* about the *means* of promoting it. They know from experience that they sometimes err; and the wonder is that they so seldom err as they do, beset as they continually are by the snares of the ambitious, the avaricious, the desperate.[42]

At the Virginia ratification convention, Madison declared that "on a candid examination of history we shall find that turbulence, violence, and abuse of power, by the majority trampling on the rights of the minority have produced factions and commotions which, in republics, have more frequently than any other cause, produced despotism."[43] Henry Lee put the matter more bluntly for the Virginia delegates: "I dread more from the licentiousness of the people, than from the bad government of rulers."[44] Tellingly, therefore, when Madison defined a "republic" in *The Federalist*, he did so without making anything but an oblique reference to majority rule: "[W]e may define a republic to be . . . a government which derives all its powers directly or indirectly from the great body of the people, and is administered by persons holding their offices during pleasure for a limited period, or during good behavior."[45]

Sentiments such as those we have just set forth are not often emphasized in civics classes and like environments because they are bluntly at odds with what we have come to think of as Jeffersonian democracy. But so deep was the concern of the framers with respect to the potential for injustice toward minorities that it is not possible to understand adequately the institutional structures they established in the Constitution without keeping their disquiet about majority rule foremost in mind. As we shall now see, this is particularly the case with regard to the judiciary they created.

Building a Better Judiciary

The problem of legislative power in a republic was, in the first place, the tendency of legislatures to assume governmental functions that were not properly within their purview. As M. J. C. Vile has said, in Revolutionary America, "legislatures soon meddled in every type of government business, including that normally reserved to the judiciary."[46] Writing for the Supreme Court, Justice Scalia has noted that "[t]he vigorous, indeed often radical populism of the revolutionary legislatures and assemblies increased the frequency of legislative correction of judgments. . . . Voices from many quarters, official as well as private, decried the increasing legislative interference with the private-law judgments of courts."[47]

The strongest of these voices was Madison's. In *Federalist* 44, he decried "legislative interference in cases affecting personal rights."[48] In *Federalist* 48, he quoted an extensive passage from Thomas Jefferson's *Notes on the State of Virginia* regarding the condition of that state's politics, including the complaint that the state legislature had on many occasions "*decided rights* which should have been left to *judiciary controversy.*"[49]

In Madison's eyes, however, it was important to acknowledge that, in a society riven by faction, the legislative process itself took on a judicial cast. In a passage in *Federalist* 10 that does not often receive much attention, Madison sets forth this idea as follows:

No man is allowed to be a judge in his own cause. . . . With equal, nay with greater reason, a body of men, are unfit to be both judges and parties, at the same time; yet, *what are many of the most important acts of legislation, but so many judicial determinations*, not indeed concerning the rights of single persons, but concerning the rights of large bodies of citizens; and what are the different classes of legislators, but advocates and parties to the causes which they determine?[50]

That is, the interplay of interests in a legislature that resulted in the passage of a particular piece of legislation was, in its implications for the rights of citizens, very much like a court case. But experience had taught Madison that, unlike a judicial proceeding presided over by an impartial judge, considerations of justice were likely to be disregarded in the legislative process. When interest dashed against interest in the legislature, as Madison further stated in *Federalist* 10, "[j]ustice ought to hold the balance, between them. Yet the parties are and must be themselves the judges; and the most numerous party, or, in other words, the most powerful faction must be expected to prevail."[51]

The point to emphasize here is that the project of the Philadelphia Convention with respect to the judiciary was more complex than is usually appreciated. The goal was only partly, as James Wilson stated at Philadelphia, to "give the judiciary a sufficient self-defensive power" such that it would be a truly independent branch of the government.[52] The object, as we shall later consider in more detail, was also to bring the judiciary into the process of legislation such that the inherently juridical character of that process might be enhanced. In other words, since the legislative process results in judgments implicating the rights of social constituencies—judgments that have a disturbing tendency to disregard the rights of minorities—would it not be sensible to involve relatively impartial judges in the process in order to ensure that disinterested reason would have a role in legislative judgments? Writing about the framers' concept of judicial power, the political theorist Shannon Stimson has made the point nicely:

The purpose of establishing an independent point of judgment outside the legislative sphere of interests was to counter demagogic appeals by bringing "disinterested" reason and reflective judgment to bear on public law and public understanding. Such a point of judgment entails that the "political" sphere is recognized to be larger than the legislative organ, *and the Court functions within this larger sphere rather than . . . in a private law sphere of its own. . . .* [T]hose who either supported it or opposed it recognized both its novel, political character and the potentially expansive latitude inherent in the new space it was to occupy within the polity.[53]

The Articles of Confederation, of course, established no federal court system. Hamilton wrote in *The Federalist* that "the want of a judiciary power" was a "circumstance that crowns the defects" of government under the Articles.[54] But what sort of judicial power did the framers believe would remedy this defect?

Tenure during Good Behavior, among Other Things

First, the judiciary under the Constitution would be an independent entity in terms of the tenure and emoluments of office. The Constitution, of course, provides in Article III, Section 1, that "Judges, both of the supreme and inferior Courts, shall hold their Offices during good Behaviour, and shall, at stated Times, receive for their Services a Compensation which shall not be diminished during their Continuance in Office." Thus, the blessings of the British Act of Settlement were finally to be established in America. Further, neither the legislative nor the executive branch was to have exclusive control over the appointment of federal judges. While the framers certainly did not want the legislature vested with sole authority to name judges, they also realized that, as one delegate said at Philadelphia, giving the power to the executive alone would cause the people to "think we are leaning too much toward Monarchy."[55] Thus, the Constitution provides, in Article II, Section 2, that the president "shall have Power, by and with the Advice and Consent of the Senate," to appoint judges. As two legal scholars have noted, "[t]he premium that the framers placed on judicial independence is reflected by the fact that these two provisions went virtually unchallenged throughout the Convention."[56]

But it is important to understand that the framers did not view the provision of life tenure as solely a self-defensive means of ensuring judicial autonomy against "the encroachments and oppressions of the representative body."[57] In *The Federalist*, Hamilton explicitly links the utility of life tenure to the fact that federal courts would be expected to impose checks upon the excesses of the legislative branch, whether or not these were directed against the judicial branch itself. While tenure during good behavior would therefore protect judges, "[t]his independence of the judges is *equally requisite* to guard the constitution and the rights of individuals from . . . dangerous innovations in the government, and serious oppressions of the minor party in the community."[58]

It is also not often noted that the framers held that life tenure did not render the judiciary anomalous within a republican polity, as Thomas Jefferson later came to believe when he opined "[t]hat there should be public functionaries independent of the nation, . . . is a solecism in a republic of the first order of absurdity and inconsistency."[59] Through the process of judicial selection conducted by the elected branches of the federal government, said Madison, "the judges, with all the other officers of the Union, will, as in the several States, be the choice, though a remote choice, of the people themselves."[60] This selection process, James Wilson told the Pennsylvania ratification convention, would compare favorably with that of Britain: "Is the judicial system of England grounded on representation? No. For the judges are appointed by the king, and he . . . derives not his majesty or power from the people."[61] But, true to the hope that judges would not be subject to the passions that might unite a majority of citizens in the pursuit of oppressive designs, Madison made it clear that "the permanent tenure by which the appointments are held in [the judicial] department must soon destroy *all sense of dependence* on the authority conferring them."[62]

The Constitution also contains provisions that in particular instances preclude what Madison called the "occlusion of Courts" by legislative action.[63] Article I, Section 9, guarantees that "the Writ of Habeas Corpus shall not be suspended, unless when in Cases of Rebellion or Invasion the public Safety may require it." Habeas corpus, of course, allows judges to command government officials to produce in court an individual within their custody for a determination of the lawfulness of continued confinement. Article I, Section 9, also provides that "No Bill of Attainder . . . shall be passed." As Leonard Levy has explained, these "are legislative findings that a named individual or an identifiable one is guilty of a crime and must suffer death as a punishment. Bills of attainder wholly circumvent the judicial system."[64]

Finally, in an effort to bolster the independence of *state* judiciaries, Article I, Section 10, extends the bans on bills of attainder and ex post facto laws to the states. Hamilton declared that the efficacy of the state judiciaries was a cause worthy of promotion specifically because "[t]he benefits of the integrity and moderation of the judiciary have already been felt in more States than one; and though they may have displeased those whose sinister expectations they may have disappointed, they must have commanded the esteem and applause of all the virtuous and disinterested."[65]

Judicial Review

Having considered the means of judicial independence, we now proceed to the means of judicial power, that is, the means by which an autonomous judiciary participates in the politics of a republican regime. Again, it is to be emphasized that the construction of judicial power must be understood against the background of the framers' persistent fear of the capacity of legislative majorities to perform acts of injustice. As Jack Rakove puts it, the framers' "grasp of the expansive uses to which legislative power could be put was itself a constitutional discovery, and it shaped much of the context within which new conceptions of judicial power . . . took shape."[66]

Most familiarly, the judiciary must possess the power to strike down legislative enactments if these are determined to be in violation of the Constitution. The classic statement here is Hamilton's in *Federalist* 78 regarding the enforcement of constitutional limitations upon legislative power:

> Limitations of this kind can be preserved in practice no other way than through the medium of courts of justice, whose duty it must be to declare all acts contrary to the manifest tenor of the Constitution void. Without this, all the reservations of particular rights or privileges would amount to nothing.[67]

The skeptic will ask at this point, if judicial review is such a wonderful thing, why does the Constitution not provide for it explicitly in the same manner that it sets forth the power of Congress to pass enumerated types of legislation? Hamilton dealt with this question in *Federalist* 81. It was true, he said, that

> there is not a syllable in the plan under consideration which *directly* empowers the national courts to construe laws according to the spirit of the Constitution. . . . I admit, however, that the Constitution ought to be the standard of construction for the laws, and that wherever there is an

evident opposition, the laws ought to give place to the Constitution. But this doctrine is not deducible from any circumstance peculiar to the plan of convention, *but from the general theory of a limited Constitution.*[68]

A number of other public statements by leading framers also made the same point. Here is John Marshall, who was later to be Chief Justice of the Supreme Court for thirty-four years, speaking to the Virginia ratification convention:

> If [the legislature] were to make a law not warranted by any of the powers enumerated, it would be considered by the judges as an infringement of the Constitution which they are to guard. They would not consider such a law as coming within their jurisdiction. They would declare it void. . . .
>
> To what quarter will you look for protection from an infringement on the Constitution, if you will not give the power to the judiciary? There is no other body that can afford such a protection.[69]

Oliver Ellsworth, the architect of the Judiciary Act of 1789, which created the federal court system, and himself a Supreme Court justice for four years, explained judicial review to the Connecticut ratification convention as a power that would restrain both Congress and the state legislatures:

> If the general legislature should at any time overleap their limits, the judicial department is a constitutional check. If the United States go beyond their powers, if they make a law which the constitution does not authorize, it is void; and the judicial power, the national judges, who to secure their impartiality are to be made independent, will declare it to be void. On the other hand, if the states go beyond their limits, if they make a law which is a usurpation upon the general government, the law is void, and upright independent judges will declare it to be so.[70]

James Wilson, who served on the Supreme Court from 1789 until his death in 1798 (in spite of being arrested twice during his term for nonpayment of debts arising from land speculation), told the Pennsylvania ratification convention that

> it is possible that the legislature . . . may transgress the bounds assigned to it, and an act may pass, in the usual mode, notwithstanding that transgression; but when it comes to be discussed before the judges—when they

consider its principles, and find it to be incompatible with the superior power of the constitution, it is their duty to pronounce it void; and judges independent, and not obliged to look to every session, for a continuance of their salaries, will behave with intrepidity, and refuse to act the sanction of judicial authority.[71]

Patrick Henry, who was the leader of the Anti-Federalist opposition to ratification in Virginia, worried that the power of judicial review would not be exercised with sufficient vigor under the Constitution:

> The honorable gentlemen did our judiciary honor in saying that they had firmness to counteract the legislature in some cases. Yes, sir, our judges opposed the acts of the legislature. . . . Are you sure that your federal judiciary will act thus? Is that judiciary as well constructed, and as independent of the other branches, as our state judiciary?[72]

But most opponents of ratification reacted with something close to horror when they contemplated the exercise of judicial review. To them, judicial review was the sure path to judicial *supremacy*. Here is the analysis of the pseudononymous "Brutus":

> [The Supreme Court] will give the sense of every article of the constitution, that may from time to time come before them. And in their decisions they will not confine themselves to any fixed or established rules, but will determine, according to what appears to them, the reason and spirit of the constitution. The opinions of the supreme court, whatever they may be, will have the force of law; because there is no power provided in the constitution, that can correct their errors, or control their adjudications. From this court there is no appeal.[73]

Brutus later made this interesting comparison to the British Constitution:

> The judges in England are under the control of the legislature, for they are bound to determine according to the laws passed by them. But the judges under this constitution will control the legislature, for the supreme court are authorized in the last resort . . . to give the constitution an explanation, and there is no power above to set aside their judgment. The framers of this constitution appear to have followed that of the British, in rendering the judges independent, by granting them their offices during good

behaviour, without following the constitution of England, in instituting a tribunal in which their errors may be corrected; and without adverting to this, that the judicial under this system have a power which is above the legislative, and which indeed transcends any power before given to a judicial by any free government under heaven.[74]

In short, Robert Bork has nothing on Brutus. But the Anti-Federalists would not agree with Bork that the Constitution is a document that, but for the obfuscations of "political" judges, is easily interpreted. On the contrary, it was one of the central contentions of the Anti-Federalists that the Constitution was vague and unspecific throughout—that it was, in the words of the leading scholar of Anti-Federalist thought, "inexplicit, obscure, and dangerously complex."[75] Thus, Virginia's Edmund Randolph, a delegate at Philadelphia who refused to sign the Constitution, declared that it contained too many "ambiguities of expression."[76] Accordingly, as declared by the Anti-Federalist firebrand Mercy Otis Warren, in her 1805 history of the Revolution, the opponents of the Constitution "were solicitous that every thing should be clearly defined" and "that every article that admitted of double confusion be amended, before it became the supreme law of the land."[77]

The Anti-Federalists expressed particular concerns about Article I, Section 8's provision that Congress could "make all laws which shall be necessary and proper for carrying into execution" the long list of enumerated powers set forth earlier in the Section. Here is James Monroe speaking at the Virginia ratification convention:

> There is a general power given to them to make all laws that will enable them to carry their powers into effect. There are no limits pointed out. . . . By this general, unqualified power, they may infringe not only on the trial by jury, but the liberty of the press, and every right that is not expressly secured or excepted from that general power.[78]

And Brutus was simply appalled when he contemplated the "necessary and proper clause":

> [H]ow is it possible to understand the extent of that power which can pass all laws which shall be necessary and proper for carrying it into execution? It is truly incomprehensible. A case cannot be conceived of, which is not included in this power.[79]

How did the proponents of ratification respond to the Anti-Federalist contention to the effect that "inexplicitness seems to pervade this whole political fabric"?[80] Not as the Imperial Judiciary theorists would wish— that is, not with assertions that the exercise of judicial review would be uncontroversial because the Constitution in fact lends itself to facile inter-pretation or with the assurance that courts would employ any particular interpretive method that would limit severely the scope of judicial discre-tion in the exercise of judicial review. Rather, the Federalists forthrightly acknowledged that the Constitution was indeed broadly worded and even ambiguous in places. This, they believed, was *inevitable.*

It was inevitable, first of all, because of the very nature of language it-self. Language, said Madison in *The Federalist*, was necessarily imprecise:

> The use of words is to express ideas. Perspicuity, therefore, requires not only that ideas should be distinctly formed, but that they should be ex-pressed by words distinctly and exclusively appropriate to them. But no language is so copious as to supply words and phrases or every complex idea, or so correct as not to include many equivocally denoting different ideas. Hence it must happen that however accurately objects may be dis-criminated in themselves, and however accurately the discrimination may be considered, the definition of them may be rendered inaccurate by an inaccuracy of the terms in which it is delivered. And this unavoidable in-accuracy must be greater or less according to the complexity and novelty of the objects defined.[81]

Oliver Ellsworth made the same point when replying directly to the Anti-Federalist charge "that some powers of the Legislature are ambiguous, and others indefinite and dangerous":

> The charge of being ambiguous and indefinite may be brought against every human composition, and necessarily arises from the imperfection of language. Perhaps no two men will express the same sentiment in the same manner, and by the same words; neither do they connect precisely the same ideas with the same words. From hence arises an ambiguity in all languages, with which the most perspicuous and precise writers are in a degree chargeable.[82]

Moreover, the framers asserted that the breadth of the Constitution's terms was a reflection of the needs of governance. When they are alarmed by the supposedly illegitimate expansion of federal legislative power, contemporary conservatives will posit that "the founding generation authorized a federal government of delegated powers only, which they enumerated in a constitution—expecting, if necessary, that judges would limit the political branches to those powers if political checks should fail."[83] And Madison in fact said that "[t]he powers delegated by the proposed Constitution to the federal government are few and defined."[84] (On the other hand, Hamilton told the New York ratifying convention that "[e]veryone knows that the objects of the general government are numerous, extensive, and important.)[85] But it is not often remembered that the Federalists were also convinced that it would be unwise, even impossible, to enumerate the *means* by which the enumerated ends of federal power would manifest themselves in practice; said Hamilton in *The Federalist*, only time and the actual experience of governance under the Constitution would reveal what means would be necessary:

> Constitutions of civil government are not to be framed upon a calculation of existing exigencies, but upon a combination of these with the probable exigencies of ages, according to the natural and tried course of human affairs. Nothing, therefore, can be more fallacious than to infer the extent of any power proper to be lodged in the national government from an estimate of its immediate necessities. There ought to be a CAPACITY to provide for future contingencies as they may happen; and as *these are illimitable* in their nature, so it is impossible safely to limit that capacity.[86]

Madison made the same point later in *The Federalist* when discussing why the Philadelphia Convention had composed the "necessary and proper clause," rather than attempt to create an exhaustive list of measures that would be necessary and proper for carrying into effect the enumerated powers afforded to Congress:

> [T]he attempt would have involved a complete digest of laws on every subject to which the Constitution relates; accommodated too not only to the existing state of things, but to all the possible changes which futurity may produce.[87]

In other words, the attempt would have been foolish.[88]

But remember that the Federalists were deeply concerned with the capacity of any legislature to abase its powers, well defined or not. When it came to a legislature, said Madison, "[i]ts constitutional power being at once more extensive, and less susceptible of precise limits, it can, with greater facility, mask, under complicated and indirect measures, the encroachments which it makes on the co-ordinate departments."[89] How, then, would anyone, a judge or a legislator, know when Congress had overstated its boundaries and performed an unconstitutional act?

The inquiry could be approached with nothing like mathematical precision. The question would inevitably involve an understanding that the constitutional text alone would often not provide definitive answers. It would therefore require the employment of what Madison called "the doctrine of *construction or implication*."[90] This doctrine recognized that it would often be the case that a *range* of plausible constructions could be derived from the constitutional text. Thus, as Madison wrote to Jefferson shortly after the Philadelphia Convention, questions concerning the proper boundary between federal and state powers would not be "free from different constructions by different interests, *or even from ambiguity in the judgment of the impartial*."[91] Similarly, when the First Congress was considering proposed amendments to the Constitution, Representative Madison spoke against an amendment that would have declared that the federal government could exercise only those powers "expressly" granted to it "because it was impossible to confine a government to the exercise of express powers, *there must necessarily be admitted powers by implication*, unless the constitution descended to recount every minutiae."[92] There could be no escape from the doctrine of construction or implication.

Even before the Constitution was ratified, the Federalists interpreted particular clauses in ways that make quite clear the scope of interpretive choice they foresaw. In *Federalist* 82, for example, Hamilton considered the following clause of Article III, Section I: "The judicial power of the United States shall be vested in one supreme court, and in such inferior courts as the congress shall from time to time ordain and establish." He noted first that "[t]his might either be construed to signify, that the supreme and subordinate courts of the union should *alone* have the power of deciding those causes, to which their authority is to extend; or simply to denote [what] the organs of the national judiciary should be."[93] In other words, Hamilton here acknowledges that the phrase can be read either to exclude or permit what lawyers call "concurrent jurisdiction," which is the notion that the jurisdiction of the federal and state courts can overlap, as opposed to being exclusive of one another. He concludes that, of the two interpretations, "as the first would amount to an alienation of state power by implication, the last appears to me the most natural and the most defensible construction."[94]

At the Philadelphia Convention itself, we find Madison engaging in an unresolved interpretive debate with his fellow delegates. As the Convention was coming to a close, two delegates from Maryland sought to protect the interest of seafaring states by proposing a provision to the effect that "no State shall be restrained from laying duties of tonnage for the purpose of clearing harbors and erecting light-houses." Gouverneur Morris of New York replied to the Marylanders that their motion was not necessary since "the States are not restrained from laying tonnage as the Constitution now stands." However, Madison spoke immediately after Morris and took issue with his interpretive position: "Whether the states are now restrained from laying tonnage duties depends on the extent of the [federal government's] power 'to regulate commerce.' *These terms are vague*, but *seem* to exclude the power of the States."[95]

Further, when they ratified the Constitution, a number of states suggested that certain amendments be considered immediately. Three of these proposed amendments sought to constitutionalize a narrow interpretation of the powers of the national government. Thus, South Carolina urged an amendment providing that "no Section or paragraph of the said Constitution warrants a Construction that the states do not retain every power not expressly relinquished by them and vested in the General Government of the Union."[96] Virginia, which wanted to be sure that prohibitions upon congressional powers would not be interpreted as license to do all that was not specifically denied, proposed this amendment: "That those clauses which declare that Congress shall not exercise certain powers be not interpreted in any manner whatsoever to extend the powers of the Congress. But that they may be construed either as making exceptions to the specified powers where this shall be the case, or otherwise as inserted for greater caution."[97] New York suggested almost precisely the same amendment.[98] Of course, none of these interpretive directives made its way into the Constitution.[99]

But the best illustration of the extent to which the framers were aware of the range of interpretations to which the Constitution is subject is their actual experience of governance under the document. During the early years of the federal government's operation, the extent of its constitutional powers was a constant source of controversy. Originalists are generally loathe to acknowledge this fact because, as Jefferson Powell asserts, it demonstrates that their "underlying assumption that the Founders 'really' had agreed, in 1787–88, on issues of interpretation about which they immediately fell into intense disagreement in 1789 is inherently implausible."[100] The reality was, however, an exasperated representative noted in 1795, that "the Constitution was introduced into every subject [of Congressional debate]. . . . Whenever a gentleman is at a loss for an argument, the Constitution is brought forward."[101]

An excellent example, among many, that demonstrates the depth of interpretive discord into which the framers quickly fell is the 1791 debate over the creation of a national bank. It is a good example in particular because it shows the primary authors of *The Federalist*, Hamilton and Madison, wholly at odds.

The Constitution contains no explicit authorization for a bank. But this did not trouble Hamilton. His primary defense of the bank's constitutionality rests upon the necessary and proper clause. In his eyes, this clause obviates any qualms arising from the fact that the creation of a bank is not among the enumerated powers of Congress because it "gives an explicit sanction to the doctrine of implied powers, and is equivalent to an admission of the proposition, that the government, as to its specified powers and objects, has plenary and sovereign authority."[102] Having said this, all that was left was for Hamilton to show that a bank was necessary by carrying out one or more of the enumerated powers. Taking necessary to mean "needful, requisite, incidental, useful, or conducive to," he made short work of the undertaking.[103] It is also interesting to note that Hamilton was not at all dissuaded by the fact that the delegates at Philadelphia had rejected the idea of giving the Congress the express power to create corporations:

> [W]hatever may have been the intention of the framers of the constitution, or of a law, that intention is to be sought for in the instrument itself, according to the usual & established rules of construction. Nothing is more common than for laws to *express* and *effect*, more or less than what was intended. If then a power to erect a corporation, in any case, be deducible by fair inference from the whole or any part of the numerous provisions of the constitution of the United States, arguments drawn from extrinsic circumstances, regarding the intention of the constitution, must be rejected.[104]

Hamilton posited a similar interpretation in his famous *Report on Manufactures*, also issued in 1791. In the *Report*, Hamilton advocated that the federal government enact a range of measures to encourage industrial development. Realizing that most of these measures had no explicit sanction in Article I's enumeration of the powers of Congress, Hamilton found grounding for his program in Article I, Section 8's mandate that Congress "may lay and collect Taxes, Duties, Imposts and Excises, to pay the Debts, and provide for the common Defense and general Welfare of the United States":

> The terms *"general Welfare"* were doubtless intended to signify more than was expressed or imported in those which Preceded; otherwise numerous exigencies incident to the affairs of a Nation would have been left without a provision. The phrase is as comprehensive as any that could have been used; because it was not fit that the constitutional authority of the Union, to appropriate its revenues shou'd have been restricted within narrower limits than the "General Welfare" and because this necessarily embraces a vast variety of particulars, which are susceptible neither of specification nor of definition.[105]

Madison's response to Hamilton's advocacy of a national bank centered upon what he believed to be Hamilton's unconstrained definition of the word "necessary." In a speech made in the House of Representatives against the bank, Madison declared that "whatever meaning [the necessary and proper] clause may have, none can be admitted, that would give an unlimited discretion to Congress."[106] Madison asserted that that such would surely be the case if necessary was defined not as *essential* but merely as *convenient*, because one could justify the constitutionality of virtually any policy measure by illustrating some manner in which it increased the federal government's facility in exercising one or more of its enumerated powers. He thus argued that "if instead of direct and incidental means, any means could be used" to carry out the enumerated powers, then "the essential characteristic of the government, as composed of limited and enumerated powers, would be destroyed."[107]

And here was the crux of the debate. In his defense of the bank, Hamilton asserted that the government's existence was threatened by Madison's (and Jefferson's) constrained view of national legislative power: "It is essential to the being of the National government, that so erroneous a conception of the meaning of the word *necessary*, should be exploded."[108] A good case can be made that this debate between relatively constrained and unconstrained visions of the national government's power has continued throughout our history. The Supreme Court acknowledged as much more than sixty years ago when it discussed the scope of the general welfare clause:

> Since the foundation of the nation, sharp differences of opinion have persisted as to the true interpretation of the phrase. Madison asserted it amounted to no more than a reference to the other powers enumerated in the subsequent clauses of the same section. . . . Hamilton, on the other hand, maintained the clause confers a power separate and distinct from those later enumerated, is not restricted in meaning by the grant of them, and Congress consequently has a substantive power to tax and to appropriate, limited only by the requirement that it shall be exercised to provide for the general welfare of the United States.[109]

The point to be made here, at least briefly, is that the meaning of the Constitution's terms has been *contested* right from the beginning of the operation of government under that document. It is a myth to assert that, in some pre-Warren Court golden age, something like unanimity regarding those terms, based upon a shared understanding of framers' intent, ever existed.

To return to the judiciary itself, this inquiry into the framers' experience with interpretive conundrums serves to make the crucial point that it is no wonder that Hamilton referred to judicial review as "so arduous a duty."[110] Interpreting the Constitution would be hard work that would yield few wholly uncontroversial answers. Indeed, said Hamilton, this was precisely why the Constitution established the Supreme Court:

> If there is in each State, a court of final jurisdiction, there may be as many different final determinations on the same point, as there are courts. There are endless diversities in the opinions of men. *We often see not only different courts, but the Judges of the same court, differing from each other.* To avoid the confusion which would unavoidably result from the contradictory decisions of a number of independent judicatories, all nations have found it necessary to establish one court paramount to the rest— possessing a general superintendence, and authorized to settle and declare in the last resort, an uniform rule of civil justice.[111]

One can only remark how far this is from the writing of someone like Robert Bork, who believes emphatically that, if all judges merely adhered to the original intention of the framers in the correct manner judicial review would indeed be something akin to an exact science.

Interpreting Statutes

Raoul Berger asserts that the framers "drew a line between the judicial reviewing function, that is, *policing* grants of power to insure that there were no encroachments beyond the grants, and legislative policymaking *within* those bounds."[112] From this, he concludes that the judiciary's role in the legislative process "was limited to *policing* constitutional boundaries."[113] On the contrary, it was their view that the legislative process would find its *necessary* culmination in the judiciary's participation because, as Jefferson Powell has written, it was their belief that "a document's meaning might become clearer and more certain over time by successive decisions that settled ambiguities and uncovered implications."[114]

Madison made the same point in *The Federalist*: "All new laws, though penned with the greatest technical skill and passed on the fullest and most mature deliberation, are considered as more or less obscure and equivocal, until their meaning be liquidated and ascertained by a series of particular discussions and adjudications."[115] Or, as Hamilton said more succinctly, "[l]aws are a dead letter without courts to expound and define their true meaning and operation."[116] It is upon the basis of statements such as these that the law professor William Eskridge has recently argued that the framers understood the notion that the goal of statutory interpretation was in part that of "creating meaning that was inchoate beforehand."[117]

And the supporters of the Constitution very much wanted judges to engage in statutory interpretation guided by considerations of equity. It was hoped that the practice of elucidating the meaning of laws through statutory interpretation would be undertaken with an eye toward the protection of minorities from the unjust acts of legislative majorities. Thus, in *Federalist* 78, Hamilton declares that

> *it is not with a view to infractions of the Constitution only* that the independence of the judges may be an essential safeguard against the effects of occasional ill humors in society. These sometimes extend no farther than to the injury of the private rights of particular classes of citizens, by unjust and partial laws. *Here also the firmness of the judicial magistracy is of vast importance* in mitigating the severity and confining the operation of such laws.[118]

Even the Anti-Federalist Brutus lauded this power when he declared that unjust statutes of the New York legislature "have uniformly received the strictest construction by the judges, and have been extended to no cases but to such as came within the strict letter of the law. In this way, have our courts, I will not say evaded the law, but *so limited it in its operation as to work the least possible injustice.*"[119]

And this is precisely what the Supreme Court did in a number of cases under the Chief Justiceship of John Marshall. As Mark Graber has demonstrated, the Marshall Court heard challenges to several state and federal statutes that attempted to determine ownership of frontier lands. The Court determined that certain of these statutes effected "naked land transfers," that is, "taking the property of worthy A and giving it to undeserving B," which was "the paradigmatic constitutional taboo during the nineteenth century."[120] Instead of exercising judicial review and striking down these laws outright, the Court applied an interpretive rule to the effect that "acts ought never to be so construed as to subvert the rights of property," even if this resulted in quite blatant disregard of the statutory text.[121] Thus, Graber concludes, "instead of ignoring statutory law, the justices engaged in statutory misconstruction solely to prevent an unconstitutional naked land transfer of property."[122]

In sum, the framers did not approve of Montesquieu's image of judges as "no more than the mouth that pronounces the words of the law, mere passive beings, incapable of moderating either its force or rigor."[123] On the contrary, Madison said that judges would be in the thick of controversy over laws that arguably worked injustice because "the success of [legislative] usurpation will depend on the executive and judiciary departments, which are to expound and give effect to the legislative acts."[124] The work of expounding laws, therefore, was not to be a mere textual exercise. Instead, as Professor Eskridge puts it, the judiciary would be "expected to strike down unconstitutional laws, trim back unjust and partial statutes, and make legislation more coherent with fundamental law."[125]

A Bill of Rights?

We now arrive at something of a paradox, but one that is more apparent than real. I have said that concerns about minority rights were central to the framers' constitutional vision. But how does this assertion square with the fact that the supporters of ratification generally *opposed* the addition of a bill of rights to the Constitution? Over time of course we have come to see the first ten amendments as the palladium of our liberties as citizens. The framers, however, were not less solicitous of the interests of minorities than I have made them out to be. On the contrary, their opposition to a bill of rights was rooted in their expansive concern for these interests.

The framers believed that legislatures, when animated by a passion to commit injustice, could be endlessly creative in enacting statutes not blatantly unconstitutional in order to effect their designs. Remember Madison's statement that the legislature can "mask under complicated and indirect measures" its unjust intents.[126] Given this capacity for oppression by stealth, the framers believed that setting down the rights of citizens in a bill of rights was unwise. The likely result would be that rights would be defined too *narrowly*, thereby affording the legislature a greater capacity to abridge them. James Wilson framed the problem perfectly for the Pennsylvania ratification convention:

> [W]ho will be bold enough to undertake to enumerate all the rights of the people? and when the attempt to enumerate them is made, it must be remembered that if the enumeration is not complete, everything not expressly mentioned will be presumed to be purposely omitted.[127]

More specifically, in *Federalist* 84, Hamilton applied Wilson's reasoning to the question of freedom of the press. As the Constitution then stood, he argued, Congress had no power *at all* to legislate with respect to the press. But inserting a provision into the Constitution regarding press freedom would afford Congress "a colorable pretext" to claim that it *could* legislate with respect to the press, except in so far as expressly limited by the prohibitive clause. And this would open the door to attacks upon press freedom because legislative majorities animated by a passion for that end would become ingenious in avoiding the prohibition. Thus, echoing Wilson, Hamilton declares, "What is the liberty of the press? Who can give it any definition which would not leave the utmost latitude for evasion? I hold it to be impracticable."[128]

In a letter to Thomas Jefferson, Madison argued in the same vein regarding the freedom of religion:

> [T]here is great reason to fear that a positive declaration of some of the most essential rights could not be obtained in the requisite latitude. I am sure that the rights of Conscience in particular, if submitted to public de-

finition would be narrowed much more than they are likely to ever be by an assumed power.[129]

Of course, we have a bill of rights. The Federalists lost this point and agreed to work for the passage of amendments in the First Congress in exchange for the ratification of the Constitution. But, as he shepherded these amendments through Congress, Madison emphasized that judges would be the sentinels of whatever enumerated rights were set forth:

> If they are incorporated into the constitution, independent tribunals of justice will consider themselves in a peculiar manner the guardians of those rights; they will be an impenetrable bulwark against every assumption of power in the legislative or executive; they will be naturally led to resist every encroachment upon rights expressly stipulated for in the constitution by the declaration of rights.[130]

Further, the framers' unease regarding a too narrow enumeration of rights was not forgotten when the Bill of Rights was composed. It is in fact embodied in the Ninth Amendment: "The enumeration in the Constitution of certain rights, shall not be construed to deny or disparage others retained by the people." Imperial Judiciary theorists are made very uneasy by the Ninth Amendment. As we saw in chapter 1, Justice Scalia has reasoned the amendment into meaninglessness. Robert Bork asserts that "[t]here is almost no history that would indicate what the Ninth Amendment was intended to accomplish."[131] Thus, like the privileges and immunities clause of the Fourteenth Amendment, the Ninth Amendment becomes another part of the Constitution that Bork says judges should simply ignore. More generally, the late Charles L. Black charged that "academic writing on this Amendment seems to me to be in great part a multidirectional fluttering flight from the Amendment's rather plain meaning."[132]

But the indeterminate quality of the Ninth Amendment—what exactly are the other rights "retained by people"?—puzzles lawyers in general. John Hart Ely has quipped that "[i]n sophisticated legal circles mentioning the Ninth Amendment is a surefire way to get a laugh. ('What are you planning to rely on to support that argument, Lester, the Ninth Amendment?')"[133] But, Ely continues, there can be no wishing away the Ninth Amendment's indeterminate quality: "that the Ninth Amendment was intended to signal the existence of federal constitutional rights *beyond those specifically enumerated* in the Constitution is the only conclusion its language seems comfortably to support."[134] Or, as Jefferson Powell asserts, the Ninth Amendment is "the quintessential case" where "the Founders consciously chose to leave a question of constitutional meaning for later interpreters."[135]

Why did they so choose? Because, as Bernard Bailyn has written, American revolutionaries were uniform in their belief that "English law did not and properly could not wholly exhaust the great treasury of human rights. *No documentary charter ever could.* Laws, grants, and charters merely stated the essentials . . . insofar, and only insofar, as they had come under attack in the course of English history. They marked out the minimum not the maximum boundaries of rights."[136] The Ninth Amendment therefore sets forth the framers' belief that the government should not presume itself free to act upon its citizens in all ways save for those expressly prohibited by the Constitution.[137] When Imperial Judiciary theorists decry "the creation of new rights" as the quintessence of judicial activism, they are wholly disregarding this belief.

Judicial Tyranny?

The claim that the framers were aware of the Constitution's broad and general terms and fully cognizant of the implications of that fact emphatically does not lead to the conclusion that they also envisioned or expected a state of anarchy with respect to constitutional interpretation. On the contrary, regarding the judiciary specifically, there was recognition that courts could not be afforded unlimited discretion in constitutional judgment. The clearest statement is Hamilton's in *Federalist* 78:

> To avoid an arbitrary discretion in the courts, it is indispensable that they should be bound down by strict rules and precedents which serve to define and point out their duty in every particular case that comes before them; and it will readily be conceived from the wickedness of mankind that the records of those precedents must unavoidably swell to a very considerable bulk and must demand long and laborious study to acquire a competent knowledge of them. Hence it is that there can be but few men in the society who will have sufficient skill in the laws to qualify them for the stations of judges.[138]

For Raoul Berger, the phrase "bound down by strict rules and precedents" is pure gold, because he takes it to be incontrovertible truth that the framers intended a throughly narrow scope for judicial review.[139] But the passage clearly doesn't support Berger's militant reading. Hamilton speaks, first of all, of the danger of "arbitrary discretion," not of the exercise of judicial discretion altogether. More important, the passage is a quite emphatic statement of how difficult Hamilton thought the proper exercise of judicial discretion would be. Over time, precedents would "swell to a very considerable bulk," a statement that, by the way, is utterly inconsistent with the notion that original intent alone, with minimal resort to precedent, should govern constitutional adjudication. Thus, says Hamilton, it would take "long and laborious study" to master the body of precedent, which again is why Hamilton believed judicial review to be "so arduous a duty."

But, as we have said, the framers also recognized that judicial discretion could become arbitrary. If so, what was the solution? Hamilton provides the answer in *Federalist* 81. He says there that judges will be subject to

> the important constitutional check which the power of instituting impeachments in one part of the legislative body, and of determining upon them in the other, would give to that body upon the members of the judiciary. This is alone a complete security. There can never be danger that the judges, by a series of deliberate usurpations on the authority of the legislature, would hazard the united resentment of the body intrusted with it, while this body was entrusted with the means of punishing their presumption by degrading them from their stations.[140]

Thus, in proposing his wholly unsuccessful 1997 campaign to seek the impeachment of purportedly activist federal judges, Representative Tom DeLay, of Texas, was on firm ground when he told Congress that "America's founders believed that impeachment would be an effective way of keeping the judiciary within its proper bounds."[141]

But he was on less firm ground than he probably thought. At the Philadelphia Convention, the delegates roundly rejected an effort to, as it were, grease the skids of judicial removal. Specifically, John Dickinson moved that a provision be added to the Constitution to the effect that judges could be removed from the bench without cause, that is, on the mere "application (by) the Senate and House of Representatives."[142]

Gouverneur Morris opposed the motion because he felt "it was fundamentally wrong to subject Judges to so arbitrary an authority,"[143] and Edmund Randolph did so out of fear of "weakening too much the independence of judges."[144] Most interesting, however, is James Wilson's response to the remark that, in Britain, judges were removable without cause upon the joint application of the House of Commons and the House of Lords. Wilson

> considered such a provision in the British Government as less dangerous than here, the House of Lords & Commons being less likely to concur on the same occasions. Chief Justice Holt, he remarked, had successively offended by his independent conduct, both houses of Parliament. Had this happened at the same time, he would have been ousted. The Judges would be in a bad situation if made to depend on every gust of faction which might prevail in the two branches of our Govt.[145]

Thus, Wilson expected—indeed, he welcomed—that judges would offend the popular branches of government. Tom DeLay notwithstanding, we deny the character of our constitutional order when we act as if we should not expect the same thing.[146]

Conclusion: "Doing Justice Equally to All in the Community"

Writing in the wake of the U.S. Supreme Court's decision in *Casey v. Planned Parenthood*, Richard John Neuhaus, the editor of *First Things*, offered this vision of America:

> We are two nations: one concentrated on rights and laws, the other on rights and wrongs; one radically individualistic and dedicated to the fulfillment of the self, the other communal and invoking the common good; one viewing law as the instrument of the will to power and license, the other affirming an objective moral order reflected in a Constitution to which we are obliged; one typically secular, the other typically religious; one elitist, the other populist.[147]

It is hard to be anything but blunt in response: this is insipid Manichaeanism. But it is also insipid Manichaeanism with an ideological purpose. *Casey* is said to be the work of "an imperial court" that has "chosen sides in the culture wars."[148] It goes without saying that the Court has enlisted on the side of radical individualism, secularism, elitism, and so on.

America is not two nations. Nor is it one nation. What America is was hinted at by the historian David Bell in a review of recent works about the history of anti-Semitism in France: "The classic canard of modern anti-Semitism (it originated, incidentally, in France) is that the Jews are 'a state within a state'; but which group, in the United States, is *not* a state within a state?"[149] That is, America is a country of many enclaves, based upon race, religion, ethnicity, class, and political belief, among other things.

In *Federalist* 10, James Madison argued famously that cultural heterogeneity was precisely the source of America's salvation as a republican society that could protect the interests of minorities. In a small republic, one that resembled one of the thirteen American states, "the fewer probably will be the distinct parties and interests composing it; the fewer the distinct parties and interests, the more frequently will a majority be found of the same party; and . . . the more easily will they concert and execute their plan of oppression."[150] In a larger republic, one the size of the United States, "you take in a greater variety of parties and interests; you make it less probable that a majority of the whole will have a common motive to invade the rights of other citizens; or if such a common motive exists, it will be more difficult for all who feel it to discover their own strength and to act in unison with each other."[151] Thus it is that Samuel P. Huntington has said that, in *Federalist* 10, "the pluralist paradigm received its classic statement."[152]

But, as we shall see in more detail in chapter 5, Madison was not a pluralist. Rather, he was particularly concerned for the security of the rights of one portion of the community, a propertied minority whose numbers, he thought, were destined to dwindle and who, as a result, would face an increasingly hostile unpropertied majority. He was very much wrong in this regard, because America has never devolved into a society dominated by such a simple class antagonism. It has become, as we have just said, a nation of many enclaves.

Of course, however, the history of the American polity has been something less than the history of vigorous, but essentially benign, competition among interest groups. At all levels of government, oppressive majorities have not infrequently formed. The history of American race relations—and I mean here not only the relations between African Americans and the white majority—is only the most obvious example. The history of American political dissent and the history of nonconformist religious sects and unassimilated ethnic groups provide several others. It therefore does no violence to our history to note, as Garry Wills has, that "running men out of town on a rail is at least as much an American tradition as declaring unalienable rights."[153] But, as Wills admits, declaring unalienable rights is also our tradition. To my knowledge, no Imperial Judiciary theorist has explained how these rights will remain secure in the absence of an independent judiciary.

It will not do to overstate the case here. Although I have tried to demonstrate that the framers very much wanted an energized national judiciary, they certainly did not see the courts as the sole means for guaranteeing the future of republican government in America. Far from it. Madison in particular expressed doubts on more than one occasion about the efficacy of judicial review in reining in legislatures engaged in acts of injustice. The depth of his doubts is demonstrated by his passionate attachment to a measure that did not win passage at Philadelphia: a veto upon state laws in the hands of the federal government. At Philadelphia, Madison and James Wilson fought a persistent but unsuccessful battle for this power. One reason that it was necessary, said Madison, was that judicial review would be a decidedly "insufficient" substitute for keeping state legislatures in check: "[I]t is more convenient to prevent the passage of a law, than to declare it void after it is passed."[154]

And Alexander Hamilton placed his hopes for successful republican government in America on the possibility that George Washington, the likely first president, would staff the federal government with capable administrators (very much including Hamilton himself): "A good administration will conciliate the confidence and affection of the people and perhaps enable the government to acquire more consistency than the proposed constitution seems to promise for so great a Country."[155] But Hamilton was not at all convinced that the Constitution, much less the courts themselves, would be able to provide sufficient protection "against domestic violence and the depredations which the democratic spirit is apt to make on property."[156]

It is against these sentiments that Hamilton's characterization of the judiciary as "the least dangerous" branch of government must be read. The full passage, remember, asserts that "the judiciary, from the nature of its functions, will always be the least dangerous to the political rights of the Constitution; because it will be least in a capacity to annoy or injure them."[157] As we have seen, the supporters of the Constitution believed that the *most* dangerous branch, the one with the greatest capacity to annoy or injure rights, would be the legislature, because, through it, a majority actuated by a sense of injustice could effect its designs. Thus, that Hamilton characterized the judiciary as the least dangerous branch cannot be taken as an endorsement of judicial weakness.

We can safely conclude that, even in the face of doubts about how strong the judiciary would be in practice, a substantive judicial power was a central element of the federalist constitutional program. Through the provision for life tenure, the framers created a more independent judiciary than had ever existed in America. Through their subsequent defense of the power of judicial review during the ratification debates, they invested it with the power to enforce constitutional limitations. Finally, once government under the Constitution began to operate, the framers resisted all efforts to add amendments that would diminish judicial power:

> Anti-Federalists . . . proposed amendments designed to . . . enervate the federal judiciary. Its original jurisdiction would be limited to cases involving the United States as a party, two or more states, foreign nations, and admiralty and maritime law. Admiralty courts were to be the only inferior courts of original jurisdiction; state courts would hear other issues, with only certain one appealable to the federal judiciary. Finally, if a decision of the Supreme Court dissatisfied a litigant, the president, under congressional regulations, could appoint a commission to review the decision.[158]

All of these amendments failed to win passage.

At the 1788 North Carolina ratification convention, a delegate named William Davie made the following assertion: "It is necessary that the Constitution should be carried into effect, that the laws should be executed, justice equally done to all the community, and treaties observed. These ends can only be accomplished by a general paramount Judiciary."[159] It is the judicial function of "doing justice equally to all the community" that the Imperial Judiciary theorists would have us devalue in the name of majority will. In a nation now composed of many more communities than William Davie could have foreseen, this would be a disaster of the first order.

3

The Judiciary in History

It is a persistent theme of the Imperial Judiciary thesis that the power wielded by American courts over the past forty or so years is orders of magnitude beyond that exercised by courts for any sustained period ever before in our history. Recall Nathan Glazer's declaration in "Towards an Imperial Judiciary?" on what judicial power has become: "The courts have truly changed their role in American life. . . . [They] are now far more powerful than ever before. . . . [They] now reach into the lives of the people, against the will of the people, deeper than they ever have in American history."[1] Max Boot tells us that, "because the law matters more" today, "what could have been shrugged off as a petty annoyance a hundred years ago—bad judges making bad decisions—today assumes the proportions of a much more substantial problem."[2] Similarly, federal appellate judge James L. Buckley has recently declared that, while "an inclination among federal judges to take policy into account is hardly new," what is unique about recent decades "is the profound impact that a number of the [Supreme] Court's more recent decisions have had on the social and political life of this country."[3]

Further, when writers of the Imperial Judiciary school acknowledge the existence of judicial power in pre-Warren Court America, they spend a disproportionate amount of time focusing on particular cases that have come to be widely considered improvident or even disastrous exercises of the judicial function. More specifically, they make frequent reference to *Dred Scott v. Sandford*,[4] the 1857 U.S. Supreme Court ruling that held that Congress had no power to halt the territorial expansion of slavery, the effect of which was to hasten, perhaps even guarantee, the outbreak of the Civil War. The ideological utility of this catastrophic ruling for Imperial Judiciary theorists is proved by the manner in which it is reflexively linked to *Roe v. Wade*,[5] a practice begun a few days after the latter decision was issued when William F. Buckley termed *Roe* "the Dred Scott decision of the twentieth century."[6] The linkage is typically followed by a statement like

Gary McDowell's assertion that "*Dred Scott* did for the moral issue of slavery what *Roe* did for the moral issue of abortion. Each case sought to cut off public debate once and for all over the vexing moral questions involved."[7]

But there is vastly more to the history of American judicial power than *Dred Scott*. To be sure, thoughtful commentators like Glazer do note that, more than handing down the occasional landmark decision, the judiciary had experienced "activist cycles" prior to the era of the Warren Court.[8] But this is still an inadequate expression of the actual record of the exercise of judicial power in the American polity. The fact is that judicial power has *never* for any sustained period been marginal in American political life.

It is the purpose of this chapter to consider three broad instances of judicial dynamism in our history that occurred before the relatively familiar history of the judiciary's role in the American polity since the New Deal. These are: (1) the role of American courts in shaping a national economic order during the first half of the nineteenth century, (2) the judicial evisceration of the amendments added to the U.S. Constitution in the wake of the Civil War, and (3) the judicial response to the rise of the American labor movement. I have chosen these three instances because, with the arguable exception of the second, they are little discussed outside academic works, which I think is highly unfortunate. Once one comes to understand that courts have often exercised a substantial influence upon great social and political questions, it becomes impossible to hold that judicial power sprang fully grown from the forehead of Chief Justice Warren.

The Nineteenth-Century Revolution in the Common Law

As already noted, Alexis de Tocqueville expressed the view that American judges wielded "immense political power."[9] In fact, at the time de Tocqueville wrote, courts were one of the few cohesive governmental institutions in an American polity whose most salient feature was institutional minimalism. In their historical contentions regarding judicial power, Imperial Judiciary theorists tend to focus almost exclusively upon the operation of the federal courts, and especially upon their exercise of judicial review. Nineteenth-century judicial power, however, was centered in the *state* courts, and here, as the current Chief Judge of New York has said, "the grand tradition has been not of constitutional but of common law decision making."[10]

Indeed, the state courts, and not any legislative body, were the chief source of American law for most of the nineteenth century. As the law professor and federal appellate judge Guido Calabresi has said, "most law was court-made. Legislatures did, of course, possess the ultimate authority, subject to constitutional requirements, to make law; however, that authority was exercised sparingly, by modern standards, and in largely revisionary capacity."[11] Calabresi's Yale colleague Grant Gilmore has put the matter succinctly: "The federal Congress did little; the state legislatures did less. The judges became our preferred problem-solvers."[12]

This is one of the themes of the pathbreaking book *Building a New American State*, by the political scientist Stephen Skowronek. Skowronek actually labels the governmental apparatus of pre–Civil War America "a state of courts and parties."[13] The hallmark of the American constitutional order was decentralization. As Skowronek says, "sovereignty was to be shared between the new central government and the old regional units of government. . . . Constitutional federalism inhibited the penetration of central power throughout the nation by ensuring the integrity of these states, each with its own institutional organization, legal code, and law enforcement apparatus."[14]

Within this maze of highly decentralized power, courts and parties were the primary vehicles of systemic cohesion and stability. Political parties provided "a regimen of voter mobilization, party coalition building, and national two-party competition."[15] "The only institutions that could stand, at least partially, outside direct party domination and claim to complement the parties in the performance of . . . basic constituent tasks were the courts."[16] Thus, says Skowronek, "[i]t fell to the courts at each level of government to nurture, protect, interpret, and invoke the state's prerogatives over economy and society as expressed in law. . . . The courts had become the American surrogate for a more fully developed administrative apparatus."[17] Or, as Cass Sunstein has said, "the vast majority of regulatory functions were undertaken by the common law courts, which elaborated the basic principles of property, tort, and contract. . . . [J]udges performed the basic regulatory functions that might otherwise have been carried out by bureaucrats."[18]

These conclusions rely upon the work of numerous legal historians who have detailed the central role of American courts—particularly state courts—in the creation of a market society through legal change. Contrary to nostalgic cant, America did not develop a market that grew of itself, governed by minimal legal intrusion. J. W. Hurst, the dean of American legal historians, stated almost half a century ago in *Law and the Conditions of Freedom in the Nineteenth Century United States*, that "[n]ot the jealous limitation of the power of the state, but the release of individual creative energy was the dominant value. Where legal regulation or compulsion might promote the greater release of individual or group energies, we had no hesitancy in making affirmative use of the law."[19] Hurst continued:

> Responding to the needs of a growing commerce, the courts in the first half of the nineteenth century enlarged the array of procedures and instruments to promote dealing at a distance and on credit, and gave a contract emphasis to relations of employment, agency and lease. . . . [J]udges exercised their invention in the law of negotiable instruments . . . of factors, of agency, of insurance, of banking. Thinking did not yet run to extensive federal legislation in economic matters; state legislatures lacked experience and during a good number of decades were under a cloud; hence state and federal court judges did most of the work.[20]

An extensive treatment of this age of judicial improvisation is not my goal here. Rather, I hope to summarize its course in several areas of the private law in order to establish at least the outlines of judicial creativity during the first half of the nineteenth century.

Property

The dilemma of property rights in a dynamic commercial society is that the rights of individual owners often conflict. Mills powered by water disturb the ability of downstream property owners to make the fullest use of their riparian rights; workshops and factories belch smoke upon their neighbors; railroads run across privately held tracts of land. Thus, in nineteenth-century American courts, "two competing conceptions of property emerged, one that emphasized its dynamic aspects, associating it with economic growth, and another that emphasized its static character, associating it with security from too rapid change."[21] Morton Horwitz describes this latter doctrine of property ownership, inherited from the eighteenth century, as "an explicitly antidevelopmental theory" that "limited property owners to what courts regarded as the natural uses of their land, and often 'natural' was equated with 'agrarian.'"[22] The rights of property ownership

according to this theory were therefore primarily "the right to absolute dominion over land, and absolute dominion, it was assumed, conferred on
an owner the power to prevent any use of his neighbor's land that conflicted with his own quiet enjoyment."[23] However, in the early decades of
the nineteenth century, "judges began to see that a conception of property
as absolute and exclusive gave a single landowner the power to prevent all
sorts of economically desirable, but injurious, modes of activity on neighboring land."[24] Increasingly, therefore, as the American economy began
growing rapidly, the dominant theory of property rights applied by courts
"underwent a fundamental transformation—from a static agrarian conception entitling an owner to undisturbed enjoyment, to a dynamic, in-
strumental, and more abstract view of property that emphasized the
newly paramount virtues of productive use and development."[25]

An excellent example of the new thinking is the 1844 opinion of the
Massachusetts Supreme Judicial Court in *Cary v. Daniels*.[26] The opinion
was written by Lemuel Shaw, the long-time chief justice of the Supreme
Judicial Court and perhaps the most influential judge of his time. In discussing the relative rights of two mill owners to use a common watercourse to provide power for their respective mills, Shaw explicitly considered not merely abstract questions of quiet enjoyment and the "natural"
use of the watercourse but also the public interest in seeing that property
rights were conceived of in a manner conducive to economic development:

> It is agreed on all hands, that the owner of a parcel of land, through which
> a stream of water flows, has a right to the use and enjoyment of the bene-
> fits to be derived therefrom. . . . But one of the beneficial uses of a water-
> course, and in this country one of the most important, is its application to
> the working of mills and machinery; a use profitable to the owner *and
> beneficial to the public*. It is therefore held, that each proprietor is entitled
> to such use of the stream, so far as reasonable, *conformable to the usages
> and wants of the community*, and having regard to the progress of im-
> provement in hydraulic works, and not inconsistent with a like reasonable
> use by other proprietors of land, on the same stream, above and below.[27]

The rise of the railroad posed another acute challenge to the traditional
idea of property, as an 1839 case from Kentucky demonstrates. In *The Lexington & Ohio Rail Road Co. v. Applegate*, a group of Louisville property
owners sued to stop a railroad from operating within the confines of the

city.[28] The railroad, they alleged, was a public nuisance that "alarmed horses, . . . endangered the security of persons passing on foot, . . . [and] had the effect of diminishing the value of real estate on Main Street, . . . and of injuring the commercial and manufacturing business of those who resided there."[29] The Kentucky Court of Appeals acknowledged that, in former times, the plaintiffs would undoubtedly have had a case. However, times had changed:

> The onward spirit of the age must, to a reasonable extent, have its way. The law is made for the times and will be made or modified by them. . . . And therefore, rail roads and locomotive steam cars—the offspring, as they will also be the parents, of progressive improvement—should not, in themselves, be considered as nuisances, although, in ages that are gone, they might have been so held, because they would have been comparatively useless, and therefore more mischievous.[30]

Or consider *Losee v. Buchanan,* a case decided in 1873 by the New York Court of Appeals.[31] The court was asked whether the owners of a paper mill could be held liable to neighboring property owners for the explosion of a steam boiler on their premises, even though there was no evidence that the boiler had been operated in a negligent fashion. In an excellent exposition of the new law of property, the court imposed no liability:

> [T]he general rules that I may have the exclusive and undisturbed use and possession of my real estate as not to injure my neighbor, are much modified by the exigencies of the social state. We must have factories, machinery, dams, canals and railroads. They are demanded by the manifold wants of mankind, and lay at the basis of all our civilization. If I have any of these upon my lands, and they are not a nuisance and are not so managed as to become such, I am not responsible for any damage they accidentally and unavoidably do my neighbor. He receives his compensation for such damage by the general good, in which he shares. and the right which he has to place the same things upon his lands.[32]

As Horwitz notes, "the desirability of maximizing economic development" as a common-law imperative had tremendous consequences because, "[o]nce the question of reasonableness became a question of efficiency, legal doctrine enabled common law judges to choose the direction of American economic development. . . . [T]hey were willing to manipulate the concept of property to conform to their own notions of the needs of industrialization."[33] In sum, in Hurst's words, property law increasingly "had less to do with protecting *holdings* than it had to do with protecting *ventures*."[34]

Contract

Hurst also notes that "[t]he years 1800–1875 were . . . above all else, the years of contract in our law."[35] William Nelson has summarized the long-term trend of the law of contract toward increasing solicitude for the imperatives of entrepreneurship:

> As the nineteenth century wore on, courts in contract cases . . . turned with increasing frequency to an analysis of the economic needs of the business and mercantile communities. The judges were, as they themselves said, "necessarily led to consider the effect of a different opinion on the commercial part of the community," for they realized that if they adopted rules disadvantageous to business "there would soon be an end of . . . very extensive class[es] of commercial enterprises."[36]

Morton Horwitz argues that the perspective of a law of contract that inclined toward the needs of entrepreneurs was one that sought to uphold contracts as actually made by the parties, without resort to objective standards. "Only in the nineteenth century," he says, "did judges and jurists finally reject the longstanding belief that the justification of contractual obligation is derived from the inherent justice or fairness of an exchange. In its place, they asserted for the first time that the source of the obligation of contract is the convergence of the wills of the contracting parties."[37] The law thus came to favor and protect the sort of autonomous bargaining undertaken by modern business enterprises, an approach that did not recognize any greater goal than that of discerning and enforcing the intentions of the contracting parties. As set forth by Grant Gilmore, the dominant imperative of contract came to be that

> courts should operate as detached umpires or referees, doing no more than to see that the rules of the game were observed and refusing to intervene affirmatively to see that justice or anything of that sort was done. . . . [I]f A, without the protection of a binding contract, improvidently relies,

to his detriment, on B's promises and assurances, that may be unfortunate for A but is no fit matter for legal concern.[38]

Therefore, says William Nelson, the new contract law encouraged the ethos of a market economy:

> The new rules of contract undermined stability primarily by giving individuals freedom to make economic bargains purely in their own interest. ... [B]argainers no longer needed to assume that they should receive only a fair equivalent in return for their goods and services; they no longer needed to assume that hard work resulting in the production of goods or services was the only legitimate means of accumulating wealth. Instead, the new law of contract permitted men to accumulate wealth by turning a sharp bargain or by anticipating the fluctuations of the market.[39]

In sum, "[t]he judicial transformation of the common law of contracts reflects with particular clarity American judges' devotion to the idea of a free market in which no-holds-barred-type competition would generate maximum growth."[40]

Tort

Labor, especially on the rapidly expanding railroads, was tremendously dangerous during the early decades of America's industrialization. As the frequency of industrial accidents soared, it became a legal question of great urgency as to who would bear their cost. As Lawrence Friedman notes, "[b]efore 1800, torts were an insignificant branch of the law," but in the nineteenth century this changed significantly because of "the industrial revolution, whose machines had a marvelous capacity for smashing the human body."[41]

In answering the question of liability, American state courts again came down on the side of encouraging entrepreneurship by squarely placing the cost of accidents upon injured workers. This was a clear departure from the common-law rule that, as Blackstone put it, maintained that, "for those things which a servant may do on behalf of his master, ... the master is answerable for the act of his servant, if done by his command, either expressly given, or implied."[42] In its stead, American judges invented the "fellow servant rule," which held that an injured worker could not sue his employer if it could be demonstrated that the accident that had occasioned his injury had been caused by the negligence of his fellow employees.

The seminal case is *Farwell v. Boston & Worcester R.R. Co.*,[43] another opinion by Chief Justice Lemuel Shaw, decided in 1842. The plaintiff was a train engineer whose train jumped the tracks because of the negligence of track bed workers. As a result, the plaintiff was "thrown with great violence upon the ground; by means of which one of the wheels of one of said cars passed over the right hand of plaintiff, crushing and destroying same."[44] Shaw begins his opinion by stating that all of the rights of the engineer against his employer, whether express or implied, are set forth in their contract of employment. (Recall here J. W. Hurst's statement of how judges "gave a contract emphasis to relations of employment.")[45] It follows, therefore, that "all such risks and perils as the employer and the servant respectively intend to assume and bear may be regulated by the express or implied contract between them."[46] Further, in the absence of any express agreement pursuant to which the employer agrees to be responsible for the negligent acts of an employee's fellow workers, Shaw held that

> we are not aware of any principle which should except the perils arising from the carelessness and negligence of those who are in the same employment. These are the perils which the servant is as likely to know, and against which he can as effectually guard, as the master. They are perils incident to the service, and which can be as distinctly foreseen and provided for in the rate of compensation as any others.[47]

In other words, Shaw held that it was only reasonable for workers to assume the ordinary risks of their employments because such risks were foreseeable to the employee, who could therefore guard against them and also seek higher pay as compensation for assuming such risks. The engineer Farwell, therefore, could not recover from his employer because the possibility of the negligence of track bed workers was foreseeable to him and was something against which he should have protected himself.

The influence of *Farwell* was vast. It, in fact, "became *the* case in the common law of employer liability, treated not only in Massachusetts but throughout the Anglo-American jurisprudential world as the requisite authoritative statement of the limits to an employer's responsibilities, the point of departure in all subsequent litigation in any industrial situation."[48] But, at the same time, "[n]o rule in the nineteenth century came to be quite so vilified and despised by organized labor and working people. After all, the net result of the rule was to make most industrial accidents noncompensable. If a train ran off the rails, or if a steamboat exploded in midstream, because of some careless mistake of an engineer or another worker, the passengers could sue the company for damages; injured employees could get nothing."[49] Writing in 1912, one commentator declared that the fellow servant rule, "as applied by our courts, [has] saved countless millions of dollars to the employing classes in this country, while [it has] killed and made paupers of untold thousands of laborers and their wives and children."[50]

But the fellow servant rule remained dominant in American law for decades. The "legislative repeal" of the rule, and its replacement by workmen's compensation regimes, was a slow process. Only six states had passed compulsory worker compensation laws by 1910; this figure more than doubled by 1920.[51]

Corporations

The primary institutional vehicle of American industrialization was the private corporation. Corporations were—and still are, for that matter—state-chartered entities. In the early decades of the nineteenth century at least, corporate charters issued by states tended to set forth corporate purposes and restrictions with great detail. Further, state legislatures "reserved power to amend or abrogate the charter, or imposed limitations on its powers. Moreover, corporations did not have innate powers; they could exercise only those powers specifically granted in the charter or necessary for the powers expressly granted."[52]

It was through the interpretation of corporate charters, says Skowronek, that "the judiciary became the chief source of economic surveillance in the nineteenth century."[53] As the century progressed, courts increasingly reached interpretive results that favored economic development over the protection of corporate rights that threatened to slow development.

The *locus classicus* here is the 1837 decision of the U.S. Supreme Court, *Charles River Bridge v. Warren Bridge*.[54] The facts of the case are well set forth by James W. Ely, Jr.:

Incorporated by the Massachusetts legislature in 1785, the Charles River Bridge Company was authorized to erect a toll bridge over the Charles River. Before this charter expired, lawmakers empowered another corporation, the Warren Bridge Company, to build a second bridge within a short distance of the original bridge. This charter provided that as soon as the cost of construction was paid, the Warren Bridge would become toll free. Because a toll bridge could not successfully compete with a free bridge, the Warren grant threatened to undercut the value of the original bridge. Nothing in the Charles River Bridge charter stated that the grant was exclusive, but the company argued that the original grant implied that it had the sole right to maintain a bridge for the life of the charter.[55]

The Charles River Bridge Company thus contended that the grant of a charter to the Warren Bridge was a violation of the federal Constitution's provision, in Article I, Section 10, to the effect that no state could pass a law "impairing the obligation of contracts." Speaking for the Court, however, Chief Justice Roger Taney refused to countenance the claim that the Charles River Bridge Company impliedly possessed an exclusive right to span the river. In a passage that expresses quite wonderfully the judicial spirit of the age, Taney held that such a finding would be anathema to the dynamism required for industrial development:

> If this court should establish the principles now contended for, what is to become of the numerous railroads established on the same line of travel with turnpike companies; and which have rendered the franchises of the turnpike corporations of no value? . . . We shall be thrown back to the improvements of the last century, and obliged to stand still, until the claims of the old turnpike corporations shall be satisfied, and they shall consent to permit these States to avail themselves of the lights of modern science, and to partake of the benefit of those improvements which are now adding to the wealth and prosperity, and the convenience and comfort of every other part of the civilized world.[56]

In short, Taney "arrayed himself unequivocally on the side of 'progress.'"[57] The economic historian Stuart Bruchey thus speaks of "Taney's ideal of publicly sponsored free competition in the interest of community welfare. His essential contribution was so to adjust constitutional law to the needs of the corporation as greatly to stimulate its use in business."[58]

In sum, then, in Lawrence Friedman's assessment, "the thrust of the law was promotional" in the first half of the nineteenth century.[59] But it is important to note that none of this went unchallenged and that the power of courts was, as today, a salient political issue. An important point of conflict between the first American political parties was "an increasing identification of Republicans with skepticism of the import of common law and Federalists with endorsement of its extension."[60] Most especially, the power of American judges to shape common law rules that governed the course of economic development was seen by many as anomalous in a county avowedly dedicated to the principle of popular sovereignty. Because it was inherited from England, populist forces saw the common law as a "product of aristocratic deviousness, [which] was incompatible with the plain republicanism of the American people."[61] Moreover, these oppositionists stressed "that common law jurisprudence put the future of the law at the mercy of the caprice, whim, class, and party passions of the men who sit on the bench."[62]

By the 1830s, opposition to judicial power took the form of movements in many states to replace the common law with legislative codes. "Codifiers challenged the common law's consensual and apolitical claims, arguing that a less arbitrary, more democratic legalism required the clear, written commands of the sovereign."[63] Karen Orren has described these movements:

> The proposals to codify, to systematize the complete body of existing law in a single code drawn up under the supervision of the legislature sprang from a jumble of purposes: to emancipate the new nation from foreign and decayed institutions; to organize the laws along a rational plan; to eliminate the arbitrariness of judges; to curb the influence and arrogance of lawyers; to mitigate the expense and delay of lawsuits; to further democratize the government.[64]

But, as Christopher Tomlins notes, judges responded by

> claim[ing] a legislative authority for the courts' common law jurisdiction, arguing that as embodiments of the sovereign will courts enjoyed an authority to expound that sovereign will no less than legislatures. . . . Indeed in important respects—flexibility in molding decision to circumstance, continuity of tenure and thus of policy perspective—judges held that their capacity to expound the sovereign will was greatly superior.[65]

The result was that, "[al]though attacked for its English provenance and old-fashioned procedures, the common law easily withstood radical threats to replace it with codified legislation. . . . [I]t survived its critics to become the most important influence upon the adjudication of contracts, wills and altercations between employers and their employees."[66] In sum, then, in spite of the attacks of the Imperial Judiciary theorists of the time, nineteenth-century American judges maintained their primary role as the shapers of the nation's economic order. As the historian Charles Sellers has concluded in his account of the triumph of the market in Jacksonian America, "[b]y taking control of the state courts and asserting through them their right to shape the law to entrepreneurial ends, lawyer/judges during the first half of the nineteenth century fashioned a legal revolution."[67]

Eventually, however, populist forces did succeed in a more radical fashion than merely establishing codes at the expense of the common law. As the nineteenth century wore on, in state after state, judiciaries were made elective. Thus, "after Iowa and New York in 1846 made all judges elective, eleven other states also did so (in whole or in part) over the next four years, and nine more did so in the succeeding decade."[68] In fact, "all states joining the Union between 1846 and 1958 adopted constitutions providing for the election of most of their judges."[69] As we shall consider in chapter 6, however, judicial elections as they are currently practiced should be troubling to anyone concerned with the integrity of state judiciaries.

The Judicial Strangulation of the Civil War Amendments

The Thirteenth Amendment, which outlaws slavery, the Fourteenth Amendment, which defines American citizenship and prevents the states from denying equal protection and due process of law to any person, and the Fifteenth Amendment, which outlaws the denial of suffrage on account of race, are known collectively in constitutional discourse as "the Civil War Amendments." Enacted by Congress and ratified by the states in the wake of a war that cost 600,000 lives, they have been—especially the Fourteenth Amendment—the subject of endless commentary regarding the intentions of those who composed them and the legitimate scope of their protections. Eric Foner, the leading historian of the Reconstruction

Era, has termed the amendments "striking departures in American law" that "transformed the Constitution from a document primarily concerned with federal-state relations and the rights of property into a vehicle through which members of vulnerable minorities could stake a claim to substantive freedom and seek protection against misconduct by all levels of government."[70] Yet, at least as regards formerly enslaved African Americans, who were certainly intended to be their immediate beneficiaries, Foner is quick to add that "two [of the Civil War Amendments] were substantially nullified in the decades that followed their ratification."[71] Nullification was the product of judicial decisions, particularly by the U.S. Supreme Court. This, says Foner, is a tragic irony "in view of the fact that Congress had placed so much of the burden for enforcing blacks' civil and political rights on the federal judiciary."[72]

This did not have to be. At a time when individual Supreme Court Justices "rode circuit" and issued opinions as lower appellate judges, the signs that the amendments would be read broadly were actually somewhat promising. In *U.S. v. Rhodes*,[73] for example, an 1866 decision, Justice Noah Swayne affirmed the right of the federal government to prosecute three white men who had terrorized an African American family in Nelson County, Kentucky. In his opinion, Swayne saw the goal of the Thirteenth Amendment as not simply the immediate abolition of slavery. Rather, the amendment had the further aim of establishing freedom itself as an imperative of America's national existence:

> The present effect of the amendment was to abolish slavery wherever it existed within the jurisdiction of the United States. In the future it throws its protection over everyone, of every race, color, and condition within that jurisdiction, and guards them against the recurrence of the evil. The Constitution, thus amended, consecrates the entire territory of the republic to freedom, as well as to free institutions. The amendment will continue to perform its function throughout the expanding domain of the nation, without limit of time or space.[74]

In *U.S. v. Hall*, an 1871 decision, Circuit Judge William Woods, who was later to sit on the Supreme Court, upheld a federal prosecution of white Alabamans for acts of racial terror. Woods declared emphatically that the newly enacted Fourteenth Amendment made the provisions of the Bill of Rights applicable to state governments:

> Before the Fourteenth Amendment, Congress could not impair [the rights secured by the Bill of Rights], but the states might. Since the Fourteenth Amendment, the bulwarks of these rights have been strengthened, and now the states are positively inhibited from impairing or abridging them, and so far as the provisions of the organic law can secure them they are completely and absolutely secured.[75]

Further, since the Fourteenth Amendment forbids a state government to "deny to any person within its jurisdiction the equal protection of the laws," Woods held that, if a state government failed to do so, the federal government was thereby empowered to prosecute private citizens who sought to impair the rights of African Americans: "Denying includes inaction as well as action, and denying the equal protection of the laws includes the omission to protect, as well as the omission to pass laws for protection."[76]

In 1870, while riding circuit, Justice Joseph Bradley decided a case brought by *white* butchers in New Orleans, who challenged a Louisiana statute that created The Crescent City Live-Stock Landing and Slaughter-House Company and charged it with undertaking the construction of a huge slaughterhouse in the city. The act further mandated that, upon the completion of the new slaughterhouse, the butchering of animals would be allowed nowhere else within the greater New Orleans area. Any independent butcher wishing to continue in his trade would have to rent space in the new slaughterhouse, subject to rates and conditions set at the sole discretion of the corporation.

In striking down the law as violative of the privileges or immunities clause of the Fourteenth Amendment, Bradley declared that "we may safely say that it is one of the privileges of every American citizen to adopt and follow such lawful industrial pursuit—not injurious to the community—as he may see fit."[77] The slaughterhouse monopoly clearly violated the freedom to labor. Moreover, with respect to the Fourteenth Amendment as a whole, Bradley posited that its broad terms were an invitation to future interpreters to apply its protections to actions not within the contemplation of the framers of the amendment:

> It is possible that those who framed the article were not themselves aware of the far reaching character of its terms. They may have had in mind but one particular phase of social and political wrong, which they desired to redress. Yet, if the amendment, as framed and expressed, does in fact bear

a broader meaning, and does extend its protecting shield over those who were never thought of when it was conceived and put in form, and does reach social evils which were never before prohibited by constitutional enactment, it is to be presumed that the American people, in giving it their imprimatur, understood what they were doing, and meant to decree what has in fact been decreed.[78]

Unfortunately, Justice Bradley's decision, along with several other suits arising from the same Louisiana statute, reached the Supreme Court in 1873, to be decided under the consolidated title *Slaughterhouse Cases*.[79] Here began the strangulation process, which is especially troubling in light of the fact that only five Justices joined the Court's opinion, leaving four Justices in dissent. By one vote, therefore, the Court issued a ruling the result of which, "as reflected in public policy, was the reduction of Southern blacks to peonage, the creation of Jim Crow, and the demise of the Republican Party in the South."[80]

In his opinion for the majority, Justice Samuel Miller begins with the declaration that state governments possess a store of regulatory power so comprehensive as to be "incapable of any exact definition or limitation."[81] The challenged statute, said Miller, which sought to provide consumers with untainted meat products through centralized slaughtering, certainly was intended to achieve a permissible regulatory goal. If the act was therefore wise, was it yet in any sense unconstitutional? Miller foreshadows his conclusion by declaring that "the one pervading purpose found in" the Civil War Amendments, indeed "lying at the foundation of each," was the liberation of African American slaves, not the enlargement of the rights of white citizens.[82]

Miller disposes of any argument based upon the Thirteenth Amendment in a few paragraphs. "[T]he obvious purpose" of the amendment "was to forbid all shades and conditions of African slavery."[83] Thus limiting the scope of the amendment to its immediate end, Miller dismissed out of hand any suggestion that its purpose might encompass the constitutionality of state-created monopolies.

Most of Miller's analysis of the Fourteenth Amendment is devoted to the privileges or immunities clause in Section 1, which protects "the citizens of the United States." He begins by noting that the Constitution as originally written, in Article IV, Section 2, provides that "[t]he citizens of each state shall be entitled to all the privileges and immunities of citizens of the several states." What are these "privileges and immunities?" For his definition, Miller relies upon *Corfield v. Coryell*,[84] the 1823 circuit opinion issued by Supreme Court Justice Bushrod Washington that, as we saw in chapter 1, is today held by Justice Clarence Thomas to be similarly definitive. Justice Washington argued that the term encompassed

> those privileges and immunities which are *fundamental*; which belong of right to the citizens of all free governments. . . . What these fundamental principles are, it would be more tedious than difficult to enumerate. They may all, however, be comprehended under the following general heads: . . . the right to acquire and possess property of every kind, and to pursue and obtain happiness and safety, subject, nevertheless, to such restraints as the government may prescribe for the general good of the whole.[85]

It was therefore the purpose of Article IV, Section 2, to ensure that the several states would not deny these fundamental rights to citizens of other states who came within their borders.

However, when Miller turns to the analogous clause in the Fourteenth Amendment, he notes that it "speaks only of the privileges and immunities of *the citizens of the United States*, and does not speak"—as does Article IV, Section 2—"of those of *the citizens of the several states*."[86] Miller thus reasons that the Fourteenth Amendment must protect a body of rights *wholly distinct* from those protected by Article IV, Section 2. They are those rights "which owe their existence to the Federal government, its National character, its Constitution, or its laws."[87]

As to what these Fourteenth Amendment rights of national citizenship might be, Miller provides a list that is decidedly more impoverished than Justice Washington's. It is a curious melange, which includes the right "to come to the seat of government" for redress of grievances, the right of free access to "seaports . . . subtreasuries, land offices, and courts of justice," the right to demand the federal government's protection "when on the high seas or within the jurisdiction of a foreign government," the privilege of habeas corpus, and the right "to use the navigable waters of the United States."[88] Miller therefore uses the distinction of national/state citizenship rights "to construe the new privileges or immunities clause so narrowly as to read it effectively out of existence."[89] In a remark typical of the great majority of commentators on *Slaughterhouse*, Michael Kent Curtis points out that "[w]hy an amendment, which Miller incorrectly thought was designed only to protect blacks, would focus on things such as traveling back and forth to Washington, D.C., and to the seaports and protection on the high seas and in foreign countries, Justice Miller does not explain."[90] Similarly, Charles L. Black points to the "tottering absurdity" of holding that "such great words, used at such a moment in history," could mean nothing "except a few little things that were already there when this Amendment became law."[91]

Miller now races to his conclusion. The claim of the butchers raised no constitutional qualms because "the rights claimed by these plaintiffs, if they have any existence, are not privileges and immunities of the citizens of the United States, within the meaning of the clause of the Fourteenth Amendment under consideration."[92] In other words, the protection of most of those rights, and certainly of those rights that could be called fundamental, remained firmly under the auspices of the several states. Furthermore, says Miller, that the Fourteenth Amendment protects but a narrow class of rights is an unqualifiedly good thing because an amendment of the scope contended for by the butchers "would constitute this court a perpetual censor upon all legislation of the States, on the civil rights of their own citizens, with the authority to nullify such as it did not approve as consistent with those rights, as they existed at the time of the adoption of the amendment."[93]

Far beyond simply denying the claim of butchers, Miller thus wishes to proclaim that the Civil War Amendments were enactments of a decidedly unrevolutionary character that wrought little change in the existing balance of federalism:

> [W]e do not see in those amendments any purpose to destroy the main features of the general system. Under the pressure of all the excited feeling growing out of the war, our statesmen have still believed that the existence of the States with powers for domestic and local government, including the regulation of civil rights—the rights of persons and property—was essential to the perfect working of our complex form of government.[94]

The majority opinion in *Slaughterhouse* thus leaves the definition and protection of the most crucial rights of citizenship within the command of the state governments.

Justice Miller's opinion in *Slaughterhouse* "powerfully reminds us that interpretations offered in 1873 can be highly unreliable evidence of what was in fact agreed to in 1866–68."[95] Even Raoul Berger, who is no advocate of the expansive judicial definition of rights, asserts that Justice Stephen J. Field's dissenting opinion "more honestly reflected the intentions of the framers."[96] A good summary of Miller's most egregious errors is given by William Nelson:

> While equality for blacks was surely the central concern of the [Fourteenth Amendment's] framers and ratifiers, it was never their sole and exclusive concern. Those who discussed the amendment were aware of its implications for other groups, such as Chinese, Indians, women, and religious minorities. . . . It was simply wrong for Justice Miller to suggest that the Fourteenth Amendment could be limited only to cases of discrimination against blacks.
>
> Miller was equally wrong in limiting the privileges or immunities clause only to rights which owed their existence to national law. No one who sat in Congress or in the state legislatures that dealt with the Fourteenth Amendment doubted that [it] was designed to put to rest any doubt about the power of the federal government to protect basic common law rights of property and contract.[97]

In all its narrowness, *Slaughterhouse* became "the major source of definitions for both the Thirteenth and Fourteenth Amendments" for decades to come.[98] And very soon even Justice Miller's concession that the amendments were intended primarily, if not exclusively, to benefit African Americans was made to ring hollow. In *U.S. v. Cruickshank*,[99] the Supreme Court held unanimously that white citizens charged with murdering some fifty African Americans during the Colfax Massacre in Louisiana in 1873, an event Eric Foner has termed "[t]he bloodiest single instance of racial carnage in the Reconstruction era,"[100] could not be prosecuted by the federal government because the massacre had been carried out by private citizens. The Fourteenth Amendment, reasoned the Court, "prohibits a State from depriving any person of life, liberty, or property, without due process of law; but this adds nothing to the rights of one citizen as against another."[101] This holding takes no account of what Judge Wood recognized in *U.S. v. Hall*, that the Fourteenth Amendment contemplated federal intervention when state governments stood by while the rights of African Americans were being destroyed by private citizens. Thus, as Foner says, "the decision rendered national prosecution of crimes committed against blacks virtually impossible, and gave a green light to acts of terror where local officials either could not or would not enforce the law."[102] Thus did the South become, as W. E. B. DuBois chillingly termed it, "an armed camp for intimidating black folk."[103]

Since it found no warrant in the Civil War Amendments for the federal prosecution of murder, it is wholly unsurprising that the Supreme Court also found no constitutional basis for the federal government to do away with merely social discrimination based on race. Although Section 5 of the Fourteenth Amendment empowers Congress "to enforce, by appropriate legislation," the provisions of the amendment, these latter simply did not mean very much in the wake of *Slaughterhouse.*

This reality was set forth most comprehensively in the *Civil Rights Cases* of 1883.[104] In the waning days of Reconstruction, Congress had passed the Civil Rights Act of 1875, which provided "that all persons within the jurisdiction of the United States shall be entitled to the full and equal enjoyment of the accommodations, advantages, facilities, and privileges of inns, public conveyances on land or water, theaters, and other places of amusement."[105] The legislation engendered a flurry of litigation by African Americans challenging exclusion from hotels, theaters, trains, ships, and so on, with mixed results.

The Supreme Court considered six of these suits in the *Civil Rights Cases.* Again, the lack of "state action" put to rest any notion that the Fourteenth Amendment could extend to the private discriminatory policies of theater owners or innkeepers:

> [U]ntil some state law has been passed, or some state action through its officers or agents has been taken, adverse to the rights of citizens sought to be protected by the Fourteenth Amendment, no legislation of the United States under said amendment, nor any proceeding under such legislation, can be called into activity, for the prohibitions of the amendment are against state laws and acts done under state authority.[106]

The Court did not forget to add the gratuitously insulting aside that it was past time for African Americans to stop expecting any favors with respect to the terms of their civic existence: "When a man has emerged from slavery, and by the aid of beneficent legislation has shaken off the inseparable concomitants of that state, there must be some stage in the progress of his elevation when he takes the rank of mere citizen, and ceases to be the special favorite of the laws."[107]

But, if the Fourteenth Amendment could not reach private acts, what of *state* laws that mandated segregation? The Court famously answered this question in *Plessy v. Ferguson,*[108] which was "universally and confidently cited" for more than half a century as "the leading authority" for the constitutionality of Jim Crow legislation.[109] The case concerned a Louisiana statute that required private railroad companies to maintain separate cars for African Americans and whites, but it became the basis for segregation in every imaginable public facility.[110]

The Court began with the proposition that "[a] statute which implies merely a legal distinction between the white and colored races . . . has no tendency to destroy the legal equality of the two races or re-establish a state of involuntary servitude."[111] From this it followed that the equal protection guaranteed by the Fourteenth Amendment "was undoubtedly to enforce the absolute equality of the two races before the law, but, in the nature of things, it could not have been intended to abolish distinctions based upon color, or to enforce social, as distinguished from political, equality, or a commingling of the two races upon terms unsatisfactory to either."[112] Thus, in a capitulation to the ideology and practice of white supremacy, the Court concluded that the states remained "at liberty to act with reference to the established usages, customs, and traditions of the people, and with a view to the promotion of their comfort, and the preservation of the public peace and good order."[113]

As we have seen, even Robert Bork admits that, in practice, the doctrine of separate but equal was a sham. But it is not often noted to what extent the Supreme Court acknowledged the principle to be a sham and allowed it to be so. This is illustrated perfectly by *Cumming v. County Bd. of Ed.*,[114] a case decided three years after *Plessy*. In *Cumming*, a group of African American plaintiffs filed suit against the school board of Richmond County, Georgia, after it had discontinued the operation of the only public high school for blacks in the county, thereby abandoning the secondary education of sixty students. The high school building, the school board decided, would be converted to an elementary school in order to train up to two hundred black children "in the rudiments of education."[115]

With virtually no analysis of the plaintiffs' claims, and without so much as mentioning *Plessy*'s mandate that equal facilities were required, the Court simply accepted the school board's decision as having been made "in the interest of the greater number of colored children."[116] The Court concluded that "the education of the people in schools maintained by state taxation is a matter belonging to the respective states, and any interference on the part of Federal authority with the management of such schools cannot be justified except in the case of a clear and unmistakable disregard of the rights secured by the supreme law of the land."[117] Thus it was that, throughout the South, "with few exceptions, the story of black schools became a case study in deliberate and criminal neglect."[118]

The Fifteenth Amendment was similarly gutted, albeit somewhat more slowly. During the years when the federal government maintained a military presence in the South, "black voters exercised their political rights in large numbers. Behind this power of the sword, blacks held a larger proportion of public offices in the South than they do today."[119] In *U.S. v. Reese*,[120] an 1875 case, the Court merely struck down the main statute that allowed the federal government to prosecute acts taken to hinder or prevent African Americans from voting. The statute, said the Court, was impermissibly overbroad because it could conceivably reach acts not motivated by racial animus, while the Fifteenth Amendment applied "only when the wrongful refusal [of suffrage] is because of race, color, or previous condition of servitude."[121]

By the time of *Plessy*, the Court was willing to place its imprimatur upon the wholesale disenfranchisement of African Americans. In *Williams v. Mississippi*,[122] decided in 1898, the Court upheld Mississippi's voter registration system, which, while making no explicit mention of race, afforded local registrars essentially unlimited discretion to refuse the vote to any citizen. Such discretion, of course, was meant to serve as the means by which African Americans would be barred from the polls. However, the Court upheld the scheme, stating that state's suffrage laws "do not on their face discriminate between the races, and it has not been shown that their actual administration was evil; only that evil was possible under them."[123]

As a result of *Williams*, Mississippi "provided a model, and in less than two decades the rest of the South in various ways followed its example."[124] During this time, even an intellect as towering as Oliver Wendell Holmes's was degraded. In the 1903 decision *Giles v. Harris*,[125] Holmes resorted to rank sophistry in order to deny the petition of African American voters in Alabama to be included in the state's voter registration lists. The plaintiffs had argued "that the whole registration scheme of the Alabama constitution is a fraud upon the Constitution of the United States," since it excluded African Americans. That being the case, asked Holmes, "how can we make the court a party to the unlawful scheme by accepting it and adding another voter to its fraudulent lists."[126] This pretty much sums up the judicial spirit of the age with respect to the constitutional mandate to protect the rights of African Americans.

When Imperial Judiciary theorists pay any attention to the decades-long judicial abandonment of African American rights, they do so in a manner that can fairly be termed bloodless. Thus, Robert Bork declares that Justice Miller's opinion in *Slaughterhouse* was animated by "a sound judicial instinct" because he rejected "an almost illimitable discretionary power" to expand the scope of the Fourteenth Amendment by limiting its protections to African Americans.[127] Bork does not even consider that, on its face alone, the amendment applies to "all persons," and he wastes no ink detailing the manner in which Miller's holding was the most Pyrrhic of victories for the Fourteenth Amendment's supposed beneficiaries. Similarly, Raoul Berger can laud the *Cruickshank* decision as embodying a reading of the Fourteenth Amendment "closer to the intention of the framers" than those set forth by liberal constitutionalists of today without the merest mention of the racial slaughter that occasioned the case.[128]

More broadly, Max Boot argues that the success of American federalism "can be measured by the more than 130 years of internal peace we've enjoyed since the Civil War," thereby tossing down the memory hole the pervasive violence that enforced white supremacist regimes in the states.[129] And Mary Ann Glendon, while acknowledging "the dismal failures of many local officials in dealing with racial issues," fails to note eight decades worth of judicial sanction for these failures.[130]

The quotation from Glendon is particularly telling. Those "dismal failures" of which she speaks were hardly viewed as such by the officials implementing them. On the contrary, these were white supremacists consciously administering white supremacist regimes. For decades, they were spectacularly successful in this pursuit, thereby refuting as a matter of history Walter Berns's blithe assertion that "[i]mmoderate and outrageous demands especially are not likely to be successful" in legislative bodies.[131] Nearly a century of Jim Crow legislation proves otherwise. And, of course, the judiciary eventually took a catalytic role in eliminating this disgrace, but only when it assumed its proper role as the guardian of minority rights.

In 1866, Frederick Douglass, probably the most prominent African American of the day, expressed unease as to whether the rights of his people could be secured:

> While there remains such an idea as the right of each State to control its local affairs—an idea, by the way, more deeply rooted in the minds of men of all sections of the country than perhaps any other political idea—no general assertion of human rights can be of any practical value.[132]

This is overstated, but, with regard to the matter of protection of the rights of African Americans and other minorities, it has proved true. As long as the federal judiciary forsook the mandate of the Civil War Amendments and left local majorities free to define rights as they wished, those amendments were of no practical value.

The Anti-Union Era

In 1905, a divided Supreme Court handed down its decision in *Lochner v. New York*.[133] At issue in the case was the constitutionality of a state law limiting bakery workers to a work week of no more than sixty hours. The statute was not a radical measure. Bakers typically worked seventy-five hours a week, and often much more, under conditions that were considered appalling even by the standards of the times. Numerous contemporary "reports and exposes of the baking industry" all confirmed that "bakeries were filthy and that the products they turned out were a danger to the consuming public."[134]

Nevertheless, the Court struck down the New York statute. First, because it applied to bakers only, and not to workers in general, and because no nonarbitrary basis for so distinguishing bakers could be discerned, the Court held that the statute violated the equal protection clause of the Fourteenth Amendment. According to the Court, there could be "no contention that bakers as a class are not equal in intelligence and capacity to men in other trades or manual occupations," and thus there was no basis for a law affording special protection to bakers.[135] Second, the Court held that the due process clause of the Fourteenth Amendment was also violated because the statute represented "an illegal interference with the rights of individuals, both employers and employees, to make contracts regarding labor upon such terms as they may think best."[136] In sum, in G. Edward White's assessment, at a time when the Court was displaying "a disinclination" to use the Fourteenth Amendment "to protect the civil rights of blacks," it "became more inclined" to use the same amendment "to safeguard the property rights of entrepreneurs."[137]

Lochner has become notorious as the foremost example of the Supreme Court's hostility to legislative efforts to regulate an unfettered market economy. Thus, legal commentators refer frequently to "the *Lochner* era." But it is easy to overstate the significance of the case. As Kermit Hall says, "[t]he *Lochner* decision was in many ways an aberration with limited impact. Judges in places as different as Montana, New York, and Missississippi sustained various hours laws, many of which by the second decade of the twentieth century applied generally to all workers in manufacturing, not just people laboring in hazardous occupations."[138] In fact, says Hall, "[a]ppellate judges did invoke laissez-faire principles in a few celebrated cases, but in most instances state and federal courts, 'moved consistently toward approval of a wide range of reform legislation' which, 'although occasionally delayed in the courts, [was] not blocked there.'"[139]

More specifically, Howard Gillman has written that "nineteenth century courts were on guard not against all regulations of the economy, but only a particular kind of government interference in market relations . . . considered [to be] 'class' or 'partial' legislation; that is, laws that (in their view) promoted only the narrow interests of particular groups or classes rather than the general welfare."[140] Courts were therefore quite willing, says Gillman, to uphold "public purpose" legislation: "Judges upheld inspection and public health laws, ordinances restricting dangerous or unhealthful businesses to certain locations, regulations of weights and measures, licensing schemes, and prohibition acts; in other words, regulations that were arguably neutral with respect to struggles going on among interests in society."[141]

Examples of this jurisprudential style are legion. In *Muller v. Oregon*,[142] decided only three years after *Lochner*, the Supreme Court upheld a maximum hours law for female laundry workers, holding that the law was an expression of the interest of the public at large in providing for maternal health and safety. Similarly, a year after the Court struck down a state minimum wage law applicable to women and children,[143] it upheld another state law that forbade restaurant owners to employ women between the hours of 10:00 P.M. and 6:00 A.M. because "night work is substantially and especially detrimental to the health of women."[144]

However, if courts were willing to uphold prolabor legislation if grounded upon a purportedly legitimate "public purpose" such as employee health or safety, in matters involving labor unions they were, as Kermit Hall puts it, "uniformly hostile."[145] Indeed, says Hall, "courts tended to treat [unions] as ongoing threats to public order, even when legislatures recognized them as legitimate."[146] The jurisprudential era that stretched from the closing decades of the nineteenth century to the opening decades of the twentieth was therefore less marked by a rigid adherence to the tenets of laissez-faire and more by a dogged effort to counter this perceived threat. The judiciary, says William Forbath, took the lead in fashioning the government's response to the rise of the American union movement: "Nowhere else among industrial nations did the judiciary hold such sway over labor relations as in nineteenth and early-twentieth century America. Nowhere else did trade unionists contend so constantly with judge-made law."[147] Or, as Forbath has written elsewhere, "[f]rom the 1880s through the 1920s, state and federal appellate judges were principal architects of the nation's industrial relations policies."[148]

Before 1890, writes Herbert Hovenkamp, "the law concerning the right to strike was clear. Workers could not be forced to accept a wage that they did not want, and they had the right to refuse to work either singly or in combination. But they could not coerce other employees to join them, or other businesses to refuse to deal with the struck employer."[149] However, as labor struggles became more frequent and disruptive, judges began to broaden the concept of coercion so as to stifle the capacity to strike: "Courts in the late nineteenth and early twentieth centuries began scrutinizing strikes very closely for evidence of 'coercion' of unwilling participants. Activities that were not generally considered coercive in the 1870s and 1880s, such as simple picketing, became so after 1900."[150]

Thus, for example, in *Gompers v. Buck's Stove & Range Co.*, decided in 1911, the Court upheld the imprisonment of union members for having organized a consumer boycott against a struck employer, a strategy that the Court held to be "a conspiracy causing irreparable damage to the business or property" of the employer.[151] Here is how the Court described the consequent necessity for judicial intervention:

> Society itself is an organization, and does not object to organizations for social, religious, business, and all legal purposes. The law, therefore, recognizes the right of workingmen to unite and to invite others to join their ranks. . . .
>
> But the very fact that it is lawful to form these bodies, with multitudes of members, means that they have thereby acquired a vast power, in the presence of which the individual may be helpless. This power, when unlawfully used against one, cannot be met, except by his purchasing peace at the cost of submitting to terms which involve the sacrifice of rights protected by the Constitution.[152]

Gompers is indicative of how, in order to facilitate judicial intervention into strikes, judges also broadened the definition of the legally compensable injury that a strike might inflict. Unions frequently argued that, in and of itself, the act of striking was merely a withdrawal of labor that resulted in no physical injury to the property of the employer. As Forbath writes, judges met this argument by transforming the very concept of property:

> In place of the inherited view limiting property rights primarily to tangible objects, they adopted the definition that held property to be anything that had "pecuniary" or "exchangeable value" including a man's business or labor. Because boycotts and strikes injured employers' profit-making activities, and therefore their "pecuniary interests," they trenched on the employers' property.[153]

Thus, where an employer had once been "merely free to run his shop, and use his machinery, as he willed, he now was found to have a property right to do so that was protected from interference created by a boycott or strike pressing for adherence to union work rules and standards."[154]

The most potent weapon in the judicial arsenal against labor was the "labor injunction," which Felix Frankfurter termed "America's distinctive contribution in the application of the law to industrial strife."[155] The labor injunction was simply a judicial order that enjoined a strike. It was used to devastating effect in the 1894 Pullman Strike, waged by Eugene V. Debs's American Railway Union against the country's largest manufacturer of railroad cars. It was Debs's strategy to have ARU members strike against railroads that used Pullman cars, a move that threatened to stop railroad traffic throughout much of the country. The judicial reaction was swift:

> Federal judges in nearly every large city west of the Allegheny Mountains . . . turned their courtrooms into police courts by issuing roughly one hundred decrees prohibiting the ARU and other unions from threatening, combining, or conspiring to quit in any fashion that would embarrass the railways' operations. They also enjoined refusals to handle the cars of other struck lines. Several of the injunctions, including that against Debs and his ARU, also forbade attempts to induce fellow workers to support the strikes or boycotts.[156]

The injunction against the ARU, which was issued by two federal judges in Chicago, was, in the words of the *Chicago Tribune*, "so broad and sweeping that interference with the railroads, even of the remotest kind, will be made practically impossible."[157]

It was this injunction that the Supreme Court upheld unanimously in *In re Debs*.[158] The injunction was perfectly proper, said the Court with admirable forthrightness, because striking was a form of political activity that could not be countenanced:

> [I]t is a lesson which cannot be learned too soon or too throughly that under this government of and by the people the means of redress of all wrongs are through the courts and at the ballot box, and that no wrong, real or fancied, carries with it legal warrant to invite as a means of redress the co-operation of a mob, with it accompanying acts of violence.[159]

Debs, who had done his utmost to ensure that strikers avoided violence, had a memorable reaction to the decision. "Every federal judge," he said, "is now made a Czar. The decision of the Supreme Court had crowned them and given them autocratic sway."[160]

Debs did not exaggerate. The labor injunction was massively applied. In Forbath's estimation "roughly 105 labor injunctions issued in the 1880s, 410 in the 1890s, 850 in the 1910s, and 2,130 in the 1920s."[161] Numerous states and localities enacted laws that sought to forbid the issuance of injunctions against a variety of peaceful strike activities. However, as Forbath says, "[a]t least twenty-five of these anti-injunction statutes were struck down on constitutional grounds. . . . Most of the measures that were not invalidated were vitiated by narrow construction."[162] Thus, in *Truax v. Corrigan*,[163] the Supreme Court struck down an Arizona statute that forbade the issuance of injunctions to enjoin peaceful picketing. The effect of the decision, said Justice Holmes in dissent, was "to prevent the making of social experiments that an important part of the community desires, in the insulated chambers afforded by the several states."[164] Or, as Mary Ann Glendon would say, Holmes thought that the majority was "wreak[ing] havoc with grass-roots politics."[165]

The labor historian David Montgomery has summed up the cumulative impact of the judicial assault upon unions:

> [B]y the 1920s almost any strike, whatever the political affiliations of its leaders, was likely to face some sort of court injunction. Court orders forbidding boycotts and sympathetic strikes had first appeared in the 1880s and then become widespread during the open-shop drive of the early twentieth century. A series of Supreme Court decisions between 1917 and 1922 gave such judicial orders the sanction of the

highest court in the land and increased both the uniformity and the anti-union quality of their subsequent impact. As a result of those decisions, mass picketing could be forbidden, yellow dog contracts were legally enforceable, and injunctions might forbid union organizers from recruiting workers who had signed one of those pledges never to join a union.[166]

For a justification of this legal course, we have no better source than Supreme Court Justice David J. Brewer, who averred, in a speech delivered in 1893, that "it must ever remain the duty of the courts, in the protection of society, and in the execution of the laws of the land, to condemn, prevent, and punish all such unlawful conspiracies and combinations."[167] Samuel Gompers, the president of the American Federation of Labor, saw things differently. In 1903, he opined that the enmity of the courts toward the labor movement amounted to "judicial usurpation and tyranny" that threatened to "destroy the American Republic."[168]

Robert Bork has suggested that never so often as today has the purportedly activist course of the judiciary "been so popular in the law schools, in the press, and in the opinions of elite groups generally."[169] This is flatly incorrect. The work of the courts in combating the rising American labor movement was wildly popular among "elite groups." Here is a typical comment from the elite bar that appeared in an 1893 issue of the *American Law Review*, lauding the recent issuance of a labor injunction by a Michigan federal court:

> The spectacle of the action of the federal judges above referred to is simply that of a new, independent, fearless, conservative force entering the arena. . . . The action of the federal judges seems to have been applauded by the best portion of the public press without distinction of party, and there is hardly any doubt that their action is largely supported by the conservative public opinion of the country.[170]

Indeed, judges themselves made no secret of their enmity toward unions. Here again is Justice David J. Brewer, in an 1891 speech, commenting upon the nature of a strike: "It is coercion, force; it is the effort of the many by the mere weight of numbers to compel the one to do their bidding. It is a proceeding outside the law."[171] It was blatantly partisan declarations such as this that caused the Progressive leader Herbert Croly to conclude, in 1909, that "the courts are as much influenced . . . by a political theory as they are by any fidelity to fundamental law, and that if they continue indefinitely in the same course, they are likely to get into trouble."[172] More broadly, the leading politician of Progressivism, Senator Robert M. LaFollette, of Wisconsin, wrote three years later that, "by usurping the power to declare laws unconstitutional and by presuming to read their own views into statutes without regard to the plain intention of the legislators," the judiciary had "become in reality the supreme law-making and law-giving institution of our government. . . . [It had] come to constitute what may indeed be termed a 'judicial oligarchy.'"[173]

What happened during this era was more than what Imperial Judiciary theorists contend has happened today with respect to matters like abortion. That is, the era saw more than a judicial arrogation of power that took political questions out of the hands of the public and imposed judicial solutions upon them. The anti-union era was marked by a judicial attempt to actually suppress a political movement.

But the labor movement did not allow itself to be suppressed. On the contrary, even in the face of decades worth of judicial animus, it continued its organizational work. It also continued to act politically, eventually becoming an important part of the New Deal coalition that experienced immense electoral success.

The New Deal coalition also achieved considerable legislative success, especially with respect to statutes that governed labor relations. Most significant here is the National Labor Relations Act, which "brought a new regime of government-sponsored collective bargaining, a regime based on a statute, to end the instability and violence that had characterized industrial relations for some six decades."[174] The constitutionality of the Act was upheld by the U.S. Supreme Court in 1937, a Court whose personnel now reflected a considerably more benign attitude toward the labor movement.[175] Of course, this change of attitude was itself the product of the success of the New Deal coalition, which had won the White House and the Senate and, with them, the ability to decisively influence the judicial selection process.

Recently, Justice Robert Young, one of the most conservative justices on the current Michigan Supreme Court, which is itself one of the most conservative state supreme courts in the country, gave a speech in which he argued that "[n]ow, as never before, it simply matters who wears a black robe,"[176] because the courts "have become a new and previously unmonitored source of social and political policymaking."[177]

Justice Young has gotten history badly wrong. Who wears black robes has *always* mattered greatly in this country. Tocqueville knew this in the 1830s. It may be that the demands of preserving the coherence of the Imperial Judiciary thesis prevent its adherents from understanding it today.

4

The Judiciary and
the Extent of Rights

Harvard University's 1978 commencement address was delivered by Alexander Solzhenitsyn, who was then still in the early years of his enforced exile from the Soviet Union. Solzhenitsyn delivered a jeremiad that received headlines around the world for its assessment of a West that had "lost its civil courage" in the struggle against Communist expansionism, a loss "particularly noticeable among the ruling groups and the intellectual elite, causing an impression of loss of courage by the entire society."[1]

A significant item in Solzhenitsyn's indictment was the claim that, in the West, "[t]he defense of individual rights has reached such extremes as to make society as a whole defenseless against certain individuals."[2] He continued:

Destructive and irresponsible freedom has been granted boundless space. Society appears to have little defense against the abyss of human decadence, such as, for example, misuse of liberty for moral violence against young people, motion pictures full of pornography, crime, and horror. It is considered to be part of freedom and theoretically counterbalanced by the young people's right not to look or not to accept. Life organized legalistically has thus shown its inability to defend itself against the corrosion of evil.

And what shall we say about the dark realm of criminality as such? Legal frames (especially in the United States) are broad enough to encourage not only individual freedom but also certain individual crimes. The culprit can go unpunished or obtain undeserved leniency with the support of thousands of public defenders. When a government starts an earnest fight against terrorism, public opinion immediately accuses it of violating the terrorists' civil rights. There are many such cases.[3]

How shocking it must have been to hear expansive individual rights de-nounced by a man who had suffered greatly at the hands of a regime that was in essence a seventy-year conspiracy against the very concept of rights as a restraint upon state power. Still, Solzhenitsyn's address was embraced immediately and enthusiastically by American conservatives, not least for its criticism of rights.

Indeed, criticisms that echo Solzhenitsyn's are now a staple of our po-litical discourse. The New York corporate attorney Philip K. Howard is well removed from Solzhenitsyn in terms of literary renown, but the same sort of thinking about rights is palpable in this passage from his best-sell-ing 1994 book, *The Death of Common Sense*:

> Rights, almost no one needs to be told, are all around us. The language of rights is used everywhere in modern America—not only in public life, but in the workplace, in school, in welfare offices, in health care. There are rights for children and the elderly; the disabled; the mentally disabled; workers under twenty-five and over forty; alcoholics and the addicted; the homeless; spotted owls and snail darters.[4]

We have already noted that the baleful effects of expansive judicial protec-tion of individual rights are a central element of the Imperial Judiciary thesis. As Max Boot puts it, judges "seem to delight in recognizing ever-ex-panding 'rights' for an ever-expanding array of minority groups."[5] The same charge made its way into the 1996 Republican Party platform, quot-ing from a speech given by the party's presidential standard-bearer, Robert Dole:

> The American people have lost faith in their courts, and for good reason. Some members of the federal judiciary threaten the safety, the values, and the freedom of law-abiding citizens. They make up laws and invent new rights as they go along, arrogating to themselves powers King George III never dared to exercise.[6]

As we have also seen, the Imperial Judiciary thesis holds that judges do not "invent new rights" at random. They implement a left/liberal *strategy* to impose through the courts what cannot be won at the polls. That is, judicial "rights creation" is the usurpation of politics. The Justices of the Supreme Court, says Robert Bork, "armed with a written Constitution and the power of judicial review, could become not only the supreme legislature of the land but a legislature beyond the reach of the ballot box."[7] And, of course, behind the judges are the cultural elite, especially the like-minded academics and litigators with whom they work in concert. Bork again: "An elite moral or political view may never be able to win an election or command the votes of a majority of a legislature, but it may nonetheless influence judges and gain the force of law in that way."[8]

This chapter seeks to debunk this kind of thinking. First, I examine the validity of the core claim being put forward: that the United States has become a rights-besotted nation. Next, to the extent that the judiciary has expanded enforceable rights over the past half-century, I consider both the ideological tenor of that development and its staying power. Specifically, I ask two questions: (1) to what extent can the most doctrinally radical decisions of the Warren Court era be characterized as victories for the left? and (2) have the Warren Court's decisions protecting the interests of politically disfavored minorities, specifically criminal defendants and welfare recipients, escaped serious contraction by later Courts?

"The Land of Rights"

So Mary Ann Glendon entitles the first chapter of her book *Rights Talk.* And, indeed, during the past half-century, Americans have been justified in viewing the Constitution as a source of judicially enforceable rights, as opposed to merely unenforced platitudes, to a much greater extent than at any time previous in our history. This is the legacy of the central operating principle of the Warren Court, as stated by G. Edward White: "a momentum toward an increasingly broad definition of the rights attaching to American citizenship."[9]

To an extent not often appreciated, however, it is only with the Warren Court that the Supreme Court began paying sustained attention to claims of individual right, other than those attaching to property ownership. A few statistics tell the tale. "As late as the mid-thirties, less than 10 percent of the Court's decisions involved individual rights other than property rights. . . . By the late sixties, almost 70 percent of its decisions involved individual rights."[10] "[W]hereas in the 1935–36 term only 2 of 160 written opinions [involved individual rights other than property rights], in the 1979–80 term the ratio had increased to 80 out of 149—a trend that has continued unabated."[11]

Glendon is therefore certainly correct when she asserts that, "[a]t least until the 1950s, the principal focus of constitutional law was not on personal liberty as such, but on the division of authority between the states and the federal government, and the allocation of powers among the branches of the central government."[12] But Glendon does not dwell upon the consequences of this inattention to individual rights, which is typical of commentators who decry the contemporary overexpansion of rights in the United States. To state the matter baldly, however, individual rights were quite fragile and neglected things. The point is well made by Richard Posner—certainly no fan of the legacy of the Warren Court—in his review of Glendon's *A Nation under Lawyers:*

> There was surprisingly little actual enforcement of constitutional rights in the 1950s. A large proportion of the criminal defendants who could not afford a lawyer had to defend themselves. . . . Many prisons and insane asylums were hellholes, and to their inmates' complaints the courts turned a deaf ear. The right of free speech was interpreted narrowly, the better to crush the Communist Party and protect the reading public from Henry Miller. Police brutality was rampant, and the tort remedies against it ineffectual. Criminal sentencing verged on randomness, and in some parts of the country capital punishment was imposed almost casually.[13]

Yet it has become common in political discussion today to exaggerate, sometimes wildly, the extent to which individual rights have received judicial recognition in recent decades. Consider first the very extensive limits upon judicially enforceable rights in the United States. A good place to start is the Supreme Court's 1989 decision in *DeShaney v. Winnebago County Dept. of Social Services*.[14] That case considered whether a young Wisconsin boy, who had suffered a series of beatings at the hands of his father, had been deprived of his constitutional rights by state officials who were aware of the father's violent tendencies. Social workers had taken certain steps along the lines of monitoring and counseling the father. They did not, however, remove the boy from his father's custody. The beatings eventually resulted in permanent brain damage.

The boy's mother, who was estranged from the father, brought a lawsuit charging that the boy had been deprived of due process in the form of adequate protection from his father's violence. According to her, the government "was categorically obligated to protect him in these circumstances."[15] The Court squarely rejected the argument:

> [N]othing in the language of the due process clause itself requires the state to protect the life, liberty, and property of its citizens against invasion by private actors. . . . Its purpose was to protect the people from the State, not to ensure that the State protected them from each other.[16]

Thus, as a general matter, there exists "no affirmative right to government aid, even where such aid may be necessary to secure life, liberty, or property interests of which the government itself may not deprive the individual."[17]

If there is no federal constitutional right to be protected from private violence, it should come as no surprise that the courts have consistently rejected claims that there is any right to the government's provision of a wide range of needs that can fairly be called fundamental. There is no federal constitutional right to housing.[18] Nor is there a federal constitutional right to be provided with an education.[19] And it almost goes without saying that no court has come close to suggesting that there is any federal constitutional duty on the part of the government to alleviate whatever level of material inequality prevails in society. On the contrary, as Justice Frankfurter asserted, "a State need not equalize economic conditions. . . . Those are contingencies of life which are hardly within the power, let alone the duty, of a State to correct or cushion."[20] Even Glendon has acknowledged that "the American Constitution, unlike the constitutions of most other liberal democracies, contains no language establishing affirmative welfare rights or obligations."[21]

Beyond these most fundamental needs, there is no general federal constitutional right to employment. In an article in the *New York Times* on the wave of layoffs in Internet companies, a prominent labor lawyer declared that "Americans instinctively believe that they can only be fired for doing something wrong, or not performing."[22] But, with respect to private employment, in the absence of any employment contract stating the contrary, the American rule remains "employment-at-will," which means that one can be refused a job or terminated for any reason or no reason. The only substantial limitation upon this is the purely statutory right not to be denied employment or fired in violation of one of the various antidiscrimination statutes. The principle is set forth in a recent decision of the U.S.

Court of Appeals for the Seventh Circuit: "The personnel decisions of [a] company may not be good ones, sometimes even harsh, but unless they violate some aspect of federal law, for instance, age, race, or gender discrimination, those business decisions are no business of this court."[23]

Even when the Supreme Court has recognized and enforced a particular federal constitutional right, it has also held consistently that the government has no duty to facilitate any citizen's enjoyment of that right. The quintessential case is *Harris v. McRae*, in which the Supreme Court upheld the Hyde Amendment, which forbids the use of Medicaid funds to pay for abortions.[24] There the Court stated bluntly that "it simply does not follow that [a woman's reproductive freedom] carries with it a constitutional entitlement to the financial resources to avail herself of the full range of protected choices."[25]

Perhaps the best evidence of the extent to which rights-conscious liberals have fallen well short of their fondest aims with respect to judicial recognition of rights is the fact that, for many years now, they have largely abandoned hope that the federal courts will be the most fruitful source of that which they seek. Justice William Brennan issued a seminal statement in this regard in a 1977 issue of the *Harvard Law Review*. There he noted "a trend in recent opinions of the United States Supreme Court to pull back from, or at least suspend for the time being," expansive conceptions of individual rights.[26] Brennan's response was to issue "a clear call to state courts to step into the breach."[27] That is, he admonished state courts to seek constitutional bases for the broad definition of rights in their own constitutions:

> [T]he point I want to stress here is that state courts cannot rest when they have afforded their citizens the full protections of the federal Constitution. State constitutions, too, are a font of individual liberties, their protections often extending beyond those required by the Supreme Court's interpretation of federal law.[28]

This has remained a frequent theme among liberal commentators. Thus, the law professor Robert Shapiro has written recently that "[a]t a time when federal courts generally take a narrow view of individual rights—a far cry from the expansive vision of the 1960s and '70s—state courts have provided a significant alternative avenue for relief."[29] But Shapiro is also well aware of the substantial limits faced by a strategy of rights expansion based on state courts. He notes first that, to a far greater extent than federal court decisions, state supreme court decisions are subject to being overruled by constitutional amendment:

> The cumbersome amendment process written into the U.S. Constitution makes that document relatively impervious to change. In more than two hundred years, the Constitution has been amended only twenty-seven times. State constitutions, in contrast, are much more subject to revision. They have, on average, been amended more than one hundred times each—some far more than that. . . . If people are outraged by a decision granting a right under a state constitution, their response might be to try to change the constitution. When the Hawaii supreme court indicated that it might recognize a right to same-sex marriage, for example, the voters approved a constitutional amendment allowing the legislature to ban such unions.[30]

The facts on the ease with which state constitutions may be amended are stunning. "In forty-four states, only a simple majority vote in a referendum is required to ratify proposed amendments. . . . In addition, in eighteen states voters can propose constitutional amendments directly, with thirteen permitting ratification of those proposals by a simple majority of those voting on the measure."[31] Kermit Hall has summarized what state constitutional pliability has meant over the course of our history:

> There have been 239 separate constitutional conventions, and since the beginning of the republic there has never been a three-year period in which at least one state constitutional convention or, more recently, a constitutional revision commission has not met. Since 1776 the fifty states have operated under no fewer than 146 constitutions and thirty-one of the fifty states have had two or more constitutions. Eighteen states have had four or more constitutions, with Louisiana topping the list with eleven.[32]

At this point, however, adherents of the Imperial Judiciary thesis will leap up to remind us that, late in 1999, the Vermont Supreme Court held that the constitution of that state mandates that homosexual unions must be granted the same legal benefits as are afforded to heterosexual marriages.[33] The Vermont constitution is atypically difficult to amend. What is more, the U.S. Constitution, in Article IV, Section 1, states that "Full faith and Credit shall be given in each State to the public Acts, Records and judicial

Proceedings of every other State." That is, it is generally the case that marriages performed in one state must be legally honored in *all* states. Thus, in the eyes of conservative critics, "the Vermont ruling is a clear and present danger to marriage everywhere in the country. . . . In other words, the long-anticipated legal crisis of the American family has arrived, and it has arrived as a nationwide crisis."[34]

Congress has already addressed this issue. In 1996, when it looked as if the Hawaii Supreme Court might give constitutional protection to same-sex unions, Congress passed the Defense of Marriage Act (DOMA), which provides that no state "shall be required to give effect to any public act, record, or judicial proceeding of any other State . . . respecting a relationship between persons of the same sex that is treated as a marriage under the laws of such other State."[35] Representative Bob Barr, of Georgia, has asserted that DOMA "provides the tools to check the spread of homosexual marriage at Vermont's borders," thereby ensuring that the state does not become "a homosexual Las Vegas, offering drive-through recognition to same-sex couples."[36] As of this writing, DOMA's constitutionality has not been judicially determined, and scholarly debate on the issue is intense.[37]

Professor Shapiro identifies a second, and more forbidding, obstacle to liberal hopes for rights expansion through state courts:

> But perhaps most significant of all is the fact that state judges enjoy less insulation from politics than their federal counterparts. Unlike federal judges, who are appointed for life, most state judges are subject to regular electoral review. State judges associated with controversial rulings have found themselves the victims of retribution. A particularly spectacular purge came in California in 1986 when voters removed three state supreme court justices, largely because of decisions overturning death sentences.
>
> It is hard for a state judge to miss the message: unpopular rulings may cost you your job. In the words of Otto Kaus, a former justice on the California Supreme Court, for a state judge to try to ignore the political consequences of a decision is like trying to ignore "a crocodile in your bathtub."[38]

As we discuss in more detail in chapter 6, since 87 percent of state judges face some form of election, this is a very potent obstacle indeed. It is becoming even more so lately, as judicial elections are coming to resemble more and more elections generally, complete with big money contributors and attack ads. It suffices for now to say that to the extent that judges are subject to the same incentives as legislators with respect to attaining and continuing in office, they will likely feel correspondingly less inclined to advance the interests of politically unpopular minorities.

Victories for Liberals Alone?

The Warren Court is universally called a "liberal" Court. More than this, any decision of the Supreme Court before, during or after the Warren Court, that is rights expansive is invariably classified as a "liberal" decision, with the large exception of cases involving property rights. These tags, however, obscure a neglected truth. If one considers the rights-expansive decisions of the past half-century that have been the most doctrinally unprecedented and that have had the greatest impact on the way in which our politics is practiced, one cannot conclude that these have exclusively furthered the substantive policy goals of liberals.

The Redistricting Cases

In *Baker v. Carr*,[39] decided in 1962, the Supreme Court held that the federal courts had jurisdiction to decide claims arising from the refusal of state officials to redraw state legislative districts so as to correct disparities of population between districts. Two years later, in *Reynolds v. Sims*,[40] the Court held that the equal protection clause of the Fourteenth Amendment requires that both houses of a state legislature be elected from districts of roughly equal population. That same year, in *Wesberry v. Sanders*, the Court held that the "one person-one vote" principle applied to congressional districts, as well.[41] Chief Justice Warren famously regarded these cases as the most important decided by the Court under his stewardship.

He did not exaggerate. Prior to *Baker* and *Reynolds*, most state legislatures were egregiously malapportioned, with rural districts exercising dominance over cities because election districts had not been redrawn to keep up with the growth of urban populations. *Baker*, for example, was a Tennessee case, a state where "districts comprising only 27 percent of the state's population could control the senate, while the comparable figure for the house was 29 percent."[42] And Tennessee was "not untypical of state legislatures of the time":

> In some states, the population disparities across districts were startling. In the California senate, one member represented more than 6 million people, while another represented fewer than 15,000. In the New Jersey senate, the largest district contained more than 923,000 people, while the smallest had under 49,000; in the Texas senate the population per senator ranged from 147,000 to 1.2 million. In New York's lower house, districts varied from 315,000 down to 15,000; in the Kansas house, the most populous district had nearly 69,000, the smallest just over 2,000.[43]

Urban centers were grossly underrepesented in numerous state legislatures because of the failure to redistribute legislative seats to reflect their frequently skyrocketing populations. Here are some examples of how things stood in 1962:

> In Connecticut, the four largest cities have 23 percent of the population and eight out of 279 members in the House. In New Jersey, the five largest counties have 53 percent of the population and five of twenty-one seats in the Senate. In Florida, the five largest counties have half the population and five of thirty-eight Senate seats. Wayne County has one-third of the population and one-fifth of the seats in the Michigan Senate. Cook County has over half the population and twenty-four of the fifty-eight Senate seats. Los Angeles has almost 40 percent of the population and one of forty seats in the Senate; the six largest counties have two-thirds of the population and six of forty Senate seats.[44]

In sum, "[w]hen the Supreme Court was asked to hear challenges to the fairness of state legislative apportionment in *Baker* . . . the maldistribution of legislative districts had become a national disgrace."[45] Even Robert Bork agrees that "the plaintiffs [in *Baker*] deserved to win" because, since "a majority of Tennessee voters could not govern, they were denied representative government."[46] But the possibility of reform through the states themselves was chimerical, because minority-dominated legislatures simply refused to act on reapportionment, and state courts were not bold enough to order them to do so. Thus, as Archibald Cox asserts, "most state legislators were more interested in self-perpetuation than electoral reform. No one could reasonably suppose that Congress would grasp the nettle. As a practical matter, either the Court must act or nothing would be done."[47]

But *Baker* was by no means the first time the Court had been asked to step into the breach on the issue of state legislative reapportionment. In earlier cases, however, the Court had refused to address the issue on the ground that it was a quintessentially political matter that a court should not decide. Thus, in the 1946 case of *Colgrove v. Green,* Justice Frankfurter famously asserted that courts "ought not to enter this political thicket."[48] Therefore, in deciding *Baker* and *Reynolds* as it did, the Court was casting aside a position of nonintervention that was widely believed to have been set in stone. Accordingly, after *Reynolds* was decided, Anthony Lewis wrote that "even some liberal-minded persons, admirers of the modern Supreme Court, find themselves stunned."[49] Since *Reynolds,* however, judicial oversight of legislative apportionment of election districts has become a familiar element of our politics. But has the liberal political program advanced as a result?[50]

Timothy O'Rourke has considered a wide range of studies that have investigated redistricting's effects over more than three decades. He notes that, by the end of the 1960s, "virtually every state legislature [had redrawn] legislative boundaries one or more times," and that "[b]y the mid-1970s only four states were left with legislatures that were egregiously malapportioned."[51] In sum, the judiciary's "continuing oversight of redistricting has produced a remarkable degree of uniformity in congressional and state legislative representation: congressional districts within states now exhibit near-perfect population equality, and state legislative districts are only slightly less perfect."[52]

However, in terms of *who wins,* O'Rourke is more cautious: "While three decades of redistricting activity have plainly enhanced minority representation, this activity, as a general matter, has had a less discernable impact on party fortunes, particularly at the congressional level."[53] With respect to Congress:

> From the perspective of 1963 through 1983, reapportionment and redistricting had little impact on the overall strength of Republicans and Democrats in the House. The Republicans were unable to make gains from the growth of suburbs and the Sunbelt as many predicted. If redistricting did not alter the balance of power between the parties, it did redistribute seats within parties, with suburban Democrats becoming more numerous and urban and southern rural Democrats less so. Republicans, both rural

and suburban in the early 1960s, became relatively more suburban from the 1960s on. These trends continued into the 1990s.[54]

And as for state legislatures:

> If Democrats, as a rule, benefitted from redistricting in northern states, Republicans ultimately gained from redistricting in southern states, such as Tennessee, where post-*Baker* redistricting fueled a GOP surge in the legislature in the late 1960s. In Florida, the percentage of Republican seats in the state senate grew from 5 to 42 percent and in the house from 9 to 33 percent in the 1967 election under a court-ordered reapportionment.[55]

Concerning actual policy outcomes, O'Rourke sees "little evidence that redistricting significantly affected ideology or policy" in Congress, while "redistricting did, in fact, produce evident change in state fiscal policies," with more money going to metropolitan areas in the wake of reapportionment.[56] The most clearcut gain, however, was that

> redistricting after 1990 made a discernable, if not overwhelming, contribution of the Republican takeover of the [U.S. House of Representatives] in 1994. The new Republican leadership of the House—heavily Sunbelt, suburban, and conservative in character—is in many ways a testament to the cumulative impact of both reapportionment and redistricting since the 1960s. Reapportionment has shifted seats from Frost Belt states to Sun Belt states, and redistricting has moved seats away from rural and central city areas to the suburbs.[57]

In sum, reapportionment did not decisively advance the goals of any ideological faction. And this is as Chief Justice Warren intended. As John Hart Ely has written, the reapportionment cases were motivated "not by a desire on the part of the court to vindicate particular substantive values it had determined were important or fundamental, but rather a desire to ensure that the political process . . . was open to those of all viewpoints on something approaching an equal basis."[58] Or, as Lani Guinier and Pamela S. Karlan lament, "the new doctrine was *procedural*; it focused on voting rather than on the fairness of political *outcomes*."[59]

Political Speech

The Warren Court is uniformly recognized for its expansive free speech jurisprudence. Imperial Judiciary theorists have paid a good deal of attention to its opinions arising from the context of protest demonstrations, partly as a means of asserting that the Court had a left-wing bent but also to suggest that it undermined the civility of our politics. The fact is, however, that the Warren Court's protest cases were not so much breaking new ground as they were building upon a tradition that had begun decades earlier. It was, after all, in 1949 that the Court held that the "function of free speech under our system of government is to invite dispute. It may indeed best serve its high purpose when it induces a condition of unrest, creates dissatisfaction with conditions as they are, or even stirs people to anger."[60]

Nor can it be said that the Warren Court's decisions in this area were particularly weighted in favor of the protest activities of the left. Imperial Judiciary adherents have a special affection for *Cohen v. California*, a 1971 post–Warren Court decision, written by the impeccably conservative Justice Harlan, in which the Court overturned the conviction of an antiwar protester who wore a jacket emblazoned with the phrase "FUCK THE DRAFT" into a courtroom.[61] Robert Bork, for example, sees the case as a sterling example of the "moral relativism" that is allegedly the central tenet of contemporary liberalism.[62] Hadley Arkes has somehow come to the conclusion that "the teaching of *Cohen* made it dangerous for people to venture out, especially at night, into public places."[63] But, in a landmark decision, the Warren Court overturned the conviction of a Ku Klux Klansman for having given a public address advocating violence as a means of political reform.[64] And, on the ground that the destruction of government property could be enjoined, the Court upheld the conviction of antiwar protesters who burned their draft cards, thereby condoning the criminalization of one of the signature acts of protest against the Vietnam War.[65]

There is little question, however, that where the Warren Court made the most decisive break with the past of First Amendment jurisprudence was in the area of libel law. In *New York Times Co. v. Sullivan*,[66] a 1964 opinion, the Court for the first time placed constitutional restrictions upon state libel laws by holding that, in order to succeed upon a libel claim, a public official—the Court would soon expand the rule to include "public figures" generally—had to prove not only that the challenged statement was false but that it was made either with knowledge of its falsity or with reckless disregard of whether or not it was true. In so holding, Archibald Cox has remarked, the Court cast aside "175 years of settled legal practice."[67]

In his book on the case, Anthony Lewis has set forth how radical a break from the past *Sullivan* represents:

> In English libel law, and until 1964 the libel law of most American states, the plaintiff was entitled to damages if a false and damaging statement was made about him, even though the defendant published the falsehood innocently. The defendant could defeat a libel action only by bearing the burden of proving a defamatory statement true. . . .
>
> The *Sullivan* rule changes both these aspects of the common law. Now the plaintiff had to show that the defendant had published a falsehood with a high degree of fault—namely knowingly or recklessly. It necessarily followed that the plaintiff first had to show that there was something false in the publication, so the burden shifted to him. This can make all the difference in the result of libel suits. In Britain, newspapers that go to court to defend against a libel suit instead of settling lose almost every time, and a major reason is that they have the burden of proving that the challenged story is true.[68]

But can *Sullivan* be called a victory for liberals alone? Lino Graglia thinks so, having listed libel as one of many jurisprudential realms in which he believes the courts have been aggressively pursuing left-wing policy goals.[69] But Professor Graglia is badly mistaken, and no less than Robert Bork tells us so.

Bork performed this salutary task in a concurring opinion he authored in *Ollman v. Evans*,[70] a 1984 case decided by the entire U.S. Court of Appeals for the District of Columbia Circuit. The case arose from a piece written by the conservative syndicated columnists Rowland Evans and Robert Novak about a Marxist political scientist, Bertell Ollman. Perhaps best known as the inventor of *Class Struggle,* a leftist version of the board game *Monopoly,* Ollman was being considered for appointment to the chairmanship of the political science department of the University of Maryland. The Evans and Novak column claimed that, far from being a scholar worthy of this distinction, Ollman was "widely viewed in his profession as a political activist" who had "the avowed desire . . . to use higher education for indoctrination." They also included a quotation, which they attributed to a "political scientist in a major eastern university, whose scholarship and reputation as a liberal are well known," to the effect that

"Ollman has no status within the profession, but is a pure and simple activist."

Ollman was eventually denied the University of Maryland post. As a consequence—apparently having decided to disregard the view that "the institutions of the state exercise a hostile domination over the individual ... because they are themselves dominated by a class of men who are alien and hostile to him"[71]—Ollman availed himself of the courts to sue Evans and Novak for libel. The case was heard by the full D.C. Circuit after a three-judge panel of the Circuit had reversed a federal district court's dismissal of Ollman's claim.

In an opinion by Judge Kenneth Starr—yes, *that* Kenneth Starr—the full circuit reinstated the dismissal. Starr looked to the rule of *Sullivan,* as developed in the case of *Gertz v. Robert Welch, Inc.,* in which the Supreme Court held that "[u]nder the First Amendment there is no such thing as a false idea."[72] Examining "the totality of circumstances" in which the Evans and Novak column appeared, particularly its status as an op-ed piece, Starr held that the authors' intentions "were not to set forth definitive conclusions, but instead meant to ventilate what in their view constituted the central questions raised by Mr. Ollman's appointment."[73] Thus, the column was not libelous; it was "plainly part and parcel of [the American] tradition of social and political criticism."[74]

Bork concurred in this result but did not join Starr's opinion because he viewed it as insufficiently protective of political speech. He begins his concurring opinion by asserting that "the First Amendment must not try to make public dispute safe and comfortable for all the participants."[75] Ollman's suit is a threat to this principle because it

> arouses concern that a freshening stream of libel actions, which often seem as much designed to punish writers and publications as to recover damages for real injuries, may threaten the public and constitutional interest in free, and frequently rough, discussion. Those who step into areas of public dispute, who choose the pleasures and distractions of controversy, must be willing to bear criticism, disparagement, and even wounding assessments.[76]

But here Bork faces a familiar originalist problem. We know little, he says, about the specific intent of the framers with respect to libel actions that seek "enormous sums" and are therefore "quite capable of silencing political commentators forever."[77] Indeed, we must acknowledge that the First

Amendment "was written by men who had not the remotest idea of modern forms of communication."[78] Thankfully, however, and amazingly in light of *The Tempting of America*, "we have a judicial tradition of a continuing evolution of doctrine to serve the central purpose of the First Amendment."[79] Bork continues:

> We know very little of the precise intentions of the framers and ratifiers of the speech and press clauses of the First Amendment. But we do know that they gave into our keeping the value of preserving free expression and, in particular, the preservation of political expression, which is commonly conceded to be the value at the core of those clauses. Perhaps the framers did not envision libel actions as a major threat to that freedom. I may grant that, for the sake of the point to be made. But if, over time, the libel action becomes a threat to the central meaning of the First Amendment, why should not judges adapt their doctrines?[80]

We in fact do know from the text of the First Amendment that its only explicit restriction is upon the legislature: "Congress shall make no law . . ." It makes no mention whatever of the applicability of the amendment to civil libel suits. It is therefore difficult to argue with Anthony Lewis's assertion that "[t]hose who drafted and ratified the First Amendment almost certainly did not have civil libel suits in mind."[81] But Bork contends that this should not bar judges from attempting to meet the threat that libel suits pose to free expression because, "unless we continue to develop doctrine to fit First Amendment concerns, we are remitted to old categories which, applied woodenly, do not address modern problems."[82]

Bork's central difficulty with Starr's opinion is that its reliance upon a "totality of circumstances" test may fail to provide sufficient protection to the nature of political conflict inherent in a democracy. Ollman's suit must fail, says Bork, because, "by his own actions, [he] has entered into a political arena in which heated discourse was to be expected and must be protected."[83] As a general matter, "in order to protect a vigorous marketplace in political ideas and contentions, we ought to accept the proposition that those who place themselves in a political arena must accept a degree of derogation that others need not."[84] Bork continues:

> Necessary to the preservation of [freedom of expression], of course, is the willingness of those who would speak to be spoken to and, as in this case, to be spoken about. This is not always a pleasant or painless experience,

but it cannot be avoided if the political arena is to remain as vigorous and robust as the First Amendment and the nature of politics require.

In deciding a case like this, therefore, one of the most important considerations is whether the person alleging defamation has in some real sense placed himself in an arena where he should expect to be jostled and bumped in a way that a private person need not expect.[85]

Within a regime of free expression, therefore, it is only to be expected that a figure such as Ollman will have opponents who will use strong language to attack him. Thus, with respect to the statement that Ollman "has no status within the profession," Bork says we must rely upon the capacity of readers to consider the source and weight the statement accordingly: "The reader does not accept [the statement] as a concrete fact. He understands that the speaker thinks poorly of Ollman. He gathers that Ollman is a controversial figure within the profession."[86]

The crucial point is that in *Ollman* Bork endorses *Sullivan* for its protection of a constitutional commitment to political speech that is unfettered in its contentiousness. This is by definition a commitment to a regime of political discourse that does not advance the cause of any single ideology. It is precisely this aspect of the regime that troubles an ideologue like Mark Tushnet, who wonders why "liberals still celebrate the First Amendment when it benefits their political opponents."[87] But it is certain that, just as the reapportionment decisions promoted the *process* of democratic elections, so *Sullivan* and its many progeny have promoted free expression in and of itself, not any particular ideological brand of expression.

Irreversible Liberal Victories?

David Luban begins a 1999 law review article on the jurisprudence of the Warren Court by declaring that "the true significance of the Warren Court . . . lies not in [its] transformation of the judicial role, but in its transformation of the concept of a legal right."[88] He continues by asserting that "the Warren Court approached the concept of a right by rethinking the nature of a remedy."[89] Luban's point here is that the Warren Court created a series of "ex ante" remedies for constitutional rights violations, which allowed those who have had their rights infringed to be compensated *before* the full potential damage of the infringement is effected. The classic example is the "exclusionary rule," which the Warren Court applied to state criminal proceedings in *Mapp v. Ohio*.[90] The rule allows a judge to exclude illegally seized evidence from a criminal trial, rather than admit it and leave the defendant with only the possibility of bringing a subsequent civil suit against the police who conducted the improper search.

But Luban also asserts that "the legacy of decisions" left to us by the Warren Court has "suffered and continue[s] to suffer erosion at the hands of subsequent Courts."[91] He leaves the statement unelaborated, but I should like to expand upon it here. Specifically, have Warren Court decisions in favor of the poor and criminal defendants—who allegedly are the quintessential objects of bleeding-heart liberal affection—remained intact? And, if not, why were they vulnerable?

The Poor

"Long, long ago in a galaxy far, far away, expanding the rights of poor people was a central goal of liberal constitutional theory."[92] In 1969, for example, Professor Frank Michelman of Harvard published an article in the *Harvard Law Review* in which he argued that the equal protection clause of the Fourteenth Amendment could be the source "of a state's duty to protect against certain hazards which are endemic in an unequal society" because it "is the constitutional text which most naturally suggests itself to one who would claim a legal right to have certain wants satisfied out of the public treasury."[93] In other words, Michelman was arguing for the constitutionalization of a duty on the part of the state to provide poor citizens with at least a minimal level of material support. Most striking from the perspective of the present, Michelman expressed a belief that the Supreme Court might actually move in this direction. He referred to the contemporary Court as "a body commendably busy with the critically important task of charting some islands of haven from economic disaster in the ocean of (what continues to be known as) free enterprise."[94]

Another law review article arguing in favor of constitutional rights for poor people appeared in a 1993 issue of the *University of Pennsylvania Law Review*. It provides an interesting contrast to Michelman's article. The author, Stephen Loffredo, argues that "the political powerlessness of the poor requires some form of enhanced judicial protection."[95] But Loffredo's assessment of the chances that his vision will be made manifest by the Supreme Court anytime soon is bleak. The current Court is said to display a "nearly limitless deference to legislation that disadvantages poor people" and "ignores the central role that wealth plays in American politics."[96] What happened?

Michelman's hopes were not without foundation. This is true in spite of an approach to the provision of welfare that a leading historian of American poverty, writing *before* the recent end of welfare as we knew it, has termed a "semiwelfare state":

> America remains the only advanced Western democracy without national health insurance or family allowances. Welfare coverage is neither universal nor comprehensive. Social welfare expenses consume a much smaller share of the Gross National Product than in other wealthy nations, and ideological resistance to social welfare remains far more virulent.[97]

Yet, in 1970, the Supreme Court decided a case that gave supporters of welfare rights a margin of hope. In *Goldberg v. Kelly*, the Court, speaking through Justice Brennan, considered "whether a State that terminates public assistance payments to a particular recipient without affording him the opportunity for an evidentiary hearing prior to termination denies the recipient procedural due process in violation of the due process clause of the Fourteenth Amendment."[98] The state welfare system at issue—New York's—provided that a welfare recipient who had been determined to be ineligible for further benefits could receive a formal hearing challenging the termination only *after* benefits had already been cut off.

Justice Brennan concluded that a *pre*termination hearing was necessary on the basis of a finding that the consequences of a termination of benefits were likely to be immediate and severe:

> For qualified recipients, welfare provides the means to obtain essential food, clothing, housing, and medical care. . . . [T]ermination of aid pending resolution of a controversy over eligibility may deprive an eligible recipient of the very means by which to live while he waits. Since he lacks independent resources, his situation becomes immediately desperate. His need to concentrate upon finding the means for daily subsistence, in turn, adversely affects his ability to seek redress from the welfare bureaucracy.[99]

Brennan also flirted with the notion that welfare benefits are so crucial to the well-being of those who must depend upon them that their receipt by eligible individuals should be considered a constitutional right:

Welfare, by meeting the basic demands of subsistence, can help bring within the reach of the poor the same opportunities that are available to others to participate meaningfully in the life of the community.... Public assistance, then, is not mere charity, but a means to "promote the general Welfare, and secure the Blessings of Liberty to ourselves and our Posterity."[100]

Thus, "[i]t may be realistic today to regard welfare entitlements as more like 'property' than a 'gratuity.'"[101]

Among liberal lawyers and legal academics, *Goldberg v. Kelly* has achieved iconic status as a triumph of common decency over bureaucratic soullessness. Sylvia Law, who as a young lawyer was a member of the victorious plaintiffs' legal team, recalls that the case "was won on the facts. Plaintiffs told dozens of stories about individuals devastated by erroneous terminations of subsistence aid. . . . The case was grounded in the real lives of ordinary poor people and the pervasive meanness and incompetency of an ordinary bureaucracy. The facts sang."[102] Justice Stephen Breyer has declared that, in writing the Court's opinion as he did, Justice Brennan "created a symbol, a symbol of the need for equality, dignity, and fairness in the individual's relation to the administrative state."[103] Justice Brennan himself declared that his decision was based upon a recognition that bureaucracies, which operate according to the dictates of "formal reason," lack "that dimension of passion, of empathy, necessary for a full understanding of the human beings affected by [their] procedures."[104]

But the limits of *Goldberg* were demonstrated in a case decided less than two weeks later. *Dandridge v. Williams* involved a challenge to Maryland's enactment of a ceiling upon the amount of welfare benefits any single family could receive, regardless of its size.[105] Certain large families sued to overturn the regulation. Instead of making the state provide anything like a compelling rationale for this clearly discriminatory regulation, the Court—with Justices Brennan, Marshall, and Douglas in dissent—held that "a State does not violate the equal protection clause merely because the classifications made by its laws are imperfect. If the classification has some 'reasonable basis,' it does not offend the Constitution simply because the classification 'is not made with mathematical nicety or because in practice it results in some inequality.'"[106]

The Court found such a basis in "the State's legitimate interest in encouraging employment and in avoiding discrimination between welfare families and the families of the working poor."[107] More generally, the Court made very clear that *Goldberg* would not be the herald of any array of constitutional rights extended to the poor:

> The Constitution may impose certain *procedural safeguards* upon systems of welfare administration. . . . But the Constitution does not empower this Court to second-guess state officials charged with the difficult responsibility of allocating limited public welfare funds among the myriad of potential recipients.[108]

The point is made with admirable conciseness: procedural fairness in the distribution of government benefits is a wholly different question, constitutionally speaking, from determining the *amount* of what should be distributed. Thus, the Court decisively rejected Justice Brennan's musings in *Goldberg* to the effect that government benefits might be considered a form of constitutionally protected property and instead "viewed [them] as merely statutory creations and preserved a large measure of legislative authority to manage and even eliminate benefit schemes."[109]

That last phrase is crucially important because, for better or worse, we have entered a time when welfare as we knew it no longer exists. The Personal Responsibility and Work Opportunity Reconciliation Act of 1996 was the catalyst for the new era. The most important features of the Act are that it: (1) repeals Aid to Families with Dependent Children, the primary federal welfare benefits program for sixty years, which was administered by the several states; (2) replaces AFDC with Temporary Assistance to Needy Families, a federal program of block grants to the states; and (3) allows the states broad discretion to administer TANF funds subject to requirements "first, that recipients eventually work or participate in work-related activities as a condition of receiving benefits and second, that welfare funds be time-limited."[110]

The Act was, of course, a centerpiece of President Clinton's successful reelection campaign in 1996. But it was also seen by many liberals as a cynical betrayal. Here is Robert Reich, Clinton's original secretary of labor:

> The original idea had been to smooth the passage from welfare to work with guaranteed health care, child care, job training, and a paying enough to live on. . . . In effect, what was dubbed welfare "reform" merely ended the promise of help to the indigent and their children which Franklin D. Roosevelt had initiated more than sixty years before. . . . Instead of

smoothing the transition from welfare to work, then, the new law simply demanded that people get off welfare.[111]

For our purposes, the crucial point is that the Act has been implemented without any significant judicial interference. In other words, contrary to a central tenet of the Imperial Judiciary thesis that courts stand ever ready to trump the political victories of conservatives, liberals have not been able to win the battle of welfare reform in the courts after having lost it in the legislature.

And this is hardly surprising, given that the judicial recognition of welfare rights has been so limited. William Forbath recently recounted the meagerness of what the justices of the Supreme Court have been willing to countenance. The justices have

> harbored no "minimum protectionist" vision. They would make welfare an enforceable statutory right and interpret it broadly; they would not make it a constitutional right—except in its procedural dimensions. . . . They would not compel states or Congress to make up any shortfall between statutory offerings and the real world of "brutal need," nor etch out a constitutional universe of just wants, nor subject state laws or practices that fell heavily or arbitrarily on the poor to any exacting constitutional standard.[112]

Thus, the "rights revolution," as it applies to welfare rights, has been a decidedly self-limiting affair.

Criminal Defendants

Writing early in the year 2000, the Georgetown University law professor David Cole provided this snapshot of America's prison population:

> This year, the total number of people in America's prisons and jails will reach 2 million. . . . The United States boasts 5 percent of the world's population, but fully 25 percent of the population behind bars. Our per capita incarceration rate is second only to Russia's, and five times higher than [that of] the next Western nation.
>
> During the first eighty years of the twentieth century, the prison population saw a slight increase, roughly matching our general population growth, and it actually fell during two decades, the 1940s and

1960s. Since 1980, however, the prison population has mushroomed. The growth in the 1990s, when we added nearly 700,000 prisoners, is nearly thirty times higher than the average growth from 1920 through 1970.[113]

Cole adds that this orgy of incarceration is not the result of rising crime rates:

> With the exception of homicide . . . our crime rates are not the highest among Western countries. And many Western nations experienced increases in crime rates equivalent to ours in the 1970s and 1980s, without coming close to America's record in locking up prisoners. Our incarceration rate has increased most dramatically in the past twenty years, even though crime rates have steadily decreased over that period.[114]

What might be called the postprison population has also been booming. The U.S. Justice Department has reported that, by the end of 1999, a record 4.5 million people were on parole or probation. Reporting this figure, the *Washington Post* noted that

> the number of people under correctional supervision stands at an all-time high of 6.3 million, with 1.86 million men and women behind bars in June 1999. . . . "The scope of the criminal justice system has increased substantially over twenty years," [Justice Department statistician Allen J.] Beck said. "It went from a little over 1 percent of the adult population back in 1980 to now up over 3 percent of all adults. That's one out of every thirty-two adults."[115]

It is therefore wholly unsurprising that "vastly expanded expenditures on corrections systems are now considered the norm, and, in fact, represent the largest growth area of state budgets. Virtually every state has engaged in a significant if not massive prison construction program over the past two decades. . . ."[116] Indeed, prisons themselves have become highly coveted municipal assets. The *Washington Post* has reported recently on "salvation through incarceration"—a prison-based development strategy that small towns all over America are pursuing:

> It's an old phenomenon that has surged in recent years: About 200 state and federal prisons have been built in small towns across the United

States since 1980, and fierce competition breaks out whenever a new prison project is announced. . . . Prison expansion has been "a major source of growth, of jobs, of economic development" . . . said Calvin Beale, senior demographer of the U.S. Department of Agriculture's Economic Research Service. . . . "Roughly speaking, you'll have ten jobs for every thirty or so prisoners," Beale said. "So if you have a prison come in with 1,400 prisoners, you're probably going to get four hundred jobs out of that, and in a rural setting that's a lot of jobs. . . . So they welcome these jobs, and they bid for them."[117]

All of this has occurred, of course, more than thirty years after the Warren Court's landmark rulings that constitutionalized many aspects of criminal procedure. Before these decisions, "remarkably little criminal procedure had been constitutionalized. . . . And so, for the generation of legal scholars coming of age before 1960, criminal procedure and federal constitutional law were rather distinct fields."[118] Or, to put the matter in more pedestrian terms, recall the dictum of a New York City police official of the late nineteenth century that "there is more law in the end of a policeman's nightstick than in a decision of the Supreme Court."[119]

Accordingly, the legal historian Lawrence Friedman has noted that it would be

> misleading to say that there was some sort of general consensus about rights of defendants, due process, and the like, in the nineteenth century. It would be more accurate to say that underdogs and losers rarely challenged the power of the law, and even more rarely succeeded. The case law, both federal and state, on constitutional rights of defendants was fairly skimpy. This continued to be true well into the twentieth century.[120]

Max Boot makes the unsupported declaration that "there's no evidence that police misconduct was worse" prior to the Warren Court "than it is today."[121] In fact, there is wide agreement that state criminal law was notable for its brutishness and inattention to procedural regularity. Richard Neely provides this graphic description:

> In the early 1960s, the average criminal defendant was treated like a piece of meat on its way to dressing and processing. A person was arrested, brought in for interrogation (seldom conducted in a gentlemanly man-

ner), threatened with the many dire consequences that awaited him if he did not cooperate . . . and encouraged to plead guilty. Of course a lawyer could do wonders for him, but ordinarily there was not any lawyer and would not be any lawyer unless he came up with the money to hire one or was accused of a capital crime. . . . If a person pleaded guilty, that was it— off he went to prison, having waived all grounds for appeal . . . and he just sat in prison until the sentence expired or the parole board released him. Often this process ran an entirely innocent man through its machine.[122]

Even two University of Chicago law professors, while severely critical of the continued application of Warren Court criminal procedure precedents, admit that these were a salutary reaction to police misconduct, especially respecting the treatment of minorities:

> Law-enforcement institutions played a vital role in reinforcing American apartheid. . . . In the late 1960s, for example, Chicago police led the nation in the slaying of private citizens, who were euphemistically characterized as "fleeing felons" to mask the routine use of excessive force by police against racial minorities. The police also exploited seemingly benign offense categories, such as disorderly conduct, vagrancy, and loitering, to bully minority youths and adults who had the audacity to challenge police authority.[123]

It is a commonplace of conservative discourse that the Warren Court's criminal procedure precedents have significantly hindered the police and the courts in their legitimate role of apprehending and punishing the guilty. In response, I make three brief points: (1) critics of the courts tend to vastly overstate the extent of the Warren Court era's solicitude for criminal defendants, such as when Justice Thomas makes the absurd claim that "our legal system accepted the general premise that social conditions and upbringing could be excuses for harmful conduct";[124] (2) the Warren Court's precedents have not prevented the march toward two million incarcerated Americans; and (3) whatever the facts, opportunistic politicians will not for the foreseeable future cease bashing judges for their alleged softness toward crime. More important for the validity of the Imperial Judiciary thesis, however, consider the fate of the three most prominent Warren Court criminal procedure precedents as they have been treated by later Courts. Without exception, they have been severely limited.

Miranda

In *Miranda v. Arizona*, a 1966 decision, the Supreme Court held that, when an individual is taken into police custody, "[p]rior to any questioning, the person must be warned that he has a right to remain silent, that any statement he does make may be used as evidence against him, and that he has a right to the presence of an attorney, either retained or appointed."[125] The Constitution required these warnings, said the Court, because "the Fifth Amendment privilege [against self-incrimination] is available outside of criminal court proceedings and serves to protect persons in all settings in which their freedom of action is curtailed in any significant way from being compelled to incriminate themselves."[126]

Thirty-four years later, amid a great deal of editorial commentary, the Supreme Court reaffirmed *Miranda* in *Dickerson v. U.S.*[127] In an opinion by Chief Justice Rehnquist, a 7-2 majority held that "*Miranda* has become embedded in routine police practice to the point where the warnings have become part of our national culture."[128] If nothing else, this is a testament to the cultural power of cop shows.

Justice Scalia, joined by Justice Thomas, dissented in a mocking tone that was not without justification. He declared that "Justices whose votes are needed to compose today's majority are on record as believing that a violation of *Miranda* is not a violation of the Constitution."[129] The Chief Justice could answer this assertion only by "conced[ing] that there is language in some of our opinions that supports [the dissenters'] view."[130]

It more than supports the view. As one commentator has asserted, "one can say fairly that the Court has retreated from the holding of *Miranda* in several significant respects. Principally, the Court has separated the warnings . . . from [their] constitutional underpinning, consequently diminishing respect for the values embodied in the Fifth Amendment."[131] That is, almost from the time the case was decided, the Supreme Court has downgraded the constitutional status of *Miranda* warnings in order to justify exception after exception to the rule that they must always be read to criminal suspects. Thus, in *Harris v. New York*, a 1971 decision, the Court held that a "mere" failure to give *Miranda* warnings would not bar prosecutors from using an uncoerced confession at trial for "impeachment" purposes on cross-examination—that is, as a means to discredit a defendant's direct testimony.[132]

In 1974, after other exceptions to the *Miranda* rule had already been upheld, the Court said explicitly that *Miranda*'s safeguards "were not themselves rights protected by the Constitution but were instead measures to insure that the right against compulsory self-incrimination was protected."[133] It then went on to hold that a statement uttered by a suspect who had not received *Miranda* warnings could be used for *all* purposes at the trial of another suspect. Ten years later, the Court held that a suspect need not be warned before being questioned if such questioning arises from a reasonable concern for public safety. Here the Court applied a cost-benefit analysis to determine whether warnings were necessary: "the need for answers to questions in a situation posing a threat to the public safety outweighs the need for a prophylactic rule protecting the Fifth Amendment's privilege against self-incrimination."[134] This is clearly a far cry from the simple majesty of a constitutionally required rule.

Quite apart from these and other limitations, it must also be noted that the Court has in no way significantly expanded *Miranda*. Thus, in *Schneckloth v. Bustamonte*, for example, the Court declined to require police to warn a suspect of his rights before asking his consent to undertake a search.[135] Nor has the Court ever held that the Fifth Amendment requires something more than simply giving warnings in order to assure a trial judge that a confession has been voluntarily obtained. As Akhil Reed Amar has argued, there is no question that much more could be done in this regard:

> While *Miranda* purported to establish propriety in police-station interrogation, our system in fact can still be quite ugly. Despite *Miranda's* promise to open up the black box in the police station, it did not require that lawyers, magistrates, or even tape or video recorders be present in interrogation rooms. In the absence of these monitors, detectives and police have often engaged in ingenious, but troubling, forms of interrogation.[136]

Amar concludes that "the more egregious forms of interrogation abuse such as beating have stopped," but "intimidation is alive and well in the police station."[137]

For our own conclusion, we cannot do better than point to the observation of the law professor Jonathan Turley, written the day after *Dickerson* was handed down:

> [W]hile the Supreme Court is clearly unwilling to pull the plug, *Miranda* lingers at best on life support. In fact, the *Miranda* of the Warren Court

died years ago. It succumbed not to a single blow of the conservative majority but to a thousand paper cuts.

Over the years, the Court has allowed a myriad of exceptions that make Miranda a mere symbolic presence in most federal cases. Because of these rulings, reversals of convictions under *Miranda* are relatively rare events. . . .

Ultimately, what saved *Miranda* from being overturned is probably more its mystique than its meaning. *Miranda* has become too interwoven in our legal and cultural fabric to simply be dispatched as no longer relevant. The Court therefore preserved the body while allowing its spirit to drain away years ago.[138]

Mapp

Stated simply, the exclusionary rule mandates that evidence seized in violation of the Fourth Amendment's prohibition upon "unreasonable searches and seizures" cannot be admitted in a criminal trial. The rule was extended to the states in *Mapp v. Ohio*, a case in which Cleveland police ransacked a criminal suspect's house without bothering to obtain a search warrant.[139] The Court held that the extension of the rule to the states was constitutionally necessary because "without [the] rule the freedom from state invasions of privacy would be so ephemeral and so neatly severed from its conceptual nexus with the freedom from all brutish means of coercing evidence as not to merit this Court's high regard as a freedom 'implicit in the concept of ordered liberty.'"[140]

In spite of this stirring declaration, the exclusionary rule has undergone a fate remarkably similar to that of *Miranda* warnings. It has been a story of burgeoning exceptions that have effectively come to swallow the substance of the rule. The Warren Court itself established the "stop and frisk" exception in *Terry v. Ohio*, where it held that police could make warrantless searches and seizures of suspects in cases where there is "an articulable suspicion of a crime of violence" in progress.[141]

The most potent exception to the exclusionary rule was established in *U.S. v. Leon*, in which the Court held that the rule does not apply when the police rely in good faith upon an improperly granted warrant in order to conduct a search.[142] As happened with *Miranda*, the Court in *Leon* downgraded the exclusionary rule from a constitutional command to a mere remedy whose application depends upon a cost-benefit analysis:

The Fourth Amendment contains no provision expressly precluding the use of evidence obtained in violation of its commands. . . . The wrong condemned by the Amendment is "fully accomplished" by the unlawful search and seizure itself, and the exclusionary rule is neither intended nor able to "cure the invasion of the defendant's rights which he has already suffered."

Whether the exclusionary sanction is appropriately imposed in a particular case . . . must be resolved by weighing the costs and benefits of preventing the use in the prosecution's case-in-chief of inherently trustworthy tangible evidence obtained in reliance on a search warrant issued by a detached an neutral magistrate that ultimately is found to be defective.[143]

The "good-faith exception" spawned so many other exceptions that the law professor George Kannar, writing in 1988, has given this assessment of Fourth Amendment jurisprudence:

Out of a misplaced zeal to punish individual malefactors, [the Burger Court] began behaving like a neighborhood police court, cluttering its docket with insignificant cases simply because it could not bear the sight of particular individuals going free. In the process, the Republican-dominated Court converted Fourth Amendment jurisprudence into the confused quagmire it is today—piling exception upon exception, creating exceptions *to* exceptions, until not even the legal treatise writers can figure out exactly what the law is, or conscientious officers figure out how to act.[144]

In sum, as Justice Brennan declared in his dissenting opinion in *Leon*, the pattern of the Fourth Amendment cases has been as follows: "First there is the ritual incantation of the 'substantial social costs' exacted by the exclusionary rule, followed by the virtually foreordained conclusion that, given the marginal benefits, application of the rule in the circumstances of these cases is not warranted."[145]

Gideon

Robert Bork has recently asserted that the rule of law in America, "as the names Bill Clinton and O. J. Simpson remind us, is giving way to the rule of politics and ethnic identity."[146] I express no opinion about Bill Clinton, but, if Bork is suggesting here that Simpson's celebrated trial was in any significant sense typical of the treatment of minority defendants in American criminal trials, he is sadly mistaken. This is even less true when one considers that Simpson was defended by a "dream team" of superstar attorneys. This is rare, whatever the race of the defendant. David Cole sets forth what *is* typical:

> The vast majority of criminal defendants are too poor to hire an attorney. In 1992, about 80 percent of defendants charged with felonies in the country's seventy-five largest counties were indigent. Approximately three-quarters of all inmates in state prisons were represented by public defenders or some other publicly provided attorney.[147]

That most of these defendants were represented at all is the result of the Supreme Court's decision in *Gideon v. Wainwright,* handed down in 1963, which held that indigent defendants must be provided with trial counsel when charged with a crime, save for certain misdemeanors that do not entail imprisonment.[148] Until *Gideon,* states were required to provide counsel only in capital cases. In its decision, the Court, through Justice Hugo Black, again used soaring terms to set forth the right:

> The right of one charged with crime to counsel may not be deemed fundamental and essential to fair trials in some countries, but it is in ours. From the very beginning, our state and national constitutions and laws have laid great emphasis on procedural and substantive safeguards designed to assure fair trials before impartial tribunals in which every defendant stands equals before the law. The noble ideal cannot be realized if the poor man charged with crime has to face his accusers without a lawyer to assist him.[149]

Gideon was substantially gutted by a single case, *Strickland v. Washington.*[150] Here the Court set forth the standard pursuant to which a criminal defendant may successfully claim that the representation he received at trail was so incompetent that his conviction cannot stand without a retrial:

> The benchmark for judging any claim of ineffectiveness must be whether the counsel's conduct so undermined the proper functioning of the ad-

versarial process that the trial cannot be relied on a having produced a just result. . . .

First, the defendant must show that counsel's performance was deficient. This requires showing that counsel made errors so serious that counsel was not functioning as the "counsel" guaranteed the defendant by the Sixth Amendment. Second, the defendant must show that the deficient performance prejudiced the defense. This requires showing that counsel's errors were so serious as to deprive the defendant of a fair trial, a trial whose result is reliable.[151]

This is a very stringent standard. Indeed, the "*Strickland* standard has proved virtually impossible to meet."[152] One comprehensive study has demonstrated that more than 99 percent of ineffective assistance of counsel claims brought in federal court fail.[153] In fact, the Supreme Court did not issue an opinion holding that the standard had been violated until 2000.

In *Williams v. Taylor*, Terry Williams had been convicted of murder and sentenced to death.[154] This is the level of ineptitude that the Court found sufficient for holding that Williams had not received effective assistance of counsel during the sentencing phase of his trial:

The record establishes that counsel did not begin to prepare for that phase of the proceedings until a week before the trial. They failed to conduct an investigation that would have uncovered extensive records graphically describing Williams' nightmarish childhood, not because of any strategic calculation but because they incorrectly thought that state law barred access to such records. Had they done so, the jury would have learned that Williams' parents had been imprisoned for the criminal neglect of Williams and his siblings, that Williams had been severely and repeatedly beaten by his father. . . .

Counsel failed to introduce available evidence that Williams was "borderline mentally retarded" and did not advance beyond sixth grade in school. They failed to seek prison records recording Williams' commendations for helping to crack a prison drug ring. . . . Counsel failed even to return the phone call of a certified public accountant who had offered to testify that he had visited Williams frequently when Williams was incarcerated as part of a prison ministry program, that Williams "seemed to thrive in a more regimented and structured environment," and that Williams was proud of the carpentry degree he earned while in prison.[155]

The stringency of the *Strickland* standard is very bad news for indigent defendants, because few would argue that the quality of representation provided to indigents is generally high. On the contrary, as a writer in the *Harvard Law Review* has asserted recently,

> nearly four decades after *Gideon*, the states have largely, and often outrageously, failed to meet the court's constitutional command. . . .
>
> [S]ince the 1963 *Gideon* decision, a major independent report has been issued at least every five years documenting the severe deficiencies in indigent defense services. The evidence is unambiguous and telling. Lawyers representing indigent defendants often have unmanageable caseloads that frequently run into the hundreds, far exceeding professional responsibility guidelines. These same lawyers typically receive compensation at the lowest end of the professional pay scale. Stories of intoxicated, sleeping, and otherwise incompetent public defenders are legion, such that it has become trite to lament the sometimes shockingly incompetent quality of indigent defense counsel in America today.[156]

Consider but one product of this situation. David Chandler was convicted in federal court of murder. In spite of the presence of mitigating evidence that might have saved him from being sentenced to death, his counsel's sole preparation for the sentencing hearing consisted of a request made on the afternoon before the hearing "to Deborah Chandler, the defendant's wife, to 'find' some character witnesses to 'stand up for Ronnie' the next morning."[157] This is a fine illustration of Justice Harry Blackmun's assertion that "practical experience establishes that the *Strickland* test, in application, has failed to protect a defendant's right to be represented by something more than a person who happens to be a lawyer."[158]

Yet, the full U.S. Court of Appeals for the Eleventh Circuit, albeit in a 6-5 vote, held that Chandler had not received ineffective assistance of counsel. The lawyer who represented him on his appeal reacted to the Circuit's decision by declaring, "You might as well do away with *Gideon*."[159]

Conclusion: "The Warren Court Is [D]ead"

This statement is literally true: no Justice who served on the Supreme Court during the Chief Justiceship of Earl Warren is alive today.[160] But the extent to which the statement is not true as a result of the efforts of both the Warren Court's supporters and detractors is astonishing. For many liberals, the Warren Court remains without peer as the model of what the Supreme Court should be within our polity. For conservatives, the Warren Court stands damned as the progenitor of an Imperial Judiciary whose power only continues to expand.

Thus, the Warren Court remains vibrantly alive in debates over the proper role of the courts in our constitutional order. But the stances of both its celebrators and its opponents have ossified into something like self-evident truths. As such, both are in serious need of critical reassessment.

It is hoped that this chapter adds something to these reassessments. To return to the questions asked at the outset, I conclude that the Warren Court's boldest decisions in the area of civil rights and liberties were not inherently liberal in effect and that the scope of its most inherently liberal decisions has been waning virtually since the day they were issued. In other words, ideologically satisfying platitudes about the Warren Court—and about the state of rights in America in general—add nothing but obfuscation to the debate about the nature and the extent of contemporary judicial power.

5

The Judiciary and
the Politics of Rights

In his memoir of his tenure as Ronald Reagan's solicitor general, the Harvard law professor Charles Fried declared that, for the Reagan administration, *Roe v. Wade*[1] was "the symbol of all that had gone wrong in law, particularly in constitutional law."[2] Somewhat famously, Robert Bork has declared that, in the entire *Roe* opinion, which runs for more than fifty pages in the U.S. Reports, "there is not one line of explanation, not one sentence that qualifies as legal argument."[3]

As we have already discussed, the Imperial Judiciary thesis holds that *Roe*'s insidiousness goes well beyond the contention that the Supreme Court reached the wrong result. Turning again to Bork, the case also represents "the greatest example and symbol of the judicial usurpation of democratic prerogatives in this century."[4] The claim here is that *Roe* stopped democratic politics with respect to the abortion question. More specifically, the argument posits that: (1) meaningful and lasting compromise on the abortion issue that will be embraced by virtually all citizens is possible; (2) legislative bodies were in fact reaching such compromise when *Roe* was decided; and (3) *Roe*'s effect has been to stifle or trivialize democratic debate with respect to the abortion issue. I suggest in this chapter that all of these assertions are misguided.

I also use this chapter to discuss *Buckley v. Valeo*,[5] a decision whose central principle—that the First Amendment proscribes the imposition of limits on the amount of money that a political campaign can expend—is all but universally applauded by conservatives. Decided in 1976, *Buckley* partially struck down the post-Watergate amendments to the Federal Election Campaign Act on First Amendment grounds, thereby placing a substantial constitutional obstacle in the way of subsequent legislative efforts to regulate campaign spending. Thus, just as *Roe* constitutionalized the debate over the abortion question by raising abortion to the status of a right, so *Buckley* raised the issue of money in political campaigns to a similar status. I do not attempt here to defend *Roe* or to attack *Buckley,* or vice versa. Nor do I wish to weigh in on the morality of abortion or the wisdom of campaign finance legislation. I also do not assert any equivalence in terms of moral importance between the issues of abortion and campaign finance reform. What I do wish to establish is that a consistent application of the Imperial Judiciary thesis must hold *both* cases to be deeply troubling.

The jurisprudence of original intent cannot countenance *Roe.* Given the legal status of women at the time of the ratification of the Constitution and of the Civil War Amendments, arguing in favor of "a woman's right to choose" on originalist grounds simply will not wash. But can *Buckley*, which held that the First Amendment substantially restricts the ability of legislatures to regulate the role of money in election campaigns, be any more successfully defended on originalist grounds? The attempt has been made, but, as I hope to show, it is not successful.

Further, the conclusion that Imperial Judiciary theorists draw from *Roe's* incompatibility with a jurisprudence of original intent is that the abortion question is a nonconstitutional moral issue that should be debated and resolved in legislative bodies without judicial intervention. But the same reasoning may be applied to *Buckley.* The manner in which elections should be conducted is without question one of the most fundamental procedural issues facing any democracy. If the holding of *Buckley* cannot be grounded upon original intent, shouldn't Imperial Judiciary theorists reexamine the role judges have played in the campaign finance debate as a result of *Buckley's* constitutionalization of the issue? To my mind, the answer is certainly yes. To my knowledge, however, the effort has not been made.

Abortion as a Right

Justice Scalia and Justices Souter, O'Connor, and Kennedy do not agree on much with respect to the issue of abortion, but they are apparently united in the belief that controversy over the issue can and should go away. In their joint opinion in *Casey v. Planned Parenthood of Southeastern Pennsylvania*, in which they reaffirmed *Roe's* recognition of a constitutional right to abortion, Justices Souter, O'Connor, and Kennedy opined that one reason for upholding *Roe* was that the decision could end contention over abortion, if only the competing sides would let it:

Where, in the performance of its judicial duties, the Court decides a case in such a way as to resolve the sort of intensely divisive controversy reflected in *Roe* and those rare, comparable cases, its decision has a dimension that the resolution of the normal case does not carry. It is the dimension present whenever the Court's interpretation of the Constitution calls the contending sides of a national controversy to end their national division by accepting a common mandate rooted in the Constitution.[6]

As we have already noted, Justice Scalia is of the view that it is the Court's involvement in the abortion debate that has prevented compromise. Before *Roe*, he argued in his dissenting opinion in *Casey*, compromise was in fact in the offing: "Profound disagreement existed among our citizens over the issue, but that disagreement was being worked out at the state level. . . . Pre-*Roe* . . . political compromise was possible."[7]

In an earlier case, *Ohio v. Akron Center for Reproductive Health*, decided in 1990, Justice Scalia asserted in a brief concurring opinion that compromise was *still* possible should the Court come to its senses:

Leaving this matter to the political process is not only legally correct, it is pragmatically so. That alone—and not lawyerly dissection of federal judicial precedents—can produce compromises satisfying a sufficient mass of the electorate that this deeply felt issue will cease distorting the remainder of our democratic process. The Court should end its disruptive intrusion into this field as soon as possible.[8]

It is a matter of no small wonder that this faith is so common, and certainly not only among judges. Mary Ann Glendon has written that the tragedy of *Roe* is that it curtailed "the process of legislative reform that was already well on the way to producing . . . compromise statutes that gave very substantial protection to women's interests."[9] Similarly, Jean Bethke Elshtain calls *Roe* "a civic debacle" because "there was promising *political* discourse going on in many states in 1973."[10] Jonathan Rauch has made a variation of this argument, suggesting not that *Roe* should not have happened but that it happened too early:

When *Roe v. Wade* was handed down, states were gradually moving toward legalization of abortion. The *Roe* decision smashed that slow but discernable progress toward consensus by leaving no place in the sun for those who dissented. Out of *Roe* sprang a deeply aggrieved prolife movement that challenged not just abortion but the very legitimacy of the courts. The cost to the country's social fabric has been immense. . . .

The great mistake in *Roe* was not that the courts became involved; judicial scrutiny was inevitable. The mistake, rather, was that the federal courts became involved, long before there was anything like a national consensus.[11]

The argument is made with particular frequency in the immediate aftermath of a Supreme Court decision of any significance on the abortion issue. Thus, in the wake of 2000's *Stenberg v. Carhart*,[12] which struck down Nebraska's statute banning "partial birth abortion," the *Chicago Tribune* editorialized as follows:

A generation ago, abortion was one of many political issues Americans were addressing through democratic institutions designed to forge consensus and compromise. But on Jan. 22, 1973, that changed. In the landmark case known as *Roe v. Wade*, the Supreme Court withdrew the subject from the political arena by declaring that abortion was protected by the Constitution.

State laws against it were swept aside, and the process of arriving at a national consensus was abruptly short-circuited. Public opinion was deprived of its rightful say on one of the central issues of our time.[13]

In the wake of President George W. Bush's "compromise" decision with respect to the future of fetal stem cell research, which satisfied few and which certainly did not put an end to the matter, the *Wall Street Journal* editorialized in precisely the same terms: "Our view is that abortion has remained such a polarizing issue for more than thirty years because a willful Supreme Court yanked it away from legislatures, which work out compromises the country can live with."[14]

The problem with this argument, in whatever variation it is made, is that it is, as the historian David Garrow says, a "fictionalized but nonetheless widely accepted version of history."[15] We shall have more to say along these lines later in the chapter. But it is also important to understand that the argument misconstrues (or ignores) the fundamental character of the political controversy over abortion. It is not a conflict over quotidian policy, like a highway bill or tax cut legislation. It is a battle of moral visions concerning the definition of life and the boundaries of individual autonomy. Troubling as this is to America's pragmatic spirit, which is summed up nicely in the cliche that politics is "the art of compromise," such battles between moral visions do not remotely lend themselves to the achievement of consensus.

The British political theorist John Dunn has with great perception defined the character of political clashes of this sort:

> If moral tenets are merely posited, adopted, and laid down, then conflicts between the moral tenets of two or more persons or social groups or political communities are fundamentally clashes of will. True, one person, group, or community may be more confused or ignorant than its opponent; and one may also (and perhaps even consequently) be worse or better placed to commend to others the values that it has posited, laid down, or adopted than its less coherent or more benighted opponent can hope to prove. *But, even after a relatively intense process of mutual persuasion or mutual abuse, the clashes of will are seldom likely simply to dissipate.*[16]

The American abortion debate is the quintessential example of the sort of controversy Dunn describes, because the two positions that anchor the debate are alike only in their clarity. They are otherwise fundamentally irreconcilable. Kristin Luker says this plainly at the beginning of *Abortion and the Politics of Motherhood*, which remains the best book yet written on the controversy: "The two sides of the abortion debate share almost no common premises and very little common language."[17]

There is a chasm between the view that a woman has a right to refuse to remain pregnant, regardless of the wish of the state that she remain so, and the assertion that human life begins at conception, which makes abortion an act of murder. Specifically, the gulf between the prolife and the prochoice positions is unbridgeable because each side accuses the other of engaging in an unconscionable denial of personhood. Here is the official position of the Catholic Church: "Human life must be respected and protected absolutely from the moment of conception. From the first moment of his existence, a human being must be recognized as having the rights of a person—among which is the inviolable right of every innocent being to life."[18] Compare this with the declaration of a feminist law professor: "Restrictions on abortion reflect the kind of bias that is at the root of the most invidious forms of stereotyping: a failure to consider, in a society always at risk of forgetting, that women are persons, too."[19]

It is of course the case that most Americans—much to the dismay of both those who hold strict prochoice or prolife positions—hold views somewhere between these two positions.[20] But two things remain correct about Americans at the poles of the issue: (1) each of the strict positions is embraced by a sizable minority of Americans, and (2) there is no evidence that this will cease to be the case at any time in the foreseeable future. Given this, the inescapable fact of the matter is that each of the suggested "compromises" of the abortion issue—and there is certainly no shortage of them—will not be accepted as dispositive, or even as legitimate, by adherents of one or both of the two strict positions.

Consider some examples. One frequent compromise strategy is the suggestion that the United States should adopt the policy of some other nation where abortion is not a source of significant political controversy. Mary Ann Glendon has been particularly eloquent in arguing that European nations have addressed the abortion issue in a far more constructive manner than has the United States. In *Abortion and Divorce in Western Law*, written in 1987, she praises various European "compromises" that have seen the liberalization of abortion laws, while allowing the government considerable leeway in discouraging abortion.

However, as Glendon herself recognizes, the capacity of European governments to discourage abortion is largely dependent upon social welfare spending. Providing extensive prenatal and postnatal care to mothers and children seriously diminishes the weight of economic hardship as a motive for abortion. Here is how one commentator contrasts the German and the American situations:

> [American] social welfare laws are considerably less developed than those of Germany. . . . Paid maternity leave, for example, is not required by federal law and is not available to most working women. Even where available under state law, paid leaves usually expire after only eight weeks. In Germany and most other European countries, maternity leaves are paid for six months. Mothers often are granted unpaid leave for an additional year with full benefits and job security. In addition, while day care for children between the ages of three and five is included in the German public school system, it is rarely provided in the American school system. Furthermore, the 1992 German abortion law guaranteed kindergarten schooling and free contraception for minors.[21]

Although she doesn't say so explicitly, one gets the very strong sense that Glendon is fully aware that a legislative program of this sort is simply not going to happen in the United States. She in fact acknowledges that, in light of America's "lonely individualism and libertarianism," "[t]he experience of these smaller and more homogeneous countries may not . . . be a reliable indicator of what our own situation would be in this respect."[22]

Then there are various technological fixes, some based upon expanding medical knowledge regarding the fetus. Gregg Easterbrook received some attention early in 2000 with such a proposal. Writing in *The New Republic*, Easterbrook asserted that, "[w]hen *Roe* was decided in 1973, medical knowledge of the physiology and neurology of the fetus was scant. . . . That is now changing, and it is time for the abortion debate to change in response." Easterbrook goes on to cite research that has found that "only about one-third of sperm-egg unions result in babies" and that "by the beginning of the third trimester the fetus has sensations and brain activity and exhibits other signs of formed humanity."[23] He thus concludes that new science provides ethical backing for both access to early-term abortion and restrictions on late-term abortion.

But this means nothing to one who holds that life begins at conception. Nor does it convince those who hold the prochoice position that to focus on the fetus is to miss the ethical point. Writing in *The Nation*, Karen Houppert made this sharp response to Easterbrook:

> Memo to Gregg: Yours is that same tiresome argument about when life begins. [The radical prolife leader] Randall Terry and his minions call them "preborn." You've simply modernized, adding the intellectual's imprimatur by invoking science to define "signs of formed humanity." . . .
>
> This is where our jaded feminist gives a weary nod and says, "Remember, this fetus is being carried inside a woman's body. The question," she'd remind him, "is not, 'When does life begin?' but 'Can it ever be moral for a woman to be pregnant against her will?'"[24]

In the same vein, Katha Pollitt has denounced all proposals that employ "the fetus-as-person argument" because "they have the effect of broadening little by little the areas of the law in which the fetus is regarded as a person, and in which the woman is regarded as its container."[25]

The ultimate technological fix is thought to be the widespread introduction into the United States of mifepristone, the "abortion pill," widely available in Europe and marketed there under the name RU-486. Mifepristone blocks production of a hormone necessary to sustain a fertilized egg, thereby providing for a nonsurgical abortion. Jean Reith Schroedel has exclaimed that "[t]hese drugs provide us with an opportunity to back away from the precipice and put much of the abortion conflict behind us."[26] Similarly, writing shortly after *Stenberg*, Martha Davis, the legal director of the NOW Legal Defense and Education Fund, asserted that RU-486 will largely preclude the need for abortion clinics, which will mean the end of any focal point for abortion protests:

> Once this drug receives FDA approval, women seeking to terminate a pregnancy early in their term will be able to return to the paradigm wishfully outlined in *Roe v. Wade* in 1974 [*sic*] but rarely achieved in the days of wholesale clinic violence: deciding in private, with their doctor's advice, whether to proceed with the pregnancy. . . .
>
> Mifepristone does not signal a new phase of the abortion wars, but the beginning of an end to this destructive, tiresome and insoluble debate that should be welcomed by all sides.[27]

This is more wishful thinking. The fact that prolife forces have been fighting tooth and nail for years to block the introduction into the United States of RU-486 is not, as Davis would have it, an act of desperate self-preservation based upon the knowledge that the movement will evaporate once the drug arrives on these shores. On the contrary, as Margaret Talbot has written, the use of the drug will simply "accelerate a shift in prolife rhetoric toward the plight of the woman who terminates her pregnancy, allowing her at least to share the stage with the photogenic late-term fetus. . . . [W]hen it comes to mifepristone, antiabortion activists have been stressing the medical (and psychological) risks they argue it poses for women at least as much as the threat to the unborn child."[28] Which is not to say that RU-486 will stop the prolife movement from focusing on the fetus. This is how Janet Parshall, of the prolife Family Research Council, describes the drug: "Each pill is loaded like ammunition to take the life of a preborn child with one painless swallow. It's not birth control, it's *life* control."[29] Vicki Saporta, of the National Abortion Federation, is thus showing a great deal more realism than Davis when she declares that "[i]mproving access is very important, but mifepristone is not a magic solution for ending the abortion debate in this country."[30] And, in fact, use of RU-486 a year after its approval by the FDA remains minimal. A survey by the Kaiser Family Foundation released late in 2001 "found that only 6 percent of gynecologists and 1 percent of general-practice physicians" were providing mifepristone to their patients.[31]

In sum, as at least Justice Stephen Breyer has recognized, the two sides in the abortion debate espouse "virtually irreconcilable points of view."[32] The abortion debate is therefore best described as a clash of absolutes, a phrase that served as the subtitle of Laurence Tribe's 1990 book on the issue. In spite of this, Tribe devoted a substantial portion of the book to the discussion of potential compromises. In her review of the book, however, Amy Gutmann rightly asserted that his efforts were not convincing because "prolife and prochoice positions taken at their strongest, that is in their most moderated forms, *are not rationally reconcilable.*"[33] And it is crucial to understand that the abortion debate has been a clash of absolutes, both before and after *Roe* was decided. *Roe* did not simply drop from the skies; it was the culmination of years of prochoice activism.

Kristin Luker sums up the nineteenth-century history of abortion in America as follows:

> At the opening of the nineteenth century, no statute laws governed abortion in America. What minimal legal regulation existed was inherited from English common law tradition that abortion before quickening was at worst a misdemeanor. . . .
>
> In contrast, by 1900 every state in the Union had passed a law forbidding the use of drugs or instruments to procure abortion at *any* stage of pregnancy "unless the same be necessary to save the woman's life."[34]

By the 1960s, abortion remained widely criminalized. David Garrow asserts that "the first major stimulus toward significant liberalization" was the American Law Institute's 1959 endorsement of a model state abortion law that would allow for the procedure "if two doctors agreed that there was a 'substantial risk that continuance of the pregnancy would gravely impair the physical or mental health of the mother.'"[35] By 1967, the *Journal of the American Medical Association* had editorialized in favor of abortion reform,[36] and the National Organization for Women had drafted a "Women's Bill of Rights" that included "[t]he right of women to control their own reproductive lives by removing from the penal code laws limiting access to contraceptive information and devices, and by repealing laws governing abortion."[37] Thus, says Laurence Tribe, "[w]hile the belief that elective abortion was every women's right originated with radical feminists, by the late 1960s it had become dominant within the movement against restrictive abortion laws."[38]

The year 1967 was also the year that "[n]ationwide the abortion agenda would turn to a legislative focus. . . . Therapeutic reform bills would be considered by the legislatures of at least *twenty-five* states during the first eight months" of the year.[39] Over the next several years, the abortion battle raged in a large number of states, resulting in liberalization victories in states as different as California, Colorado, and North Carolina.[40] In Washington state, full repeal was won by popular referendum in 1970. And there were defeats for abortion law reform as well, including crushing losses in 1969 in New York and Texas.[41] "By 1973," however, "fourteen states had adopted some version of the Model Penal Code's abortion law, and four others had completely decriminalized abortion."[42]

What is striking about all of this debate is that its tone, if less orchestrated by organized prochoice and prolife groups, was every bit as fierce as post-*Roe* debate. Take the case of New York, which in 1970 repealed its restrictive abortion statute. Laurence Tribe writes that "[f]or the first time a strong feminist bloc made its political presence felt. On the other side, the Roman Catholic Church took a strong public position against legalization." Tribe continues:

> The forces opposing repeal included among their targets those Catholic legislators like Mary Ann Krupsack . . . who took a position in favor of abortion rights. As a result of her stance, Krupsak's father's neighborhood business was picketed, even by her in-laws, and she was singled out by the bishop of Albany in a day of mourning for legislators who supported the legalization of 'murder.'"[43]

Tribe also quotes from the account in the *New York Times* of the bill's passage in the lower house of the New York legislature, where the deciding vote was cast by an assemblyman who represented a district 65 percent of whose population was Catholic:

> Assemblyman George M. Michaels of Auburn, his hands trembling and tears welling in his eyes, stopped the rollcall only seconds before the clerk was to announce that the reform bill had been defeated for lack of a single vote. . . . "I realize, Mr. Speaker," Mr. Michaels said, "that I am terminating my political career, but I cannot in good conscience sit here and allow my vote to be the one that defeats the bill—I ask that my vote be changed from 'no' to 'yes.'"[44]

Neither side viewed this as a resolution of the abortion issue. On the contrary, a repeal of New York's abortion reform measure the following year was defeated only by the veto of Governor Nelson Rockefeller, who noted that "the extremes of personal vilification and political coercion brought to bear on members of the Legislature raise serious doubts that the votes to repeal the reforms represented the will of the majority of the people of New York State."[45] The same year in Pennsylvania, only the veto of Democratic governor Milton Schapp prevented the enactment of a law that would have allowed abortions only in the case where three doctors concurred that the abortion was necessary to save the mother's life.[46]

Pennsylvania in particular demonstrates the fallacy of the contention that an organized prolife movement arose only after *Roe.* "Beginning in 1967, the Pennsylvania Catholic Conference (PCC) built a well-organized, comprehensive campaign on the state and local levels that preempted its opponents and generated broad-based legislative support for restrictive abortion policy."[47] And, as Jean Reith Schroedel has written, Pennsylvania was not unique:

> The first permanent community-based prolife group was established in 1967 when New York antiabortion activists mobilized against efforts to reform the state's abortion law. Although eventually defeated in their attempt to halt liberalization in New York, prolife groups expanded rapidly in the late 1960s, as mass-based prolife organizations sprang up in New York, Virginia, Minnesota, California, Florida, Colorado, Michigan, Illinois, Ohio, and Pennsylvania. The Minnesota Citizens Concerned for Life (MCCL), one of the largest of the state prolife groups, had ten thousand members in the early 1970s before *Roe.*[48]

In sum, Justice Scalia's recollection of a concerted pre-*Roe* effort on all hands toward political compromise is not accurate. It is no more correct to assert, as does Judge James L. Buckley, that the intervention of the courts into the abortion issue "unleashed the most divisive political issue since *Dred Scott v. Sandford.*"[49] The issue had been "unleashed" years before, and not because of any judicial decision.

And then came *Roe.*[50] In their vilifications of the decision, prolife polemics frequently make claims along the lines that abortion "has been imposed on the nation by judicial fiat."[51] This is an ideologically comforting but historically obfuscatory position in light of the years of legislative struggle before *Roe*. Much more correct, but far less common among the critics of *Roe*, is the view of Bruce Fein:

> The high court invented a constitutional right to an abortion by a 7 to 2 margin in *Roe v. Wade* (1973), but the decision generally echoed the moral and ideological currents of the time. State laws were toppling abortion restrictions like tenpins, and then-California Governor Ronald Reagan had signed a virtual carbon copy of *Roe* in 1967.[52]

And, as already mentioned, prolife commentary is also replete with such assertions as this: "[b]y creating the most permissive national rule imaginable, the Supreme Court [in *Roe*] paralyzed the democratic process. The basic political problem with *Roe* is that it dismantled American democracy—it prevented the people from expressing their will on abortion."[53] But *Roe* did not establish an unqualified right to abortion, far from it. That is, in its often derided "trimester analysis," the decision allowed for state restrictions on abortion in the second trimester of pregnancy and for the outright banning of abortion in the third trimester.[54] This is certainly not to say that *Roe* was not a tremendous victory for prochoice forces. It is simply to say that the politics of abortion did not stop on *Roe*'s account.

The organizational strength of the prolife movement grew rapidly in response to *Roe*.[55] Within two years after *Roe*, 449 abortion restriction bills were considered by state legislatures, and fifty-eight became law.[56] The movement also won passage of the Hyde Amendment in 1976, which prohibited the use of Medicaid funds for most abortions. Fully 33 percent of the abortions performed in the United States were thereby defunded.[57] Prolife votes were of course also crucial to the 1980 election of Ronald Reagan, who referred to *Roe* during the campaign as "an abuse of power worse than Watergate."[58]

But the prolife movement has fallen short of the central aim of overruling *Roe*. After years of internal argument over what sort of amendment to put forward, prolife forces saw the defeat in 1983 of a constitutional amendment that would have overturned *Roe* and allowed the several states to regulate or ban abortion as they chose. The vote in the Senate was 50-49, eighteen votes short of the two-thirds majority needed for passage. Those voting against the amendment included thirteen Republicans.[59] No antiabortion constitutional amendment has reached the Senate floor since 1983.

And prochoice forces have had considerable victories as well. In 1986, antiabortion referenda were defeated in Massachusetts, Oregon, Arkansas, and Rhode Island, the last of which has the greatest percentage of Catholic citizens of any state in the Union.[60] Also in 1986, Robert Bork's nomination to the Supreme Court was defeated. Bork and his champions have, of course, long charged that he was the victim of an unprincipled smear campaign, but some facts are not in doubt. Bork excoriated *Roe* in his nomination hearings as a decision "that contains almost no legal reasoning."[61] As opinion polls found that Americans were opposed to Bork's nomination by an almost 2-1 margin, the Senate voted it down 58-42. It is difficult to argue with David Garrow's assessment that Bork's "public image as an unyielding foe of constitutional privacy had become perhaps the single greatest negative in spoiling his chances for Senate confirmation."[62]

Since Bork, *every* nominee to the Supreme Court—save for Bork's immediate successor, the hapless Douglas Ginsburg, who withdrew before reaching the stage of Senate hearings—has stated in his or her nomination hearings a belief in a constitutional right to privacy, the basis of *Roe's* holding:

> Anthony Kennedy noted that "the concept of liberty in the due process clause is quite expansive, quite sufficient, to protect the values of privacy that Americans legitimately think are part of their constitutional heritage. The first question asked of David Souter concerned privacy; and he unhesitatingly replied, "I believe the due process clause of the Fourteenth Amendment does recognize and does protect an unenumerated right of privacy." Even Clarence Thomas told Senator Biden on the first day of his hearings that "my view is that there is a right to privacy in the Fourteenth Amendment." Needless to say, Clinton nominees Ruth Bader Ginsburg and Stephen Breyer embraced privacy rights at their confirmation hearings. For Ginsburg, privacy, and with it, abortion, "is something central to a woman's life, to her dignity. It's a decision she must make for herself."[63]

It is also well to remember that, during his confirmation hearings, Justice Thomas asserted that he had reached no conclusion as to the correctness of *Roe*.[64]

In *Webster v. Reproductive Health Services*,[65] decided in 1989, and *Casey*,[66] decided in 1992, the Supreme Court reaffirmed *Roe* but also held that states could enact a range of legislation to discourage abortion. Both cases brought forth forceful political responses by prochoice forces. After *Webster*, an effort by Florida's governor to enact strict antiabortion statutes went down to defeat, while Virginia and New Jersey elected staunchly prochoice governors.[67] Both Connecticut and Washington state codified *Roe*, the latter by popular referendum.[68]

After *Casey*, Bill Clinton was elected to the White House on a strong prochoice platform. The Clinton years saw the passage of such prochoice measures as the Freedom of Access to Clinic Entrances Act[69] and the executive repeal of federal regulations that banned family planning organizations that receive federal funds from counseling clients with regard to abortion. Finally, in 1999, the Senate, by a vote of 51-48, for the first time passed a nonbinding resolution that endorsed *Roe v. Wade*.[70]

As we have seen, *Casey* is reviled by conservatives because it did not overrule *Roe*. However, in upholding Pennsylvania's regulations that mandated informed consent, waiting periods, and the notification of a minor's parents in order to obtain an abortion, the Court significantly devalued abortion's status as a constitutional right. As Garrow asserts, *Casey* is "an opinion in which invocation of the constitutional concept of 'liberty' completely and utterly supplanted the Court's previous employment of 'privacy' as the operative legal construct."[71] The practical effect of making a woman's access to abortion a "liberty interest" and not a privacy right is substantial. Here is a typical prochoice assessment:

> By upholding the portions of the Pennsylvania Abortion Control Act that require a woman to listen to a state-scripted, prochildbirth lecture given by a physician, and to wait twenty-four hours before going ahead with her abortion, the Court has now left it to fifty state legislatures to cook up more "pieces" of the abortion pie, so some state will have larger and others smaller abortion rights packages.
>
> . . . Regulations will be written, debated, passed, challenged, overturned, refined, challenged again, in a never-ending stream of laws, executive orders, legal briefs, bureaucratic forms, and data sheets.[72]

Since *Casey*, numerous states have in fact opted for regulations that hinder or discourage access to abortion. The current situation, in brief, is that

> abortion would be flatly illegal in eleven states if *Roe v. Wade* were overturned. Only six states and the District of Columbia are fully prochoice. Sixteen states require waiting periods, and twenty-one states mandate

"informed consent," which requires abortion providers to give women specific materials about abortion and its risks, benefits, and alternatives before performing an abortion. Currently, thirty-two states require the involvement of an adult before a minor can obtain an abortion, and in twenty states it is an offense for a nonparent to take a minor across state lines to get an abortion.[73]

Again, this discussion is not meant to defend or to criticize *Roe v. Wade*. It is meant to defend the judiciary from the attacks launched against it by many of *Roe*'s critics. The point is not that *Roe* should not be criticized but that its power should not be overestimated and the history of its origins, and the history of its impact, obliterated.

As at least some conservatives have recognized, criticism of *Roe* and its progeny can serve as a means to avoid facing an unpleasant truth, which is that, for all the talk of abortion having been "imposed" on the nation through "judicial tyranny," it is folly to believe that, if *Roe* were overruled, abortion in America would disappear. One does not have to go as far as the conservative commentator Christopher Caldwell, who asserts that abortion is now "an indispensable part of the normal middle-American toolkit," to acknowledge that the contemporary United States is not a culture that would give up abortion but for its judicial imprimatur.[74] Or, as one of the conservative critics of the *First Things* symposium on "The End of Democracy?" declared, "[w]hat we are dealing with is, in short, a cultural, rather than primarily a judicial, problem."[75] But bashing judges is easy; transforming culture is hard.

Money and Speech

In 1974, in the wake of the Watergate scandal, Congress substantially amended the Federal Election Campaign Act.[76] First, the amendments established a regime of limits upon campaign contributions. Ceilings of $1,000 for individuals and of $5,000 for political action committees were placed upon the amount that could be contributed to a candidate for federal office during a single election. Limits were also placed upon the amounts that could be contributed to the national committees of political parties during a single year, $20,000 for individuals and $15,000 for political action committees. Further, the amendments imposed a $25,000 annual limit upon an individual's aggregate contributions to federal candidates, political action committees, and national political parties.

The 1974 amendments also placed ceilings upon expenditures that could be made by campaigns for federal offices. That is, specific spending caps were established for races for the White House and for House and Senate seats. In addition, specific caps were also placed upon the amount of campaign expenditures that could be drawn from a candidate's personal funds.

As already noted, the Supreme Court in *Buckley v. Valeo* partially invalidated FECA on First Amendment grounds. Specifically, the Court drew a distinction between contribution limits and expenditure limits, upholding the former and invalidating the latter. The Court held that expenditure limits necessarily limited political speech protected by the First Amendment, while contribution limits did not have the same impact:

> The expenditure limitations . . . represent substantial rather than merely theoretical restraints on the quantity and diversity of political speech. . . . By contrast, . . . [a] limitation on the amount of money a person may give to a candidate or campaign organization . . . involves little direct restraint on his political communication, for it permits the symbolic expression of support evidenced by a contribution but does not in any way infringe the contributor's freedom to discuss candidates and issues.[77]

The Court also found that the government had a far more substantial interest in limiting contributions than in limiting expenditures. Limits upon contributions were justifiable as a means of pursuing the legitimate end of preventing "the actuality and appearance of corruption resulting from large individual financial contributions."[78] On the other hand, the Court held that the government had no similarly legitimate interest in limiting the amount that campaigns could spend as a means of equalizing electoral competition between candidates:

> [T]he concept that government may restrict the speech of some elements of our society in order to enhance the relative voice of others is wholly foreign to the First Amendment, which was designed "to secure 'the widest possible dissemination of information from diverse and antagonistic sources,'" and "'to assure unfettered interchange of ideas for the bringing about of political and social changes desired by the people.'" *New York Times Co. v. Sullivan.*[79]

The impact of *Buckley* and its progeny upon the manner in which elections are conducted in America has been considerable. A brief description has been set forth by the law professor Burt Neuborne:

> By upholding FECA's contribution limits, while striking down its expenditure ceilings, the *Buckley* Court created a campaign financing system very different from the one Congress intended. . . . [C]ontribution limits . . . made raising money harder, but the lack of spending caps maintained the system's voracious need for money. In simple economic terms, the *Buckley* Court limited supply (contributions), while leaving demand (expenditures) free to grow without limit. The predictable effect has been to increase the pressures on candidates to satisfy the ever-increasing demand for campaign cash. Inadvertently, the *Buckley* opinion took a congressional program designed to minimize the impact of wealth on campaigns and turned it into an engine for the glorification of money.[80]

Because *Buckley* has had such a palpable effect on the workings of American democracy, one would think that Imperial Judiciary theorists would be terrifically exercised over the fact that the opinion makes nothing like a comprehensive effort to establish that the intent of the framers of the First Amendment dictates its result. *Buckley* is, after all, a case where unelected judges largely took the regulation of campaign finance away from elected legislators. But, if they were to become so exercised, would they be able to make the argument from original intent that the Court did not? Could they demonstrate that the framers of the First Amendment would have viewed the act of spending money on election campaigns as clearly beyond substantial government regulation?

I think that they could not. To begin with, reliance upon original intent "is especially ill suited in the context of campaign finance. It is highly unlikely that the ratifiers of the First Amendment had any specific intentions at all on the topic."[81] Indeed, "the Constitution is silent on virtually all the important issues regarding elections, from how ballots are to be cast, to the electoral system for all public offices save the President and the Senate, to issues of how elections are to be run and financed, to the eligibility for voting, and so forth."[82]

The Constitution in fact contemplates a much more limited role for popular elections than that which we are used to. Article I, Section 3 provides for the selection of senators by the state legislatures, not by popular election. This arrangement was not altered until the passage of the Seventeenth Amendment in 1913. Article II, Section 1 declares that the election of the president shall be by the votes of "a Number of Electors" chosen by several states. Each state is directed to choose its electors "in such manner as the Legislature thereof may direct." For some time after government under the Constitution began to operate, popular election was not the favored means of choosing electors. On the contrary, a majority of state legislatures opted for the selection of electors by the legislature itself through the first four presidential elections.[83]

Further, the ethos and mechanisms of modern elections, or even rough equivalents thereof, were almost wholly unknown to the framers and ratifiers of the First Amendment. On the contrary, "[e]lectioneering techniques developed slowly in early America."[84] This is especially true with respect to the very idea of an election "campaign." In pre-Revolutionary America, politics remained an affair governed by social deference, not freewheeling vote solicitation:

> Prior to their revolution, Americans presumed that social, political, and cultural authority should be united in an order of gentlemen. Artisans and common farmers could vote and hold offices in their locality. . . . But it was unthinkable that any man without all the attributes of gentility should seek the more honorific and lucrative public offices at the county or provincial level. . . . Almost universal and unquestioning expectation, rather than formal law, underlay the unitary authority of the genteel in America.[85]

Thus, "a well-to-do planter or merchant could secure a legislative seat without openly appealing for votes. In colonial times the common person's deference toward members of the elite was particularly strong. . . . Moreover, custom dictated that a provincial office seeker remain above the conflict and not actively solicit support."[86]

In the northern colonies in particular, elections were "pretty tame affairs," largely limited to the vote itself.[87] The "conventional mode of politics" held that it was "inappropriate and demeaning for those virtuous and eminent enough to occupy positions of public trust to scramble for votes."[88] Nor, as we shall consider presently, did the contemporary citizenry look with favor upon robust competition for votes. This remained so even as the Revolution approached, as is demonstrated in Robert Gross's classic study of Concord, Massachusetts, during the Revolutionary Era. Here is how Gross describes voter reaction to Joseph Lee, who campaigned vigorously in a 1771 election for a seat in the state legislature held by a respected incumbent:

> Concordians were republicans, *not* democrats. Despite the upsurge in popular power, they still regarded as illegitimate those values and practices we now consider essential to modern democratic politics. As Joseph Lee's failed challenge to representative Barrett demonstrated, organized competition for power between opposing candidates occasioned the most intense anxiety. Lee and his supporters were a "faction"—designing men in league against the common good. The voters simply could not accept that open expression of differences about men and measures that is required for full discovery of the majority will and its translation into public policy.[89]

In some parts of the South, particularly Virginia, a form of campaigning existed in that candidates for office were expected to "treat" voters with gifts of food and (especially) alcoholic beverages.[90] But this practice was denounced by orthodox Republicans like James Madison, who referred disapprovingly in *Federalist* 10 to "the vicious arts by which elections are too often carried."[91]

After the Revolution, as well, the consensus was that "the solicitation of the suffrages of voters" was improper.[92] As the historian Gil Troy has written, it continued to be the case that "proper candidates stood for election; they did not run":

> This pristine approach to campaigning suited early American society. Most inhabitants lived in farming communities scattered along the Atlantic coast. Information traveled only as quickly as individuals could. . . . In these self-sufficient polities, people usually knew one another intimately, obviating the need for spectacular campaigning. All knew their place in society, with commoners expected to defer to their betters.

Thus, concludes Troy, "[i]n the early republic, national politics was remarkably primitive and relatively cheap."[93] Bradley Smith, who as a law professor and now as a commissioner of the Federal Election Commission has been perhaps the leading academic critic of campaign finance reform, appears to agree: "In the colonial period and early years of the Republic, campaign finance was not an issue. . . . In those early days, such campaign expenses as existed were typically paid from the candidate's own pocket, and went for food and drink, or the occasional pamphlet or piece of campaign literature."[94]

Consider in this light the first three national elections under the Constitution. In 1788, George Washington achieved the presidency more or less by acclamation and certainly did not engage in the least bit of campaigning for the office. In 1792, Washington won reelection under similar circumstances, while, with respect to congressional elections, there remained "the widest range of inhibitions against out-and-out party activity."[95] In 1796, Thomas Jefferson faced off against John Adams for the presidency. But Jefferson "did not stir out of Monticello the whole times, and avoided making any commitments whatever," while Adams did not campaign because he believed the office "was simply the recognition to which he was entitled for nearly thirty years of meritorious public service."[96]

Even with Jefferson's triumph over Adams in the election of 1800, an election which has attained the status of a democratic uprising in our national memory, things remained very much the same. In her recent account of the contest, Joanne Freeman notes that "[t]he proper stance for a candidate for high office" remained "complete and utter silence, the sort of republican display of obedience to the public will that came so naturally to Jefferson."[97] Indeed, when Aaron Burr, Jefferson's ostensive running mate, engaged in some actual campaigning, it was seen by his contemporaries "as evidence of his willingness to take extreme measures."[98]

In sum, the notion of a "campaign contribution" and of "campaign expenditures" beyond very modest amounts did not exist because there was very little activity that we recognize today as campaigning. As a result, we cannot hope to state with any large measure of certainty whether the framers would have opposed campaign finance regulation. And we surely cannot know whether such opposition would have been grounded upon the belief that political money is "speech" within the purview of the First Amendment.

Besides dealing with the fact of a wholly different politics prevailing at the time of the Founding, the originalist must also confront the political mentality of that time. As we have noted, the Supreme Court in *Buckley* recognized a legitimate government interest in preventing "the actuality and appearance of corruption" in public affairs.[99] To the framers, however, the fear of public corruption amounted to something like an obsession. As Gordon Wood has observed, it was a central feature of eighteenth-century Republicanism that republics "were very fragile polities, extremely liable to corruption."[100] Hamilton noted in the *Federalist* that, in light of "the disorders that disfigure the annals" of republican government," the "advocates of despotism" had had an easy time arguing against "not only the forms of republican government, but against the very principles of civil liberty."[101]

Republics were unlike other governments in that their end was not the pursuit of the good of a ruler, or of a particular class. Rather, republics pursued a highly idealized notion of the common good. As Wood has described it, Republican theory held that the common good was "an entity in itself, prior to and distinct from the various private interests of groups and individuals. . . . [P]olitics was conceived to be not the reconciling but the transcending of the different interests of the society in the search for a single common good."[102]

To be capable of pursuing the common good, therefore, it was necessary that a man be *disinterested*, that is, independent and virtuous enough to rise above the furtherance of mere partial interests. John Adams expressed the point perfectly in 1776 when he declared that a republican must possess

> a positive passion for the public good . . . this public passion must be superior to all private passions. Men must be ready, they must pride themselves, and be happy to sacrifice their private pleasures, passions, and interests, nay, their private friendships and dearest connections, when they stand in competition with the rights of society.[103]

It is attitudes like this that engendered the belief that republics were so fragile. As Wood says, republics "demanded far more morally from their citizens than monarchies did of their subjects."[104]

The originalist who seeks to justify the unregulated role of money in politics will have a hard time coming to terms with this ideological universe. Even if the framers had no real sense of the concept of the campaign contribution, it is not hard to imagine that they would have looked highly askance at a candidate for public office who accepted unlimited donations from private individuals and entities. How could such a person be trusted to pursue the common good, as opposed to the good of his donors?

Similarly, is it not plausible that a candidate who lavished his own funds upon an election campaign would be viewed as pursuing his own glory and as engaging in an unseemly quest for votes, rather than presenting himself as one capable of the disinterested pursuit of society's common interest? It is in fact the case that Americans of the Revolutionary Era were quite concerned that voters make their electoral choice on the basis of dispassionate judgment, and not as a result of mere persuasion by the candidates. Here is Theophilus Parsons, one of the premier lawyers of the time, writing in 1778:

> Elections ought to be free. No bribery, corruption, or undue influence should have place. They stifle the free voice of the people, corrupt their morals, and introduce a degeneracy of manners, a supineness of temper, and an inattention to their liberties, which pave the road for the approach of tyranny, in all its frightful forms.[105]

How does one square a sentiment like this with campaigns of unlimited expense?

In spite of all this, the current Supreme Court's adherents of originalist jurisprudence have argued, in a recent campaign finance case, that the framers of the First Amendment would have viewed legislative measures to restrict the role of money in politics as plainly unconstitutional. In *Nixon v. Shrink Missouri Government PAC*, the Court upheld a Missouri statute that limits campaign contributions to candidates for state offices.[106] Justice Thomas wrote a dissenting opinion, which Justice Scalia joined.[107] Justice Thomas begins credibly enough by quoting a passage from James Madison's 1799 "Virginia Resolutions":

> The value and efficacy of [the right to elect the members of government] depends on the knowledge of the comparative merits and demerits of the candidates for the public trust, and on the equal freedom, consequently, of examining and discussing these merits and demerits of the candidates respectively.[108]

Although this has no direct relation to the question of campaign finance, it is at least an avowal that the First Amendment should be broadly construed to provide for the fullest possible provision of relevant information to voters. On the other hand, Justice Thomas makes no mention of the reason why Madison composed the Virginia Resolutions. They were a statement of opposition to the Alien and Sedition Acts, the latter of which made it a federal crime to "write, print, utter, or publish . . . any false, scandalous, and malicious writing or writings against the government of the United States."[109] Shortly after the passage quoted, Madison makes it plain that the constitutional flaw of the Sedition Act is that it ensures an unequal electoral competition between incumbents and challengers: "the former will be covered by the 'sedition act' from animadversions exposing them to disrepute among the people; whilst the latter may be exposed to the contempt and hatred of the people, without a violation of the act."[110] It is therefore not at all clear that Madison would see a law that establishes public funding for campaigns and that applies to challengers and incumbents *equally* as suffering from the same constitutional infirmity.[111]

From here, Justice Thomas goes downhill fast. He quotes a passage from *Federalist* 35 in the following context:

> [Campaign] donors seek to disseminate information by giving to an organization controlled by others. Through contributing, citizens see to it that their views on policy and politics are articulated. In short, "they are aware that however great the confidence they may justly feel in their own good sense, their interests can be more effectively promoted by [another] than themselves."[112]

This is nothing but sleight of hand. The quoted passage has nothing whatever to do with campaign donors and candidates but deals with the political relation between two classes: "mechanics" and "manufacturers."[113] Alexander Hamilton is making the argument that the former have an interest in giving the latter their votes, not their money.

Federalist 35 actually contains an excellent synopsis of the sort of deferential politics that prominent framers hoped would continue in America under the Constitution. In that essay Hamilton considered the political relationship between citizens engaged in "the mechanic and manufacturing arts" and affluent merchants. The former

> know that the merchant is their natural patron and friend; and they are aware that . . . their interests can be more effectually promoted by the merchant than by themselves. They are sensible that their habits of life have not been such as to give them those acquired endowments, without which in a deliberative assembly the greatest natural abilities are for the most part useless; and that the influence and weight and superior acquirements of the merchants render them more equal to a contest with any spirit which might happen to infuse itself into the public counsels, unfriendly to the manufacturing and trading interests. [Mechanics and manufacturers will therefore] bestow their votes upon merchants and those whom they recommend. We must therefore consider

merchants as the natural representatives of all these classes of the community.[114]

Hamilton continues by asserting that a similar commonality of interest exists "from the wealthiest landlord to the poorest tenant" and that the well-being of the "landed interest" as a whole will best be served by the election of large landholders to political office.[115] The point for us is that Hamilton looked forward to an electoral politics under the Constitution that would consist of the decorous recognition of "the natural representatives" of the people. Elections consisting of loud, expensive campaigns which competed for popular favor by pandering to popular desires would not have been pleasing to him.

Justice Thomas concludes with a plain misreading of *Federalist* 10 in an effort to show that the framers actually were very much in favor of robust electoral competition under the aegis of political parties. He contends that contribution caps would have been "contemptuously dismissed" by Madison because he would have lauded unfettered campaign contributions as an aid to healthy factional competition: "The framers preferred a political system that harnessed . . . faction for good, preserving liberty while also ensuring good government."[116]

What we have here is a failure to understand the mental universe in which the framers were operating and to remember that, as the great Madison scholar Douglass Adair put it half a century ago, *Federalist* 10 "is eighteenth-century political theory directed to an eighteenth-century problem."[117] That mental universe, as we have seen, was one in which the pursuit of the common good was perpetually threatened by merely partial interests. "Faction" and "party" were forces of political dysfunction. The project of *Federalist* 10 is emphatically not to "harness faction for good" by allowing for expansive competition between factions. On the contrary, Madison makes it as plain as possible that "*the public good is disregarded in the conflict of rival parties.*"[118]

Let us consider this in more detail. The framers possessed decidedly negative views about political parties, which they characterized as a species of faction. A "faction," said Madison in *Federalist* 10, was "a number of citizens . . . who are united and actuated by some common impulse of passion, or of interest, adverse to the rights of other citizens, or to the permanent and aggregate interests of the community."[119] The reason why small republics were inherently unstable, thought Madison, was that they made it too easy for parties to achieve power: "The smaller the society, the fewer probably will be the distinct parties and interests composing it; the fewer the distinct parties and interests, the more frequently will a majority be found of the same party; and . . . the more easily will they concert and execute their plans of oppression."[120] Conversely, a large republic might possibly succeed because it would encompass "a greater variety of parties and interests," thereby making it "less probable that a majority of the whole will have a common motive to invade the rights of other citizens."[121]

In other words, Madison's goal in *Federalist* 10 is to argue in favor of a large republic, one that would contain so many factions and interests that it would be likely that no one faction could control the government and use it as a vehicle of oppression, as any faction inevitably would. Further, Madison also believed that, in a large republic, it would be more likely that voters would elect "a chosen body of citizens, whose wisdom may best discern the true interest of their country and whose patriotism and love of justice will be least likely to sacrifice it to temporary or partial interests."[122] In other words, the people would, one would hope, not elect "[m]en of factious tempers."[123]

Madison therefore did not want to "harness faction for good"; he wanted to build a republic that would "*break and control the violence of faction*."[124] Daniel Howe gives an excellent exposition of Madison's thought in this regard: "All factions, even those that do not originally derive from passion, have the effect of unduly strengthening passion over reason. Partisanship comes to substitute for independent judgment. . . . *Narrow or short-sighted interests are not ennobled in Publius's presentation*; a good government will 'break and control' their violence, *not be the vehicle for their expression and rule*."[125]

In accordance with this disposition, it is hardly surprising that "the framers specifically intended the constitutional structure to preclude the rise of political parties, which were considered the quintessential form of 'faction.'"[126] Richard Hofstadter makes the point succinctly in his classic study of the rise of political parties in the United States:

> While most of the Fathers did assume that partisan opposition would form from time to time, they did not expect that valuable permanent structures would arise from them which would have a part to play in the protection and exercise of liberties or in reconciling the stability and effectiveness of government with the exercise of popular freedoms. . . . The Fathers hoped to create not a system of party government under a con-

stitution but rather a constitution that would check and control parties.[127]

To return to Justice Thomas, it almost goes without saying that he is unable in his *Shrink Missouri* dissent to quote anything from the Founding Era that specifically concerns campaign contributions. As we have seen, the very notion—like the notion of campaigning itself—did not really exist. And he cites nothing at all from the debates that accompanied the framing and ratification of the First Amendment. If one wanted to be irascible about it, one might assert that Justice Thomas has used a patina of original intent in order to argue for a judicial veto upon legislative measures to regulate money in politics.[128]

Yet, in spite of its lack of a plausible originalist pedigree, *Buckley*'s ethos of opposition to the regulation of money in politics is, it is fair to say, wildly popular among conservatives.[129] Senator Mitch McConnell, Republican of Kentucky, expresses the view wonderfully: "Campaign finance is synonymous with constitutional freedom."[130] (And when Congress actually passed major campaign finance reform legislation in 2002, Senator McConnell led the charge to federal court as a plaintiff in a lawsuit seeking to overturn the legislation.) George F. Will opines that "enthusiasm for [campaign finance reform] is applied liberalism, the impulse to have the state put a leash on everything, in the name of equality."[131] And when the conservative litigator Clint Bolick celebrated his recent victory in which he persuaded an Arizona court to declare the state's program of providing public funds for campaigns to be a violation of the First Amendment, he did not express any unease over the fact that the program had been established not merely by the state legislature, but by popular referendum. On the contrary, he referred to the program as a "scheme" that had been "cynically designed."[132] Finally, even the court-bashing Tom DeLay is quite willing to recognize an exception for matters of campaign finance: "We must recognize, *as have the courts,* that no debate is free without the freedom to dedicate resources to the promulgation of ideas."[133] As far as I am aware, however, none of these gentlemen has gotten any further than Justice Thomas in justifying *Buckley* on originalist grounds.

The abortion issue and the question of money in politics have both been constitutionalized by the courts. That is, both matters are no longer left to legislative determination alone. In neither case can it be argued that the framers would have wished it so. Instead, in both cases, judges have been confronted with claims that constitutional principles should be applied to social realities—expanding equality for women and highly expensive political campaigns—of which the framers had no inkling.

In both cases, judges have satisfied these claims, at least in part, and have thereby greatly altered the parameters of legislative and popular debate with respect to the issues of abortion and money in politics. They have not, however, shut off debate. The opponents of *Roe* and the opponents of *Buckley* both continue—by engaging in public debate, voting, influencing the judicial selection process, and even engaging in litigation—to press for their policy goals and for their preferred constitutional vision. This is what we call democracy.

6

The Judiciary and the Polity

The *Laws* is Plato's longest and far and away his most tedious philosophical dialogue. Plato's aim in the *Laws*, as in the more widely read *Republic*, is to set forth the workings of an ideal state. In contrast to the *Republic*, however, the *Laws* posits a state that is meant to be an attainable ideal. It is to be governed not by a cadre of philosopher-kings but, as the title suggests, by a legal code.

Still, after having described in numbing detail a code that embraces just about all aspects of social existence, Plato cannot resist returning to the *Republic*'s spirit. In the closing passages of the *Laws*, he introduces the "Nocturnal Council," which is essentially a stripped-down version of the *Republic*'s philosopher-kings. The Nocturnal Council is an unelected body of elders who have held high positions elsewhere in state officialdom. They "meet before dawn, when people are least beset by other business, public or private."[1] Through rigorous legal and philosophical study, they "are more highly qualified than the man in the street to explain what virtue is, and to put it into practice."[2] Most important, in a manner that Plato does not make at all clear, the Nocturnal Council is to function as an "organ of protection"; it will impose its insights into philosophy and law upon state officialdom in order to keep the latter from committing actions at odds with the aim of promoting virtue.[3]

Imperial Judiciary theorists often write about the U.S. Supreme Court in particular, and the judiciary in general, as if it approximates Plato's Nocturnal Council. This is not to say that certain features of the judicial branch don't lend themselves to the analogy. Federal judges are, of course, unelected and life tenured. Although most of them have the good sense not to deliberate before dawn, their deliberations do take place in *chambers*, a term with a cabalistic ring to it. So perhaps it should not be at all surprising to see a conservative law professor label the federal judiciary "a secretive and unaccountable cadre."[4] And why do you think many courthouses look like temples? Because, according to the *Wall Street Journal's*

Tunku Varadarajan, "the judges who sit in them now constitute a priest-hood, an oracular class that shapes the way we behave, or, more accurately, the way we are allowed to behave."[5]

Most important, of course, it is easy to depict the exercise of judicial review as akin to an act of the Nocturnal Council. The courts can be characterized as standing apart and above the polity, descending on occasion, as do the members of the Nocturnal Council, to impose their purportedly superior legal and ethical comprehension upon the wayward popular branches of government. The Nocturnal Council itself has been described by an eminent Plato scholar as "the real sovereign of State, since it can control the law, which was before regarded as sovereign; and by its introduction the law-state is really destroyed."[6] In the same fashion, another conservative law professor describes the Supreme Court as "nine unelected Law Lords imposing their will on more than 270 million Americans," in violation of "the original, simple conception of the Constitution, to wit, that legislatures were supposed to legislate and judges were supposed to judge."[7]

The purpose of this chapter is to argue that descriptions of this sort do not by a long shot accurately situate the judiciary within the contemporary American polity. If one focuses upon particular exercises of judicial review with which one does not agree, it is easy to portray the judiciary as an institution residing in Olympian detachment from the rest of the political system. But the judiciary does not so reside. It is in fact *embedded* in the political process. To demonstrate this, I outline here the manner in which judicial power is subject to both expansion and contraction at the hands of the popular branches of government.

First, much of the judiciary's contemporary power has been conferred upon it by the people's representatives; they have made it both the over-seer of the actions of a vast array of regulatory bodies and the adjudicator of disputes arising from a range of statutory rights. Further, even if one focuses upon the exercise of judicial review, any realistic assessment of judicial power must take into account the influence of the popular branches. The course of judicial review is determined in no small part by the fact that, unlike the Nocturnal Council, judges of the federal courts are not a self-selecting group but are individuals who have won the approval of the people's representatives. Further, even given the judiciary's role as the final interpreter of the constitutional text, our history demonstrates over and over again that the *implementation* of constitutional decisions issued by the courts is highly contingent upon the will of the popular branches.

The chapter concludes by making note of three matters regarding the limits of judicial power in the American polity that should be obvious but that do not receive much attention in Imperial Judiciary commentary. First, with respect to the conduct of foreign and military affairs, which are no small matters in the contemporary United States, the judiciary plays no appreciable role whatever. Second, in the realm of criminal law, the power of federal judges as definers of criminal punishment has been severely contracted by the Federal Sentencing Guidelines, versions of which have been enacted in several states in order to limit the sentencing discretion of state judges. Finally, as to the judiciaries of the fifty states, a large majority of their members are chosen through popular elections, which have grown increasingly rancorous in recent years and which do no small amount of violence to the ideal of an independent judiciary. It suffices to say that the supreme court of any state that has judicial elections is no Nocturnal Council.

In sum, this chapter *contextualizes* the judiciary within the American polity. The hope is that this will demonstrate that the courts "are one standard component of our democratic regime as it has evolved through time."[8]

Policing the Administrative State

In his review of Tocqueville's *Democracy in America*, John Stuart Mill contended that "America needs very little government. She has no wars, no neighbours, no complicated international relations; no old society with its thousand abuses to reform; no half-fed and untaught millions crying for food and guidance."[9] The framers of the Constitution would not have quarreled with Mill's assessment. As the historian Jack Rakove has written, "the creation of the national Leviathan of 1787–1789 was followed by a near century-long desuetude in which the business of the national government was reduced to collecting some duties, delivering the mail (albeit on Sunday, at least for a while), and governing western territories."[10]

Since then, for better or worse, the federal government has become an entity that can be called a Leviathan without irony. No one can argue with Justice Souter's contention the "[t]he proliferation of Government, State and Federal, would amaze the framers, and the administrative state with its reams of regulations would leave them rubbing their eyes."[11] It is difficult to express briefly the scope of federal government activity in modern

America, particularly with respect to its role as a regulator of the market, but the following is a good attempt:

> Over the years the federal government . . . has come to regulate a variety of economic activities. The Interstate Commerce Commission (ICC) was established in 1887 and given power over railroad rates. The Federal Trade Commission (FTC), overseeing general trade practices, and the Federal Reserve Board (FRB), regulating bank assets, were set up in 1914. Many new agencies were established during the New Deal of the 1930s, including the Civil Aeronautics Board (CAB), Federal Communications Commission (FCC, absorbing the Federal Radio Commission of 1927), the National Labor Relations Board (NLRB), Securities and Exchange Commission (SEC), and the Federal Power Commission (FPC). Others were added later: the Atomic Energy Commission (AEC, subsequently transformed in the Nuclear Regulatory Commission [NRC]), the Consumer Product Safety Commission (CPSC), the Environmental Protection Agency (EPA), and the Occupational Safety and Health Administration (OSHA). Much regulating is done by agencies within regular branch departments, such as the Antitrust Division of the Justice Department and the Food and Drug Administration.[12]

This was written in 1983. Since then, declarations along the lines of "the era of Big Government is over" have become a rhetorical standard for politicians across the political spectrum, Ralph Nader excepted. But I note that all of these agencies are still with us.

After wielding power for decades, the federal government's regulatory agencies administer a body of rules that "now occupies an importance equal to statutory law."[13] Nevertheless, the agencies remain anomalous entities within our constitutional order, as the law professor Nicholas Zeppos notes:

> While Article I empowers Congress to legislate, Article II empowers the president to execute the law, and Article III empowers the courts to adjudicate, administrative agencies exercise all three constitutional powers in one entity. For example, the National Labor Relations Board (NLRB)— the agency empowered by statute to regulate union activities—is authorized to promulgate rules that are indistinguishable from legislative enactments. The NLRB also exercises executive power, in the broadest sense of carrying out legislative policies, as well as exercising particular functions

long recognized as quintessentially executive, such as making prosecutorial decisions. Finally, the NLRB exercises judicial functions in adjudication disputes between unions and employers.[14]

Thus could Justice Robert Jackson argue as early as 1952 that administrative agencies "have become a veritable fourth branch of the Government, which has deranged our three-branch legal theories much as the concept of a fourth dimension unsettles our three-dimensional thinking."[15]

This clearly raises a problem of the legitimacy of agency power within a democratic polity, especially since, as Guido Calabresi has asserted, agencies "are not so majoritarian as we assume legislators to be, and they are not so conscious of principle in lawmaking as we have traditionally asked our courts to be."[16] That is, the bureaucrats who populate regulatory agencies are unelected. Except for the officials at the highest levels of the organizational chart, who are appointed by the incumbent president, they are employed through the civil service system. Agencies themselves are not democracies. Decisions are instead made pursuant to a chain of command. But the nature of the directives that come through the chain are subject to reversal with the change of presidential administrations and statutory directives.

While agencies are established by Congress, the statutes by which they are brought into being generally do not set forth agency responsibilities with precision. Far from it. As a leading scholar of administrative law puts it, "federal legislation establishing agency charters has, over the past several decades, often been strikingly broad and nonspecific," and, as a result, Congress has afforded "sweeping powers to a host of new agencies under legislative directives cast in the most general terms."[17]

Consider some examples. The Food and Drug Administration has been afforded the authority to regulate drugs, which according to its charter statue include "articles intended for use in the diagnosis, cure, mitigation, treatment, or prevention of disease in man or other animals" and "articles (other than food) intended to affect the structure or any function of the body of man or other animals."[18] One can certainly work a great deal into a definition like that without too much imagination. Not to be outdone, the charter statute of the National Highway Transportation Safety Administration directs that agency to promulgate equipment standards for motor vehicles that "shall be practicable, shall meet the need for motor vehicle safety, and shall be stated in objective terms."[19] Finally, the Clean Air Act empowers the Environmental Protection Agency to ensure that a range of airborne pollutants are kept at levels "requisite to protect the public health" with an "adequate margin of safety."[20]

It has also frequently been the case that, once Congress has established an agency, it declines to revise the statutory definition of the agency's responsibilities. Here, for example, is how the labor historian David Brody has recently described government regulation of labor relations: "Congress has not significantly amended the law in more than forty years, and regarding basic doctrine—the rights of workers to organize, choose their own representatives, and bargain collectively—the Taft-Hartley amendments (1947) to the original National Labor Relations Act (1935) are the last word."[21]

Charged with responsibilities of such scope, the administrative state, as already noted, "may appropriately be regarded as the fourth effective branch of government."[22] The question then becomes, given that these statutes and others like them do not afford *absolute* discretion to agencies, who determines when an agency has exceeded its statutory authority or when an agency has committed an act in violation of the Constitution itself? Stated another way, agency actions "constitute a buzzing infinity of rules, adjudications, exceptions, initiatives, inspections, prosecutions, suggestions, and admonitions whose democratic nature is ensured only by the general government context in which they exist."[23] But who determines when an agency has departed the democratic context?

In a nice illustration of Judge Calabresi's dictum that "[a]s the 'sources of law' expand, so, it would seem, does judicial power," the political branches have given the judiciary the authority to make determinations concerning the permissible scope of agency lawmaking.[24] The primary grant of authority in this regard is the Administrative Procedure Act (APA),[25] enacted in 1946, which has justly been called "akin to a Bill of Rights in the administrative state."[26] The APA provides that a "final agency action" is "subject to judicial review" in the context of a lawsuit that may be brought by any person "adversely affected or aggrieved" by such action.[27] Broadly speaking, the APA allows courts to "veto" regulatory decisions in two ways:

> First, the court can find procedural irregularity on the part of the agency [in making the decision], such as failure to give notice, lack of a fair hearing, or inadequate findings of fact to support the agency's conclusion. Second, if the agency has been careful to protect its procedural flanks, the

court can find the action by the agency in excess of its authority, "arbitrary," or contrary to the weight of the evidence.[28]

The APA is thus the supervisory mechanism pursuant to which the vast statutory discretion granted to agencies is policed. The late Judge Harold Leventhal, a longtime member of the U.S. Court of Appeals for the District of Columbia Circuit, spoke of this linkage between broad delegation and judicial oversight as a tradeoff between the dual necessities of administrative flexibility and the curbing of arbitrary power: "Congress has been willing to delegate its legislative powers broadly—and courts have upheld such delegation—because there is court review to assure that the agency exercises the delegated power within statutory limits, and that it fleshes out objectives within those limits by an administration that is not irrational or discriminatory."[29]

As Judge Leventhal implies, the tenor of court review of agency action under the APA has long been one of deference toward an agency's interpretation of its statutory authority. The leading case of recent years is *Chevron U.S.A. Inc. v. Natural Resources Defense Council*, in which the Supreme Court held that, while the judiciary "is the final authority on issues of statutory construction," courts should nevertheless uphold an agency's interpretation of its statutory powers that is not "arbitrary, capricious, or manifestly contrary to the statute."[30] In other words, "a court may not substitute its own construction of a statutory provision for a reasonable interpretation made by the administrator of an agency."[31] The rationale for this deferential stance—beyond the fact that regulators are presumed to be far more knowledgeable concerning what they are regulating than are judges—is that decisions made by regulatory agencies are deeply influenced by the political process. As a result, agency policies are believed to reflect the results of deliberation and bargaining among the people's representatives. As the Court stated in *Chevron*, since each presidential administration—with the approval of Congress, or in spite of its opposition—attempts to direct the federal bureaucracy to pursue policies it favors, reviewing courts should acknowledge that agencies may "properly rely upon the incumbent administration's views of wise policy to inform its judgments.[32]

But we may now be in the midst of a move away from judicial deference to agency action. During its 1999–2000 term, the Supreme Court handed down a 5-4 decision in *FDA v. Brown & Williamson Tobacco*

Corp.,[33] that involved a challenge to the Food and Drug Administration's promulgation of a range of restrictions upon the sale of tobacco products, rules greatly favored by the Clinton administration. As we have seen, the statute under which the FDA operates allows it to regulate drugs, a term the statute defines very broadly. Relying upon this statutory discretion, the FDA argued before the Court that it had the authority to regulate tobacco as a drug because cigarettes are "intended to affect" certain functions of the body.[34] The Court noted, however, that the FDA's charter statute provides as well that the agency must ban any drug that cannot be made "safe and effective" and that the agency itself had found that a safe cigarette could not be made. In fact, prior to promulgating the very regulations in question, "the FDA quite exhaustively documented that 'tobacco products are unsafe,' 'dangerous,' and 'cause great pain and suffering from illness.'"[35] The Court thus reasoned that the FDA had no statutory authority to "conclude that a drug . . . cannot be used safely for any therapeutic purpose and yet, at the same time, allow the product to remain on the market."[36] Thus, the only agency policy that would comport with its statutory authority would be to ban cigarettes. But the Court held that the FDA could not do this because any ban would be in violation of congressional intent expressed in other statutes that explicitly contemplate the marketing of cigarettes.

Going even further than this, a 1999 decision of the U.S. Court of Appeals for the District of Columbia Circuit held not merely that the Environmental Protection Agency, in issuing regulations regarding acceptable levels of air pollution, had overstepped the limits of its discretion under the Act but that Congress had delegated too much discretion to the EPA.[37] This is a really radical departure from the norms of judicial oversight of agency action because, as the Court declared in 1989, "[since 1935] we have upheld . . . *without deviation*, Congress' ability to delegate power under broad standards."[38] The D.C. Circuit Court, however, found the language of the Clean Air Act, cited earlier, that empowers the EPA to restrict certain air pollutants to a level "requisite to protect the public health" with an "adequate margin of safety"[39] amounted to an unconstitutional delegation of legislative power because it afforded essentially total discretion to the EPA:

> Here it is as though Congress commanded EPA to select "big guys," and EPA announced that it would evaluate candidates based on height and weight, but revealed no cut-off point. The announcement, though sensi-

ble in what it does say, is fatally incomplete. The reasonable person responds, "How tall? How heavy?"[40]

Delegation without any effective limit upon agency discretion, the court reasoned, granted the EPA the authority to pursue any policy it chose regarding air quality. This would afford the agency the same level of discretion as that possessed by Congress with respect to the issue of air quality. But Congress cannot cede all of its discretion over an issue to a regulatory agency because this would violate the provision of Article I, Section 1, that vests "all legislative powers" in Congress.

Whatever the wisdom of this holding, it is significant that it received hosannas from sources that can be trusted to take the Imperial Judiciary line whenever a court adopts a broad vision of civil rights or civil liberties. Thus, while review of the D.C. Circuit's decision was pending before the Supreme Court, the Washington Legal Foundation, in one of its polemical advertisements on the op-ed page of the *New York Times*, described the EPA case as one that poses the question of "who actually runs our government—elected leaders or unelected bureaucrats." This strikes me as completely missing (or misrepresenting) the point of the case. It is really about whether elected leaders have neglected their responsibility to legislate with sufficient specificity to ensure that unelected bureaucrats do not have unrestrained discretion. Nevertheless, the piece concludes by speculating darkly that, "[u]nless the Supreme Court puts EPA in its place, regulators will continue to hijack the legislative power that rightfully belongs in the hands of our elected representatives."[41] The *Wall Street Journal* similarly editorialized in favor of judicial assertiveness against the EPA because the agency "has gone far beyond what Congress intended" with respect to enforcing the Clean Air Act. (The editorial then argues that Congress "let" the EPA go astray by failing to provide the agency with "meaningful guidance" in the wording of the Act. It is not clear how one can conclude that EPA has violated congressional intent while at the same time asserting that Congress "[gave] the bureaucrats carte blanche.")[42]

One who has steeped himself in the writings of Imperial Judiciary theorists might at this point leap up to suggest that going to court to implore unelected federal judges to rein in unelected bureaucrats does not demonstrate fidelity to the thesis. One might point out that the true acolyte would lobby *Congress* to amend the relevant statutes to limit agency discretion in the manner desired. Indeed, if one were in a churlish mood, one might charge that the plaintiffs in these cases are acting just like liberal culture warriors by trying to achieve something through the courts that they cannot achieve through the political process.[43] However, being that churlishness is usually in bad taste, it might be best to just recognize that, with respect to these cases at least, many conservatives lack the doctrinaire's compulsion to be consistent. It would be in particular bad taste here because the Supreme Court, speaking through no less than Justice Scalia, upheld decades worth of precedent and reversed the D.C. Circuit's holding that Congress had unconstitutionally delegated its legislative authority to the EPA.[44]

Adjudicating Statutory Rights

In 1990, Cass Sunstein published *After the Rights Revolution*. Knowing that Sunstein is a prominent liberal law professor, one might expect from the title that the book is a love letter to the Warren Court and a lament for its demise. But, as Sunstein declares at the outset, the "rights revolution" to which his book is devoted is "the creation, by Congress and the President, of a set of legal rights departing in significant ways from those recognized at the time of the framing of the American Constitution."[45] The scope of this revolution has been vast:

> The catalogue is a long one, but the most prominent examples include rights to clean air and water; safe consumer products and workplaces; a social safety net including adequate food, medical care, and shelter; and freedom from public and private discrimination on the basis of race, sex, disability, and age. The rights revolution was presaged by the New Deal and by President Roosevelt's explicit proposal of a Second Bill of Rights in 1944; it culminated, at least thus far, in the extraordinary explosion of statutory rights in the 1960s and 1970s.[46]

In their focus upon the exercise of judicial review and upon the purportedly illegitimate "creation" of constitutional rights through its exercise, Imperial Judiciary theorists pay insufficient attention to this statutory rights revolution. But this revolution has, as in the case of the expansion of the administrative state itself, been accompanied by a conferral of vast power upon the judiciary by the popular branches of government. The power granted the judiciary in this regard is not only the role of adjudicator of the myriad lawsuits arising under consumer and environmental laws and antidiscrimination statues effecting employment, housing, and public accommodations. It is also the power arising from the fact that these statutes, as with the regulatory charter statutes already considered, are written in uniformly broad terms that are given specific meaning through judicial interpretation. In the case of these statutes, Alexander Hamilton's dictum that laws "are a dead letter without courts to expound their true meaning and operation" is true with a vengeance.[47]

Take Title VII of the Civil Rights Act of 1964. This enactment, along with state human rights laws, represents the primary exception to the American doctrine of employment at will, which allows private employers to hire and discharge employees with complete discretion. Title VII's central provision states as follows:

> It shall be an unlawful employment practice for an employer—
> (1) to fail or refuse to hire or to discharge any individual, or otherwise to discriminate against any individual with respect to his compensation terms, conditions, or privileges of employment, because of such individual's race, color, religion, sex, or national origin; or
> (2) to limit, segregate, or classify his employees or applicants for employment in any way which would deprive or tend to deprive any individual of employment opportunities or otherwise adversely affect his status as an employee, because of such individual's race, color, religion, sex, or national origin.[48]

As Benjamin Cardozo put it eighty years ago, cases that arise from a statute such as this "are cases where the creative element in the judicial process find its opportunity and power. . . . Here it is that the judge assumes the function of the lawgiver."[49] Or, as Sunstein says with respect to Title VII itself, the statute by its terms raises a multitude of questions to which judges supply answers that will be, at least in part, policy driven:

> The statutory prohibition of "discrimination" is uninformative about the role of discriminatory effects, the appropriate burdens of proof and production, and the mechanisms for filtering out discriminatory treatment. Judicial answers to these questions sometimes purport to be relatively mechanical responses to congressional commands, but in fact they amount to judge-made implementing devices responsive to the judges' own, necessarily value-laden views about how the statute is best understood. In light of the existence of textual gaps on the relevant questions,

this is inevitable. Much of the law of Title VII is a fully legitimate (because unavoidable) norm-ridden exercise of developing gap-filling rules.[50]

Consider some examples of Title VII "gap filling." Can an African American plaintiff bring a Title VII claim of race discrimination, even if he has no evidence of outright discriminatory intent on the part of an employer? Title VII as originally enacted is silent on the question. But the Supreme Court has held that the claim is viable if the plaintiff is able to present evidence that a particular practice of the employer, such as the use of written tests to obtain promotions, has resulted in largely cutting African Americans off from promotions. In *Griggs v. Duke Power Co.*, the Supreme Court said that such a suit based upon so-called disparate impact discrimination could succeed, but only if the test in question "cannot be shown to be related to job performance," that is, only if the employer fails to show that the test actually measures qualifications an employee needs to perform a certain job.[51]

Does Title VII's prohibition of discrimination based on "race" prohibit private employers from implementing affirmative action programs that encourage the hiring of racial minorities, even if such programs result in narrowed employment opportunities for the white majority? In *United Steelworkers of America v. Weber*,[52] the Court answered this critically important question in favor of the establishment of affirmative action programs. Its decision was based upon two rationales: (1) Title VII's manifest purpose was to aid racial minorities, especially African Americans, who had historically faced pervasive discrimination in employment; and (2) the statutory provision that mandates that Title VII shall not "be interpreted to *require* any employer . . . to grant preferential treatment" to any racial group was taken to be evidence that Congress wished to leave private employers the option to adopt affirmative action programs *voluntarily*.[53]

Finally, can a plaintiff succeed on a Title VII claim of sex discrimination if she has been subject to unwanted sexual advances from a superior even if her refusal to accede to these has not resulted in her demotion or firing? The Supreme Court said yes in *Meritor Savings Bank v. Vinson*, but only if the plaintiff can demonstrate that the harassment she suffered was "sufficiently severe or pervasive to alter the conditions of [her] employment and create an abusive working environment."[54]

But the crucial thing to remember about power conferred upon courts to adjudicate statutory rights is that, as with power conferred upon regulatory agencies through charter statutes, what Congress gives it can take away. Specifically, the legislative branch remains free to overturn any statutory interpretation it wishes by means of statutory amendment. And this is not merely a theoretical possibility. One study has demonstrated that between 1967 and 1990 Congress overturned a total of 121 Supreme Court decisions through statutory amendment.[55]

The most dramatic example of legislative override in recent years is surely the Civil Rights Act of 1991.[56] Much to the dismay of conservatives, this enactment overturned certain of the Rehnquist Court's restrictive readings of Title VII and other civil rights statutes. The statute was particularly directed at *Wards Cove Packing Co. v. Atonio*.[57] Here the Court altered the standards applicable to disparate impact cases set forth in *Griggs* by both heightening the quantum of proof a Title VII plaintiff need present with respect to establishing that a certain employment practice has resulted in restricted employment opportunities and by lowering the quantum of proof that an employer need present in order to establish that the challenged employment practice was utilized for sound business reasons.

The Civil Rights Act of 1991 explicitly declared the sense of Congress that "the decision of the Supreme Court in *Wards Cove Packing Co. v. Atonio* . . . has weakened the scope and effectiveness of Federal civil rights protections."[58] It went on to specifically define the respective burdens of proof for plaintiffs and defendants in a Title VII disparate impact case in a manner that essentially reinstated *Griggs*.[59]

In this light, consider that conservatives have long excoriated the Court's holding in *Weber* that Title VII does not prohibit private employers from implementing affirmative action programs. Bruce Fein, for example, has asserted that *Weber* is an example of "freestyle interpretation" in which the Court "ignored unambiguous non-discriminatory language and legislative history of the 1964 Civil Rights Act in favor of an interpretation authorizing racial discrimination against while male employees."[60] Even more caustically, Richard E. Morgan asserts that *Weber* effects a "pious fraud" upon Title VII in the service of "fashionable opinion among legal and civil rights elites."[61]

But Fein also admits that "[t]he traditional remedy when courts misinterpret statutes is for legislatures to pass new, superseding legislation."[62] Thus, the libertarian law professor Richard Epstein has written that, "[w]hile *Griggs* was something of a thunderbolt on the legal horizon when it first hit, it has now, more or less, been codified in the 1991 Civil Rights

Act."[63] The lesson is clear: if you want to defeat a statutory interpretation undertaken at the behest of "legal and civil rights elites," enlist Congress in your cause.

Reining in "the Imperial Judiciary"

The Constitution of course employs the principles of separation of powers and checks and balances as means of preventing the power of the federal government from degenerating into tyranny. James Madison sums this up in two sentences in *The Federalist*:

> It will not be denied that power is of an encroaching nature and that it ought to be effectually restrained from passing the limits assigned to it. After discriminating, therefore, in theory, the several classes of power. as they may in their nature be legislative, executive, or judiciary, the next and most difficult task is to provide some practical security for each, against the invasion of the others.[64]

Imperial Judiciary theorists believe that the Constitution is in terminal crisis because the courts have passed the limits assigned to them. But at least the formal constitutional securities meant to prevent this haven't been done away with yet. Some of these, however, while appearing quite substantial as abstract propositions, are simply off the table in contemporary political practice.

For example, Article III, Section 1, of the Constitution provides for the existence of only a single federal court—the U.S. Supreme Court—and "such inferior Courts as the Congress may from time to time ordain and establish." On the theory that the power to create implies the power to destroy, it is plausible to conclude from this provision that Congress might enact legislation to dismantle the federal court system, save for the constitutionally required Supreme Court. It is certainly not inconceivable that such legislation might be proposed. After all, segregationist members of Congress used to run on the platform that the Fourteen Amendment should be repealed. The court-dismantling legislation would have about an equal chance of success.

Only slightly more likely to succeed would be so-called jurisdiction-stripping measures, which forbid the courts from hearing certain specified classes of cases. The theory here is that (1) Congress may limit the appellate jurisdiction of the Supreme Court because Article III, Section 2, provides that it is subject to "such Exceptions, and under such Regulations as the Congress shall make" and (2) Congress may limit the jurisdiction of the lower federal courts because the power to create these courts implies a plenary power to determine the scope of their jurisdiction.

During the early days of the first Reagan administration, a flurry of jurisdiction-stripping bills were introduced in Congress regarding such issues as abortion, school prayer, and school desegregation. With the federal courts prevented from hearing cases on these issues, the thinking went, "[s]tate supreme courts would thus possess the final authority on the meaning of particular parts of the Constitution in their respective states."[65] However, in no small part because of their dubious constitutionality, none of these bills came close to passage.[66]

The procedure for amending the Constitution set forth in Article V has been more effective as a means to overturn particular court decisions. The Eleventh Amendment, added to the Constitution in 1798, forbids lawsuits in the federal courts "commenced or prosecuted against one of the United States by citizens of another State, or by citizens or subjects of any foreign state." This overturned the Supreme Court's opinion to the contrary in the 1793 case of *Chisholm v. Georgia*.[67] The Civil War Amendments—the Thirteenth, Fourteenth, and Fifteenth—all overturned the Court's holdings in *Dred Scott v. Sanford* to the effect that African Americans were not citizens of the United States and that the Constitution afforded them no rights.[68] The Sixteenth Amendment, enacted in 1913, gives Congress the power to pass income tax legislation, which had been declared unconstitutional by the Supreme Court in the 1895 case of *Pollack v. Farmers' Loan and Trust Co.*[69] Finally, the Twenty-Sixth Amendment, enacted in 1971, giving eighteen-year-olds the right to vote, overturned *Oregon v. Mitchell*, which held that Congress had no authority to enact legislation allowing eighteen-year-olds the right to vote in state and local elections.[70]

But, as we saw in the preceding chapter with respect to the efforts of prolife forces to overturn *Roe v. Wade*—and, lest it be forgot, as women's rights advocates found out when their immense effort to enact the Equal Rights Amendment failed—amending the Constitution is both a slow process and one very uncertain of success. It was *meant* to be because, as Madison put it, "extreme facility" of amendment "would render the Constitution too mutable."[71]

Under its general budgetary power, Congress can seek to influence the behavior of the federal courts by diminishing funds allocated for court operations and by declining to raise judicial salaries. (Under Article III, Section 1, Congress cannot reduce a federal judge's salary during her tenure on the bench.) There has in fact been successful congressional resistance in recent years to fulfilling the budgetary requests of the federal courts and to approving judicial salary increases. But this has not caused much more than grumbling among federal judges, most notably Chief Justice Rehnquist, who wrote a member of the Senate in April 2000 to complain that "in today's legal market a first-year associate in a law firm could make as much in salary as a federal judge."[72]

As we saw in chapter 2, Article I, Section 3, vests the House of Representatives with the power to impeach federal judges and provides that the Senate shall conduct trial proceedings to determine whether an impeached judge should be removed from the bench. No one questions the wisdom of impeachment and removal of manifestly corrupt federal judges. But, as we also noted earlier, Representative Tom DeLay of Texas caused a bit of a stir in 1991 by advocating the impeachment and removal of federal judges who have issued purportedly activist decisions with no basis in law. DeLay told the *New York Times* that he advocated "impeaching judges who consistently ignore their constitutional role, violate their oath of office, and breach the separation of powers."[73] Speaking to the *Washington Post*, DeLay was pugnacious: "The judges need to be intimidated. . . . They need to uphold the Constitution. If they don't behave, we're going to go after them in a big way."[74]

DeLay's proposal was welcomed by some of the more vociferous adherents of the Imperial Judiciary thesis. Somewhat cautiously, Terry Eastland declared that, "[i]n light of the modern judiciary's encroachment into areas once exclusively claimed by the elective branches, it would be odd to insist Congress should continue to rule out impeachment as a response to particular decisions."[75] Similarly, Dennis Shea, of the Heritage Foundation, opined that "[a] very careful and highly selective use of this authority would send a powerful message to the federal bench that its renegade days are over."[76] In spite of this welcoming rhetoric, however, DeLay's effort went nowhere.

We finally arrive at the manner in which judges are placed on the federal bench. According to Article II, Section 2, federal judges are appointed to the bench by the President "with the Advice and Consent of the Senate." Imperial Judiciary theorists, obsessed with the failure of the Supreme Court to overrule *Roe v. Wade* and to explicitly overturn various Warren Court precedents, tend to discount the potential for the strategic use of federal court appointments to decisively influence the course of jurisprudence. Imperial Judiciary commentary tends to focus upon the notion that, once on the bench, basking in luxurious life tenure, a federal judge is at any time prone to become an ideological free agent. This perception is quite at odds with the historical record.

The first mistake that Imperial Judiciary adherents make here is to assume that presidents always pursue ideological goals at the expense of all others when it comes to judicial appointments. But this is not the case, as is illustrated by the circumstances surrounding the appointments of two of the most liberal Justices in Supreme Court history, Earl Warren and William Brennan. The story is frequently told of how the retired Dwight Eisenhower quipped that the two biggest mistakes he made as chief executive were sitting on the Supreme Court. The fact is, however, that ideological factors played a decidedly secondary role in both of these appointments.

When it came to federal court appointments in general, Eisenhower displayed "a willingness to abandon ideological compatibility in the service of other goals."[77] Thus, the appointment of Warren, who was the governor of California at the time of his ascension to the Court, was made largely in appreciation of his considerable aid to Eisenhower in winning the Republican presidential nomination in 1952.[78] The appointment of Brennan was largely motivated by Eisenhower's desire to name a Catholic to the Court in hopes of securing the support of this crucial voting block in the 1956 election.[79]

Imperial Judiciary adherents also tend to forget that, even if a president is ideologically motivated in his judicial nominations, his nominees must still win Senate approval. Hence, "to the degree that a president is confronted with a Senate that is opposition controlled or generally hostile to his views, the president's freedom of choice in his appointments is accordingly restricted."[80] In fact, the comparative success rates for Supreme Court nominees when control of the White House and the Senate is in the hands of a single party and when control is divided are 87.9 percent and 54.5 percent.[81]

The best recent example of a Justice arriving on the Court as a compromise candidate after an ideological showdown between the Senate and the White House is Anthony Kennedy, who was Ronald Reagan's third choice to replace Justice Lewis Powell. In 1986, a Republican-controlled Senate approved the staunchly conservative Antonin Scalia by a vote of 98-0. But it was a very different story the following year when Reagan attempted to

replace Justice Powell, because control of the Senate had shifted to the Democrats in the 1986 midterm elections.

Reagan's first choice was, of course, Robert Bork, who was rejected by a
record margin in the Senate because of his presumed ideological extrem-
ism. Next up was the ardent conservative Douglas Ginsburg, Bork's colleague on the U.S. Court of Appeals for the D.C. Circuit. Ginsburg withdrew after his dalliances with marijuana were brought to light. Then came
Anthony Kennedy, who had earlier been eliminated from White House
consideration because of the perceived inconstancy of his conservatism.
Indeed, an internal White House memorandum devoted to Kennedy's
opinions as judge on the U.S. Court of Appeals for the Ninth Circuit
warned that his "easy acceptance of privacy rights as something guaranteed by the Constitution is really very distressing."[82] His nomination
therefore represented a bow to the reality that Kennedy was the most conservative nominee that the Senate would approve in the wake of the Bork
imbroglio.

The two terms of Bill Clinton's presidency demonstrate the truth of
several of the points just made. Clinton displayed little substantive interest
in staffing the federal judiciary, and, unlike the Bush and Reagan administrations that preceded him, Clinton employed no comprehensive ideological screening process for federal judicial nominees. He also faced a Senate
controlled by Republicans for six of his eight years in the White House,
and, as even the conservative Clint Bolick had to admit near the end of
Clinton's tenure, Clinton "has not expended significant capital on judicial
nominations."[83] Indeed, Clinton actually withdrew no fewer than nine
federal court nominees in the face of Republican complaints about their
purported extreme liberalism.[84]

Hence the frequent anger expressed by liberals over Clinton's lack of effort in this regard. The liberal law professor Herman Schwartz charged
that Clinton betrayed "a surprising indifference to trying to undo the
sharp tilt to the right of the Reagan and Bush administrations."[85] The unabashedly liberal judge Steven Reinhardt, of the U.S. Court of Appeals for
the Ninth Circuit, declared similarly that it was "one of the greatest disap-
pointments of Clinton's presidency that the judiciary was not one of his
concerns."[86]

But, in keeping with his rigid adherence to ideological "triangulation,"
Clinton never gave in to liberal demands with respect to staffing the federal courts. A comprehensive review of "Clinton's Judicial Legacy" in the
magazine *Judicature* bears this out. Clinton's two Supreme Court nomi-

nees, Ruth Bader Ginsburg and Stephen Breyer, "appear to have been carefully considered, although perhaps more for their ability to pass senatorial muster than for their ability to lead the Court in a more liberal direction."[87] His "typical" nominee to the federal appellate courts was "a moderate Democrat with conservative career experiences."[88] Finally, a thorough study of the opinions of federal district court judges appointed by Clinton shows them to be a shade more liberal than those appointed by Gerald Ford.[89]

It is also readily demonstrable that a president who *does* have clear ideological goals and who is successful in achieving Senate approval for his nominees is usually not displeased by the overall behavior of these nominees on the bench. The most dramatic illustration of the point in recent decades is surely the success of Nixon, Reagan, and Bush appointees in turning the federal courts decisively away from the vision of racial justice pursued by the Warren Court. Numerous elements of this vision have undergone contraction or outright reversal over the past several years. Thus, the Supreme Court has made it extremely difficult for public employers to undertake affirmative action programs as a means of enhancing the employment opportunities of minorities.[90] The Court has also repeatedly invalidated electoral districts, with large minority populations, created to encourage the election of minority candidates. These are said to amount to an expression of racism: "When the State assigns voters on the basis of race, it engages in the offensive and demeaning assumption that voters of a particular race, because of their race, 'think alike, share the same political interests, and will prefer the same candidates at the polls.'"[91]

But no element of the Warren Court's racial justice jurisprudence has been more effectively dismantled than that of court-enforced efforts to desegregate public schools. This is directly attributable to the fact that a series of Republican White House administrations were radically opposed to these efforts and were determined to use judicial appointments as the primary means of turning the tide. Their success has been tremendous.

To understand how tremendous, let's return to 1968. In that year, after more than a decade of Supreme Court torpor in the face of segregationist resistance to the *Brown* decision, the Court issued its opinion in *Green v. New Kent County.*[92] In *Green*, the Court declared unconstitutional a soidisant "freedom of choice" method of assigning students to schools within a county school district. These plans allowed students regardless of race to request to attend any school they chose. What this meant in practice was that the schools remained as segregated as ever, because no whites requested to attend schools in African American residential areas and few African Americans wished to face the social scorn or worse that would face them should they ask to attend a white school.

The Court declared that merely giving up the form of segregating students according to race while allowing the reality of segregation to continue was not sufficient to accord with what Jeffrey Rosen has called "the central premise of the *Brown* decision—that integrated public schools are the most important institution in a pluralistic society."[93] Therefore, the Court declared, school districts have "the affirmative duty to take whatever steps might be necessary to convert to a [desegregated school] system in which racial discrimination would be eliminated root and branch. . . . The burden on the school board today is to come forward with a plan that promises realistically to work, and promises realistically to work *now*."[94]

Three years later, in *Swann v. Charlotte-Mecklenburg Board of Education*,[95] the Supreme Court explicitly upheld the constitutionality of desegregation plans that use racial assignment for the purpose of achieving integration. As Owen Fiss describes it, the Court in *Swann* emphasized that "integration is in such a constitutionally favored position that states will be denied the power to enact laws restricting the method of achieving that goal—i.e., laws forbidding the local boards to make assignments for that end."[96] Further, and most important in understanding the political firestorm that the case engendered, the Court declared that, when making student assignments, a school board *had* to favor the goal of integration over consideration of the geographic proximity of a particular school to a student's home. In other words, the prospect that rapid integration would require large numbers of students to be assigned to schools other than those closest to home was of no constitutional significance. Because "desegregation plans cannot be limited to the walk-in school," those students would have to be bused, and *Swann* empowered federal courts overseeing desegregation plans to order busing.[97] Two years later, in *Keyes v. District No. 1, Denver, Colorado*,[98] the Court extended *Swann* to northern and western states, holding that "school districts in states with no recent history of de jure segregation were nonetheless obligated to desegregate if the districts themselves had engaged in any type of discriminatory behavior."[99]

I think that anyone who lived in the United States during the time these cases were decided will have memories of the anger and civil unrest brought about by court-ordered busing of schoolchildren for the purpose of achieving integration. To adherents of the Imperial Judiciary thesis, the experience was, at least until *Roe v. Wade* had been around for a while, the quintessential example of the damage wrought by an out-of-control judiciary. In his 1975 article "Towards an Imperial Judiciary?," Nathan Glazer refers repeatedly to the desegregation decisions as supporting his conclusion that "the [Supreme] Court, and the subordinate courts, are now seen as forces of nature, difficult to predict and impossible to control."[100] Lino Graglia devoted an extraordinarily vituperative book to the subject. Here is a representative sample:

> [T]he very principle that best and most easily justifies *Brown's* prohibition of segregation—that all racial discrimination by government is prohibited—presented perhaps the greatest obstacle to justification of the Court's decisions, beginning with *Green*. . . . The difficulty was so great that the Court has never openly admitted the new requirement or attempted to justify compulsory integration on its own merits. The Court has, instead, attempted to disguise its new requirement as a continuation and enforcement of the old prohibition. This impossible task has required it to resort to methods—unfair and inaccurate statements of fact, patently fallacious reasoning, and perversion of the 1964 Civil Rights Act—that would be considered scandalous in any other institution or official of American government.[101]

But unpopular Supreme Court jurisprudential trends have political consequences. Indeed, as the political scientist Walter Dean Burnham has written, throughout our history "[o]ne of the most important indicators of critical realignment" in American politics "is the eruption of political controversy centering on the Supreme Court."[102] Thus, whatever the wisdom of the desegregation decisions, there is no question that, beginning with the 1968 presidential election, opposition to busing became a central element of the Republican Party's very potent appeal. Thomas Byrne Edsall has described the eventual result:

> [The busing issue] fell like an axe through the Democratic Party, severing long-standing connections and creating a new set of troubled alliances: white, blue-collar northerners with southerners against blacks and upper-middle class liberals. A dwindling band of northern liberals found that they were defending a policy with no real constituency: poll after poll found decisive white opposition to busing, and only lukewarm support in the black community, which was generally split down the middle on the issue.[103]

Richard Nixon did not make busing a core issue of his 1968 campaign. Still, he made no bones about where he stood. "I believe," he said then, "that *Brown* was a correct decision, but on the other hand, while that decision . . . said that we should not have segregation, when you go beyond that and say that it is the responsibility of the federal government and the federal courts to, in effect, act as local school districts . . . then I think we are going too far."[104] Further, as noted earlier, opposition to the Warren Court was a constant theme of Nixon's 1968 run, leading him to promise to name only "strict constructionist" judges to the federal courts.

In 1972, the busing issue was the centerpiece of Nixon's domestic program. In March 1972, "in a nationwide television and radio address, Nixon boldly called on Congress to impose a 'moratorium' on the federal courts to prevent them from ordering any new busing to achieve racial balance."[105] Soon after this, he decided to press Congress to consider an amendment to the Constitution to prohibit busing. He asserted that "[c]ross-city and cross-county busing is wrong; it is harmful to education; it does not unite races and communities; . . . If the Congress continues to refuse to act on the proposal I have made to solve this problem—moratorium on all busing orders—we will have no choice but to seek a constitutional amendment."[106]

Nixon was able to name four Justices to the Supreme Court in spite of a Senate controlled by Democrats throughout his White House tenure. (The Senate rejected two of his nominees—Clement Haynsworth and Harold Carswell—thereby thwarting Nixon's campaign promise that he would put a Justice from the Deep South on the Court.) Even though, much to Nixon's distress, two of these four Justices—Warren Burger and Harry Blackmun—joined the Court's unanimous opinion in *Swann*, these two, when joined by Lewis Powell and William Rehnquist, moved quickly to direct the Court's school desegregation jurisprudence to a radically different course.

In *Milliken v. Bradley*,[107] decided in 1974, the Court considered a federal district judge's order that the public schools of Detroit be integrated. The problem with achieving this goal was that, because of the migration of whites from Detroit to the surrounding suburbs, a movement that had been going on for years but that had gained particular force after Detroit's 1967 race riots, there were few white students left in Detroit's public schools. As a result, the district judge "ordered a metropolitan-area-wide desegregation remedy, encompassing fifty-three suburban school districts, in order to desegregate Detroit schools."[108]

In a 5-4 decision, with the four Nixon Justices voting with Justice Potter Stewart, the Court overturned this plan. It held that a district court could not order desegregation *across* school districts in the absence of evidence that school district lines had been drawn with discriminatory intent or that the suburban school districts were engaging in discriminatory conduct with respect to the racial composition of their *own* schools. In other words, the federal courts were largely without authority to remedy the consequences of "white flight" from America's large cities. As Davison Douglas described in 1997, the results have been dramatic:

> More than 80 percent of the nation's minority students live in metropolitan areas, which, in most instances, are divided into majority-black inner-city school districts and majority-white suburban school districts. In the nation's largest cities, fifteen of every sixteen black and Latino students are in schools where most of the students are non-white. The four states with the most extreme school segregation—Illinois, Michigan, New York, and New Jersey—each contain large metropolitan areas where majority-black urban school districts are cut off from neighboring majority-white suburban school districts. *No court decision has influenced patterns of racial isolation in America's schools in more than* Milliken.[109]

In the 1980 presidential election, which ended the Carter interregnum, Ronald Reagan ran on a Republican Party platform that "condemn[ed] the forced busing of school children to achieve arbitrary racial quotas . . . which has been a prescription for disaster."[110] The Supreme Court stayed out of the busing controversy in the 1980s, declining to review numerous decisions issued by an increasingly conservative federal judiciary that allowed school districts to abandon school desegregation plans.[111] When the Court revisited the issue in the 1990s, the result, supported by all of the Reagan and Bush Justices except for Justice Souter, was a trio of cases that greatly facilitated the dissolution of desegregation orders. In *Board of Education of Oklahoma City Public Schools v. Dowell*, the Court held that a district court could dissolve a desegregation plan if it found that "the Board had complied in good faith with the desegregation decree since it was entered, and whether the vestiges of past discrimination had been eliminated to the extent practicable."[112] This is a lenient standard that gives district courts considerable capacity for absolving school boards of not having fulfilled the goals of a desegregation plan as originally written.[113] In *Freeman v. Pitts*, the Court gave federal district courts the capacity to dissolve desegregation orders "in incremental stages before full compliance has been achieved in every area of school operations."[114] Finally, in *Missouri v. Jenkins*,[115] the Court reversed a federal district judge's desegregation order that sought to attract suburban whites to the public schools of Kansas City by ordering the establishment of "magnet schools" that would offer superior facilities and specialized curriculums. As in *Milliken*, the Court here denied the district court's power to attempt to reverse the effects of "white flight." Taken together, Gary Orfield argues, this trio of cases "view[s] racial integration not as a goal that segregated districts should strive to attain, but as a merely temporary punishment for historic violations, an imposition to be lifted after a few years."[116]

The dissolution of federal court desegregation orders continues apace. Here are the results:

> In the 1996–97 school year, the average white public school student attended a school that was more than 80 percent white. Meanwhile, 69 percent of black students were attending a school defined as majority-minority—a school whose nonwhite population ranges from 50 percent to 100 percent of the student body. And 35 percent of black students were attending a school with a student body that was overwhelmingly minority—defined as 90 percent to 100 percent—a figure not seen since the mid-1970s.[117]

The court decisions that have made statistics like this possible, Gary Orfield argues, "are the natural product of five national administrations elected on anticivil rights platforms."[118] This is a bit strong, but the course of school desegregation jurisprudence over the course of the past forty years is a wonderful affirmation of Terri Jennings Peretti's assertion that, "[g]iven turnover on the Court and a membership that has passed the partisan and ideological litmus test applied by elected officials, it can concluded that the values of the Justices mirror and certainly lie within the range of those values currently or recently receiving official representation in other branches of government."[119]

How Many Divisions Do the Courts Have?

It was noted earlier that the Supreme Court's 1968 decision in *Green v. New Kent County*, in which the Court demanded that a school district take immediate steps toward integration, was issued after years of virtual inaction by the Court on the issue of school desegregation. What had happened during the time since the *Brown* decision in 1954?

A year after *Brown*, in the so-called *Brown II* decision, the Court set forth the manner in which desegregation was to be implemented.[120] It was here that the Court famously mandated that desegregation take place with "all deliberate speed."[121] Less famously, however, *Brown II* provided next to no specific details as to how the Court expected local school districts to go about desegregating themselves. This was surely the result of the Court's consciousness of its extraordinarily perilous position with respect to ending segregation. Congress and the Eisenhower administration were, at best, very reluctant to aid in the implementation of *Brown*, and southern politicians were prepared to use all available means, including violence, to block its implementation. This, says Lucas Powe, explains the Court's mushy stance in *Brown II*:

> The Court's solution here—because no other solution presented itself—was placing southerners in charge of how *Brown* was implemented. First, the local school board would devise a plan; then the local federal judge would approve or reject that plan. The Court was placing a lot of faith in the southern establishment—if for no other reason than there appeared nowhere else to turn.[122]

This faith, if indeed it existed, was misplaced. Southern resistance to *Brown* was spectacularly successful, and the Court itself retreated in its wake. From 1955 through 1964, Gerald Rosenberg notes, "the Court issued only three full opinions in the area of segregation of elementary and secondary schools. It routinely refused to hear cases or curtly affirmed or reversed lower court decisions."[123] The result was a mockery of the notion of "all deliberate speed":

> The statistics from the Southern states are truly amazing. For ten years, 1954–64, virtually *nothing happened*. Ten years after *Brown* only 1.2 percent of black schoolchildren in the South attended school with whites. Excluding Texas and Tennessee, the percent drops to less than one-half of 1 percent (.48 percent). Despite the unanimity and forcefulness of the *Brown* opinion, . . . its decree was flagrantly disobeyed. After ten years of Court-ordered desegregation, in the eleven Southern states barely one out of every 100 black children attended school with whites.[124]

By 1964, however, the White House and Congress had both moved decisively in the direction of enforcing the civil rights of African Americans. Title VI of the Civil Rights Act of 1964 provided that no recipient of federal funds could practice discrimination based on race.[125] Faced with the cutoff of federal funds for education, which were burgeoning in the years of Lyndon Johnson's Great Society, segregated school districts began to take their first serious steps toward reform. Indeed, "the percentage of black children attending desegregated schools in the South increased tenfold, from 2 to 20 percent, between 1964 and 1968."[126] It was in this context that *Green* was decided.

Imperial Judiciary theorists do not pay much attention to the decade-long resistance to *Brown*, presumably because it clashes so abruptly with their perspective.[127] Nonetheless, outright defiance of the Supreme Court's constitutional decisions has a long history in American politics.

Two of the most notorious examples both involve Georgia. Soon after the Republic began, the Court decided *Chisholm v. Georgia*, which held that the State of Georgia could be sued in federal court by a citizen of another state.[128] The Georgia legislature passed a law in response that declared that anyone who attempted to enforce the Supreme Court's ruling would be "guilty of a felony and shall suffer death, without benefit of clergy, by being hanged."[129] In 1830, the Court issued an order staying the death sentence of a Cherokee Indian who had been prosecuted by Georgia pursuant to a law of dubious constitutionality that gave the state's courts jurisdiction over lands that the Cherokee tribe held pursuant to a treaty with the federal government. Georgia carried out the execution in direct defiance of the Court.[130]

Barry Friedman argues that, while an extreme case, the execution was nevertheless "emblematic of the times. In several notable instances when called to the bar of the Court, states simply failed to appear or denied jurisdiction."[131] Nor is resistance to federal court decisions a thing of the dark past. In June 2000, the Supreme Court held, in *Santa Fe Independent School District v. Doe*, that the Santa Fe, Texas, school district had violated the First Amendment by allowing a purportedly student-initiated prayer to be read over the public address system at school football games.[132] Within weeks, as the new high school football season approached, the *New York Times* reported that, "throughout [the South], where the line between religion and high school football has never been particularly well marked, grass-roots efforts are under way to restore prayer to its traditional position just before the kick-off."[133] (I would not expect that Congress will anytime soon pass a statute cutting off federal funds to any school district that defies the Court's ruling.)

But a weapon far less crude than outright resistance can also be used to roll back judicial power in cases involving constitutional rights. This weapon is not the ability of the popular branches to force certain interpretations of the Constitution upon the courts but their capacity to limit the scope of permissible remedies that a court may order for violations of constitutional rights. A successful target in this regard has been the power of courts to order relief in cases brought by prison inmates who allege that a correctional facility is being operated in a manner that violates the Eighth Amendment's prohibition on "cruel and unusual punishments."

For more than thirty years, an extensive campaign of prison reform has been carried out, primarily through the federal courts, and particularly with regard to correctional institutions in the South and in the West. These cases are the quintessential example of what the Harvard law professor Abram Chayes famously termed "a new model of civil litigation" in which trial court judges "increasingly become the creator and manager of complex forms of ongoing relief."[134]

The story is told brilliantly by Malcolm Feeley and Edward Rubin in their book *Judicial Policy Making and the Modern State*, where they forthrightly describe prison reform litigation as "our nation's most aggressive campaign of judicial policy making."[135] They argue persuasively, however, that federal judges in these cases did not simply use the Eighth Amendment's four-word prohibition as a means to implement their own ideas as to how prisons should be run. Rather, they show that, by the mid-1960s, professional organizations such as the American Correctional Association and the U.S. Bureau of Prisons had developed detailed standards for the operation of correctional institutions and that "federal judges adopted this agenda as the basis for their remedial orders" in the prison cases.[136]

Although Feeley and Rubin generally applaud the changes wrought by these cases, they do not assert that federal judges had either the desire or the ability to transform America's prisons into models of how correctional facilities should be operated. They particularly note that the vast increase in America's prison population, which was considered in chapter 4, has to a significant degree overwhelmed the changes that federal judges have ordered:

> Cells designed for one person now house two or three, school rooms and
> gymnasiums have been converted into dormitories, tent camps and trailer

parks for inmates have sprouted in the prison yard, training and rehabilitation programs have been either overwhelmed with participants or restricted to small fractions of eligible inmates, and prison officials have been compelled to shift from management to coping strategies.[137]

Feeley and Rubin also record that a more conservative Supreme Court "has produced a number of decisions that decrease the scope of the specific constitutional guarantees that federal courts had previously established. Prisoners' rights of free speech, due process, legal access, and free exercise of religion have all been scaled back."[138]

But the legislative contribution to the rollback of prison reform through litigation in the federal courts has been at least as significant. In 1996, Congress enacted the Prison Legal Reform Act (PLRA), which, in the words of two conservative commentators, in an article entitled "How to Put Lawmakers, Not Courts, Back in Charge," "revolutionizes the administration of state and municipal prisons nationwide."[139]

For our purposes, the PLRA makes two procedural changes of crucial significance in the manner in which prison litigation in the federal courts is conducted. First, it precisely limits the scope and duration of relief that federal judges may order to correct violations of constitutional rights in state prison facilities:

> Preliminary injunctive relief must be narrowly drawn, extend no further than necessary to correct the harm the court find requires preliminary relief, and be the least intrusive means necessary to correct that harm. The court shall give substantial weight to any adverse impact on public safety or the operation of a criminal justice system caused by the preliminary relief and shall respect [state officials and the operation of state law] in tailoring any preliminary relief. Preliminary injunctive relief shall automatically expire on the date that is ninety days after its entry, unless the court makes [a specific finding that prison facilities remain in violation of the original injunctive order].[140]

Second, in an effort to limit the capacity of federal courts to supervise prison facilities for an indefinite period, the PLRA allows state officials to seek termination of any order of injunctive relief two years after it has been entered. The court *must* terminate its order unless "it makes written findings based on the record that prospective relief remains necessary to correct a current and ongoing violation of the federal right, extends no further than necessary to correct the violation of the federal right, and is the least intrusive means necessary to correct the violation of the federal right."[141]

The PLRA has been quite successful. First, even though it mandates specific limitations upon the capacity of the federal courts to redress violations of constitutional rights, the courts have without significant exception upheld its constitutionality. Indeed, as of this writing, all eight of the federal circuit courts of appeal that have considered the termination provisions of the PLRA have upheld their constitutionality.[142] More important, the statute is achieving its intended results. As the *New York Times* reported early in 2000, "[s]everal states, including Washington, Florida, and Arkansas, have already ended court supervision of parts of their prison systems. . . . In Alabama, the attorney general has successfully sued to dismiss twenty-two jail cases since 1996."[143]

Needless to say, conservatives have heralded the PLRA, seeing it as a model for rolling back federal court power in other areas of constitutional litigation. In a typical encomium, Spencer Abraham, a Republican senator from Michigan, called the PLRA "the crucial first step toward restoring limits on judicial power and taking the judicial activists out of the game."[144] For our purposes, however, the point is that the PLRA demonstrates that the powers of the federal courts are in yet another way limited. As Feeley and Rubin put it, "Congress' ability to take action of this sort demonstrates that the courts are not nearly so imperial, or unstoppable, as their critics have claimed, even when grounding their authority on the Constitution."[145]

A Note on Foreign and Military Matters

For more than half a century, no nation has played a more important role in world affairs than the United States. It is uncontroversial to declare that a great portion of the federal government's money, personnel, and intellectual effort is devoted to questions of diplomacy and war. Simply stated, the role of the judiciary in all of this is negligible. The Supreme Court stated the basic principle in this regard as early as 1918:

> The conduct of foreign relations of our government is committed by the Constitution to the executive and legislative—"the political"—departments of the government, and the propriety of what may be done in the

exercise of this political power is not subject to judicial inquiry or decision.[146]

Consider first the judicial branch's stance toward the armed forces' treatment of its personnel. The Supreme Court once held famously that "children do not shed their constitutional rights . . . at the schoolhouse gate."[147]
The Court has consistently held that pretty much the opposite is true for
recruits entering the military base. My favorite example is *Goldman v.
Weinberger*, in which the Court considered a U.S. Air Force policy that
mandated that headgear could not be worn indoors "except by armed security police in the performance of their duties."[148] The Court held that
this policy did not result in a denial of freedom of religion when applied
to an Air Force clinical psychologist, who was also an ordained Orthodox
rabbi, who claimed a right to wear a yarmulke while on duty. Such a holding would be virtually unthinkable had the case involved a civilian agency
of the government. However, the Court declared, the military is different:

> [W]hen evaluating whether military needs justify a particular restriction
> on religiously motivated conduct, courts must give great deference to the
> professional judgment of military authorities concerning the relative im-
> portance of a particular military interest. . . . Not only are courts ill
> equipped to determine the impact upon discipline that any particular in-
> trusion upon military authority might have, but the military authorities
> have been charged by the executive and legislative branches with carrying
> out our nation's military policy. *Judicial deference is at its apogee* when leg-
> islative action under the congressional authority to raise and support
> armies and make rules and regulations for their governance is
> challenged.[149]

This passage pretty much sums up the stance of the courts with respect to
military affairs generally. It is therefore wholly unsurprising that the most
controversial military personnel policy of recent years—the so-called
don't ask, don't tell approach with regard to homosexual soldiers—has
been upheld by each of the four federal circuit courts of appeal that has
considered it.[150] This clearly does some damage to the notion that federal
judges have enlisted in "the culture wars" on the side of the left.

The story is much the same with respect to the conduct of foreign affairs. Article III, Section 2, does give the federal courts jurisdiction over
"all Cases affecting Ambassadors, . . . Controversies to which the United

States shall be a Party; . . . and [Controversies] between a State, or the Citizens thereof, and foreign States, Citizens or Subjects." Thus, the federal courts are certainly no strangers to cases involving foreign litigants and international transactions. But, in any matter touching the federal government's conduct of foreign policy, almost total judicial deference is the rule. The point is well summed up in a Supreme Court opinion of 1948:

> [T]he very nature of executive decisions as to foreign policy is political, not judicial. Such decisions . . . are delicate, complex and involve large elements of prophecy. . . . They are decisions of a kind for which the judiciary has neither aptitude, facilities nor responsibility.[151]

Interestingly, however, if one were to compose a list of ways in which contemporary political practice clashes—not merely differs but actually clashes—with the intent of the framers of the Constitution, near the top of the list would certainly be the manner in which the United States commits its troops to violent conflict. Article I, Section 8, gives Congress the power "To declare War." As John Hart Ely has said, "the 'original understanding' of the [Constitution's] framers and ratifiers can be obscure to the point of inscrutability. Often this is true. In this case, however, it isn't."[152]

There is a good deal of evidence to the effect that the framers did not wish to prevent the president—who is made "Commander in Chief of the Army and Navy of the United States" in Article II, Section 2—from repelling sudden attacks upon the territory of the United States or upon American soldiers or citizens abroad. Beyond this, however, they were quite emphatic that the solemn and awful decision to commit troops to conflict for an indefinite period of time must rest with the Congress, the branch of the federal government most representative of the people. Indeed, it was a commonplace among the framers that one of the surest paths to tyranny was to grant the executive the sole power of deciding to go to war. The King of England, declared Blackstone, has "the sole prerogative of making war and peace."[153] America, however, was to work on a different principle. Here is Alexander Hamilton, himself perhaps the primary voice among the framers in favor of a powerful executive, speaking in *The Federalist*:

> The President is to be commander-in-chief of the army and navy of the United States. In this respect his authority would be nominally the same

with that of the King of Great Britain, but in substance much inferior to it. It would amount to nothing more than the supreme command and direction of the military and naval forces, as first general and admiral of the Confederacy; while that of the British king extends to the *declaring* of war and to the *raising* and *regulating* of fleets and armies—all which, by the Constitution under consideration, would appertain to the legislature.[154]

And here is James Wilson speaking in the Pennsylvania ratifying convention:

> This system will not hurry us into war; it is calculated to guard against it. It will not be in the power of a single man, or a single body of men, to involve us in such distress; for the important power of declaring war is vested in the legislature at large; . . . from his circumstance we may draw a certain conclusion that nothing but our national interest can draw us into war.[155]

The point is summed up perfectly by James Madison in a letter written in 1798: "The constitution supposes, what the History of all Govts. demonstrates, that the Ex. is the branch of power most interested in war, & most prone to it. It has accordingly with studied care, vested the question of war in the Legisl."[156]

We have moved from this to the boast of President George H. W. Bush to the effect that "I didn't have to get permission from some old goat in the United States Congress to kick Saddam Hussein out of Kuwait."[157] Thus can Laurence Tribe conclude that, "[c]ontrary to the Constitution's text, structure, and history, the Executive has, since the advent of the Cold War, made decisions to go to war without much congressional participation and, even when Congress has participated, it has often done so without much exercise of independent judgment."[158]

One would think that originalists would be outraged. But here is Robert Bork in an address delivered in 1990:

> [T]here is the desire of Congress to make or to invoke law with respect to the use of American troops abroad. No nation is more devoted to the rule of law than is the United States, but there are areas of life, and the international use of armed force seems to be one of them, in which the entire notion of law . . . is out of place. The pretense that there is such law, and that it has been constantly violated, has debilitating effects upon our foreign

policy, on the vigor of the presidency, and the rightful place of the president in our system of government.[159]

One can argue that contemporary world conditions, which allow a band of fanatics to inflict great harm upon a nation's citizenry by means of hijacking passenger jets and slamming them into buildings, requires that the president be afforded great leeway in committing American forces to combat.[160] One cannot, however, argue that Article I, Section 8, is a "pretense."

The Federal Sentencing Guidelines

In their excellent book on criminal sentencing in the federal courts, Kate Stith and Jose Cabranes note that, "[f]or almost two centuries, trial judges in the American federal system bore much of the burden—and at times all of the burden—of achieving a just sentence within the maxima set by a statute."[161] There is no question that such broad discretion brought about a great deal of disparity in severity of sentences handed out to those convicted in federal court. This has been noted in a recent address by Justice Breyer:

> In a well-known 1974 Second Circuit "experiment," fifty district court judges each sentenced twenty offenders on the basis of the same set of presentence reports. And the results diverged dramatically. Where one judge sentenced a defendant to three years, another judge chose twenty years; where one imposed a suspended sentence for an immigration crime, another imposed a three-year prison term. The Department of Justice, later repeating the experiment with 208 federal judges, found them unanimous about whether to impose a prison term in only three of sixteen hypothetical cases. It also found serious disparity as to length. For example, while the judges sentencing one particular hypothetical fraud defendant imposed a 1.1-year prison term on average, one judge gave the same defendant fifteen years.[162]

In response to this situation, a reform effort was launched by federal legislators who spanned the political spectrum from tough-on-crime conservatives to civil libertarians. In 1984, they enacted a bill establishing the Federal Sentencing Commission and charged it with composing a comprehensive set of regulations to guide federal judges in the imposition of criminal sentences. The Commission, with Justice Breyer as one of its main drafters, produced the Federal Sentencing Guidelines. Stith and Cabranes provide a brief description of how the Guidelines determine a sentence:

> The centerpiece of the Guidelines is a 258-box grid that the Commission calls the Sentencing Table. . . . The horizontal axis of this grid, entitled "Criminal History Category," adjusts severity on the basis of the offender's past criminal record. The vertical axis, entitled "Offense Level," reflects a base severity score for the crime committed, adjusted for those character-istics of the defendant's criminal behavior that the Sentencing Commis-sion has deemed relevant to sentencing. The Guidelines, through a com-plex set of rules requiring significant expertise to apply, instruct the sen-tencing judge on how to calculate each of these factors. The box at which the defendant's Criminal History Category and Offense Level intersect then determines the range within which the judge may sentence the de-fendant.[163]

The Federal Sentencing Guidelines were implemented in the federal courts in November 1987. "The purpose of the new regime," Stith and Cabranes argue, "was to divest the independent federal judiciary of the power to de-termine criminal sentences, . . . to strip them of authority to determine the purposes of criminal sentencing, the factors relevant to sentencing, and the proper type and range of punishment in most cases."[164] In this quest, the Guidelines have been quite successful:

> With a far more limited role, the federal trial judge in today's sentencing ritual has little or no opportunity to consider the overall culpability of the defendant before him. The Guidelines themselves determine not only which factors are relevant (and irrelevant) to criminal punishment, but also, in most circumstances, the precise quantitative relevance of each factor.
> . . . The judge's prescribed role is largely limited to factual determina-tions and rudimentary arithmetic operations.[165]

The Guidelines are widely despised among federal judges, who see them as sacrificing individual justice in sentencing to the tyranny of a 258-box grid. A 1992 poll of federal judges found that 86 percent of 640 respon-dents thought that the Guidelines should be amended to give more discretion to the sentencing judge, while slightly more than half favored getting rid of them altogether.[166] More than one federal judge has been bold enough to excoriate the Guidelines publicly. In 2001, for example, a federal district court judge in Massachusetts, who had the discretion to decline to hear criminal cases because of his "senior status," announced that he would do so because he could no longer tolerate implementing the Guidelines:

> In the long tradition of the common law, it was the judge, the neutral arbiter, who possessed the authority to impose sentences which he deemed just within the broad perimeters established by the legislature. Under the Sentencing Commission Guidelines the power to impose a sentence has been virtually transferred from the court to the government, which, as the prosecuting authority, is an interested party to the case. This transfer constitutes an erosion of judicial power and a breach in the wall of the doctrine of the separation of powers.
> . . . There is a maxim of the law that no party can be a judge in his own case. That maxim is violated by the Sentencing Commission Guidelines.[167]

But, in spite of the Imperial Judiciary's opposition, more than forty thousand individuals per year convicted of crimes in federal court are sentenced pursuant to them.[168]

A Note on State Judiciaries

In his book *How Courts Govern America*, Richard Neely describes his decision in 1972 to seek election to a seat on the Supreme Court of West Virginia. One of West Virginia's U.S. senators had indicated that he was going to retire, and Neely, the grandson of a longtime senator from the state, decided to enter the race for his seat. Eventually, however, the incumbent senator changed his mind:

> It was at that point . . . that I decided it was better to be a winning state supreme court justice than a losing United States senator, so I took my small organization and the statewide name recognition I had bought with the campaign contributions into a lower stakes game which I could win. I outspent my opponents ten to one and won the primary election for

judge by thirty-five thousand votes and the general election by fifty-four thousand. The outcome had nothing to do with my legal ability, but with inherited name recognition, the enthusiasm and charm of youth, and money—most of it either mine or my father's.[169]

What is interesting about this passage is Neely's attitude toward making the switch to seeking a judgeship. One senses that he feels that he might as well have sought a seat on a city council or in the state legislature. However, the Imperial Judiciary thesis notwithstanding, we still tend to believe that there are functional differences between judges on the one hand and legislators on the other. The latter make promises as to policy in order to get elected and represent constituents by attempting to pass (or block) statutes. Judges, however, decide lawsuits, and we expect that they will do so from a perspective of impartiality that does not seek to advance anyone's policy preferences, especially those of the judge.

To use an imperfect analogy from sports, legislators are players and judges are referees. However, as Justice John Paul Stevens puts it, subjecting judges to popular election "is comparable to allowing football fans to elect the referees."[170] This may yield popular referees, but not necessarily impartial ones. Consider the following campaign pitch taken from the 1982 election for the Ohio Supreme Court:

> Thirty million dollars—that's what the Democratic Supreme Court saved us in just one year by saying no to utility rate hikes. This has been the people's court. Let's keep it that way. Vote Sweeney, Locher, and Celebrezze. . . . A quarter-century of judicial experience, insisting on tough safety standards for the worker, holding the line on unfair taxes, backing our police to fight crime. Let's keep the people's court Democratic.[171]

I have no knowledge that Sweeney, Locher, and Celebrezze were not judges of the highest ability and integrity, but I might think differently were I a lawyer for a utility company.

Lawrence Friedman declares that the "idea of electing judges strikes Europeans as very peculiar—as odd as if we elected doctors or policemen or government chemists."[172] Yet the practice has deep roots in our political culture. In *The Federalist*, Alexander Hamilton warns against popular election of judges because it would engender "too great a disposition to consult popularity to justify a reliance that nothing would be consulted [by judges] but the Constitution and the laws" in deciding cases.[173] On the other hand, Thomas Jefferson, Hamilton's great adversary, took the opposite view: "That there should be public functionaries independent of the nation . . . is a solecism in a republic, of the first order of absurdity and inconsistency."[174] As we saw in chapter 3, it was Jefferson's view that won out in the states.

Today, some 87 percent of state judges, at both the trial and the appellate levels, face some form of election in order to attain and/or remain on the bench.[175] The types of election they face vary widely among partisan races, nonpartisan ones, and "retention elections," where a judge does not run against another candidate but runs upon the question of whether she should remain on the bench after the completion of a fixed term. Whatever the mode of election, however, there is increasing reason to agree with Paul Carrington's assertion that, "[i]n whatever form, elections tend to empower persons or groups outside the judiciary to reward or to intimidate judges for their decisions, and thus to bend the administration of the law."[176]

As the political scientist Anthony Champagne has described, most judicial elections used to be polite affairs:

> The old-style judicial campaign was a low-budget affair where the judicial candidate spoke to any group willing to hear a dull speech about improving the judiciary or about judicial qualifications. There were numerous hands to shake, bar and newspaper endorsements to obtain, and that was about it. . . . If the candidate was an incumbent who had avoided scandal or attack for a highly visible, controversial decision, victory was likely. Indeed, such a candidate would not likely have an opponent. . . . For an open seat, if the judicial candidate had an attractive name, a popular political party affiliation, or a good ballot placement . . . the candidate had a good chance to be elected.[177]

However, as numerous stories in the press in recent years have documented, the amount of money being spent in judicial campaigns has skyrocketed, as has the level of campaign rhetoric.[178] This has occurred because groups that wish to see particular judges elected or defeated have discovered that running a judicial campaign in the manner of any other political campaign produces results. Paul Carrington describes the new dispensation:

The cost of [state supreme court] campaigns is doubling almost every bi-ennium so that judicial candidates in several states are regularly spending millions, much of it on spot advertising on commercial television pre-pared by highly paid craftsmen skilled in the art of disparaging public persons. Funds sufficient for such races cannot be raised by small individ-ual contributions but only by contributions of sufficient size to confirm the widely shared suspicion that the donor expects something in return. Also, the time and effort expended by judges in fundraising can be a seri-ous distraction from the work of the court that the judge is employed to perform.[179]

The 2000 elections yielded a number of examples that demonstrate the point. In Michigan, a campaign in which more than $20 million was spent saw a successful effort by the Republican Party, insurance companies, and business groups to reelect three justices who have turned the Michigan Supreme Court into one of the most conservative in the country.[180] In Ohio, however, a similar effort to defeat the Ohio Supreme Court justice who wrote the opinion striking down the state's tort reform bill was un-successful, in no small part because she was able to raise considerable funds from labor unions and trial lawyers.[181] In Idaho, for the first time in more than forty years, a sitting state supreme court justice was defeated for reelection. The judge had been targeted for defeat by business interests specifically because she had decided for the federal government in a law-suit over water rights, an issue that constitutes the third rail of Idaho poli-tics.[182]

The U.S. Supreme Court has long held that due process requires that litigants in any American courtroom be guaranteed "a neutral and de-tached judge."[183] The increasingly contentious nature of state judicial elec-tions is casting considerable doubt upon the capacity of many state court systems to comply with this requirement. Numerous recent studies are feeding this doubt. For example, it has been demonstrated, in a study of a sample of more than seven thousand cases, that states with elected judicia-ries impose significantly higher damages upon out-of-state defendants who lose tort suits than do states with appointed judiciaries.[184] Another study has investigated cases decided by the Alabama Supreme Court that raise the question of whether a business can require consumers to submit legal claims to arbitration, as opposed to bringing an action in court. It concludes as follows: "Justices whose campaigns are funded by plaintiffs' lawyers are all Democrats and oppose arbitration, while justices whose campaigns are funded by business are nearly all Republicans and favor arbitration."[185] Finally, a comprehensive study of how environmental issues have figured in recent judicial elections finds "grounds for concern about disproportionate influence by well-heeled special interest groups, conscious efforts to disguise or misrepresent the ideological or financial interests being served by certain advocacy efforts, and misleading reports and rhetorical attacks on judicial candidates."[186]

Further, numerous recent opinion polls have uniformly revealed a growing unease among the public regarding the quality of justice one may receive from an elected judiciary. Anthony Champagne has summarized these:

> A recent national survey of public opinion and the court system found that 81 percent of respondents believed that "[j]udges' decisions are influenced by political considerations." Seventy-eight percent believe "[e]lected judges are influenced by having to raise campaign funds." These national survey findings are supported by state surveys. In Texas, 83 percent of respondents thought judges were influenced by contributions in their decisions. A Pennsylvania poll showed that 88 percent thought judicial decisions were influenced by contributions made to judicial campaigns. An Ohio poll found that 90 percent of Ohians believed political contributions affected judicial decisions. A Washington poll found that 76 percent of the respondents believed judges were influenced by political decisions and 66 percent by having to raise campaign funds.[187]

Indeed, judges themselves have come to express outright cynicism with respect to the role of money in judicial elections. In a case that challenged certain changes made to court rules by the Louisiana Supreme Court that had the effect of seriously hindering the ability of an environmental law clinic to bring suits against industrial polluters, a federal district judge, in an opinion dismissing the challenge, declared that, "in Louisiana, where state judges are elected, one cannot claim complete surprise when political pressure somehow manifests itself with the judiciary."[188]

Recent developments in state judicial elections, however, have not altered one venerable fact: no judge facing election can afford to be anything less than "tough on crime." This may be a laudable stance in the abstract, but it is not an impartial one, as is demonstrated by the realities of being a judge in Los Angeles:

Judges are . . . under tremendous pressure to keep their jobs. "If a judge is labeled soft on crime, it's a sure ticket to no longer being a judge," said [a Los Angeles criminal defense attorney]. A judge who doesn't seem tough enough can pretty much expect an election challenge from an ambitious prosecutor, a daunting prospect in Los Angeles County where even a bare-bones campaign can cost $100,000.[189]

The late Otto Kaus, who served on the California Supreme Court, famously declared that, for an elected judge, ignoring the political consequences of his decisions is like trying to "ignore a crocodile in your bathtub."[190] Gerald Uelmen has correctly noted that an elected judge's opinions in criminal matters, especially in death penalty cases, are "the fattest crocodile."[191] It is not for nothing that the chief justice of North Carolina announced in the early 1990s that he would not seek another term of office because the overturning of even a single death penalty conviction could likely mean his defeat.[192]

Imperial Judiciary theorists are convinced that it is the unelected federal judiciary that represents the greatest threat to the Republic's continued vigor, if not its very existence. It is well to remember, however, that, in the 1830s, Alexis de Tocqueville looked at the growing trend in the American states toward elected judiciaries and legislative recall of judges and was more than a little concerned: "I venture to predict that sooner or later these innovations will have dire results and that one day it will be seen that by diminishing the magistrates' independence, not judicial power only but the democratic republic itself has been attacked."[193]

Conclusion
Why the Courts

In the Introduction I declared that I hoped to convince readers, regardless of their political leanings, that the institution of an independent judiciary is worth defending. I think that there are two broad reasons why this is so.

First, from the beginnings of the American republic, we have simply found a vigorous judiciary to be *useful*. Most obviously, this has been true with respect to the necessity of resolving private disputes between citizens and for the trying of criminal defendants. (I take it to be uncontroversial that judicial resolution of the former is preferable to flipping a coin and that criminal trials are preferable to leaving the determination of guilt and innocence to prosecutorial discretion.) But, as I have tried to show, the judiciary's utility goes well beyond this.

Statutes produced by legislative bodies with large memberships almost inevitably employ a certain amount of vague and general language, both to facilitate compromise among legislators and to make the statute applicable to a range of particular factual circumstances. We have placed the burden of statutory interpretation, which is the act of actually applying statutes to particular factual circumstances, upon the courts. Alexander Hamilton has already been quoted to the effect that statutes "are a dead letter without courts to expound and define their true meaning."[1]

We have also seen that the popular branches of government have conferred tremendous powers upon the courts, in terms of both oversight of the administrative state and adjudication of claims arising from the numerous statutes that Congress has passed over the past several decades that allow citizens to seek court relief for a range of injuries, from racial discrimination to securities fraud. Grant Gilmore writes that, at the dawn of the modern administrative state in the 1930s, conventional wisdom among legal thinkers held that "judicial power was a relic of the dead past" that would eventually yield to adjudication and problem solving by bureaucratic expertise alone, unaided by generalist judges.[2] Gilmore continues: "What happened, as is frequently the case, is the opposite of what the conventional wisdom assumed."[3]

Second, I think that the American polity has long realized that robust judicial power, if not actually necessary for the system to operate, is certainly conducive to its operation. In one of his addresses in which he railed against purportedly illegitimate judicial power, Lino Graglia opined that "there is no alternative to majority rule except minority rule."[4] This is not, as the saying goes, the American Way.

I know of no better succinct description of the central operating principle of the American polity than what Robert Dahl termed the "Madisonian" conception of democracy:

> What I am going to call the "Madisonian" theory of democracy is an effort to bring off a compromise between the power of majorities and the power of minorities, between the political equality of all adult citizens on the one side, and the desire to limit their sovereignty on the other.[5]

From our national beginnings, we have recognized—in principle at least—as has no other nation on Earth that, if dreadful consequences are to be avoided, majority rule cannot be a principle applied without restraint or exception. As we have seen, it was in fact the evil of "faction," when the latter came to constitute a majority, that the framers viewed as the central problem of popular government:

> Indeed, it was this factious majoritarianism, an anomalous and frightening conception, for republican government, grounded as it was on majority rule, that was at the center of the Federalist perception of politics. In the minds of the Federalists the measure of a free government had become its ability to control factions, not, as used to be thought, those of a minority, but rather those of "an interested and overbearing majority." "To secure the public good and private rights against the danger of such a faction, and at the same time to preserve the spirit and form of popular government," said Madison, "was the great desideratum of republican wisdom."[6]

As a nation, we have understandably never been wholly at ease with the recognition that our society can produce "factions" that, when able to command a majority of the people's representatives, will do harm to relatively defenseless minorities and individuals. In the main, we are very receptive to politicians who pledge "I'm a uniter, not a divider," and it is not for nothing that the national motto is "*E pluribus unum.*"

I think, however, that, if we are honest, we must agree with Oliver Wendell Holmes: "This tacit assumption of the solidarity of the interests of society is very common, but seems to us to be false."[7] We need not be as pessimistic about human nature as was Holmes to admit that a lack of thoroughgoing social solidarity in a polity that employs majority rule means that minorities and individuals will not infrequently believe that they have been treated unjustly at the hands of the majority.

To my knowledge, no one has suggested a feasible way for a democratic polity to ensure the possibility that minority and individual interests will be protected from majoritarian excess—I am positive that no one knows how to ensure the *certainty* that they will be protected—other than through mechanisms that resemble judicial review and the tempering of laws by the application of equity.[8] Further, I am unaware of any convincing argument that these mechanisms are not best operated by adjudicators who are insulated from continual pressure to please a majority of whomever their constituents might be. One can argue that the American judiciary has not operated these mechanisms particularly well over the course of our history, but I am unconvinced that we can do without the institutional capacity itself.

But, to accept the need for this institutional capacity means that we must also face the reality that judges will make choices in their adjudications. As I have argued, the originalist assumption that judging can be reduced to something like a math problem is illusory. We must also accept that, in their exercise of discretion, individual judges will be influenced by things like ideology and personal prejudice of one kind or another.

But, again, we remain uncomfortable with this notion. I think, however, that the response to this unease made by Benjamin Cardozo eighty years ago remains valid. We must acknowledge, he argued, the existence of

the likes and the dislikes, the predilections and the prejudices, the complex of instincts and emotions and habits and convictions, which make the man, whether he be litigant or judge.... There has been a certain lack of candor in much of the discussion of [this] theme, or rather perhaps in the refusal to discuss it, as if judges must lose respect and confidence by the reminder that they are subject to human limitations. I do not doubt the grandeur of the conception which lifts them into the realm of pure reason, above and beyond the sweep of perturbing and deflecting forces. None the less, if there is anything of reality in my analysis of the judicial process, they do not stand aloof on these chill and distant heights; and we shall not help the cause of truth by acting and speaking as if they do.[9]

And, if judges are human beings, they will inevitably disappoint us, even outrage us, at one time or another. They will sometimes issue decisions that we perceive to be gravely unjust. What is the wisest response when this happens? Having written about the numerous ways in which the American judiciary is constrained by the democratic process, I think that the answer is that one should seek to use the latter to effect the desired jurisprudential change. It strikes me as utterly unconstructive to instead respond by first attributing to judges vast and unrestrained powers that they do not in reality possess and then proceeding to blame them for what one believes is wrong with the society at large.

Notes

Note: For the convenience of the reader, I have tried to cite to the most accessible sources in my use of writings from the era of the Constitution's formation. For example, instead of citing to the multivolume scholarly editions of the writings of various framers, which are generally available only in research libraries, I have whenever possible used sources such as the recently published Library of America anthologies of the works of Madison and Hamilton. The following abbreviations will be used in the notes:

AH LOA: *Hamilton: Writings*, selected by Joanne B. Freeman (The Library of America 2001).

APWFE: *American Political Writing during the Founding Era*, edited by Charles S. Hyneman and Donald S. Lutz, 2 vols. (Liberty Fund 1983).

DC LOA: *The Debate on the Constitution*, selected by Bernard Bailyn, 2 vols. (The Library of America 1993).

Elliot: *The Debates in the Several State Conventions, on the Adoption of the Federal Constitution . . .* , edited by Jonathan Elliot, 4 vols. (Washington 1836).

Farrand: *The Records of the Federal Convention of 1787*, edited by Max Farrand, 3 vols. (Yale University Press 1966).

Fed: *The Federalist Papers*, edited by Clinton Rossiter (Mentor 1961).

JM LOA: *Madison: Writings*, selected by Jack N. Rakove (The Library of America 1999).

Notes to Introduction

1. William Kristol, "Crowning the Imperial Judiciary," *New York Times*, November 28, 2000, at A29.

2. William Kristol, "Judicial Tyranny," *Washington Post*, December 10, 2000, at B7.

3. William Kristol and Jeffrey Bell, "Against Judicial Supremacy," *Weekly Standard*, December 4, 2000, 11.

4. Ramesh Ponnuru, "The Judicial-Activist State," *National Review*, December 18, 2000, at 20.

5. Paul Gigot, "Liberals Discover the Tyranny of the Courts," *Wall Street Journal*, December 15, 2000, at A16.

6. Maggie Gallagher, "Liberals Aren't Used to Losing in Court," *Detroit Free Press*, December 15, 2000, at http://www.freep.com/voices/editorials/egall15 _2001215.htm.

7. Tunku Varadarajan, "Judges or Priests?," *WSJ.com*, May 11, 2001.

8. Roger Pilon, "Judges and the Constitution," *NationalReview.com*, September 4, 2001.

9. Robert H. Bork, "Adversary Jurisprudence," *New Criterion*, May 2002, 4.

10. Max Boot, *Out of Order: Arrogance, Corruption, and Incompetence on the Bench*, 93 (1998) (emphasis in original).

11. David Frum, "The Justice Americans Demand," *New York Times*, February 4, 2000, at A29. This piece was written after a decision by the governor of Illinois to suspend the imposition of the state's death penalty after no fewer than thirteen death row prisoners were found to have been wrongfully convicted. Frum asserts that the governor "acted properly," but, almost incredibly, he does not pause to consider how many of these thirteen men would now be dead but for "never-ending procedural review."

12. Don Feder, "Today's Liberals Loathe Democracy," *Boston Herald*, August 9, 1999, at 23. Feder deserves special mention because, among all conservative critics of the judiciary, he has no peer as a purveyor of mindless demagoguery. For example, he has opined that, "[t]o see a dictatorship in action, you don't have to go to Havana or Beijing. Instead, look to the American judiciary, with power a politburo would envy and a disdain for democracy a commissar would appreciate." Don Feder, "A Faulty Judgment Call against N.H.," *Boston Herald*, March 15, 1999, at 23. He has also characterized President Clinton's judicial nominees as follows: "Intellectually, they reflect all the variety of Stalinists at a party congress, not to mention the same political leanings." Don Feder, "Clinton's Judges: Peas Out of a Pod," *Boston Herald*, June 9, 1999, at 31.

13. Robert Bork, "Our Judicial Oligarchy," *First Things*, November 1996, 24.

14. Lino Graglia, "Constitutional Law: A Ruse for Government by an Intellectual Elite," 14 *Ga. St. U. L. Rev.* 767, 776 (1998).

15. Fed 78 at 465.

16. Which is not to say that conservatives hold a monopoly upon its use, especially in the wake of *Bush v. Gore*. Thus, after the Supreme Court's decision in that case, the Harvard law professor Randall Kennedy wrote that "many liberals have come to believe that there is something peculiarly virtuous about the third branch of government, the supposedly least dangerous branch. A reconsideration of that

particular dogma is long overdue." Randall Kennedy, "Contempt of Court," *American Prospect*, January 1, 2001, at http://www.prospect.org/print-friendly/print/v12/1/kennedy-r.html.

17. Forrest McDonald, *Novus Ordo Seclorum: The Intellectual Origins of the Constitution*, 253, n. 69 (1985). As will be shown in chapter 2, McDonald is mistaken; certain Anti-Federalist opponents of the ratification of the Constitution did indeed predict that "judicial activism" would develop, and they expressed this perception in terms quite similar to those used by today's adherents of the Imperial Judiciary thesis.

18. George F. Will, "Myth of the Solomonic Senate," *Washington Post*, December 27, 1998, at C7.

19. Quoted in Kirk Victor, "Bashing the Bench," *National Journal*, May 31, 1997, 1078.

20. Quoted in Stephan O. Kline, "Judicial Independence: Rebuffing Congressional Attacks on the Third Branch," 87 *Ky. L.J.* 679, 679–80 (1999).

21. 1 *Democracy in America* 270 (Anchor ed. 1969).

22. *Id.* at 100.

23. Judith Shklar, "Positive Liberty, Negative Liberty in the United States," in *Redeeming American Political Thought*, 112 (1998).

24. Grant Gilmore, *The Ages of American Law*, 35 (1977).

25. *Buckley v. Illinois Judicial Inquiry Bd.*, 997 F.2d 224, 229 (7th Cir. 1993) (Posner, J.).

26. I should also perhaps mention that I will have nothing much to say about the role of the courts in the 2000 presidential election. In the first place, there is already an avalanche of commentary on this matter, with more coming every day. More important, I don't believe the litigation that arose from the Florida voting debacle says much about judicial power as it is normally exercised in contemporary America. *Bush v. Gore* was, let us hope, a once-in-a-lifetime event occasioned by the fact that the lackadaisical approach we have taken to the accurate expression of popular will through elections finally caught up with us. This shameful disregard for the integrity of elections should spur legislative and executive officials into action. On the other hand, in the months since *Bush v. Gore* was decided, I have not noticed that the nature of American judicial power, or the assessment of it by commentators of various political stripes, has been much altered.

NOTES TO CHAPTER 1

1. Mark Tushnet, "Is Judicial Review Good for the Left?" *Dissent*, Winter 1998, 65.

2. *Id.* at 70.

3. *Id.*

4. Mark Tushnet, *Taking the Constitution Away from the Courts*, x (1999).

5. *Id.* at 194.

6. *Id.* at xi.

7. *Id.* at 183.

8. *Id.* at 169.

9. *Id.* at 183.

10. Lino Graglia, Letter to the Editor, *Commentary*, November 1999, 5.

11. *Id.* Nor is Graglia the only Tushnet fan on the right. David Orgon Coolidge has pointed to *Taking the Constitution Away from the Courts* as a salutary example that "[p]eople across the political spectrum are recognizing that judicial tyranny jeopardizes democracy." David Orgon Coolidge, "What the Vermont Court Has Wrought," *Weekly Standard*, January 17, 2000, 22.

12. It was this position that caused the Reagan administration to withdraw Professor Graglia's name from nomination for a seat on the U.S. Court of Appeals for the Fifth Circuit. *See* Sheldon Goldman, *Picking Federal Judges*, 326 (1997).

13. Fed 49 at 315.

14. Lucas A. Powe, Jr., *The Warren Court and American Politics*, 1 (2000).

15. Morton Horowitz, "The Warren Court and the Pursuit of Justice," 50 *Wash. & Lee L. Rev.* 5, 10 (1993). As many scholars have pointed out, the Warren Court's tenure as a whole cannot be characterized as revolutionary. Kermit Hall argues correctly that "[t]here were, in fact, two Warren Courts. During the first phase, from 1953 to 1962, the Court did not have a major public presence with the notable exception of *Brown v. Board of Education.* . . . The early Warren Court was indifferent to the rights of the accused in state courts and inconsistent in its protection of First Amendment rights. . . . After the 1962 term, the Warren Court emerged as the powerful institution of liberal change against which Nixon and others railed." Kermit Hall, "The Warren Court: Yesterday, Today, and Tomorrow," 28 *Indiana L. Rev.* 309, 314–15 (1995).

16. Quoted in John Anthony Maltese, *The Selling of Supreme Court Nominees*, 109 (1998).

17. Quoted in Peter Irons, *A People's History of the Supreme Court*, 482 (1999).

18. Philip B. Kurland, *Politics, the Constitution, and the Warren Court*, 186–87 (1970).

19. *Id.* at 204–5.

20. *Id.* at 204.

21. Archibald Cox, *The Warren Court*, 12 (1968).

22. *Id.* at 13.

23. *Id.* at 21.

24. *Id.* at 88.

25. *Id.* at 23. Kermit Hall has asserted similarly that "[t]he Warren Court Justices were remarkable for their lack of concern about the main currents of consti-

tutional thought." Kermit Hall, "The Warren Court: Yesterday, Today, and Tomorrow," 28 *Indiana L. Rev.* 309, 315 (1995).

26. Nathan Glazer and Irving Kristol, eds., *The American Commonwealth: 1976* (1976).

27. Nathan Glazer, "Towards an Imperial Judiciary?" *Public Interest*, Fall 1975, 106.

28. *Id.* at 108.

29. *Id.* at 109 (emphasis in original).

30. *Id.* at 111.

31. *Id.* at 119.

32. *Id.* at 106.

33. *Id.* at 108.

34. Vincent Blasi and Anthony Lewis, eds., *The Burger Court: The Counter-Revolution That Wasn't* (1986).

35. G. Edward White, "The Supreme Court and Constitutional Law, 1925–2000: Changing Stances of Constitutional Review," *Virginia Quarterly Review*, Spring 2000, 323–24.

36. On the ideologically charged selection process for federal judicial nominees employed by Reagan administration officials, *see* Sheldon Goldman, *Picking Federal Judges*, 296–307 (1997). For the Bush administration's approach, *see* Robert Carp, Donald Songer, C. K. Rowland, Ronald Stidham, and Lisa Richey-Tracy, "The Voting Behavior of Judges Appointed by President Bush," *Judicature*, April-May 1993, 298.

37. G. Edward White, "The Supreme Court and Constitutional Law, 1925–2000: Changing Stances of Constitutional Review," *Virginia Quarterly Review*, Spring 2000, 328.

38. Quoted in Donald Grier Stephenson, Jr., *Campaigns and the Court*, 208 (1999).

39. Terry Eastland, "Deactivate the Courts," *American Spectator*, March 1997, 60.

40. Don Feder, "Even GOP Justices Can't Get It Right," *Boston Herald*, June 26, 2000, at 21.

41. *Planned Parenthood v. Casey*, 505 U.S. 833, 996 (1992) (Scalia, J., dissenting).

42. Quoted in Dick Lehr, "Souter Raises Ire on the Right," *Boston Globe*, July 1, 1992, at 1.

43. "Chief Justice Souter?" *Wall Street Journal*, February 29, 2000, at A22.

44. Mary Ann Glendon, *Rights Talk*, 2 (1991).

45. *Id.* at 4.

46. *Id.*

47. *Id.* at 9.

48. Mary Ann Glendon, *A Nation under Lawyers*, 141(1994).

49. *Id.*

50. *Id.* at 142.

51. *Id.* at 168.

52. *Id.*

53. Mary Ann Glendon, *Rights Talk*, 6 (1991).

54. Mary Ann Glendon, *A Nation under Lawyers*, 68 (1991).

55. *Casey v. Planned Parenthood*, 505 U.S. 833, 995 (1992) (Scalia, J., dissenting).

56. *Id.* at 1002.

57. "Introduction," *First Things*, November 1996, 18. The editors tell us that the symposium was immediately occasioned by a decision of the U.S. Court of Appeals for the Ninth Circuit that overturned the state of Washington's criminalization of assisted suicide. *Compassion in Dying v. Washington*, 79 F.3d 790 (9th Cir. 1996). A unanimous Supreme Court overturned the decision the following year. *Washington v. Glucksberg*, 521 U.S. 702 (1997).

58. "Introduction," *First Things*, November 1996, 19.

59. *Id.* at 19, 20.

60. The entire symposium and many of the responses it elicited are collected in Mitchell S. Muncy, ed., *The End of Democracy?* (1997).

61. *Id.* at 84.

62. Thomas Sowell, "Political Dangers: Lessons of History Weren't Learned," *Atlanta Journal-Constitution*, January 9, 2001, at http://www.accessatlanta.com /partners/ajc/epaper/editio.../opionion_a3a5fbd971a7e0a90096.htm.

63. *Romer v. Evans*, 517 U.S. 620, 636 (1996) (Scalia, J., dissenting) (citations omitted). Justice Scalia's neat distinction between a Kulturkramf and a fit of spite is a markedly clumsy one. "Kulturkramf" is the name given to Chancellor Bismarck's campaign of the 1870s to rid the newly unified German nation of the supposedly un-German influence of the Roman Catholic Church. The campaign included state interference in the ordination of Catholic clergy, the banning of certain Catholic religious orders, and the jailing of priests and bishops. *See* Gordon Craig, *Germany 1866–1945*, 69–78 (1978). It was, in sum, a spite-filled initiative.

64. *Romer v. Evans*, 517 U.S. at 652–53 (1996) (Scalia, J., dissenting).

65. Thomas Sowell, "How the Cultural Elite Undermine Traditional Values," *Indianapolis Star*, October 4, 1992, at F2.

66. *Ga. St. U. L. Rev.* 767 (1998). Robert Bork has similarly opined that "[t]he point of the academic exercise" of constitutional theory "is to be free of democracy in order to impose the values of an elite upon the rest of us." Robert Bork, *The Tempting of America*, 145 (1990).

67. Lino Graglia, "Constitutional Law: A Ruse for Government by an Intellectual Elite," 14 *Ga. St. U. L. Rev.* 767, 776 (1998). Graglia goes on to assert specifically that "the American Civil Liberties Union (ACLU), the paladin of far-left

causes and paradigmatic constitutional litigator of our time, never loses in the Supreme Court, even though it does not always win." *Id.* A dose of reality is useful here. During the 2000–01 Term of the Supreme Court, the ACLU, "which [filed] eighteen amicus briefs and five cases in which it represented a party, won eleven and lost twelve." Jonathan Groner, "Familiar Friends of the Court Have a Mixed Year," *Legal Times*, July 2, 2001, at 13. Contrast this with the record of the conservative Washington Legal Foundation, which "took part in twelve cases, with seven wins, four losses, and one that had both positive and negative elements." *Id.* Further, despite conservative mythology, such ACLU positions as opposition to most sorts of campaign finance reform and support for the free speech rights of any number of far-right-wing organizations disqualify it for the title of "paladin of far-left causes."

68. Lino Graglia, "The Legacy of Justice Brennan: Constitutionalization of the Left-Liberal Political Agenda," 77 *Wash. U. L. Q.* 183, 188–89 (1999).

69. *Id.* Note the similarity of Graglia's depiction of the "nightmare" of American liberalism with that of a leftist commentator: "[N]othing is more terrifying to American civil libertarians than the prospect of opening the Bill of Rights to political review, an idea that, for them, conjures up images of slack-jawed rednecks asking themselves if the U.S. really needs protection after all these years against compulsory self-incrimination or double jeopardy." Daniel Lazare, "America the Undemocratic," *New Left Review*, November-December 1998, 30.

70. Gary McDowell, "Reading the Letter of the Law," *Times Literary Supplement*, June 8, 1997, 7.

71. John Kekes, "Dangerous Egalitarian Dreams," *City Journal*, Autumn 2001, 102. A search of the Westlaw databases that contain the reported decisions of all American federal and state courts for the year 2000 reveals but a single inconsequential citation in a nonmajority opinion to Dworkin's works. *See U.S. v. Serafini*, 233 F.3d 758, 779 (3d Cir. 2000) (Rosenn, J., concurring in part and dissenting in part).

72. David Frum, "Canada's Reckless Supreme Court," *Wall Street Journal*, November 15, 1999, at A51. This sort of reflexive lumping together of supposed "gurus" obscures the fact that these people often don't agree on very much. For example, Tribe and Michael Dorf have written dismissively of Dworkin's approach to constitutional interpretation, asserting that, "[t]he moment you adopt a perspective as open as Dworkin's, the line between what you think the Constitution *says* and what you wish it *would* say becomes so tenuous that it is extraordinarily difficult, try as you might, to maintain that line at all." Laurence Tribe and Michael C. Dorf, *On Reading the Constitution*, 17 (1991) (emphases in original). Further, Frum's identification of MacKinnon as a "guru" of legal liberalism is ludicrous. MacKinnon's scholarship is based upon the contention that the liberal regime of free expression has allowed for the ubiquity of pornography and has thereby legitimated conditions of pervasive unfreedom for women. She has, in fact, contended

that "[s]ocial inequality is substantially created—that is, *done*—through words and images. Social hierarchy cannot and does not exist without being embodied in meanings and expressed in communications." Catharine A. MacKinnon, *Only Words*, 13 (1993) (emphasis in original). This is a view that horrifies liberal supporters of freedom of expression. *See* Ronald Dworkin, "Women and Pornography," *New York Review of Books*, October 21, 1993, 36.

73. John Leo, "Politics of the Bench," *U.S. News and World Report*, November 6, 2000, 14.

74. Jeremy Rabkin, "Partisan in the Culture Wars," 30 *McGeorge L. Rev.* 105, 107 (1998). Rabkin also declares in this piece that the Supreme Court "is afraid to disappoint its feminist constituency." *Id.* at 113. I note that he makes no mention of this when writing in praise of the Court's 2000 decision that invalidated the federal Violence Against Women Act, which Rabkin described as "a statute that was, only yesterday, a feminist icon." Jeremy Rabkin, "Sex, Violence, and the Supreme Court," *Weekly Standard*, May 29, 2000, 18.

75. Maggie Gallagher, "Liberals Aren't Used to Losing in Court," *Detroit Free Press*, December 15, 2000, at http://www.freep.com/voices/editorial/egall15 _20011215.htm.

76. Mary Ann Glendon, who actually teaches in an elite law school, was far closer to reality when she spoke in 1993 of "a legal academic establishment that is woefully out of touch with American culture and political life." Mary Ann Glendon, "What's Wrong with Elite Law Schools," *Wall Street Journal*, June 8, 1993, at A16. It is in fact the case that there is a lot of left-wing scholarship being undertaken at elite law schools that is, depending on your perspective, visionary or wacky. It simply doesn't follow, however, that any of this stuff ends up being adopted by the courts. For a critical perspective on this scholarship, *see* Daniel A. Farber and Suzanna Sherry, *Beyond All Reason* (1997). For a useful, if somewhat dated, reassurance that elite law schools are graduating not hordes of leftist cadres but hordes of corporate attorneys, *see* Robert Granfield, *Making Elite Lawyers* (1992).

77. *Harmelin v. Michigan*, 501 U.S. 957 (1991).

78. *Adarand Constructors, Inc. v. Pena*, 515 U.S. 200 (1995). Nathan Glazer himself has noted "the crumbling of the legal support that colleges and universities have relied upon to justify the almost universal practice among selective institutions of giving some kind of preference to black and Hispanic students." Nathan Glazer, "Should the SAT Account for Race? Yes.," *New Republic*, September 27, 1999, 26.

79. *Shaw v. Hunt*, 517 U.S. 899 (1996).

80. *National Endowment for the Arts v. Finley*, 524 U.S. 569 (1998).

81. *Washington v. Glucksberg*, 521 U.S. 702 (1997); *Vacco v. Quill*, 521 U.S. 793 (1997).

82. *See, e.g., Federal Maritime Comm. v. S. Carolina Ports Auth.*, 2002 WL 1050457 (U.S. May 28, 2002), *Bd. of Trustees of the Univ. of Alabama v. Garrett*, 531

U.S. 356 (2001); *Kimel v. Florida Bd. of Regents*, 528 U.S. 62 (2000); *Alden v. Maine*, 527 U.S. 706 (1999); *College Savings Bank v. Florida Postsecondary Ed. Expense Bd.*, 527 U.S. 666 (1999).

83. Cass Sunstein, *One Case at a Time*, 9 (1999).

84. Gary McDowell, "Judicial Activism Masquerading as Minimalism?" *Washington Times*, April 11, 1999, at B8.

85. Richard Hofstader, *The Paranoid Style in American Politics and Other Essays*, 23 (1965).

86. Robert Bork, *Slouching toward Gomorrah*, 96 (1996). Note the use of "abetted," which is clearly chosen to suggest the existence of a kind of criminal enterprise. Also, it appears that Bork believes that the pace is quickening. Late in 1999, he wrote that "American courts, enforcing liberal relativism, are leading the parade to Gomorrah." Robert Bork, "Activist Judges Strike Again," *Wall Street Journal*, December 22, 1999, at A18 (emphasis added).

87. Robert Bork, *Slouching toward Gomorrah*, 108 (1996).

88. *Id.* at 5.

89. J. Budzizewski, "The Future of the End of Democracy," *First Things*, March 1999, 15.

90. Robert Bork, *Slouching toward Gomorrah*, 109 (1996).

91. Robert Bork, "Our Judicial Oligarchy," *First Things*, November 1996, 23.

92. Robert Bork, *Slouching toward Gomorrah*, 109 (1996).

93. Sheldon Goldman, *Picking Federal Judges*, 198 (1997).

94. Robert Bork, *The Tempting of America*, 143 (1990).

95. Edwin Meese III, "Address before the D.C. Chapter of the Federalist Society Lawyers Division," in Steven Mailloux and Sanford Levinson, eds., *Interpreting Law and Literature: A Hermeneutic Reader*, 29 (1988).

96. *Id.* at 28.

97. *Id.* at 30.

98. Gary McDowell, "The True Constitutionalist," *Times Literary Supplement*, May 25, 2001, 15. It should be noted that Berger himself was not a conservative, and he was quite strict about acknowledging when his view of constitutional meaning conflicted with his political preferences. As his obituary in the *New York Times* put it, "Mr. Berger called himself a moderate Democrat, and it sometimes pained him that 'my conclusions are not infrequently at war with my predilections.' But it did not stop him. His advice was that people should change the Constitution rather than stretch its meaning." Douglas Martin, "Raoul Berger, 99, an Expert on Constitution in 2nd Career," *New York Times*, September 28, 2000, at C27.

99. For an effective account of the history of incorporation, *see* Henry F. Abraham and Barbara A. Perry, *Freedom and the Court: Civil Rights and Liberties in the United States*, 47–83 (7th ed. 1998). It is important to note that, while a number of provisions of the Bill of Rights have never been made applicable

against state governments, *all* of the provisions that have been made applicable were made so *before* the advent of the Warren Court. *See id.* at 60.

100. *See* Akhil Reed Amar, *The Bill of Rights,* esp. 193–97 (1998); Michael Kent Curtis, *No State Shall Abridge: The Fourteenth Amendment and the Bill of Rights,* esp. 113–128 (1986).

101. Akhil Reed Amar, *The Bill of Rights,* 303 (1998). For a discussion of the interaction between Reconstruction historiography and the law, *see* Randall Kennedy, "Reconstruction and the Politics of Scholarship," 98 *Yale L.J.* 521 (1989).

102. Raoul Berger, *Government by Judiciary,* 249 (1977).

103. *Id.* at 302.

104. Walter Berns, *Taking the Constitution Seriously,* 214 (1987).

105. Paul Craig Roberts, "Benchmarks for Impeachment," *Washington Times,* March 20, 1997, at A16.

106. Raoul Berger, *Government by Judiciary,* 336 (1977). Both of Berger's allusions here are in fact wonderful examples of what can happen when judges lack the courage or capacity to oppose the "saviors" of the day. The historian Ingo Muller has shown how the judiciary of pre-Nazi Germany forsook the rule of law in favor of furthering National Socialism. Ingo Muller, *Hitler's Justice: The Courts of the Third Reich,* 10–24 (1991). Muller points to numerous judicial proceedings in which Weimar judges sided openly with the Nazis and concludes that "[t]he fundamental legal principle of Nazi dictatorship—'Whatever benefits the people is right'—had been established by the highest courts in the land five years before the Nazis seized power." *Id.* at 24.

The reference to Indira Gandhi further demonstrates the fragility of democracy in the absence of an independent judiciary. In 1975, Prime Minister Gandhi declared a state of national emergency during which India was placed under virtual martial law. Under the guise of national salvation, Gandhi's government imprisoned thousands of political opponents and effectively banned independent press organs. The event that triggered what came to be known as "the Emergency" was a verdict of the Allahabad High Court finding that Prime Minister Gandhi had committed illegal acts in connection with her 1971 campaign for a seat in parliament. Conviction carried with it a ban on holding any political office for six years. Needless to say, calling the Emergency allowed Gandhi to ignore the verdict. *See* Stanley Wolpert, *A New History of India,* 396–400 (6th ed. 2000).

107. Raoul Berger, *Government by Judiciary,* 410 (1977).

108. *Id.* at 412.

109. Robert Bork, *The Tempting of America,* 349 (1990).

110. Henry V. Jaffa, *Storm over the Constitution,* 1 (1999).

111. Robert Bork, *The Tempting of America,* 143 (1990).

112. *Id.* at 158. Unsurprisingly, Bork believes that judges should pay no similar deference to *Roe v. Wade* and like cases that recognize a constitutional right to privacy "because they remain unaccepted and unacceptable to large segments of the

body politic, and judicial regulation could at once be replaced by restored legislative regulation of the subject." *Id.*

113. *Id.*

114. *Id.* at 94. Elsewhere in the book, however, Bork writes that the Supreme Court applied faulty reasoning in not using the First Amendment to overturn a state statute, thus implying that he does not believe incorporation to be illegitimate. *See* his discussion of *Pierce v. Society of Sisters*, 268 U.S. 510 (1925). *Id.* at 48–49.

115. 17 U.S. 316 (1819).

116. Robert Bork, *The Tempting of America*, 27 (1990).

117. Raoul Berger, *Government by Judiciary*, 386 (1977).

118. Raoul Berger, "Robert Bork's Contribution to Original Intention," 84 *N.W. U. L. Rev.* 1167 (1990).

119. *Id.*

120. *Id.*

121. *Id.* at 1174. For a description of the extent to which Bork ignores the range of historical materials that should form the basis of originalist analysis, *see* Bruce Ackerman, "Robert Bork's Grand Inquisition," 99 *Yale L.J.* 1419, 1422–25 (1990).

122. Raoul Berger, "Robert Bork's Contribution to Original Intent," 84 *N.W. U. L. Rev.* 1167, 1174.

123. Robert George, "Revisionism Revisited," *First Things*, December 1999, 53.

124. *Id.*

125. McConnell, a law professor at the University of Utah, is at the time of this writing President George W. Bush's nominee for a seat on the U.S. Court of Appeals for the Tenth Circuit. On the controversy occasioned by McConnell's nomination, *see* William Glaberson, "In New Senate, New Scrutiny of Judicial Nominees," *New York Times*, May 30, 2001, at A20.

126. Michael McConnell, "Originalism and the Desegregation Decisions," 81 *Va. L. Rev.* 947, 984 (1995).

127. *Id.* (emphasis added).

128. *Id.* at 1093.

129. Earl Maltz, "*Brown v. Board of Education* and 'Originalism,'" in Robert George, ed., *Great Cases in Constitutional Law*, 145 (2000). *See also* Earl Maltz, "Originalism and the Desegregation Decisions—A Response to Professor McConnell," 13 *Cons. Comment.* 223 (1996).

130. Raoul Berger, "The 'Original Intent'—As Perceived by Michael McConnell," 91 *N.W. U. L. Rev.* 242 (1996).

131. 347 U.S. 483, 489 (1954).

132. *Id.* at 495 (emphasis added).

133. Robert Bork, *The Tempting of America*, 76 (1990).

134. *Id.* at 75–76.

135. *Id.* at 82.

136. 163 U.S. 537 (1896).

137. To add to the confusion, it is certainly arguable that a Court imbued with Borkian principles would not have reached this conclusion. As the historian James T. Patterson has recently written, in the years following World War II, "public expenditures for black schools had increased, reflecting belated efforts by white officials to deflect mounting legal challenges to segregation." James T. Patterson, *Brown v. Board of Education: A Civil Rights Milestone and Its Troubled Legacy*, xvii (2001). Indeed, the *Brown* opinion itself recognizes that "there are findings below that the Negro and white schools involved [in the litigation] have been equalized, or are being equalized, with respect to buildings, curricula, and other 'tangible' factors." 347 U.S. at 492. Thus, a Court adhering to the principle of judicial self-restraint could well have concluded that "separate but equal" might be beginning to work at last and that the overturning of *Plessy* must await further developments.

138. Michael McConnell, "Originalism and the Desegregation Decisions," 81 *Va. L. Rev.* 947, 951 n. 11 (1996).

139. Robert Bork, *The Tempting of America*, 39 (1990).

140. 526 U.S. 489 (1999).

141. *Id.* at 523 n. 1 (Thomas, J., dissenting).

142. *Id.* at 526 (Thomas, J., dissenting).

143. *Id.* at 527 (Thomas, J., dissenting).

144. *Corfield v. Coryell*, 6 F. Cas. 546, 552 (C.C.E.D. Pa. 1825) (No. 3,230) (emphasis added).

145. Cong. Globe, 39th Cong. 1st Sess., 2765 (May 23, 1866) (emphasis added).

146. *Id.* at 1835 (April 7, 1866) (emphasis added). Michael McConnell has also noted that Justice Washington made no pretense of setting forth an exhaustive list of privileges and immunities. *See* Michael McConnell, "Originalism and the Desegregation Decisions," 81 *Va. L. Rev.* 947, 1027–28 (1996).

147. 526 U.S. at 527 (Thomas, J., dissenting).

148. Antonin Scalia, "Common-Law Courts in a Civil Law System: The Role of United States Federal Courts in Interpreting the Constitution and Laws," in Amy Gutmann, ed., *A Matter of Interpretation*, 22, 38 (1997). Which is not to say that Justice Scalia is a fanatic in this regard. For example, the Eleventh Amendment bars suits in federal court "commenced or prosecuted against one of the United States by Citizens of another State, or by Citizens or Subjects or any foreign states." Yet, although the Eleventh Amendment is silent in this regard, Justice Scalia wrote for the Court in holding that the Amendment bars suits brought in federal court by Indian tribes against the state in which a tribe resides. *Blatchford v. Native Village of Noatak*, 501 U.S. 775 (1991). His reasoning was that the Amendment "stand[s] not so much for what it says, but for the presupposition of our constitutional structure which it confirms: that the States entered the federal

system with their sovereignty intact . . . and that a State will therefore not be subject to suit in federal court unless it has consented to suit." *Id.* at 779. This purported "presupposition," however, itself has no textual basis, since the Constitution's makes no mention of the "sovereignty" of the states. For a prominent historian's explanation as to why it has no other sound basis, *see* Pauline Maier, "Alexander Hamilton as He Was Never Meant To Be," *New York Times*, July 3, 1999, at A11.

149. 530 U.S. 57 (2000).

150. *Id.* at 72–73.

151. *Id.* at 80 (Thomas, J., concurring).

152. *Id.* at 91, 93 (Scalia, J., dissenting).

153. Richard W. Garnett, "A Victory for the Family," *Wall Street Journal*, June 6, 2000, at A26. It is interesting to compare Professor Garnett's embrace of the unenumerated rights of "family privacy" and "parents' rights" with his reaction to the Court's 2002 finding that the application of the death penalty to retarded individuals violates the Eighth Amendment's prohibition upon "cruel and unusual punishments." *See Atkins v. Virginia,* 2002 WL 1338045 (U.S. June 20, 2002). Writing on the day of the decision, Garnett termed it "a breathtakingly arrogant assumption of power" because it trumps the will of "the legislatures of 20 states—and millions of our fellow citizens" who favor the execution of the retarded. Richard W. Garnett, "Personal Problems," *National Review Online*, June 20, 2002. In *Troxel,* the Court noted that "[a]ll 50 states have statutes that provide for grandparent visitation in some form." 530 U.S. at 73.

154. George F. Will, "The Grandparent Dissent," *Washington Post*, June 7, 2000, at A31. By contrast, Earl Maltz has no hesitancy in declaring *Troxel* "a classic example of everything that is wrong with activist judicial review." Earl M. Maltz, "The Trouble with *Troxel*," 32 *Rutgers L.J.* 695, 710 (2001).

155. 514 U.S. 334 (1995).

156. *Id.* at 343.

157. *Id.* at 359 (emphasis added; Thomas, J., concurring).

158. *Id.* at 361.

159. *Id.* at 374 (Scalia, J., dissenting).

160. *See Clinton v. New York,* 524 U.S. 417 (1998).

161. *See U.S. v. Bajakajian,* 524 U.S. 321 (1998).

162. 515 U.S. 646 (1995).

163. *Id.* at 652.

164. *Id.* at 652 n. 1.

165. *Id.* at 653 (citations omitted).

166. 121 S. Ct. 2038 (2001).

167. *Id.* at 2046.

168. George Will, "Not Too Strict to Apply Justice," *Washington Post*, June 17, 2001, at B7.

169. For an excellent discussion of the scope of free expression in late-eighteenth-century America, *see* Michael Kent Curtis, *Free Speech, "The People's Darling Privilege,"* 23–116 (2000).

170. David Yassky, "Eras of the First Amendment," 91 *Colum. L. Rev.* 1699, 1700 (1991).

171. Michael Kent Curtis, *Free Speech, "The People's Darling Privilege,"* 2 (2000).

172. H. L. Mencken, "Morals and the Moron," in Marion Elizabeth Rodgers, ed., *The Impossible H. L. Mencken*, 87 (1991).

173. *U.S. v. Debs*, 249 U.S. 211 (1919).

174. William H. Rehnquist, *All the Laws but One*, 221 (1998).

175. *Palko v. Connecticut*, 302 U.S. 319, 326–27 (1937).

176. Cass R. Sunstein, *Democracy and the Problem of Free Speech*, 8 (1993).

177. David A. Strauss, "Freedom of Speech and the Common Law Constitution," in Lee C. Bollinger and Geoffrey R. Stone, eds., *Eternally Vigilant: Free Speech in the Modern Era*, 38 (2002).

178. 530 U.S. 703 (2000).

179. Colorado Rev. Stat. § 18-9-122(3).

180. 530 U.S. at 763 (Scalia, J., dissenting).

181. *Id.* at 762 (Scalia, J., dissenting).

182. *Id.* at 754 (Scalia, J., dissenting).

183. *Id.* at 765 (Scalia, J., dissenting).

184. Quoted in Larry Dougherty, "Justice Presides over Annual Bar Dinner Meeting," *St. Petersburg Times*, December 13, 1998, at 3B.

185. Quoted in Patricia Manson, "High Court 'Originalist' Has Recipe for Making Good Law," *Chicago Daily Law Bulletin*, March 12, 1998, at 1.

186. Laurence Tribe, "Comment," in Amy Gutmann, ed., *A Matter of Principle*, 81 (1997).

187. The best book-length treatment is Leonard Levy, *Original Intent and the Framers' Constitution* (1988). An important article that sets forth a host of originalism's limitations is Jefferson Powell, "Rules for Originalists," 73 *Va. L. Rev.* 659 (1987). For an account of the extent to which documentary evidence exists pursuant to which original intent may be discerned, *see* James H. Hutson, "The Creation of the Constitution: The Integrity of the Documentary Record," 65 *Texas L. Rev.* 1 (1986). Jefferson Powell has also argued that the framers of the original Constitution conceived of original intent in a manner quite at odds with that of today's originalists. Jefferson Powell, "The Original Understanding of Original Intent," 98 *Harv. L. Rev.* 885 (1985).

188. Saikrishna B. Prakash, "Unoriginalism's Law without Meaning," 15 *Const. Comment.* 529, 530 (1998).

189. Keith E. Whittington, *Constitutional Interpretation: Textual Meaning, Original Intent, and Judicial Review*, 174 (1999).

190. Gary L. McDowell, "Blessings of Liberty," *Times Literary Supplement*, August 31, 2001, 26.

191. Quoted in Todd J. Gillman, "Court Confirmation Process Was 'Vicious,' Thomas Says," *Dallas Morning News*, September 10, 1999, at 32A.

192. Antonin Scalia, "Originalism: The Lesser Evil," 57 *U. Cin. L. Rev.* 849, 852 (1989) (emphasis added).

193. Robert Bork, *The Tempting of America*, 2 (1990).

194. *Id.* at 355.

195. Richard Hofstadter, *The Paranoid Style in American Politics and Other Essays*, 30 (1965).

196. Robert Bork, *Slouching toward Gomorrah*, 117 (1996). It is of no small interest that Mark Tushnet thinks Bork's proposal is fine as far as it goes but that it does not go far enough. Tushnet counters, "Why not go all the way?" and proposes his own amendment: "'The provisions of this Constitution shall not be cognizable by any court.'" Mark Tushnet, *Taking the Constitution Away from the Courts*, 175 (1999). Talk about the temptations of utopia!

197. Robert Bork, *Slouching toward Gomorrah*, 119 (1996). Justice Scalia said with respect to Bork's proposed amendment that "Bork essentially has given up. . . . I'm not so pessimistic. I'm not ready to throw in the towel. . . . We can get back." Quoted in Richard Carelli, "A Speechless Scalia Puts Unlikely 'Spin' on His Conservatism," *Washington Post*, May 23, 1997, at A27.

198. Robert H. Bork, "Adversary Jurisprudence," *The New Criterion*, May 2002, 18.

199. Robert Bork, "Forward," in Max Boot, *Out of Order*, vi–vii (1998). *The Economist* has recently viewed the same developments in a more dispassionate manner: "Established and emerging democracies display a puzzling taste in common: both have handed increasing amounts of power to unelected judges. . . . Despite continued attacks on the legitimacy of judicial review, it has flourished in the past fifty years. All established democracies now have it in some form, and the standing of constitutional courts has grown almost everywhere." "The Gavel and the Robe," *Economist*, August 7, 1999, 43.

200. Robert Bork, "Forward," in Max Boot, *Out of Order*, xiii–xiv (1998). In writing about the Vermont Supreme Court's decision extending the protections of state law to homosexual unions, Bork displayed an even greater degree of condescension. The case was an indication that "activism is now raging in the state courts. That activism prevails in those courts, even though many of them are manned by elected judges, suggests either that the public is ill informed about the shift in power from democratic institutions to authoritarian bodies or that there is a general weariness with democracy and the endless struggles it entails." Robert Bork, "Activist Judges Strike Again," *Wall Street Journal*, December 22, 1999, at A18.

201. In a variation of the "moral intimidation" argument, federal judge James L. Buckley has argued as follows: "There is a fundamental difference between a

practice that society condemns and may or may not choose to forbid, and one that the Court has declared to be constitutionally protected. The latter tips the psychological as well as the legal balance in favor of a newly defined right, because that which society may not forbid will inevitably acquire the presumption of moral legitimacy. After all, how can one condemn the exercise of a constitutional right." James L. Buckley, "The Constitution and the Courts: A Question of Legitimacy," 24 *Harv. J. Law & Pub. Pol'y* 189, 193–94 (2000). This must explain such things as our national acceptance of the practice of burning the American flag as a form of protest and the virtual absence of any criticism of the practice of abortion.

Notes to Chapter 2

1. Gordon Wood, *The Radicalism of the American Revolution*, 323 (1992).

2. Fed 9 at 72.

3. Fed 78 at 465.

4. *Second Treatise*, ¶¶ 144–48.

5. Peter Laslett, "Introduction" to John Locke, *Two Treatises of Government*, 133 (Mentor ed. 1960). But Locke did have some understanding of an independent judiciary. He wrote that, in a proper commonwealth, "whoever has the Legislative or Supream Power," would be "bound to govern according to establish'd *standing Laws*, promulgated and known to the People" and "by *indifferent* and upright *Judges*, who are to decide Controversies by those Laws." *Second Treatise*, ¶ 131 (emphases in original). I thank my friend Robert Amdur for this point.

6. 1 *The Spirit of the Laws* 152 (Hafner ed. 1949).

7. *Id.* at 156.

8. 1 *Commentaries on the Laws of England* 259–60 (1765).

9. For a brief treatment, *see* Bernard Bailyn, *The Origins of American Politics*, 68–70 (1970).

10. Merrill Jensen, ed., *Tracts of the American Revolution*, 149–50 (1967) (emphases in original).

11. Quoted in Shannon Stimson, *The American Revolution in the Law*, 50 (1990).

12. The Declaration of Independence, ¶2. The Supreme Court has noted that this passage "clearly foreshadowed" the guarantees of judicial independence set forth in Article III of the Constitution. *Northern Pipeline Construction Co. v. Marathon Pipe Line Co.*, 458 U.S. 50, 60 (1982).

13. 1 APWFE 407.

14. M. J. C. Vile, *Constitutionalism and the Separation of Powers*, 132 (2d ed. 1998).

15. Fed 48 at 308, 309.

16. David Currie, "Separating Judicial Power," 61 *Law & Contemp. Probs.* 7, 9–10 (1998).

17. Gordon Wood, "Comment," in Amy Gutmann, ed., *A Matter of Interpretation*, 50, 51 (1997).

18. Quoted in Gordon Wood, "The Origins of Vested Rights in the Early Republic," 85 *Va. L. Rev.* 1421, 1438 (1999).

19. Gordon Wood, "Interests and Disinterestedness in the Making of the Constitution," in Richard R. Beeman, Stephen Botein, and Edward C. Carter, eds., *Beyond Confederation*, 73 (1987) (emphasis added).

20. JM LOA 149. At the Philadelphia Convention itself, Madison remarked to the delegates that it was the need "for the security of private rights, and the steady dispensation of Justice . . . which had more perhaps than any thing else, produced this convention." 1 Farrand 134.

21. John Zvesper, *Political Philosophy and Rhetoric: A Study in the Origins of American Party Politics*, 44 (1977).

22. 1 DC LOA 9.

23. 1 DC LOA 74–75.

24. James W. Ely, Jr., *The Guardian of Every Other Right*, 37 (2d ed. 1998).

25. Fed 10 at 84. The Constitution in fact ensures that the state legislatures would no longer be free to enact what Madison called "the pestilent effects of paper money, on the necessary confidence between man and man." Fed 44 at 281. Article I, Section 10, forbids the states from "mak[ing] any Thing but gold and silver Coin a Tender in Payment of Debts." Article I, Section 10, also forbids the states from passing laws "impairing the Obligation of Contracts," a measure directed against debtor-relief legislation.

26. 1 DC LOA 822.

27. Bernard Bailyn, *The Ideological Origins of the American Revolution*, 173 (1967) (emphasis in original).

28. 2 DC LOA 759.

29. Fed 48 at 309.

30. 2 DC LOA 418. James Wilson made the same point at the Philadelphia Convention by appealing to the specific historical example of the English Civil War: "After the destruction of the King in Great Britain, a more pure and unmixed tyranny sprang up in the parliament than had been exercised by the monarch." 2 Farrand 301.

31. 2 DC LOA 157.

32. Helen C. Veit, Kenneth R. Bowling, and Charlene Bangs Bickford, eds., *Creating the Bill of Rights*, 81 (1991) (emphasis added).

33. Jack Rakove notes that, at the Philadelphia Convention, Madison raised the issue of "interested majorities" no fewer than five times. Jack Rakove, *Original Meanings*, 61 (1996).

34. Fed 10 at 79.

35. 3 Elliot 309–10.

36. 1 Farrand 422–23.

37. Fed 10 at 77.

38. Drew McCoy, *The Elusive Republic*, 131 (1983).

39. Gordon Wood, *The Creation of the American Republic*, 411 (1969).

40. Letter to James Monroe, October 5, 1786, in William T. Hutchinson and William Rachal, eds., 9 *The Papers of James Madison* 141 (1962–).

41. 1 Farrand 299 (notes of Robert Yates).

42. Fed 71 at 432 (emphasis in original).

43. 3 Elliot 87.

44. 2 DC LOA 646.

45. Fed 39 at 241.

46. M. J. C. Vile, *Constitutionalism and the Separation of Powers*, 158 (2d ed. 1998).

47. *Plaut v. Spendthrift Farm, Inc.*, 514 U.S. 211, 219–20 (1995).

48. Fed 44 at 282.

49. Fed 48 at 311 (emphasis by Madison).

50. Fed 10 at 79–80 (emphasis added).

51. Fed 10 at 80.

52. 2 Farrand 301.

53. Shannon Stimson, *The American Revolution in the Law*, 124–25 (1990) (emphasis added).

54. Fed 22 at 150.

55. 1 Farrand 119.

56. James S. Liebman and William F. Ryan, "'Some Effectual Power': The Quantity and Quality of Decisionmaking Required of Article III Courts," 98 *Colum. L. Rev.* 696, 713 (1998).

57. Fed 78 at 465.

58. Fed 78 at 469 (emphasis added).

59. Paul Leicester Ford, ed., *The Works of Thomas Jefferson* 256 (1904).

60. Fed 39 at 242.

61. 1 DC LOA 795.

62. Fed 51 at 321 (emphasis added).

63. JM LOA 70.

64. Leonard Levy, *Origins of the Bill of Rights*, 68 (1999).

65. Fed 78 at 470.

66. Jack Rakove, "The Origins of Judicial Review: A Plea for New Contexts," 49 *Stan. L. Rev.*, 1031, 1060 (1997).

67. Fed 78 at 466.

68. Fed 81 at 482 (first emphasis in original; second emphasis added).

69. 3 Elliot 553, 554.

70. 1 DC LOA 883.

71. 1 DC LOA 823.

72. 3 Elliott 324–25. Further, as David Currie notes, members of the First Congress repeatedly acknowledged that statutes would be subject to judicial review, and they were not at all surprised when the Supreme Court actually began to apply constitutional scrutiny to federal and state statutes. David Currie, *The Constitution in Congress*, 120, 155 (1997). On the contrary, Section 25 of the Judiciary Act of 1789 explicitly provided for the exercise of judicial review. Specifically, it mandated that the U.S. Supreme Court might review any decision of the highest court of a state "on the ground of [it] being repugnant to the Constitution . . . or where is drawn in question the construction of any clause of the Constitution." 1 Stat. 73, § 25 (1789). It is on the basis of this provision that, "[b]y 1802 the lower federal courts, in over twenty cases, had invalidated statutes of eleven of the fifteen states." Charles Sellers, *The Market Revolution*, 55 (1991).

73. Herbert Storing, ed., 2 *The Complete Anti-Federalist* 138 (1981).

74. *Id.* at 188.

75. Herbert Storing, *What the Anti-Federalists Were For*, 54 (1981).

76. 1 DC LOA 610.

77. Mercy Otis Warren, *History of the Rise, Progress, and Termination of the American Revolution*, 658–59 (Liberty Fund ed. 1988).

78. 3 Elliot 218.

79. Herbert Storing, ed., 2 *The Complete Anti-Federalist* 136 (1981).

80. 1 DC LOA 399.

81. Fed 37 at 229.

82. 1 DC LOA 239.

83. Roger Pilon, "Letter to the Editor: The Great American Behemoth," *Wall Street Journal*, September 15, 1999, at A33.

84. Fed 45 at 292.

85. AH LOA 505.

86. Fed 34 at 207 (emphasis added).

87. Fed 44 at 284–85.

88. The Virginia Plan, the original set of constitutional proposals offered for debate at the Philadelphia Convention, dispensed with *any* attempt at enumeration of powers. It simply provided that the federal government be empowered "to legislate in all cases to which the separate States are incompetent." 1 Farrand 21. Hamilton also expressed skepticism about the entire enterprise of enumeration because it "must ever be the case when you attempt to define powers.—Something will always be wanting." 1 Farrand 298 (notes of Robert Yates).

89. Fed 48 at 310.

90. Fed 44 at 284 (emphasis in original).

91. 1 DC LOA 198 (emphasis added).

92. Helen E. Veit, Kenneth R. Bowling, and Charlene Bangs Bickford, eds., *Creating the Bill of Rights*, 197 (1991) (emphasis added).

93. Fed 82 at 492 (emphasis added).

94. Fed 82 at 492.

95. 2 Farrand 625 (emphasis added).

96. Helen E. Veit, Kenneth R. Bowling, and Charlene Bangs Bickford, eds., *Creating the Bill of Rights*, 15 (1991).

97. *Id.* at 21.

98. *Id.* at 22.

99. The Tenth Amendment does declare that "The powers not delegated to the United States by the Constitution . . . are reserved to the States respectively, or to the people." Note, however, that, unlike South Carolina's proposed amendment, the Ninth Amendment omits the constricting phrase "*expressly* delegated."

100. Jefferson Powell, "The Modern Misunderstanding of Original Intent," 54 *U. Chi. L. Rev.* 1513, 1543 (1987).

101. Quoted in Joseph M. Lynch, *Negotiating the Constitution*, 139 (1999).

102. AH LOA 620.

103. AH LOA 618.

104. AH LOA 625. Hamilton also argued that, although the Philadelphia Convention had taken place less than five years ago, the true intentions of the delegates could not be ascertained with precision. The rejection of the proposal to empower Congress to create corporations might have been meant "either generally, or for some special purpose. What was the precise nature or extent of this proposition, or what the reasons for refusing it, is not ascertained by any authentic document, or even by accurate recollection." AH LOA 624. It should be noted here that Madison's notes on the Philadelphia Convention, which are the only record of the debates that comes anywhere near comprehensiveness, were not published until shortly after Madison's death in 1836. *See* Drew R. McCoy, *The Last of the Fathers*, 73–74, 163–70 (1989).

105. AH LOA 702.

106. "The Bank Bill," February 2, 1791, in William T. Hutchinson and William Rachal, eds., 13 *The Papers of James Madison*, 377 (1962–).

107. *Id.* at 376.

108. AH LOA 618 (emphasis in original).

109. *U.S. v. Butler*, 297 U.S. 1, 65–66 (1936). Speaking for the Court a year later, Justice Cardozo maintained that this debate was now "settled" and that "[t]he conception of the spending power advocated by Hamilton . . . has prevailed over that of Madison." *Helvering v. Davis*, 301 U.S. 619, 640 (1937). But of course the debate continues, in the courts and in the political culture at large.

110. Fed 78 at 469.

111. Fed 22 at 150 (emphasis added).

112. Raoul Berger, *Government by Judiciary*, 302 (1977) (emphases in original). As conclusive proof that the framers intended for the judiciary to have no other role in the lawmaking process, Berger cites the fact that the Philadelphia Convention rejected a proposal, favored by Madison and James Wilson, to establish a "Council of Revision" that would have actually involved the judiciary in the vetoing of acts of Congress. *Id*. at 300–2. Bork makes the same argument. Robert Bork, *The Tempting of America*, 154 (1990). But, of course, the defeat of this proposal does not establish that the framers foresaw *no* role for the judiciary in the legislative process beyond the narrow exercise of judicial review.

113. *Id*. at 304 (emphasis in original).

114. Jefferson Powell, "The Modern Misunderstanding of Original Intent," 54 *U. Chi. L. Rev*. 1513, 1537 (1987).

115. Fed 37 at 229.

116. Fed 22 at 150. Hamilton also made the same point with respect to treaties entered into by the United States: "Their true import, as far as respects individuals, must, *like all other laws*, be ascertained by judicial determinations." *Id*. (emphasis added).

117. William Eskridge, Jr., "All about Words: Early Understandings of the 'Judicial Power' in Statutory Interpretation, 1776–1806," 101 *Colum. L. Rev*. 990, 1096–97 (2001).

118. Fed 78 at 470 (emphases added).

119. 2 DC LOA 264 (emphasis added).

120. Mark A. Graber, "Naked Land Transfers and American Constitutional Development," 53 *Vand. L. Rev*. 73, 73 (2000) (quotations omitted).

121. *Id*. at 89.

122. *Id*. at 95.

123. 1 *The Spirit of the Laws* 159 (Hafner ed. 1949).

124. Fed 44 at 28.

125. William Eskridge, Jr., "All about Words: Early Understandings of the 'Judicial Power' in Statutory Interpretation, 1776–1806," 101 *Colum. L. Rev*. 990, 995 (2001).

126. Fed 48 at 310.

127. 1 DC LOA 808.

128. Fed 78 at 514.

129. JM LOA 420.

130. Helen E. Veit, Kenneth R. Bowling, and Charlene Bangs Bickford, eds., *Creating the Bill of Rights*, 83–84 (1991).

131. Robert Bork, *The Tempting of America*, 183 (1990).

132. Charles L. Black, Jr., *A New Birth of Freedom*, 10 (1997).

133. John Hart Ely, *Democracy and Distrust*, 34 (1980).

134. *Id*. at 38 (emphasis added).

135. Jefferson Powell, "Rules for Originalists," 73 *Va. L. Rev*. 659, 670 (1987).

136. Bernard Bailyn, *The Ideological Origins of the American Revolution*, 78 (1967). Recall here that the Declaration of Independence makes no attempt to compile an exhaustive list of human rights: "We hold these truths to be self-evident; that all men are created equal; that they are endowed by their Creator with certain inalienable rights; that *among these* are life, liberty, and the pursuit of happiness . . ."

137. Mark Graber notes that the Marshall Court effectively invalidated a number of state laws that effected improper land transfers between rival holders even though the original Constitution "lacked explicit bans on all uncompensated state government takings of private property." Mark Graber, "Naked Land Transfers and American Constitutional Development," 53 *Vand. L. Rev.* 73, 74 (2000). From this, Graber concludes convincingly that "fundamental rights jurisprudence has played a role in constitutional adjudication from the beginning of the Republic. The antebellum Supreme Court protected a right against government expropriation of land that was not explicitly mentioned in the federal constitution." *Id.* at 119.

138. Fed 78 at 471.

139. Raoul Berger, *Government by Judiciary*, 308, 365 (1997).

140. Fed 81 at 485.

141. "Testimony of the Honorable Tom Delay before the Subcommittee on Courts and Intellectual Property Regarding Judicial Impeachment," May 15, 1997, 1997 WL 10571464, at 2.

142. 2 Farrand 428.

143. 2 Farrand 428.

144. 2 Farrand at 429.

145. 2 Farrand 429 (emphasis added). Chief Justice Sir John Holt was celebrated and vilified for a series of decisions in which he asserted that the British Parliament, although sovereign, could not legislate in violation of natural law. Most famous among these is his opinion in a 1702 case in which he held that Parliament could not create a court in which the Lord Mayor of London acted both as a litigant and judge. *See* Philip A. Hamburger, "Revolution and Judicial Review: Chief Justice Holt's Opinion in *City of London v. Wood*," 94 *Colum. L. Rev.* 2091 (1994).

In yet another admission that original intent can be less than pellucid, Robert Bork states that "it is not settled" whether federal judges were meant to be subject to the threshold standard for presidential impeachment set forth in Article II, Section 4 ("Treason, Bribery, or other high Crimes and Misdemeanors"). Robert Bork, *The Tempting of America*, 22 (1990).

146. Between 1808 and 1816 anticourt forces in Congress made four attempts to amend the Constitution to provide for the removal of federal judges by order of the president upon a two-thirds vote of each house of Congress. All these attempts were unsuccessful. *See* Donald Grier Stephenson, Jr., *Campaigns and the Court*, 51 (1999).

147. Richard John Neuhaus, "The Dred Scott of Our Time," *Wall Street Journal*, July 2, 1992, at A8.

148. *Id.*

149. David A. Bell, "The Ordeal of Legitimacy," *New Republic*, February 28, 2000, 37 (emphasis in original).

150. Fed 10 at 83.

151. *Id.*

152. Samuel P. Huntington, *American Politics: The Promise of Disharmony*, 8 (1983).

153. Quoted in John Hart Ely, *Democracy and Distrust*, 60 (1980).

154. JM LOA 148.

155. AH LOA 169.

156. AH LOA 168.

157. Fed 78 at 465.

158. Kenneth R. Bowling, "'A Tub to the Whale': The Founding Fathers and the Adoption of the Federal Bill of Rights," in Ralph D. Gray and Michael A. Morrison, eds., *New Perspectives on the Early Republic*, 52 (1994).

159. 2 DC LOA 896.

NOTES TO CHAPTER 3

1. Nathan Glazer, "Towards an Imperial Judiciary?," *Public Interest*, Fall 1975, 106.

2. Max Boot, *Out of Order*, 10 (1998).

3. James L. Buckley, "The Constitution and the Courts: A Question of Legitimacy," 24 *Harv. J.L. & Pub. Pol'y* 189, 193 (2000).

4. 60 U.S. 393 (1857).

5. 410 U.S. 113 (1973).

6. Quoted in David Garrow, *Liberty and Sexuality*, 606 (1994).

7. Gary McDowell, "Lincoln Didn't Defer to Court on Moral Issue," *Wall Street Journal*, December 18, 1984, at 34. McDowell reminds us in this piece of Abraham Lincoln's refusal to recognize the Supreme Court's decision in *Dred Scott* as the definitive constitutional statement on the institution of slavery. He fails to note, however, that *before* the decision was issued, Lincoln took a contrary position. In his magisterial Lincoln biography, David Herbert Donald writes that, as late as 1856, Lincoln "invoked the judiciary as the ultimate arbiter of disputes over slavery. 'The Supreme Court of the United States is the tribunal to decide such questions,' he announced, and, speaking for the Republicans, he pledged, 'We will submit to its decisions; and if you [the Democrats] do also, there will be an end of the matter.'" David Herbert Donald, *Lincoln*, 200 (1995).

And Lincoln was hardly alone. On the contrary, "party leaders openly appealed to the Supreme Court for a legal resolution. Several bills in the 1850s ceded authority to the Court to adjudicate individual conflicts over slave ownership, and the newly elected president James Buchanan declared the status of slavery in the territories was a 'judicial question, which legitimately belongs to the Supreme Court of the United States.'" Michael McCann, "How the Supreme Court Matters in American Politics," in Howard Gillman and Cornell Clayton, eds., *The Supreme Court in American Politics: New Institutionalist Interpretations,* 70 (1999). In sum, "it was Congress itself, and not merely the gratuitous intervention by the Court, that handed over to the constitutional status of slavery in the territories." Henry V. Jaffa, *Storm over the Constitution,* 19 (1999).

8. Nathan Glazer, "Towards an Imperial Judiciary?" *Public Interest,* Fall 1975, 109.

9. 1 *Democracy in America* 100 (Anchor ed. 1969).

10. Judith S. Kaye, "Forward: The Common Law and State Constitutional Law as Full Partners in the Protection of Individual Rights," 23 *Rutgers L.J.* 727, 728 (1992). Which is not to say that nineteenth-century state courts did not exercise judicial review. Far from it. William Nelson has recently detailed their frequent resort to the practice: "By 1820, eleven of the original thirteen states were publishing reports of their cases, and the courts of ten of them had either invalidated acts of their legislatures or unequivocally asserted their right to do so. Moreover, all five of the states admitted to the Union between 1790 and 1815 had accepted judicial review by 1820, while the four states admitted between 1815 and 1819 all accepted the doctrine in cases published in the first two volumes of their reports." William E. Nelson, *Marbury v. Madison: The Origins and Legacy of Judicial Review,* 75 (2000).

11. Guido Calabresi, *A Common Law for the Age of Statutes,* 4 (1982).

12. Grant Gilmore, *The Ages of American Law,* 36 (1977).

13. Stephen Skowronek, *Building a New American State,* 24 (1982).

14. *Id.* at 21–22.

15. *Id.* at 25.

16. *Id.* at 26–27.

17. *Id.* at 27–28.

18. Cass Sunstein, *After the Rights Revolution,* 17–18 (1990).

19. J. W. Hurst, *Law and the Conditions of Freedom in the Nineteenth-Century United States,* 7 (1956).

20. *Id.* at 13.

21. G. Edward White, *The American Judicial Tradition,* 48–49 (1976).

22. Morton Horwitz, *The Transformation of American Law,* 32 (1977).

23. *Id.* at 31.

24. *Id.* at 132.

25. *Id.* at 31.

26. 49 Mass. 466 (1844).

27. *Id.* at 476–77 (emphases added).

28. 38 Ky. 289 (1839).

29. *Id.* at 292–93.

30. *Id.* at 309.

31. 51 N.Y. 476 (1873).

32. *Id.* at 484–85.

33. Morton Horwitz, *The Transformation of American Law,* 42 (1977) (emphases added).

34. J. W. Hurst, *Law and the Conditions of Freedom in the Nineteenth-Century United States,* 24 (1956).

35. *Id.* at 18.

36. William E. Nelson, *Americanization of the Common Law,* 154 (1975).

37. Morton Horwitz, *The Transformation of American Law,* 160 (1977).

38. Grant Gilmore, *The Death of Contract,* 15 (1974).

39. William E. Nelson, *Americanization of the Common Law,* 143 (1975).

40. Charles Sellers, *The Market Revolution,* 54 (1991).

41. Lawrence M. Friedman, *A History of American Law,* 409 (1st ed. 1973).

42. 1 *Commentaries on the Laws of England* 417 (1765).

43. 45 Mass. 49 (1842).

44. *Id.*

45. J. W. Hurst, *Law and the Conditions of Freedom in the Nineteenth-Century United States,* 13 (1956).

46. 45 Mass. at 56.

47. *Id.* at 57.

48. Christopher L. Tomlins, *Law, Labor, and Ideology in the Early American Republic,* 303 (1993) (emphasis in original).

49. Lawrence M. Friedman, "Losing One's Head: Judges and the Law in Nineteenth-Century American Legal History," 24 *Law and Soc. Inquiry,* 253, 264–65 (1999).

50. Gilbert E. Roe, *Our Judicial Oligarchy,* 112–13 (1912).

51. Kermit Hall *The Magic Mirror: Law in American History,* 201–2 (1989).

52. Harold M. Hyman and William M. Wiecek, *Equal Justice under Law,* 27 (1982).

53. Stephen Skowronek, *Building a New American State,* 27 (1982).

54. 36 U.S. 420 (1837).

55. James W. Ely, Jr., *The Guardian of Every Other Right,* 69 (2d ed. 1998).

56. 36 U.S. at 549, 552–53. The Massachusetts Supreme Judicial Court's opinion in the case, from which the Charles River Bridge Company appealed to the U.S. Supreme Court, similarly noted that finding an implied right of exclusivity "would [have] amount[ed] to a stipulation, that the channels of communication and course of business, and in fact the state of society and of the country itself,

should remain stationary." Quoted in William E. Nelson, *Americanization of the Common Law,* 161–62 (1975).

57. Henry F. Graff, "The Charles River Bridge Case," in John A. Garrity, ed., *Quarrels That Have Shaped the Constitution,* 74 (1962).

58. Stuart Bruchey, *The Roots of American Economic Growth, 1607–1861,* 137 (1965).

59. Lawrence M. Friedman, *A History of American Law,* 158 (1st ed. 1973).

60. Linda Kerber, *Federalists in Dissent,* 140 (1970).

61. Richard F. Ellis, *The Jeffersonian Crisis,* 176 (1971).

62. Robert M. Cover, *Justice Accused,* 141–42 (1975).

63. William J. Novak, *The People's Welfare,* 246 (1996).

64. Karen Orren, *Belated Feudalism,* 62 (1991).

65. Christopher L. Tomlins, *Law, Labor, and Ideology in the Early American Republic,* 93–94 (1993).

66. Joyce Appleby, *Inheriting the Revolution,* 50–51 (2000).

67. Charles Sellers, *The Market Revolution,* 48 (1991).

68. G. Alan Tarr, *Understanding State Constitutions,* 52 (1998).

69. Steven P. Croley, "The Majoritarian Difficulty: Elective Judiciaries and the Rule of Law," 62 *U. Chi. L. Rev.* 689, 716–17 (1995).

70. Eric Foner, "The Strange Career of the Reconstruction Amendments," 108 *Yale L.J.* 2003, 2006 (1999).

71. *Id.* at 2003. Because formal slavery was not reestablished, it cannot be said that the Thirteenth Amendment was nullified. Still, the brutally exploitative system of sharecrop agriculture that developed after slavery's demise was not much of a qualitative advance. As Leon Litwick says, "whites eager to retain their laborers found that a 'slavery of debt' worked almost as effectively as the old slavery of legal ownership." Leon Litwack, *Trouble in Mind: Black Southerners in the Age of Jim Crow,* 116 (1998).

72. Eric Foner, *Reconstruction, 1863–1877,* 529 (1988).

73. 27 F. Cas. 785 (C.C.D. Ken. 1866) (No. 16,151).

74. *Id.* at 791.

75. *U.S. v. Hall,* 29 F. Cas. 79,81 (C.C.S.D. Ala. 1871) (No. 15,282).

76. *Id.*

77. *Livestock Dealers and Butchers Association,* 15 F. Cas. 649, 652 (C.C.D. La. 1870) (No. 8,408).

78. *Id.*

79. 83 U.S. 6 (1873).

80. Robert Kaczorowski, "Revolutionary Constitutionalism in the Era of the Civil War and Reconstruction," 61 *N.Y.U. L. Rev.* 863, 938 (1986).

81. 83 U.S. at 62.

82. *Id.* at 71.

83. *Id.* at 69.

84. 6 F. Cas. 546 (C.C.E.D. Pa 1823) (No. 3,230).

85. *Id.* at 551–52 (emphasis in original).

86. 83 U.S. at 74 (emphasis supplied).

87. *Id.* at 79.

88. *Id.*

89. Robert J. Reinstein, "Completing the Constitution: The Declaration of Independence, Bill of Rights, and Fourteenth Amendment," 66 *Temple L. Rev.* 361, 402 (1993).

90. Michael Kent Curtis, *No State Shall Abridge*, 176 (1986). Kevin Christopher Newsome has argued provocatively that Justice Miller's analysis of the scope of the privileges or immunities clause in *Slaughterhouse* does not purport to give an exhaustive list of rights protected by the clause and that Miller "saw neither a need or a justification for a comprehensive explanation of federal privileges or immunities." Kevin Christopher Newsome, "Setting Incorporationism Straight: A Reinterpretation of the Slaughterhouse Cases," 109 *Yale L.J.* 643, 675 (2000). But even Newsome acknowledges that "the conventional reading" of Miller's opinion—that it reduced the privileges or immunities clause to a nullity—"is by no means an unreasonable reading" and that it was in fact the benchmark of the Court's Fourteenth Amendment jurisprudence for decades. *Id.* at 687.

91. Charles L. Black, Jr., *A New Birth of Freedom*, 69 (1997).

92. 83 U.S. at 80.

93. *Id.* at 78.

94. *Id.* at 82.

95. Akhil Reed Amar, *The Bill of Rights*, 213 (1998).

96. Raoul Berger, *Government by Judiciary*, 49 (1977). Writing for the Supreme Court, even then-Associate Justice William Rehnquist, a constant proponent of devolving power to state governments, has acknowledged that "the substantive provisions of the Fourteenth Amendment . . . embody significant limitations on state authority" and were meant to authorize "intrusions by Congress . . . into the judicial, executive and legislative spheres of autonomy previously reserved to the States." *Fiizpatrick v. Bitzer*, 427 U.S. 445, 455–56 (1976).

97. William E. Nelson, *The Fourteenth Amendment*, 163 (1988). Which is not to say that Justice Miller was alone in holding that the protections of the Fourteenth Amendment accrued almost exclusively to African Americans. Around the time of *Slaughterhouse*, a federal court in New York and the Supreme Court of California both held that the Fourteenth Amendment's equal protection clause did not grant women the right to vote. *U.S. v. Anthony*, 24 F. Cas. 829 (C.C.N.D.N.Y. 1873) (No. 14,459); *Van Valkenburg v. Brown*, 43 Cal. 43 (1872). The defendant in *Anthony* was the feminist leader Susan B. Anthony, who had been arrested for attempting to register to vote. The California Supreme Court also upheld the state's ban on court testimony offered by persons of Chinese descent. *People v. Brady*, 40 Cal. 198 (1870).

98. Harold M. Hyman and William M. Wiecek, *Equal Justice under Law*, 475 (1982).

99. 92 U.S. 542 (1875).

100. Eric Foner, *Reconstruction, 1863–1877*, 437 (1988).

101. 92 US. at 554.

102. Eric Foner, *Reconstruction, 1863–1877*, 531 (1988).

103. W. E. B. DuBois, *The Souls of Black Folk*, 88 (Penguin ed. 1989).

104. 109 U.S. 3 (1883).

105. 18 Stat. 335 (1875).

106. 109 U.S. at 13.

107. *Id.* at 25. The Civil Rights Cases have never been overruled. Indeed, the Court, speaking through Chief Justice Rehnquist, cited them recently for the proposition that Congress had no authority under the Fourteenth Amendment to enact the Violence against Women Act because, in providing a federal remedy for victims of gender-motivated violence, the act "is directed not at any State or state actor, but at individuals who have committed criminal acts motivated by gender bias." *U.S. v. Morrison*, 529 U.S. 598, 626 (2000).

108. 163 U.S. 537 (1896).

109. C. Vann Woodward, "The Case of the Louisiana Traveler," in John A. Garraty, ed., *Quarrels That Have Shaped the Constitution*, 158 (1962).

110. The Louisiana statute, however, did not command *complete* segregation. It thoughtfully provided that "nothing in this act shall be construed as applying to nurses attending children of the other race." Quoted in 163 U.S. at 541.

111. *Id.* at 543.

112. *Id.* at 544.

113. *Id.* at 550. As further testament to his great influence, the Court in *Plessy* relied in no small part on Lemuel Shaw's 1849 ruling in *Roberts v. City of Boston*, which "held that the general school committee of Boston had power to make provision for the instruction of colored children in separate schools established exclusively for them, and to prohibit their attendance upon other schools." 163 U.S. at 544.

114. 175 U.S. 528 (1899).

115. *Id.* at 532.

116. *Id.* at 544.

117. *Id.* at 545.

118. Leon Litwack, *Trouble in Mind: Black Southerners in the Age of Jim Crow*, 106 (1998). The Court later held that *private* schools that sought to opt out of the prevailing system of educational apartheid could be forbidden from doing so. Berea College was a small institution in Kentucky that began providing biracial education in 1859. In 1908, the Supreme Court upheld a state statute that forbade the school to continue the practice. *Berea College v. Commonwealth of Kentucky*, 211 U.S. 45 (1908).

119. James M. McPherson, *Abraham Lincoln and the Second American Revolution*, 145 (1991).

120. 92 U.S. 214 (1875).

121. *Id.* at 218.

122. 170 U.S. 213 (1898).

123. Id. at 225.

124. Leon Litwack, *Trouble in Mind: Black Southerners in the Age of Jim Crow*, 225 (1998).

125. 189 U.S. 475 (1903).

126. *Id.* at 486.

127. Robert Bork, *The Tempting of America*, 37, 39 (1990). Since, as we have already noted, Raoul Berger is critical of Miller's opinion, here is yet another example of the two originalists at loggerheads. For a thoroughly convincing argument that *Slaughterhouse* is in fact a horribly misconceived opinion in originalist terms, *see* Michael W. McConnell, "Originalism and the Desegregation Decisions," 81 *Va. L. Rev.* 947, 998–1000 (1995).

128. Raoul Berger, *Government by Judiciary*, 183 (1977).

129. Max Boot, *Out of Order*, 96 (1998).

130. Mary Ann Glendon, *A Nation under Lawyers*, 183 (1994).

131. Walter Berns, *Taking the Constitution Seriously*, 224 (1987).

132. Quoted in Harold M. Hyman and William M. Wiecek, *Equal Justice under Law*, 426 (1982).

133. 198 U.S. 45 (1905).

134. Paul Kens, *Lochner v. New York: Economic Regulation on Trial*, 9 (1998).

135. 198 U.S. at 57.

136. *Id.* at 61.

137. G. Edward White, *The American Judicial Tradition*, 86 (1976).

138. Kermit Hall, *The Magic Mirror: Law in American History*, 242 (1989). It is well to remember in this regard that *Lochner* itself was a 5–4 decision that struck down a statute the constitutionality of which had been upheld by all three levels of the New York state court system.

139. *Id.* at 226 (quoting Melvin Urofsky, "State Courts and Protective Legislation during the Progressive Era: A Reevaluation," 72 *Journal of American History* 64 (1985)).

140. Howard Gillman, *The Constitution in Crisis*, 7 (1993).

141. *Id.* at 55.

142. 208 U.S. 412 (1908).

143. *Adkins v. Children's Hospital*, 261 U.S. 525 (1923).

144. *Radice v. New York*, 264 U.S. 292, 294 (1924). The Court distinguished *Adkins* by stating that the earlier case involved "a wage-fixing law, pure and simple. It had nothing to do with the hours or conditions or labor." *Id.* at 295.

145. Kermit Hall, *The Magic Mirror: Law in American History*, 232 (1989).

146. *Id.* at 244.

147. William Forbath, *Law and the Shaping of the American Labor Movement*, 6 (1991).

148. William Forbath, "Labor," in Kermit Hall, ed., *The Oxford Companion to the Supreme Court of the United States*, 489 (1992).

149. Herbert Hovenkamp, *Enterprise and American Law, 1836–1937*, 226 (1991).

150. *Id.*

151. 221 U.S. 418, 437 (1911).

152. *Id.* at 439.

153. William Forbath, *Law and the Shaping of the American Labor Movement*, 85 (1991).

154. *Id.* at 88.

155. Quoted in *id.* at 59.

156. *Id.* at 75.

157. Quoted in David Ray Papke, *The Pullman Case*, 42 (1999). One of the judges who issued the injunction had recently delivered a speech in which he opined that a worker who joins a union "has effectively sunk his will into the general will of his trade and has cast away for organization all the advantages and inspiration of independent individuality." Quoted in *id.* at 40–41.

158. 158 U.S. 564 (1895).

159. *Id.* at 598–99.

160. Quoted in David Ray Papke, *The Pullman Case*, 77 (1999).

161. William Forbath, *Law and the Shaping of the American Labor Movement*, 193 (1991).

162. *Id.* at 151–52.

163. 257 U.S. 312 (1921).

164. *Id.* at 344 (Holmes, J., dissenting).

165. Mary Ann Glendon, *A Nation under Lawyers*, 168 (1994).

166. David Montgomery, *Workers' Control in America*, 160 (1980). "Yellow dog contracts" were pledges not to join a union. They were required by employers as a condition of hiring. In 1908, the Supreme Court struck down a federal law forbidding such contracts as an unconstitutional interference with "the right of the purchaser of labor to prescribe the conditions upon which he will accept . . . labor from the person offering to sell it." *Adair v. United States*, 208 U.S. 161, 174 (1908). A similar state statute was struck down six years later as being unconstitutional "class" legislation that "is intended to deprive employers of a part of their liberty of contract, to the corresponding advantage of the employed and the upbuilding of labor organizations." *Coppage v. Kansas*, 236 U.S. 1, 16 (1914).

167. Quoted in Arnold M. Paul, *Conservative Crisis and the Rule of Law*, 122 (1960).

168. Quoted in William G. Ross, *A Muted Fury*, 41 (1994).

169. Robert Bork, *The Tempting of America*, 7 (1990).

170. Quoted in Arnold M. Paul, *Conservative Crisis and the Rule of Law*, 123 (1960). Paul's book quotes scores of similar expressions of support for judicial intervention into labor relations.

171. Quoted in *id*. at 82 n.3.

172. Herbert Croly, *The Promise of American Life*, 394 (Capricorn ed. 1964).

173. Robert M. LaFollette, "Introduction," in Gilbert E. Roe, *Our Judicial Oligarchy*, vi–vii (1912).

174. Karen Orren, *Belated Feudalism*, 29 (1991).

175. *N.L.R.B. v. Jones & McLaughlin Steel Corp.*, 301 U.S. 1 (1937).

176. Robert Young, "Reflections of a Survivor of State Judicial Election Warfare," *Civil Justice Report of the Center for Legal Policy at the Manhattan Institute*, June 2001, 3.

177. *Id*. at 1–2.

NOTES TO CHAPTER 4

1. Alexander Solzhenitsyn, "A World Split Apart," June 8, 1978, www.hno.harvard.edu/hno.subpages/speeches/solzhenitsyn.html, at 2.

2. *Id*. at 4.

3. *Id*.

4. Philip K. Howard, *The Death of Common Sense*, 116 (1994).

5. Max Boot, *Out of Order*, 101 (1998).

6. "The Republican Platform 1996," adopted August 12, 1996, http://hcl.chass.ncu.edu/garson/election2000/rplat96.htm, at 16 No less expansively, the 2000 Republican Party platform criticizes judges who "disregard the safety, values, and freedom of law-abiding citizens. At the expense of our children and families, they make up laws, invent new rights, free vicious criminals, and pamper felons in prison. . . . The sound principle of judicial review has turned into an intolerable presumption of judicial supremacy." Republican Platform 2000, http://www.dallasnews.com/img/daily/preamble.htm, at 21.

7. Robert Bork, *Slouching toward Gomorrah*, 109 (1996).

8. Robert Bork, *The Tempting of America*, 16–17 (1990).

9. G. Edward White, *The American Judicial Tradition*, 318 (1976).

10. Charles R. Epp, *The Rights Revolution*, 2 (1998).

11. Henry J. Abraham and Barbara A. Perry, *Freedom and the Court*, 5 (7th ed. 1998).

12. Mary Ann Glendon, *Rights Talk*, 4 (1991).

13. Richard Posner, "Barflies," *New Republic*, October 31, 1994, 40.

14. 489 U.S. 189 (1989).

15. *Id*. at 195.

16. *Id.* at 195–96.

17. *Id.* at 196.

18. *Lindsey v. Normet*, 405 U.S. 56, 74 (1972). In this regard, consider the statement of Michael Southwick, a U.S. State Department human rights official, speaking in opposition to a United Nations effort to define housing as a "human right": "'There's the right to housing, the right to food, there's a right to everything, sometimes, that you can think of,' he said. 'It tends to become an entitlement and a legally enforceable kind of thing.' Instead, Mr. Southwick said, 'an economy, good government, the rule of law, democracy—these are the kinds of things that create housing.'" Betsy Pisik, "U.N., U.S. at Odds over Housing as a 'Right,'" *Washington Times*, June 8, 2001, at A1.

The extent to which housing is not a "legally enforceable kind of thing" in America is demonstrated by the fact that "since the late 1970s, the amount of federal money available for providing low-income housing has decreased by around 90 percent. . . . As for rent subsidies: in the late 1970s, the federal government provided 300,000 new units of rental assistance each year. . . . By the 1990s, the number of additional new vouchers had fallen to 40,000 a year, and for two years beginning in 1995, the federal government eliminated the creation of new vouchers entirely." Jennifer Egan, "To Be Young and Homeless," *New York Times Magazine*, March 24, 2002, 57–58. Needless to say, judicial intervention did not halt these budget cuts.

19. *San Antonio Indep. School Dist. v. Rodriguez*, 411 U.S. 1, 30–31 (1973).

20. *Griffin v. Illinois*, 351 U.S. 12, 23 (1956) (Frankfurter, J., concurring). This general principle is of course fully applicable to our politics, since there is certainly no constitutional obligation on the part of the government to "equaliz[e] the relative abilities of individuals and groups to influence the outcome of elections," even if it can be demonstrated that these relative abilities are greatly dependent upon the amount of money that an individual or group can contribute to an election campaign. *Buckley v. Valeo*, 424 U.S. 1, 48 (1976) (per curiam).

21. Mary Ann Glendon, "Rights in Twentieth-Century Constitutions," 59 *U. Chi. L. Rev.* 519, 521 (1992).

22. Quoted in Jennifer Lee, "Discarded Dreams of Dot-Com Rejects," *New York Times*, February 21, 2001, at C1.

23. *Murphy v. I.T.T. Educational Servs., Inc.*, 176 F.3d 934, 938 (7th Cir. 1999). Government employment is afforded constitutional protection only in cases where the government itself "conditions dismissal only for specific reasons," in which case a public employee must be afforded some measure of due process before termination. *Stone v. FDIC*, 179 F.3d 1368, 1374 (D.C. Cir. 1999) If a public employee is hired "at will," he or she is in the same boat as an at-will private employee. *Id.* at 1375.

24. 448 U.S. 297 (1980).

25. *Id.* at 316.

26. William J. Brennan, Jr., "State Constitutions and the Protection of Individual Rights," 90 *Harv. L. Rev.* 489, 495 (1977).

27. *Id.* at 503.

28. *Id.* at 491.

29. Robert A. Shapiro, "Looking for a Way to Expand Rights? Try State Courts," *Washington Post,* March 26, 2000, at B2.

30. *Id.*

31. G. Alan Tarr, *Understanding State Constitutions,* 34 (1998). Tarr also notes that the average state constitution contains more than 120 amendments. *Id.* at 10.

32. Kermit Hall, "Mostly Anchor and Little Sail: The Evolution of American State Constitutions," in Paul Finkelman and Stephen E. Gottlieb, eds., *Toward a Usable Past: Liberty under State Constitutions,* 394 (1991).

33. *Baker v. State,* 744 A.2d 864 (Vt. 1999). Whatever one thinks of the result reached by the Vermont Supreme Court, accounts of the opinion by its many critics tend to badly misrepresent the court's reasoning. The constitution of Vermont, drafted in 1777, declares that government is for the "common benefit" of the whole community, not for the "particular emolument or advantage" of any individual or group. The usually fair-minded Stuart Taylor commented that *Baker* rested upon this clause alone and was therefore nothing but a case of "judges read[ing] their values into a 223-year-old document." Stuart Taylor, "A Vote for Gay Marriage—But Not by Judicial Fiat," *National Journal,* February 19, 2000, 522.

But *Baker* rests upon much more than the "common benefit" clause. The state argued that it could grant special benefits to opposite-sex couples who marry because of the state's legitimate interest in ensuring that children are raised properly. The court agreed that the state has such an interest. However, the Vermont legislature had removed all restrictions upon adoption by same-sex couples and had also acted to establish the interests of same-sex parents and their children when such couples end their relationship. In light of these measures, the court held that the state's assertions "that Vermont public policy favors opposite-sex over same-sex parents . . . are patently without substance." 744 A.2d at 885. In other words, Vermont's legislature, not its judiciary, had determined that there is no rational basis for the state to promote parenting by opposite-sex couples over parenting by same-sex couples. Since the legislature has not similarly removed restrictions upon other types of parents, it is flatly incorrect to assert, as does Don Feder, that *Baker* "[o]f course" validates legal equality "for incestuous couples, polygamous couples [*sic*], and so on." Don Feder, "Democracy under Attack in Vermont," *Boston Herald,* December 22, 1999, at 37.

34. "The End of Marriage?" *Weekly Standard,* January 17, 2000, 7.

35. 110 Stat. 2419 § 2(a) (1996).

36. Robert Barr, "1 Man + 1 Woman = Marriage," *Washington Times,* February 9, 2000, at A7.

37. *Compare* Andrew Koppelman, "Dumb and DOMA: Why the Defense of Marriage Act Is Unconstitutional," 83 *Iowa L. Rev.* 1 (1997) *with* Ralph U. Whitten, "The Original Understanding of the Full Faith and Credit Clause and the Defense of Marriage Act," 32 *Creighton L. Rev.* 255 (1998).

38. Robert A. Shapiro, "Looking for a Way to Expand Rights? Try State Courts," *Washington Post*, March 26, 2000, at B2.

39. 369 U.S. 186 (1962).

40. 377 U.S. 533 (1964).

41. 376 U.S. 1 (1964).

42. Timothy G. O'Rourke, "The Impact of Reapportionment on Congress and State Legislatures," in Mark E. Rush, ed., *Voting Rights and Redistricting in the United States,* 198 (1998).

43. *Id.*

44. Malcolm E. Jewell, "Political Patterns in Apportionment," in Malcolm E. Jewell, ed., *The Politics of Reapportionment,* 17–18 (1962).

45. Morton Horwitz, *The Warren Court and the Pursuit of Justice,* 82 (1998). Horwitz further notes that, "[i]n eleven state senates, a voting majority could be elected by less than 20 percent of the population. . . . In only seventeen states was as much as 40 percent of the population required for majority control." *Id.* at 83.

46. Robert Bork, *The Tempting of America,* 85 (1990).

47. Archibald Cox, *The Warren Court,* 118 (1968).

48. 328 U.S. 549, 556 (1946). In *Baker,* the Court noted the several occasions on which it had decided the question in identical fashion. 369 U.S. at 270 n.1.

49. Quoted in Lucas Powe, *The Warren Court and American Politics,* 252 (2000).

50. The redistricting decisions have received no small amount of criticism on the left. Most notably, Lani Guinier has criticized the principle of one person-one vote as "deference to a tradition of according individual rights a higher value" than rights that adhere to groups. Thus, by establishing districts of equal population as the goal of electoral fairness, the principle "discuss[es] everything in terms of individual voters," thereby ignoring the possibility that minority groups that constitute a majority in no single election district will fail to have their interests represented in government. Lani Guinier, *The Tyranny of the Majority,* 139 (1994). Further, Alexander Cockburn has charged that *Reynolds v. Sims* "turned many rural counties into Third World latifundia." Alexander Cockburn, "Scaremongering and the Court," *Nation,* July 24/31, 2000, 8. I have no idea what he means by this, but it sure sounds like a criticism.

51. Timothy G. O'Rourke, "The Impact of Reapportionment on Congress and State Legislatures," in Mark E. Rush, ed., *Voting Rights and Redistricting in the United States,* 201, 202 (1998).

52. *Id.* at 209.

53. *Id.* at 213.

54. *Id.* at 214.

55. *Id.*

56. *Id.* at 217.

57. *Id.*

58. John Hart Ely, *Democracy and Distrust*, 74 (1980).

59. Lani Guinier and Pamela S. Karlan, "The Majoritarian Difficulty: One Person, One Vote," in E. Joshua Rosenkranz and Bernard Schwartz, eds., *Reason and Passion: Justice Brennan's Enduring Influence*, 210 (1997) (emphases added).

60. *Terminiello v. Chicago*, 337 U.S. 1, 4 (1949).

61. 403 U.S. 15 (1971).

62. Robert Bork, *The Tempting of America*, 248–49 (1990); *Slouching toward Gomorrah*, 99 (1996).

63. Hadley Arkes, "Liberalism and the Law," in Hilton Kramer and Roger Kimball, eds., *The Betrayal of Liberalism*, 103 (1999).

64. *Brandenburg v. Ohio*, 395 U.S. 444 (1969) (per curiam).

65. *U.S. v. O'Brien*, 391 U.S. 367 (1968).

66. 376 U.S. 254 (1964).

67. Archibald Cox, *The Role of the Supreme Court in American Government*, 38 (1980).

68. Anthony Lewis, *Make No Law*, 157 (1991).

69. Lino Graglia, "Constitutional Law: A Ruse for Government by an Intellectual Elite," 14 *Ga. St. L. Rev.* 767, 776 (1998).

70. 750 F.2d 970 (D.C. Cir. 1984) (en banc), *cert. denied*, 471 U.S. 1127 (1985).

71. Bertell Ollman, *Alienation: Marx's Conception of Man in Capitalist Society*, 219 (1971).

72. 418 U.S. 323, 339–40 (1974).

73. 750 F.2d at 987.

74. *Id.* at 986.

75. *Id.* at 993 (Bork, J., concurring).

76. *Id.* (Bork, J., concurring).

77. *Id.* at 995 (Bork, J., concurring). In a notorious 1971 law review article, Bork made a more general statement in this regard, asserting that "[t]he framers seem to have had no coherent theory of free speech and appear not to have been overly concerned with the subject." Robert H. Bork, "Neutral Principles and Some First Amendment Problems," 47 *Indiana L. J.* 1, 22 (1971). Indeed, Bork continues, "[t]he First Amendment, like the rest of the Bill of Rights, appears to have been a hastily drafted document upon which little thought was expended. . . . We are, then, forced to construct our own theory of the constitutional protection of speech." *Id.* We are obviously a long way from the positions taken in *The Tempting of America*, in which Bork describes this article as "theoretical, tentative, and speculative." Robert H. Bork, *The Tempting of America*, 333 (1990). It is explicitly so, but one might expect some discussion in the later work of how Bork came to realize

the falsity of the positions taken in the earlier work, which are expressions of the unworkability of the originalist enterprise, at least as it applies to the First Amendment. One doesn't get it, however.

78. 750 F.2d at 996 (Bork, J., concurring).

79. *Id.* at 995 (Bork, J., concurring) (emphasis added).

80. *Id.* at 996 (Bork, J., concurring). In his dissenting opinion in *Ollman*, Judge Antonin Scalia—yes, *that* Antonin Scalia—has no tolerance for Bork's position that judges should stay abreast of current threats to the general principle of free expression in order to determine when the general principle should be invoked in the exercise of judicial review. The identification of threats, says Scalia "is quintessentially legislative rather than judicial business—largely because *it is such a subjective judgment.* . . . [R]emedies [to such threats] are to be sought through democratic change rather than through judicial pronouncement that the Constitution now prohibits what it did not prohibit before." 750 F.2d at 1038 (Scalia, J., dissenting) (emphasis added).

81. Anthony Lewis, *Make No Law*, 153 (1991).

82. 750 F.2d at 995 (Bork, J., concurring).

83. *Id.* at 1002 (Bork, J., concurring).

84. *Id.* (Bork, J., concurring).

85. *Id.* (Bork, J., concurring).

86. *Id.* at 1009 (Bork, J., concurring). By contrast, Judge Scalia terms the same statement "a classic and cooly crafted libel." *Id.* at 1036 (Scalia, J., dissenting). The statement in question libels Professor Ollman, Scalia opines, because Evans and Novak "put it in the mouth of one whom they describe as (1) an expert on the subject of status in the political science profession, and (2) a political liberal, i.e., *one whose view of Ollman would not be distorted on the basis of greatly differing political opinion.* They were saying, in effect, 'This not merely our prejudiced view; it is the conclusion of an impartial *and indeed sympathetic* expert.'" *Id.* at 1037 (Scalia, J., dissenting; emphases added). Thus, for Scalia, Marxists and liberals are ideological kissing cousins.

87. Mark Tushnet, *Taking the Constitution Away from the Courts,* 131 (1999).

88. David Luban, "The Warren Court and the Concept of a Right," 34 *Harv. C.R.-C.L. L. Rev.*, 7 (1999).

89. *Id.* at 11.

90. 367 U.S. 643 (1961). *Mapp* did not "create" the exclusionary rule. The rule had been applied to *federal* criminal prosecutions more than forty years earlier. *Weeks v. U.S.*, 232 U.S. 383 (1914).

91. David Luban, "The Warren Court and the Concept of a Right," 34 *Harv. C.R.-C.L.L. Rev.* 7, 9 (1999).

92. Mark A. Graber, "The Clintonification of American Law: Abortion, Welfare, and Liberal Constitutional Theory," 58 *Ohio St. L.J.* 731, 738 (1997). As Graber notes, the liberal law professors Cass Sunstein, Laurence Tribe, and Ronald

Dworkin currently all deny that there is a constitutional basis for welfare rights. *Id.* at 735, 742–43.

93. Frank Michelman, "Foreword: On Protecting the Poor through the Fourteenth Amendment," 83 *Harv. L. Rev.* 7, 9, 11 (1969).

94. *Id.* at 33.

95. Stephen Loffredo, "Poverty, Democracy, and Constitutional Law," 141 *U. Pa. L. Rev.* 1277, 1278 (1993).

96. *Id.*

97. Michael B. Katz, *In the Shadow of the Poorhouse*, x (1986).

98. 397 U.S. 254, 255 (1970).

99. *Id.* at 264.

100. *Id.* at 265.

101. *Id.* at 262, n. 3.

102. Sylvia A. Law, "Some Reflections on *Goldberg v. Kelly* at Twenty Years," 56 *Brook. L. Rev.* 805, 807 (1990).

103. Stephen G. Breyer, "*Goldberg v. Kelly:* Administrative Law and the New Property," in E. Joshua Rosenkranz and Bernard Schwartz, eds., *Reason and Passion: Justice Brennan's Enduring Influence,* 256 (1997).

104. William J. Brennan, "Reason, Passion, and 'The Progress of the Law,'" 10 *Cardozo L. Rev.* 3, 21 (1988).

105. 397 U.S. 471 (1970).

106. *Id.* at 485 (quoting *Lindsley v. Natural Carbonic Gas Co.,* 220 U.S. 61, 78 (1911)).

107. *Id.* at 486.

108. *Id.* at 487 (emphasis added).

109. James W. Ely, Jr., *The Guardian of Every Other Right*, 158 (2d ed. 1998). Thus, it is flatly incorrect to assert, as Max Boot does, that one of the "newfangled rights" the Court has recognized is "a 'right' to welfare benefits." Max Boot, *Out of Order*, 97 (1998). The point is illustrated even in cases in which the Court has found in favor of welfare recipients. In *Shapiro v. Thompson*, for example, the Court struck down the statutes of three states that prohibited any individual from receiving welfare benefits until he or she had resided within the state for a year. 394 U.S. 618 (1969). Justice Brennan's majority decision, however, was based upon the right of travel, which was held to be violated by the statutes because they discouraged poor people from moving to these states. Thus does one critic on the left argue that "only by neutralizing the language of class and of economic entitlement did Justice Brennan secure a majority vote [in *Shapiro*]. The consequence, however, was to strip *Shapiro* of any need-based theory of economic justice and of its downwardly redistributive policy implications." Elizabeth Bussiere, "The Supreme Court and the Development of the Welfare State: Judicial Liberalism and the Problem of Welfare Rights," in Cornell Clayton and Howard Gillman, eds., *Supreme Court Decision-Making: New Institutionalist Approaches,* 165–66 (1997).

110. Sheryll D. Cashin, "Federalism, Welfare Reform, and the Minority Poor: Accounting for the Tyranny of State Majorities," 99 *Colum. L. Rev.* 552, 559 (1999).

111. Robert E. Reich, "Clinton's Leap in the Dark," *Times Literary Supplement*, January 22, 1999, 3.

112. William E. Forbath, "Constitutional Welfare Rights: A History, Critique, and Reconstruction," 69 *Fordham L. Rev.* 1821, 1870 (2001).

113. David Cole, "Two Million and Counting," www.lawnewsnetwork.com, January 19, 2000. According to a report issued in October 2000 by the Sentencing Project, the United States has now surpassed Russia to achieve the highest incarceration rate on the planet. Stuart Taylor, "The Issue Politicians Are Ignoring: 2 Million Prisoners," *National Journal*, October 21, 2000, 3299. After several years of declining crime rates, the number of prisoners in America began to decline slightly in 2001. *See* Fox Butterfield, "Number of People in State Prisons Declines Slightly," *New York Times*, August 13, 2001, at A1; David Firestone, "U.S. Figures Show Prison Population Is Now Stabilizing," *New York Times*, June 9, 2001, at A1.

114. *Id.* These are figures that stun even conservatives. Timothy Lynch, of the Cato Institute, has noted that "[i]t took more than 200 years for American to hold 1 million prisoners all at once. And yet we have managed to incarcerate the second million in only the past 10 years." Timothy Lynch, "All Locked Up," *Washington Post*, February 20, 2000, at B7.

115. Ellen Nakashima, "Number of Probationers, Parolees at Record High," *Washington Post*, July 24, 2000, at A2. With respect to parole, a criminal law corollary of *Goldberg v. Kelly* has occurred. Almost thirty years ago, the Supreme Court held that parole hearings must afford prisoners a degree of procedural due process. *Morrissey v. Brewer*, 408 U.S. 471 (1972). However, the Court has long held that "[t]here is no constitutional or inherent right of a convicted person to be conditionally released before the expiration of a valid sentence." *Greenholtz v. Inmates of the Nebraska Penal and Correctional Complex*, 442 U.S. 1, 7 (1979). Facing no federal constitutional bar to doing so, "[t]hirteen states and the federal government have gone as far as doing away with parole altogether, replacing it with a system of predetermined sentences and release times. . . . In 1980, more than 70 percent of prisoners were paroled for good behavior after serving part of their sentence, according to the Association of Paroling Authorities International. Today, only about 30 percent are given discretionary release." Alexandra Marks, "For Prisoners, It's a Nearly No-Parole World," *Christian Science Monitor*, July 10, 2001, at 1.

116. Marc Mauer, *Race to Incarcerate*, 11 (1999).

117. Lynne Duke, "Building a Boom behind Bars," *Washington Post*, September 8, 2000, at A1.

118. Akhil Reed Amar, *The Constitution and Criminal Procedure*, ix (1997).

119. Quoted in Herbert Asbury, *The Gangs of New York*, 219 (1927).

120. Lawrence M. Friedman, *Crime and Punishment in American History*, 296 (1993).

121. Max Boot, *Out of Order*, 88 (1998).

122. Richard Neely, *How Courts Govern America*, 154–55 (1982).

123. Tracey L. Meares and Dan M. Kahan, "When Rights Are Wrong," *Boston Review*, April-May 1999, 4.

124. Clarence Thomas, "Federalist Society Symposium: The Rights Revolution: Keynote Address," 1 *Mich. L. & Pol'y Rev.* 269, 275 (1996).

125. 384 U.S. 436, 444 (1966). While the Warren Court may have constitutionalized "Miranda warnings," they were not the Court's invention. As Chief Justice Warren noted in his majority opinion, "the Federal Bureau of Investigation has compiled an exemplary record of effective law enforcement" while for years requiring that suspects be informed of their rights. *Id.* at 483.

126. *Id.*

127. 530 U.S. 428 (2000).

128. *Id.* at 430. Shortly after the Supreme Court's opinion, the defendant, Charles Dickerson, was retried and convicted of bank robbery in federal district court in spite of the prosecution's inability to introduce his confession. Brooke A. Masters, "Miranda Win Fails to Free Robber," *Washington Post*, October 7, 2000, at B1.

129. *Id.* at 445 (Scalia, J., dissenting).

130. *Id.* at 438.

131. Charles D. Weisselberg, "Saving *Miranda*," 84 *Cornell L. Rev.* 109, 126 (1998). Weisselberg also quotes a widely distributed police training video, produced in 1990: "When you violate *Miranda*, you're not violating the Constitution. *Miranda* is not in the Constitution. It's a court-created decision that affects that admissibility of testimonial evidence and that's all it is. So you don't violate any law." *Id.* at 110.

132. 401 U.S. 222 (1971).

133. *Michigan v. Tucker*, 417 U.S. 433, 444 (1974)

134. *New York v. Quarles*, 467 U.S. 649, 657 (1984).

135. 412 U.S. 218 (1973).

136. Akhil Reed Amar, *The Constitution and Criminal Procedure*, 56 (1997). "Only two states require that all custodial interrogations of suspects be electronically recorded—Minnesota and Alaska, although taping has been standard practice in Great Britain for more than a decade." Steven A. Drizin, "Coerced Confessions Shine Light on Taping," *Chicago Sun-Times*, February 1, 2001, at 29.

137. Akhil Reed Amar, *The Constitution and Criminal Procedure*, 67 (1997). It is certainly no small thing, however, that "the more egregious forms of interrogation abuse" have had their day. Lawrence Friedman declares that "[p]olice brutality has a long, dishonorable history, not only on the street, but also in the station house. Here was the domain of the 'third degree'—various ways of getting

information out of suspects by inflicting suffering, physical or mental. This rather bland phrase conceals a whole world of torture and abuse—beatings with nightsticks and rubber hoses, and sometimes worse." Lawrence Friedman, *Crime and Punishment in American History,* 261 (1993).

138. Jonathan Turley, "*Miranda*—Confirmed But Barely Alive," *Washington Post,* June 27, 2000, at A23.

139. *Mapp v. Ohio,* 367 U.S. 643 (1963)

140. *Id.* at 649 (quoting *Palko v. Connecticut,* 302 U.S. 319, 325 (1937)).

141. *Terry v. Ohio,* 392 U.S. 1, 33 (1968).

142. 468 U.S. 897 (1984).

143. *Id.* at 906–7 (citations omitted).

144. George Kannar, "Liberals and Crime," *New Republic,* December 19, 1988, 20–21 (emphasis in original). Writing in 1997, Akhil Reed Amar, a severe critic of the exclusionary rule, has flatly declared that the "[t]he Fourth Amendment today is an embarrassment." Akhil Reed Amar, *The Constitution and Criminal Procedure,* 1 (1997).

145. 468 U.S. at 949 (Brennan, J., dissenting).

146. Robert Bork, "Slouching toward Bush Won't Save Us from Gomorrah," *Wall Street Journal,* October 11, 1999, at A22.

147. David Cole, *No Equal Justice,* 66 (1999).

148. 372 U.S. 335 (1963).

149. *Id.* at 344. It is well to remember, however, what the Court has never required, notwithstanding *Gideon.* The Court has never held that there is "a right to counsel when many defendants most needed it—*before* they were indicted, but after the state had singled them out for investigation and arrest. . . . [Nor must the state] provide appointed counsel for most appeals." David Cole, *No Equal Justice,* 71 (1999).

150. 466 U.S. 668 (1984).

151. *Id.* at 686–87.

152. David Cole, *No Equal Justice,* 78 (1999).

153. *See* Victor E. Flango and Patricia McKenna, "Federal Habeas Corpus Review of State Court Convictions," 31 *Cal. W. L. Rev.* 237 (1995).

154. 529 U.S. 362 (2000).

155. *Id.* at 395–96.

156. "Note: *Gideon's* Promise Unfulfilled: The Need for Lititgated Reform of Indigent Defense," 113 *Harv. L. Rev.* 2062, 2062, 2064 (2000). Some prime examples of this legion of stories are set forth in Jeffrey L. Kirchmeier, "Drink, Drugs, and Drowsiness: The Constitutional Right to Effective Assistance of Counsel and the *Strickland* Prejudice Requirement," 75 *Neb. L. Rev.* 425 (1996).

157. *Chandler v. U.S.,* 218 F.3d 1305, 1345 (11th Cir. 2000) (*en banc*) (Barkett, J., dissenting), *cert. denied,* 531 U.S. 1204 (2001).

158. *McFarland v. Scott*, 512 U.S. 1256,1259 (1994) (Blackmun, J., dissenting from denial of certiorari).

159. Quoted in Richmond Eustis, "11th Circuit Splits 6–5 on Death Case," *National Law Journal*, August 14, 2000, at A5.

160. David Luban, "The Warren Court and the Concept of a Right," 34 *Harv. C.R.-C.L. L. Rev.* 7 (1999).

NOTES TO CHAPTER 5

1. 410 U.S. 113 (1973).
2. Charles Fried, *Order and Law*, 72 (1991).
3. Robert Bork, *The Tempting of America*, 72 (1990).
4. *Id.* at 116.
5. 424 U.S. 1 (1976) (per curiam).
6. *Casey v. Planned Parenthood of Southeastern Pennsylvania*, 505 U.S. 833, 866–67 (1992).
7. *Id.* at 995 (Scalia, J., dissenting).
8. 497 U.S. 502, 520–21 (1990) (Scalia, J., concurring).
9. Mary Ann Glendon, *Rights Talk*, 58 (1991).
10. Jean Bethke Elshtain, "*Roe v. Wade*: Speaking the Unspeakable," in Robert P. George, ed., *Great Cases in Constitutional Law*, 175 (2000) (emphasis in original).
11. Jonathan Rauch, "The Right Approach to Gay Marriage," *Washington Post*, December 28, 1999, at A23.
12. 530 U.S. 914 (2000).
13. Democracy, Abortion, and the Court," *Chicago Tribune*, July 2, 2000, at 14.
14. "Splitting the Embryo," *Wall Street Journal*, August 13, 2001, at A12.
15. David Garrow, "Abortion before and after *Roe v. Wade*: An Historical Perspective," 62 *Alb. L. Rev.* 833, 840 (1999).
16. John Dunn, "Rights and Political Conflict," in *Interpreting Political Responsibility*, 50 (1990) (emphasis added).
17. Kristin Luker, *Abortion and the Politics of Motherhood*, 2 (1984).
18. *Catechism of the Catholic Church*, § 2270 (Image/Doubleday ed. 1995).
19. Reva Siegel, "Reasoning from the Body: A Historical Perspective on Abortion Regulation and Questions of Equal Protection," 44 *Stan. L. Rev.* 261, 379 (1992).
20. It is further evidence of the irreconcilable nature of the prolife and prochoice stances that the positions of those in the middle are often irreconcilable in themselves precisely because they appropriate values from both stances. Thus did a recent nationwide poll conducted by the *Los Angeles Times* report these "competing sets of feelings": "More than half of those surveyed say abortion should either

be illegal in all circumstances or legal only in cases of rape incest or when a woman's life is in danger. At the same time, more than two-thirds say that, regardless of their own feelings on the subject, the highly personal decision to obtain an abortion should be left to a woman and her doctor." Alissa J. Rubin, "Americans Narrowing Support for Abortion," *Los Angeles Times,* June 18, 2000, at A1. Thus also does Christopher Caldwell note that, with respect to abortion, great numbers of Americans "want to register their moral disapproval and keep the procedure available at the same time." Christopher Caldwell, "Pro-Lifestyle," *New Republic,* April 5, 1999, 14.

21. Florian Miedel, "Is West Germany's 1975 Abortion Decision a Solution to the American Abortion Debate?: A Critique of Mary Ann Glendon and Donald Kommers," 20 *N.Y.U. Rev. L. & Soc. Change* 471, 505 (1993–1994).

22. Mary Ann Glendon, *Abortion and Divorce in Western Law,* 52, 55 (1987).

23. Gregg Easterbrook, "Abortion and Brain Waves," *New Republic,* January 31, 2000, 21.

24. Karen Houppert, "The Meaning of Life," *Nation,* March 13, 2000, 7.

25. Katha Pollitt, *Reasonable Creatures,* 177 (1994).

26. Jean Reith Schroedel, *Is the Fetus a Person?* 190 (2000).

27. Martha Davis, "Between a Woman and Her Doctor," www.msnbc.com, June 29, 2000.

28. Margaret Talbot, "The Little White Bombshell," *New York Times Magazine,* July 11, 1999, 38.

29. Janet Parshall, "Daily Radio Commentary," www.frc.org, August 17, 2000 (emphasis in original).

30. Quoted in Shari Roan, "The Abortion Pill: Finally at Hand?" *Los Angeles Times,* August 14, 2000, at S1.

31. Rita Rubin, "RU-486," *USA Today,* October 1, 2001, at 5D.

32. *Stenberg v. Carhart* 530 U.S. at 921 (2000).

33. Amy Gutmann, "No Common Ground," *New Republic,* October 22, 1990, 43 (emphasis added). And this works both ways. In his review of Tribe's book, Michael McConnell correctly argues that the prochoice Tribe's proposed compromises amount to positing "that one side's absolutes should be adopted and the other side's rejected." Michael McConnell, "How Not to Promote Serious Deliberation about Abortion," 58 *U. Chi. L. Rev.* 1181, 1183 (1991). But McConnell goes on to offer areas of "common ground," such as abortion counseling and waiting periods, that have long been rejected out of hand by the prochoice movement as unsubtle attempts to dissuade women from exercising free choice. *Id.* at 1195–97. (Try to formulate the contents of an abortion counseling message that would be considered a "compromise" by both sides.) McConnell goes on to suggest establishing "cutoff dates for abortion somewhere between conception and birth." *Id.* at 1197. He acknowledges that, "for abortion opponents, such compromises would be difficult," but I think it is more accurate to say that the prolife movement,

which recently declared its overwhelming opposition to any fetal stem cell research, would find such "compromises" utterly unacceptable. *Id.*

34. Kristin Luker, *Abortion and the Politics of Motherhood*, 14–15 (1984).

35. David Garrow, *Liberty and Sexuality*, 277 (1994).

36. *Id.* at 312. The American Medical Association as a whole went on record for abortion law reform in 1967 and in 1970 endorsed the actual repeal of abortion laws. *Id.* at 333, 455.

37. "NOW Bill of Rights," in Robin Morgan, ed., *Sisterhood Is Powerful*, 514 (1970).

38. Laurence Tribe, *Abortion: The Clash of Absolutes*, 45 (1990).

39. David Garrow, *Liberty and Sexuality*, 310 (1994) (emphasis in original).

40. *Id.* at 332.

41. *Id.* at 369.

42. Neal Devins, *Shaping Constitutional Values*, 59 (1996).

43. Laurence Tribe, *Abortion: The Clash of Absolutes*, 47–48 (1990).

44. *Id.* at 48.

45. Quoted in David Garrow, *Liberty and Sexuality*, 546 (1994).

46. *Id.* at 578.

47. Rosemary Nossiff, *Before* Roe, 106 (2001).

48. Jean Reith Schroedel, *Is the Fetus a Person?* 38–39 (2000).

49. James L. Buckley, "The Constitution and the Courts: A Question of Legitimacy," 24 *Harv. J. Law & Pub. Pol'y* 189, 196 (2000). This is a confused statement, but, if Judge Buckley is suggesting that *Dred Scott* "unleashed" the issue of slavery, he is, as we have noted earlier, incorrect.

50. It is important to remember that *Roe* was the result of an extensive campaign in the courts for reproductive rights. David Garrow notes that *"Roe v. Wade* in Texas, and its eventual Supreme Court companion case of *Doe v. Bolton* from Georgia, were only two out of approximately fifteen to twenty roughly simultaneous cases." David Garrow, "Abortion before and after *Roe v. Wade:* An Historical Perspective," 62 *Alb. L. Rev.* 833, 836 (1999). Charles Epp has argued perceptively that this campaign of litigation is partially explained by the entry into the legal profession of "substantial numbers of women" in the years immediately prior to *Roe.* Charles R. Epp, *The Rights Revolution*, 57 (1998).

51. Robert P. George, "Justice, Legitimacy, and Allegiance: 'The End of Democracy?' Symposium Revisited," 44 *Loy. L. Rev.* 103, 104 (1998).

52. Bruce Fein, "As the Supreme Court Turns," *Washington Times*, July 18, 2000, at A16. A number of prochoice critics of *Roe*, of whom there are several, take this history to mean that the momentum toward legislative repeal of abortion laws was inexorable. Thus, Gerald Rosenberg argues that, pre-*Roe*, "there was little opposition to abortion on the federal level, widespread support for it among relevant professional elites and social activists . . . and growing public support." Gerald Rosenberg, *The Hollow Hope*, 182 (1991). In this view, all *Roe* did was galvanize

the prolife movement. Or, as the *New Republic* has editorialized, "[i]n the early 1970s antiabortion laws were on the way out," but *Roe* "killed off the movement for abortion." "Good News on Abortion," *New Republic*, July 31, 1989, 5. This view has been criticized by Peter Schuck in his review of Rosenberg's book. Schuck argues that "the pre-*Roe* liberalizations of state abortion laws typically had been quite modest, leaving significant restrictions in place," and that even these were not "as powerful and irreversible as Rosenberg suggests." Peter Schuck, "Public Law Litigation and Social Reform," 102 *Yale L.J.* 1763, 1778 (1993).

53. Clarke D. Forsythe, "A New Strategy," *Human Life Review*, September 1999, 15.

54. Precisely because *Roe* did not establish a right considered sufficiently broad, more than a few prominent feminists contend that the prochoice movement should welcome *Roe*'s demise. Here is the law professor Susan Estrich: "What *Roe v. Wade* now means is that if you're lucky enough to live in a place where doctors aren't afraid to do abortions and you have the money to pay for one, you don't have to bring cash in a plain envelope. It's safe and legal, until viability. . . . If *Roe* were actually to be overruled, every state would be required to go through a full-blown debate about whether and when to permit or prohibit abortions. . . . I can't think of an easier way to motivate women to take over American politics, to recognize that they have the power to do it. Imagine what a real movement of women using their power could accomplish." Susan Estrich, "For Some, Choice Gets Harder," *Nation*, October 9, 2000, 19–20. Similarly, in defending her decision to back Ralph Nader's presidential bid, Ellen Willis declared that "more and more I am coming to the conviction that *Roe v. Wade*, in the guise of a great victory, has been in some respects a disaster for feminism. We might be better off today if it had never happened, and we had had to continue a state-by-state political fight. *Roe v. Wade* resulted in a lot of women declaring victory and going home. In the meantime we have been losing abortion rights on the ground, both in terms of access and funding and on the ideological and psychological fronts." Ellen Willis, "Vote for Ralph Nader!" *Salon.com*, November 6, 2000.

55. As Michael McCann has noted, American history has often seen "opposition to the Court" serve as "a critical rallying cry around which citizens and official representatives mobilized. Examples include the Populist movement's response to various procorporate decisions in the late nineteenth century, the white prosegregation movement defying *Brown* . . . in the 1950s, the right-to-life movement following *Roe v. Wade* since the 1970s, and the antipornography coalition in the 1980s." Michael McCann, "How the Supreme Court Matters in American Politics," in Howard Gillman and Cornell Clayton, eds., *The Supreme Court in American Politics: New Institutionalist Approaches*, 76 (1999).

56. N. E. H. Hull and Peter Charles Hoffer, Roe v. Wade: *The Abortion Rights Controversy in American History*, 189 (2001).

57. Laurence Tribe, *Abortion: The Clash of Absolutes,* 151 (1990).

58. Quoted in Donald Grier Stephenson, *Campaigns and the Court,* 204 (1999).

59. Laurence Tribe, *Abortion: The Clash of Absolutes,* 165 (1990). Further, by 1978 only thirteen of the necessary thirty-four states had called for a constitutional convention for the purpose of passing an amendment to overrule *Roe.* David Garrow, *Liberty and Sexuality,* 631 (1994).

60. *Id.* at 668.

61. Quoted in *id.* at 669.

62. David Garrow, "Privacy and the American Constitution," *Social Research,* April 2001, 72.

63. Neal Devins, *Shaping Constitutional Values,* 92 (1996). With respect to Justice Kennedy's nomination, Morton Horwitz contends that Kennedy, who won confirmation to the Supreme Court seat for which Bork was nominated, "seemed to agree that there had been a sea change in American constitutional understanding and that the Constitution now embodied penumbral, unspecified rights. . . . Judge Bork was defeated, above all, because he rejected these views on rights." Morton Horwitz, "The Meaning of the Bork Nomination in American Constitutional History," 50 *U. Pitt. L. Rev.* 655, 664 (1989).

64. John Anthony Maltese, *The Selling of Supreme Court Nominees,* 111 (1998).

65. 492 U.S. 490 (1989).

66. 505 U.S. 833 (1992).

67. David Garrow, *Liberty and Sexuality,* 680–81 (1994).

68. *Id.* at 682, 689.

69. 18 U.S.C. § 248.

70. "Senate Backs *Roe v. Wade* Decision," www.msnbc.com, October 21, 1999.

71. David Garrow, "Privacy and the Constitution," *Social Research,* April 2001, 56. Garrow further notes that *Stenberg,* the Court's most recent abortion decision, "failed to mention the word 'privacy' even once." *Id.*

72. Iris Marion Young, "The Supreme Court and Abortion," *Dissent,* Fall 1992, 425–26.

73. Anna Greenberg, "Will Choice Be Aborted?" *American Prospect,* Fall 2001, 25. For a full description of the range of antiabortion regulations that have been passed by the states, *see* Jean Reith Schroedel, *Is the Fetus a Person?* 66–96 (2000).

74. Christopher Caldwell, "Pro-Lifestyle," *New Republic,* April 5, 1999, 14.

75. Midge Decter, "Response," in Mitchell S. Muncy, ed., *The End of Democracy?* 79 (1997).

76. 88 Stat. 1291 (1974).

77. 424 U.S. at 19–21.

78. *Id.* at 26.

79. *Id.* at 48–49.

80. Burt Neuborne, *Campaign Finance Reform and the Constitution: A Critical Look at* Buckley v. Valeo, Brennan Center Campaign Finance Reform Series, 12 (1997).

81. Edward B. Foley, "Philosophy, the Constitution, and Campaign Finance," 10 *Stan. L. & Pol'y Rev.* 23, 25 (1998).

82. Samuel Issacharoff and Richard H. Pildes, "Not by 'Election' Alone," 32 *Loy. L.A. L. Rev.* 1173, 1175 (1999).

83. *See* Samuel Issacharoff, Pamela S. Karlan, and Richard H. Pildes, *The Law of Democracy*, 244 (2d ed. 2001).

84. Robert J. Dinkin, *Campaigning in America*, 1 (1989).

85. Alan Taylor, "From Fathers to Friends of the People: Political Personas in the Early Republic," in Ralph D. Gray and Michael A. Morrison, eds., *New Perspectives on the Early Republic*, 139 (1994).

86. Robert J. Dinkin, *Campaigning in America*, 2 (1989).

87. Edmund S. Morgan, *Inventing the People*, 183 (1988).

88. Gary B. Nash, *The Urban Crucible*, 90 (1979).

89. Robert A. Gross, *The Minutemen and Their World*, 66 (1976).

90. And even this practice should be seen within the context of the deferential politics of the age: "'Treating' was not simply a way of buying support. The paternalistic dominance of the gentry was expressed in their acceptance of an obligation to show 'liberality' toward their poorer neighbors. The candidates confirmed their characters as magnanimous gentlemen when they stood to treat all voters, regardless of how they voted." Rhys Isaac, *The Transformation of Virginia, 1740–1790*, 113 (1982).

91. Fed 10 at 82.

92. Noble Cunningham, *The Jeffersonian Republicans*, 250 (1957).

93. Gil Troy, "Money and Politics: The Oldest Connection," *Wilson Quarterly*, Summer 1997, 18.

94. Bradley Smith, "The Sirens' Song: Campaign Finance Regulation and the First Amendment," 6 *J. L. & Pol'y* 1, 8 (1997).

95. Stanley Elkins and Eric McKitrick, *The Age of Federalism*, 289 (1993).

96. *Id.* at 515.

97. Joanne B. Freeman, *Affairs of Honor*, 249 (2001).

98. *Id.* at 212.

99. 424 U.S. at 26.

100. Gordon Wood, *The Radicalism of the American Revolution*, 105 (1992).

101. Fed 9 at 72.

102. Gordon Wood, *The Creation of the American Republic, 1776–1787*, 58 (1969).

103. Letter to Mercy Otis Warren, April 16, 1776, in Adrienne Koch and William Peden, eds., *The Selected Writings of John Adams and John Quincy Adams*, 57–58 (1946).

104. Gordon Wood, *The Radicalism of the American Revolution,* 105 (1992). Wood also notes just how far we are today from this way of thinking: "Republicanism . . . put an enormous burden on individuals. They were expected to suppress their private wants and interests and develop disinterestedness—the term the eighteenth century most often used as a synonym for civic virtue. . . . Perhaps we cannot quite conceive of the characteristic that disinterestedness describes: we cannot quite imagine someone who is capable of rising above private profit and private advantage and being unselfish and unbiased where a personal interest might be present." *Id.* at 104–5.

105. 1 APWFE 498.

106. 528 U.S. 377 (2000).

107. In its most recent campaign finance case, the Court upheld certain federal limitations upon the expenditure of political party funds when undertaken in co-ordination with individual candidates for office. *Federal Election Comm'n. v. Colorado Republican Fed. Campaign Comm.,* 121 S. Ct. 2351 (2001). Justice Thomas, along with Justices Scalia and Kennedy, and Chief Justice Rehnquist in part, dissented. But Justice Thomas makes no originalist argument here beyond the declaration that he is engaged in protecting "core speech and associational rights that our Founders sought to defend." *Id.* at 2372 (Thomas, J., dissenting).

108. 528 U.S. at 411 (Thomas, J., dissenting).

109. 1 Stat. 596 (1798). The unabashedly repressive Sedition Act presents a problem in itself for any originalist seeking to avoid the embarrassment of arguing that a similar statute enacted today should survive constitutional challenge. While the Sedition Act's constitutionality was debated extensively before passage, it was approved by both Houses of Congress and signed by President John Adams. Nor was it declared unconstitutional by any of the several federal courts that handled prosecutions under it. It was also never repealed but was simply allowed to expire on its own terms during the first administration of Thomas Jefferson. *See* Michael Kent Curtis, *Free Speech, The People's Darling Privilege,* 52–104 (2000); David Currie, *The Constitution in Congress,* 260–62, 269–73 (1997); Joseph Lynch, *Negotiating the Constitution,* 185–90, 200–1 (1999). The Act was not explicitly recognized as incompatible with the First Amendment until *New York Times v. Sullivan.* 376 U.S. 254, 273–77 (1964). The fact is that it was anything but an uncommon belief that the First Amendment allowed the government to jail its critics because, as one member of the House put it, "every independent Government has a right to preserve and defend itself" against critics. Quoted in David Currie, *The Constitution in Congress,* 260 (1997).

110. JM LOA 655.

111. The argument is in fact frequently made that the current campaign finance regime operates with a heavy bias toward incumbents. "Because PAC money is generally an investment in the decision-making process in Congress, it flows overwhelmingly to incumbent members of Congress who, unlike chal-

lengers, are in a position to make decisions affecting the PAC's interests. For most PACs, contributions to challengers are seen as a waste of money." Fred Wertheimer and Susan Weiss Manes, "Campaign Finance Reform: A Key to Restoring the Health of Our Democracy," 94 *Colum. L. Rev.* 1126, 1135 (1994).

112. 528 U.S. at 413 (Thomas, J., dissenting) (quoting Fed 35 at 214).

113. Fed 35 at 214.

114. Fed 35 at 214–15.

115. Fed 35 at 215.

116. 528 U.S. at 424, n. 9 (Thomas, J., dissenting).

117. Douglass Adair, "The Tenth Federalist Revisited," in Trevor Colbourn, ed., *Fame and the Founding Fathers: Essays by Douglass Adair,* 131 (Liberty Fund ed. 1974). For a demonstration that "pluralist" readings of *Federalist* 10 are the product of modern political science and not of Madison's intent, *see* Paul F. Bourke, "The Pluralist Reading of James Madison's Tenth Federalist," 9 *Perspectives in American History* 271 (1975).

118. Fed 10 at 77 (emphasis added).

119. Fed 10 at 78.

120. Fed 10 at 83.

121. Fed 10 at 83.

122. Fed 10 at 82.

123. Fed 10 at 82.

124. Fed 10 at 77.

125. Daniel W. Howe, "The Political Psychology of the Federalist," 44 *William and Mary Quarterly* 503 (1987).

126. Samuel Issacharoff and Richard H. Pildes, "Not by 'Election' Alone," 32 *Loy. L. A. L. Rev.* 1173, 1175 (1999).

127. Richard Hofstadter, *The Idea of a Party System*, 53 (1969). In *California Democratic Party v. Jones,* the Supreme Court struck down California's "blanket primary" law, which allowed voters to cast ballots in primary elections without regard to their party affiliation, thereby resulting in elections where party nominees could be chosen without having obtained the support of a majority of those party members who cast ballots. 530 U.S. 567 (2000). Writing for the Court, Justice Scalia makes no effort to argue that the framers were in favor of vigorous parties that could choose standard-bearers uninfluenced by independent voters or voters affiliated with rival parties. Rather, he limits his originalist analysis to the single statement that "[t]he formation of national political parties was almost concurrent with the formation of the Republic itself." *Id.* at 574.

And it is in fact true that, as the passionate political struggles of the 1790s developed, embryonic political parties began to form behind the respective political programs of the Federalist Hamilton and the Republican Jefferson. But it was by no means yet the case that men of public affairs saw party competition as *legitimate.* On the contrary, given that "party and faction in any form were seen as disruptive, subversive, and wicked," "any public man of probity and conscience in the America of the 1790s who engaged in factional politics would have had to persuade himself, not to say others, that what he was doing in practice did not controvert a theoretical view to which everyone, himself included, subscribed." Stanley Elkins and Eric McKitrick, *The Age of Federalism*, 263 (1993). Such persuasion usually took the form of convincing oneself, and others, that the party one supported had formed merely to oppose the designs of the other party, which was undoubtedly attempting to destroy the very existence of republican government in America. Thus did James Madison, writing in 1792, refer to the Republicans as "friends to the authority of the people, the sole foundation on which the union rests," while condemning the Federalists as "those who avow or betray principles of monarchy and aristocracy, in opposition to the republican principles of the Union." JM LOA 518.

128. In a recent law review article, Professor John O. McGinnis attempts to establish that "powerful support" for *Buckley* can be found "in the original understanding of the First Amendment." John O. McGinnis, "Against the Scribes: Campaign Finance Reform Revisited," 24 *Harv. J. Law & Pub. Pol'y* 25, 31 (2000). McGinnis first asserts that "the First Amendment was conceived as a property right of all individuals" and not as "a collective right [of society] to govern itself." *Id.* at 33, 34. Beyond the fact that he makes no attempt to demonstrate how widely held such a belief was among the framers, it would seem to prove nothing regarding campaign finance, since the framers were certainly not averse to the idea that the government could legitimately *regulate* property rights for the benefit of the common good. McGinnis then notes that the First Amendment was written against the background of struggles in Great Britain to resist government attempts to limit access to printing presses. He concludes that "a special rule limiting campaign expenditures restricts citizens' rights to rent the printing press and their contemporary equivalents. Campaign expenditure limitations are thus flatly inconsistent with the historic core of the First Amendment's protections." *Id.* at 34. But renting printing presses has no direct relation to the electoral context and therefore does nothing to address the matter of how the framers thought elections should be conducted, especially with respect to their deep distaste for the very idea of candidates soliciting votes. McGinnis ends with a reading of *Federalist* 10 that falsely claims, in the same manner as Justice Thomas in *Shrink Missouri*, that Madison longed for healthy factional competition, presumably free of any campaign finance regulation, and the possibility that "factions would replace one another [in power] with regularity." *Id.* at 35. Also like Justice Thomas, McGinnis refers to nothing from the actual debates over the First Amendment's ratification; nor does he refer to any materials from the Founding Era that deal explicitly with elections. This is an originalism of shreds and patches.

129. The only problem that conservatives tend to have with *Buckley* is that it did not go far enough. In this view, the Court should not have upheld limits upon

contributions to individual candidates as a means of negating the appearance and/or reality of corruption. Instead, public disclosure of contributions received "provides the necessary information for the citizenry to manage the problem by refusing to vote for a candidate who accepts large contributions or who seems to cast legislative votes in return for contributions." Bradley A. Smith, "Money Talks: Speech, Corruption, Equality, and Campaign Finance," 86 *Geo. L.J.* 45, 61 (1997).

130. Mitch McConnell, "Donor Limits Are Unrealistic," *USA Today*, June 14, 2000, at 26A. McConnell has spoken in Congress with equal candor: "'Soft money' . . . 'hard money' . . . and all the other terms of art tossed about in this debate are euphemisms for Constitutionally protected speech. It is no more complicated than that." Hearing of the Senate Committee on Rules and Finance on Campaign Finance Revision, March 22, 2000, 2000 WL 11070065.

131. George F. Will, "Is Free Speech Only for the Media?" *Washington Post*, October 17, 1999, at B9.

132. Clint Bolick, "If You Want the Money, Ask for It," *Arizona Republic*, June 19, 2002.

133. Tom DeLay, "Rationing Speech as Campaign Reform," *Media Studies Journal*, Fall 2000, 3 (emphasis added).

Notes to Chapter 6

1. Plato, *Laws*, 518 (Penguin ed. 1970).

2. *Id.* at 523.

3. *Id.* at 520.

4. Saikrishna B. Prakash, "America's Aristocracy," 109 *Yale L.J.* 541, 584 (1999).

5. Tunku Varadarajan, "Judges or Priests?," *WSJ.com*, May 11, 2001.

6. Sir Ernest Barker, *The Political Thought of Plato and Aristotle*, 202 (1959 ed.).

7. Stephen B. Presser, "How Bush Would Fix the Supremes," *Chicago Tribune*, November 5, 2000, at 21.

8. Malcolm M. Feeley and Edward L. Rubin, *Judicial Policy Making and the Modern State*, 335 (1999).

9. John Stuart Mill, "M. de Tocqueville on Democracy in America," in Geraint L. Williams, ed., *John Stuart Mill on Politics and Society*, 213 (1976).

10. Jack Rakove, "The Origins of Judicial Review: A Plea for New Contexts," 49 *Stan. L. Rev.* 1031, 1042 (1997).

11. *Alden v. Maine*, 527 U.S. 706, 807 (1999) (Souter, J., dissenting).

12. Benjamin I. Page, *Who Gets What from Government*, 159–60 (1983). A useful statistical synopsis of the growth of the administrative state through the course of the nation's history is set forth in an appendix to Cass Sunstein, *After the Rights Revolution*, 242–44 (1990).

13. Nicholas Zeppos, "Administrative State," in Kermit Hall, ed., *The Oxford Companion to the Supreme Court of the United States*, 11 (1992).

14. *Id.*

15. *FTC v. Rubberoid Co.*, 343 U.S. 470, 487 (1952) (Jackson, J., dissenting).

16. Guido Calabresi, *A Common Law for the Age of Statues*, 46 (1982).

17. Richard B. Stewart, "The Reformation of American Administrative Law," 88 *Harv. L. Rev.* 1669, 1677 (1975).

18. 21 U.S.C. § 321(g)(l).

19. 15 U.S.C. § 1392(f)(1).

20. 42 U.S.C. § 7409(b).

21. David Brody, "What Next for Labor Rights?" *Dissent*, Spring 2001, 18.

22. Peter L. Strauss, "The Place of Agencies in Government: Separation of Powers and the Fourth Branch," 84 *Colum. L. Rev.* 573, 582 (1984).

23. Malcom M. Feeley and Edward L. Rubin, *Judicial Policy Making and the Modern State*, 333 (1999).

24. Guido Calabresi, *A Common Law for the Age of Statues*, 99 (1982).

25. 60 Stat. 237 (1946) (codified as amended in scattered sections of 5 U.S.C.).

26. John A. Rohr, *To Run a Constitution*, 157 (1986).

27. 5 U.S.C. §§ 702, 704.

28. Richard Neely, *How Courts Govern America*, 82 (1981).

29. *Ethyl Corp v. EPA*, 541 F.2d 1, 68 (D.C. Cir.) (Leventhal, J., concurring), *cert. denied*, 426 U.S. 941 (1976).

30. 467 U.S. 837, 843 n.9, 844 (1984).

31. *Id.* at 844.

32. *Id.* at 865.

33. 529 U.S. 120 (2000).

34. 21 U.S.C. § 32l(g)(1).

35. 529 U.S. at 121.

36. *Id.* at 142.

37. *American Trucking Assns., Inc. v. EPA*, 175 F.3d 1027 (D.C. Cir. 1999).

38. *Mistretta v. United States*, 488 U.S. 361, 373 (1989) (emphasis supplied).

39. 42 U.S.C. § 7409(b).

40. 175 F.3d at 1034.

41. "Who Elected the EPA?" *New York Times*, October 2, 2000, at A27.

42. "Rein in the Regulators," *Wall Street Journal*, November 7, 2000, at A26.

43. Indeed, one lawyer supporting the EPA's position in the case argues that that is precisely what has happened: "They tried for thirty years to get Congress to change the language of the statute and they tried to get it changed through agency implementation and they didn't succeed. . . . Now they're trying to get the court to do it, through constitutional interpretation." Quoted in Margaret Kriz, "Trying to Roll Back the Regulators," *National Journal*, November 4, 2000, 3487.

44. *Whitman v. American Trucking Assns., Inc.*, 531 U.S. 457, 473–76 (2001). With the constitutionality of the Clean Air Act no longer in doubt, the D.C. Circuit on remand upheld the EPA's regulations regarding air quality that had been challenged in the case. *American Trucking Assns, Inc. v. EPA*, 283 F.3d 355 (D.C. Cir. 2002).

45. Cass Sunstein, *After the Rights Revolution*, v (1990).

46. *Id.*

47. Fed 22 at 150.

48. 42 U.S.C. § 2000e-2(a). The central provision of the Age Discrimination in Employment Act adopts this language verbatim in prohibiting discrimination against employees forty years of age and older, 29 U.S.C. § 623(a). The central provision of the Americans with Disabilities Act (ADA), which was enacted in 1990, is even more imprecise. The ADA prohibits discrimination against persons with disabilities and defines "disability" as a "physical or mental impairment that substantially limits one or more . . . major life activities." 42 U.S.C. § 1210(1). But the ADA contains no definition of the phrases "substantially limits" or "major life activities." Disabled-rights activists charge that the Supreme Court has construed the statutory language in a manner that is much too protective of employers. Thus, a unanimous Court, speaking through Justice O'Connor, held recently that "major life activities" includes such things as household chores and personal grooming activities, not merely activities that are relevant to holding a job. *Toyota Motor Mfg., Kentucky, Inc. v. Williams*, 122 S. Ct. 681 (2002). Writing shortly after *Williams* was decided, Representative Steny Hoyer, who was one of the leading legislative sponsors of the ADA, criticized the decision as being at odds with legislative intent: "Is this what we had in mind when we passed the ADA—that lawyers for businesses and individuals should spend time and money arguing about whether people can brush their teeth or take out the garbage? Not at all." But even Representative Hoyer conceded that "[i]t is difficult to say, based solely upon the letter of the law as we wrote it, that O'Connor is wrong." Steny H. Hoyer, "Not Exactly What We Intended, Justice O'Connor," *Washington Post*, January 20, 2002, at B1.

49. Benjamin N. Cardozo, *The Nature of the Judicial Process*, 165–66 (1921).

50. Cass Sunstein, *After the Rights Revolution*, 118 (1990).

51. 401 U.S. 424, 431 (1971).

52. 443 U.S. 193 (1979).

53. 42 U.S.C. § 2000e-2(j) (emphasis added).

54. 477 U.S. 57, 67 (1986) (quotation omitted). That Title VII prohibits sex discrimination *at all* is a fascinating story that is a salutary reminder of the idiosyncrasies to which the legislative process is sometimes prone. The prohibition against discrimination based on sex was proposed as an amendment to Title VII by a segregationist representative as a last-ditch effort to defeat passage of the Civil Rights Act. His thought was that the addition of a prohibition on sex discrimina-

tion would be considered so radical as to ensure the defeat of the entire bill. In other words, he was hoping sexism would preserve racism. The Civil Rights Act passed anyway, but with nothing but the most minimal debate or deliberation as to the effect of the inclusion of a prohibition upon sex discrimination. James T. Patterson, *Grand Expectations: The United States*, 1945–1974, 545 (1996). Thus, as the Court noted in *Vinson*, "there is little legislative history to guide us in interpreting the Act's prohibition against discrimination based on 'sex.'" 477 U.S. at 64.

55. William N. Eskridge, Jr., "Overriding Supreme Court Statutory Interpretation Decisions," 101 *Yale L.J.* 331, 337 (1991).

56. 105 Stat. 1071 (1991).

57. 490 U.S. 642 (1989).

58. 105 Stat. 1071 § 2(2).

59. 105 Stat. 1071 § 105(a).

60. Bruce Fein, "Bush's Supreme Error," *New York Post*, November 26, 2000, at 55. In *Weber* itself, Justice Rehnquist asserted in his dissent that the Court's interpretation of Title VII was "a tour de force reminiscent not of jurists such as Hale, Holmes, and Hughes, but of escape artists such as Houdini." 443 U.S. at 222 (Rehnquist, J., dissenting). This, it must be admitted, is quite a wonderful quip.

61. Richard E. Morgan, "Coming Clean about *Brown*," *City Journal*, Summer 1996, 51.

62. Bruce Fein, "Bush's Supreme Error," *New York Post*, November 26, 2000, at 55.

63. Richard A. Epstein, *Simple Rules for a Complex World*, 342, n.4 (1995).

64. Fed 48 at 308.

65. Donald Grier Stephenson, Jr., *Campaigns and the Court*, 205 (1999).

66. For a succinct account of the various positions in this arcane constitutional debate, see Erwin Chemerinsky, *Federal Jurisdiction*, 167–202 (2d ed. 1994). On at least one occasion, the *threat* of the passage of a jurisdiction-stripping bill may have influenced the Court's rulings. In an angry response to the Supreme Court's issuance of opinions upholding the associational rights of Communists, the Jenner-Butler bill, introduced in the Senate in 1957, would have removed the Court's appellate jurisdiction over such cases. Although the bill was defeated in the Senate, Morton Horwitz argues that the Court got the message and "reverted to Cold War orthodoxy after 1957." Morton Horwitz, *The Warren Court and the Pursuit of Justice*, 64 (1998).

67. 2 U.S. 419 (1793).

68. 60 U.S. 93 (1857).

69. 157 U.S. 429 (1895).

70. 400 U.S. 112 (1970).

71. Fed 43 at 278.

72. Quoted in Dan Morgan, "Bill Would End Ban on Honoraria for Judges," *Washington Post*, September 14, 2000, at A1.

73. Tom DeLay, Letter to the Editor, *New York Times*, April 6, 1997, at A18. The impeachment of federal judges for issuing opinions that Congress deems illegitimate has been tried. In 1802 the Jeffersonian-controlled House of Representatives impeached Supreme Court Justice Samuel Chase because of his quite real inability to conceal his Federalist sympathies while on the bench. Although the Senate was also controlled by Jeffersonians, cooler heads prevailed there, and Chase was acquitted in "a clear repudiation" of the "attempt to broaden the interpretation of what the Constitution indicated were impeachable offences." Richard Ellis, *The Jeffersonian Crisis*, 102 (1977).

74. Joan Biskupic, "Hill Republicans Take Aim at 'Judicial Activism,'" *Washington Post*, September 15, 1997, at A8.

75. Terry Eastland, "Impeachment DeLay," *American Spectator*, June 1997, 58.

76. Dennis Shea, "Impeaching Abusive Judges," *Policy Review*, May 1997, 62.

77. Terri Jennings Peretti, *In Defense of a Political Court*, 123 (1999).

78. *See* David Yalof, *Pursuit of Justices*, 44–51 (1999).

79. *See id.* at 55–61. In somewhat the same vein, Ronald Reagan's appointment of Sandra Day O'Connor to the Court was done in fulfillment of a campaign promise that he would name the first female Justice to the Court. O'Connor fit the requirement of being female. However, as her conservative critics forget when they accuse her of ideological perfidy on the issue of abortion, her appointment was made in spite of more than a little unease among Reagan aides with respect to her record on the issue as a state legislator and judge. *See id.* at 135–42.

80. Terri Jennings Peretti, *In Defense of a Political Court*, 124 (1999).

81. John Anthony Maltese, *The Selling of Supreme Court Nominees*, 5 (1998).

82. Quoted in David Yalof, *Pursuit of Justices*, 146 (1999).

83. Clint Bolick, "The Judicial Tipping Point," *American Lawyer*, March 2000, 89.

84. *See* Evan P. Schultz, "The Case for Mudslinging," *Legal Times*, January 21, 2002, at 58.

85. Quoted in David Byrd, "Clinton's Untilting Federal Bench," *National Journal*, February 19, 2000, 555.

86. Quoted in *id.*

87. Karen O'Connor and Barbara Palmer, "The Clinton Clones," *Judicature*, March-April 2001, 273.

88. Susan B. Haire, Martha Anne Humphries, and Donald R. Songer, "The Voting Behavior of Clinton's Courts of Appeals Appointees," *Judicature*, March-April 2001, 277. For a demonstration that Clinton's appellate court nominees have been "statistically indistinguishable" from those appointed by President George H. W. Bush in criminal law matters, *see* Nancy Scherer, "Are Clinton's Judges 'Old' Democrats or 'New' Democrats?" *Judicature*, November-December 2000, 151.

89. Robert A. Carp, Kenneth L. Manning, and Ronald Stitham, "President Clinton's District Judges: 'Extreme Liberals' or Just Plain Moderates," *Judicature*, March-April 2001, 284.

90. *See Adarand Constructors, Inc. v. Pena*, 515 U.S. 200 (1995). Certain Imperial Judiciary adherents are forthrightly stunned by the degree of reversal here. Two of these have declared that "the law [as determined by the Supreme Court] is becoming so indisputable, and the attempts to justify [affirmative action programs] so specious, that even many Democrat-appointed judges are now striking down these programs." Roger Clegg and John Sullivan, "Color Them Colorblind," *Weekly Standard*, May 29, 2000, 22. The unsubtle implication here is that, were the law not "becoming so indisputable," these judges would be using all manner of semantic and polemical tricks in order to evade less than indisputable precedent.

91. *Miller v. Johnson*, 515 U.S. 900, 911–12 (1995) (quoting *Shaw v. Reno*, 509 U.S. 630, 647 (1993)).

92. 391 U.S. 430 (1968).

93. Jeffrey Rosen. "The Lost Promise of School Integration," *New York Times*, April 2, 2000, Section 4, at 1.

94. 391 U.S. at 437, 439 (emphasis in original).

95. 402 U.S. 1 (1971).

96. Owen Fiss, "School Desegregation: The Uncertain Path of the Law," in Marshall Cohen, Thomas Nagel, and Thomas Scanlon, eds., *Equality and Preferential Treatment*, 164 (1977). Thus, in a companion case decided on the same day as *Swann*, the Court struck down a North Carolina statute that forbade local boards to engage in any assignment of schoolchildren according to race. *North Carolina State Bd. of Education v. Swann*, 402 U.S. 43 (1971).

97. 402 U.S. at 30.

98. 413 U.S. 189 (1973).

99. Davison M. Douglas, "The End of Busing?" 95 *Mich. L. Rev.* 1715, 1720 (1997).

100. Nathan Glazer, "Towards an Imperial Judiciary?" *Public Interest*, Fall 1975, 110.

101. Lino Graglia, *Disaster by Decree*, 259 (1976).

102. Walter Dean Burnham, "Critical Realignment: Dead or Alive?" in Byron E. Shafer, ed., *The End of Realignment?*, 124 (1991).

103. Thomas Byrne Edsall, *Chain Reaction*, 89 (1992).

104. Quoted in Donald Grier Stephenson, *Campaigns and the Court*, 180 (1999).

105. Stephen Ambrose, *Nixon: The Triumph of a Politician 1962–1972*, 523 (1989).

106. Quoted in *id*. at 555–56.

107. 418 U.S. 717 (1974).

108. Davison Douglas, "The End of Busing?" 95 *Mich. L Rev.* 1715, 1721 (1997).

109. *Id.* at 1721–22 (emphasis added; citations omitted).

110. Quoted in Donald Grier Stephenson, *Campaigns and the Court,* 202 (1999).

111. *See* Davison Douglas, "The End of Busing?" 95 *Mich. L. Rev.* 1715, 1716, n. 7 (1997).

112. 498 U.S. 237, 249–50 (1991).

113. Compare this standard with the tenor of *Green* and its progeny, which one scholar has described as "convey[ing] the Supreme Court's unmistakable impatience with the long delay in ending school segregation that followed its 1954 *Brown* decision, a deep skepticism toward official assurances of 'good faith,' and a steely-eyed demand for objective, measurable results in the desegregation of students, faculties, administrative personnel, and other aspects of public school life." John Charles Boer, "Willful Colorblindness: The New Racial Piety and the Desegregation of the Public Schools," 78 *N.C. L. Rev.* 1719, 1735 (2000).

114. 503 U.S. 467, 490 (1992).

115. 515 U.S. 70 (1995).

116. Gary Orfield, Susan E. Eaton, and The Harvard Project on School Desegregation, *Dismantling Desegregation,* 2 (1996).

117. Megan Twohey, "Desegregation Is Dead," *National Journal,* September 18, 1999, 2615–16.

118. Gary Orfield, Susan E. Eaton, and The Harvard Project on School Desegregation, *Dismantling Desegregation,* 49 (1996).

119. Terri Jennings Peretti, *In Defense of a Political Court,* 100 (1999).

120. 349 U.S. 294 (1955).

121. *Id.* at 301.

122. Lucas Powe, *The Warren Court and American Politics,* 55 (2000).

123. Gerald N. Rosenberg, *The Hollow Hope,* 43–44 (1991) (emphasis in original).

124. *Id.* at 52.

125. 42 U.S.C. § 2000d.

126. Davison Douglas, "The End of Busing?" 95 *Mich. L. Rev.* 1715, 1720 (1997).

127. This failure of attention, however, results in considerable damage to the contention of many Imperial Judiciary adherents that *Brown* is the jurisprudential equivalent of the Fall of Man. Max Boot, for example, declares that "modern judicial activism" stems "ineluctably" from *Brown*. Max Boot, *Out of Order,* 126 (1998). But he makes no mention whatever of segregationist resistance to *Brown* and then, as his first example of illegitimate activism, discusses a 1969 lower court desegregation order in *Swann*. *Id.* at 127. The reader is left to wonder what went on during the fifteen years after *Brown* was decided. George F. Will similarly as-

serts that "the reasoning by which the Court [decided *Brown*], combined with the moral prestige the ruling gave the Court, has produced an era of anti-constitutional judicial policymaking, and of racial discrimination by government." George F. Will, "Where *Brown v. Board* Fell Short," *Washington Post*, May 15, 1994, at C7. And Paul Craig Roberts contends that "[t]he rise of the robed masters and the demise of equality in law date from this decision" because it "introduced the use of judicial coercion on behalf of just causes." Paul Craig Roberts, "Loss of Self-Rule to the Lords of Law," *Washington Times*, August 17, 2000, at A18. Of the many things one might say in response to Will and Roberts, the most immediate are that "moral prestige" is not power and that "judicial coercion" was nonexistent in the implementation of *Brown* until the popular branches of government decided to ally themselves with the Court.

128. 2 U.S. 419 (1793). As already noted, *Chisholm* was overturned by the passage of the Eleventh Amendment in 1798.

129. Quoted in David Currie, *The Constitution in Congress*, 196 (1997).

130. *See* Jill Norgren, *The Cherokee Cases*, 95–98 (1996).

131. Barry Friedman, "The History of the Countermajoritiarian Difficulty, Part One: The Road to Judicial Supremacy," 73 *N.Y.U. L. Rev.* 333, 396–97 (1998).

132. 530 U.S. 290 (2000). The plaintiffs in the case were not secular humanists but a Mormon family and a Catholic family. The district court issued an order allowing them to sue anonymously in order to protect them from intimidation or harassment. But, as the Fifth Circuit Court of Appeals noted in its review of the case, this was an order that school district officials "apparently neither agreed with nor particularly respected." Indeed, after several attempts had been made to elicit the names of the plaintiffs, the district court was forced to issue an order threatening criminal sanctions for anyone engaged in this activity. *See id.* at 294, n. 1. The school officials of Santa Fe, Texas, are thus anything but supine before the power of the Imperial Judiciary.

133. David Firestone "South's Football Fans Still Stand Up and Pray," *New York Times*, August 27, 2000, Section 1, at 1. And such resistance is itself something of a tradition. Lucas Powe notes that, in response to the Supreme Court's 1962 decision barring classroom prayer in public schools, "two-thirds of [Southern] schools continued as they had before, with decided encouragement from political leaders. . . . The most vocal politician was George Wallace. He suggested that, if necessary, he would stage a 'pray-in' at schools." Lucas Powe, *The Warren Court and American Politics*, 363 (2000).

134. Abram Chayes, "The Role of the Judge in Public Law Litigation," 89 *Harv. L. Rev.* 1281, 1282, 1284 (1976).

135. Malcolm M. Feeley and Edward L. Rubin, *Judicial Policy Making and the Modern State*, 263 (1999).

136. *Id.* at 165.

137. *Id.* at 379.

138. *Id.* at 48.

139. Ross Sandler and David Schoenbrod, "How to Put Lawmakers, Not Courts, Back in Charge," *City Journal*, Autumn 1996, 61. If the PLRA indeed effects a revolution, it has done so with something less than comprehensive legislative reflection. As one commentator notes, the statute "was enacted as part of a supplemental appropriations bill and was adopted by a conference committee without receiving the benefit of public debate, hearings, or even a separate vote." Stephan O. Klein, "Judicial Independence: Rebuffing Congressional Attacks on the Third Branch," 87 *Ky. L.J.* 679, 730 (1999).

140. 18 U.S.C. § 3626(a)(2).

141. 18 U.S.C. § 3626(b)(2). One commentator has likened this provision to a phenomenon we considered in chapter 2: the efforts of Revolutionary Era state legislatures to force courts to rehear cases in which unpopular decisions had been rendered: "The attempt, though ultimately unsuccessful, to pass a law in Massachusetts in the early 1780s directing the Massachusetts Supreme [Judicial] Court to rehear a case in which it had declared slavery unconstitutional is but a portent of the legislation that could follow on the coattails of a Supreme Court decision upholding the constitutionality of the PLRA's immediate-termination provision." Lynn S. Branham, "Keeping the 'Wolf Out of the Fold': Separation of Powers and Congressional Termination of Equitable Relief," 26 *Journal of Legislation* 185, 214 (2000).

142. *See Inmates of Suffolk Cty. Jail v. Rouse*, 129 F.3d 649 (1st Cir. 1997), *cert. denied*, 524 U.S. 951 (1998); *Benjamin v. Jacobson*, 172 F.3d 144 (2d Cir.), *cert. denied*, 528 U.S. 824 (1999); *Imprisoned Citizens v. Ridge*, 169 F.3d 178 (3d Cir. 1999); *Ruiz v. U.S.*, 243 F.3d 941 (5th Cir. 2001); *Hadix v. Johnson*, 133 F.3d 940 (6th Cir.), *cert. denied*, 524 U.S. 952 (1998); *Gavin v. Branstad*, 122 F.3d 1081 (8th Cir. 1997), *cert. denied*, 524 U.S. 955 (1998); *Gilmore v. People of the State of Calif.*, 220 F.3d 987 (9th Cir. 2000); *Dougan v. Singletary*, 129 F.3d 1424 (11th Cir. 1997), *cert. denied*, 524 U.S. 956 (1998).

The Supreme Court has not yet considered the constitutionality of these termination provisions. It has, however, upheld a PLRA provision that requires a federal district judge to decide a motion for termination of injunctive relief with thirty days of its being filed. (The deadline may be extended to ninety days if the district judge finds there is "good cause" to do so.) If the judge fails to meet this deadline, the injunction terminates automatically until the motion is decided. *See Miller v. French*, 530 U.S. 327 (2000). In a statutory ruling, the Court has also interpreted the PLRA broadly to require a prisoner to complete a prison's grievance procedure before being able to sue in federal court over prison conditions, even if the grievance procedure is empowered to provide only minimal relief. *See Booth v. Churner*, 532 U.S. 731 (2001).

143. John Sullivan, "States and Cites Removing Prisons from Courts' Grip," *New York Times*, January 30, 2000, Section 1, at 1.

144. Spencer Abraham, "The Case for Needed Legal Reform," *USA Today Magazine*, July1, 1998, 24.

145. Malcolm M. Feeley and Edward L. Rubin, *Judicial Policy Making and the Modern State*, 383 (1999) (emphasis added).

146. *Oetjen v. Central Leather Co.*, 246 U.S. 297, 302 (1918).

147. *Tinker v. Des Moines Independent Community School Dist.*, 393 U.S. 503, 506 (1969). As one might expect, however, this declaration been greatly limited by later cases. *See, e.g., Hazelwood School Dist. v. Kuhlmeier*, 464 U.S. 260 (1988).

148. 475 U.S. 503, 505 (1986).

149. *Id.* at 507–8 (emphasis added; citations omitted).

150. *See Able v. U.S.*, 155 F.3d 628 (2nd Cir. 1998); *Thomasson v. Perry*, 80 F.3d 915 (4th Cir.), *cert. denied*, 519 U.S. 948 (1996); *Richenberg v. Perry*, 97 F.3d 256 (8th Cir.), *cert. denied*, 522 U.S. 807 (1997); *Philips v. Perry*, 106 F.3d 1420 (9th Cir. 1997).

151. *Chicago & S. Air Lines v. Watterman S.S. Corp.*, 333 U.S. 103, 111 (1948). It is true, however, that the judiciary can be forceful in declaring that the federal government has a monopoly over the conduct of the foreign policy of the United States. The Supreme Court recently issued a unanimous judgment striking down a Massachusetts law that forbade state agencies to purchase goods and services from companies that do business in the country of Burma, which is called Myanmar by the military thugs who rule it. The state law was held to be an invasion of the federal government's exclusive authority to impose sanctions on foreign states. *Crosby v. National Foreign Trade Council*, 530 U.S. 363 (2000).

152. John Hart Ely, *War and Responsibility*, 3 (1993).

153. 1 *Commentaries on the Laws of England* 249 (1765).

154. Fed 69 at 417–18 (emphasis in original).

155. 2 Elliot 284.

156. JM LOA 586.

157. Quoted in John Hart Ely, *War and Responsibility*, 3 (1993).

158. Laurence Tribe, *American Constitutional Law*, 667 (3d ed. 2000). As for the War Powers Resolution of 1973, 87 Stat. 555, which was meant to preclude the president from committing U.S. troops abroad for extended periods without congressional approval, it must be regarded as one of the premier standing jokes in the U.S. Code. As Tribe notes, no president has recognized it as binding, and no Congress has seriously attempted to enforce it. *Id.* at 662, n. 28.

159. Robert H. Bork, "Erosion of the President's Power in Foreign Affairs," 68 *Wash. U. L.Q.* 693, 695 (1990).

160. And in keeping with our by now established historical practice, the role of Congress in formulating the nation's response to the attacks of September 11, 2001, has been minimal. Here is the lament of a prominent Democratic senator writing six months after the attacks: "[I]n this war on terrorism, Congress, by and large, has been left to learn about major war-related decisions through newspaper articles. One day we hear that American military advisers are heading to the

Philippines. Another day we read that military personnel may go into the former Soviet republic of Georgia. The next day we are sending advisers into Yemen." Robert C. Byrd, "Why Congress Has to Ask Questions," *New York Times*, March 12, 2002, at A27.

161. Kate Stith and Jose Cabranes, *Fear of Judging*, 79 (1998).

162. Stephen Breyer, "Federal Sentencing Guidelines Revisited," *Criminal Justice*, Spring 1999, 29.

163. Kate Stith and Jose Cabranes, *Fear of Judging*, 3 (1998).

164. *Id.* at 11. Sentencing judges are allowed to depart from the sentencing range mandated by the Guidelines in cases where "the court finds that there exists an aggravating or mitigating circumstance . . . that should result in a sentence different than that described." 18 U.S.C. § 3553(b). However, the Supreme Court has cautioned sentencing judges not to get carried away with this, because the Sentencing Commission "provides considerable guidance as to the factors that are apt or not to make a case atypical" with respect to the imposition of sentence. *Koon v. U.S.*, 518 U.S. 92, 94 (1996).

165. Kate Stith and Jose Cabranes, *Fear of Judging*, 82–83 (1998).

166. Joan Biskupic and Mary Pat Flaherty, "Loss of Discretion Fuels Frustration on Federal Bench," *Washington Post*, October 8, 1996, at A1.

167. *U.S. v. Sidhom*, 144 F. Supp.2d 41 (D. Mass. 2001).

168. Although many states also use sentencing guidelines, Stith and Cabranes note that "no other jurisdiction has produced sentencing guidelines that come close to matching the United States Sentencing Guidelines in complexity and rigidity." Kate Stith and Jose Cabranes, *Fear of Judging*, 177 (1998).

169. Richard Neely, *How Courts Govern America*, 35 (1982).

170. John Paul Stevens, "Opening Assembly Address, American Bar Association Annual Meeting, Orlando, Florida, August 3, 1996," 12 *St. John's J. Legal Comment.* 21, 22 (1996).

171. Quoted in "Note: Popular Justice: State Judicial Elections and Procedural Due Process," 31 *Harv. C.R.-C.L. L. Rev.* 187, 197 (1995).

172. Lawrence Friedman, *American Law*, 65 (1984). An interesting exception here is Karl Marx, who praised the Paris Communards because, under their rule, "judicial functionaries were to be divested of that sham independence" that arose from their appointment to the bench. They were instead "to be elective, responsible, and revocable." Karl Marx, "Address of the General Council of the International Working Men's Association on the Civil War in France, 1871," in Karl Marx and V. I. Lenin, *Civil War in France: The Paris Commune*, 58 (1993).

173. Fed 78 at 471.

174. Letter to William T. Barry, July 2, 1822, in *The Writings of Thomas Jefferson* 256 (1859).

175. Roy A. Schotland, "Comment," 61 *Law & Contemp. Probs.* 149, 154 (1998).

176. Paul D. Carrington, "Big Money in Texas Judicial Elections: The Sickness and Its Remedies," 53 *SMU L. Rev.* 263, 266 (2000).

177. Anthony Champagne, "Interest Groups and Judicial Elections," 34 *Loy. L.A. L. Rev.* 1391, 1393 (2001).

178. *See* Deborah Goldberg, Craig Holman, and Samantha Sanchez, *The New Politics of Judicial Elections*, Justice at Stake Campaign (2002); Roy A. Schotland, "Financing Judicial Elections; 2000: Change and Challenge," 2001 *L. Rev. Mich. St. U. Det. C.L.*, 849. Louis Jacobson, "Lobbying for 'Justice' in State Courts," *National Journal*, November 18, 2000, 3678; William Glaberson, "Fierce Campaigns Signal a New Era for State Courts," *New York Times*, June 5, 2000, at A1; Alexander Wohl, "Justice for Rent," *American Prospect*, May 22, 2000, 34.

179. Paul D. Carrington, "Judicial Independence and Democratic Accountability in Highest State Courts," 61 *Law & Contemp. Probs.* 79, 112 (1998).

180. *See* Jesse Green and Kelly A. McCauley, "Republicans Keep Control of Michigan Supreme Court," *Michigan Lawyers Weekly*, November 13, 2000, at 1; Curt Guyette, "Justice at Any Price?" *Detroit Metro Times*, October 10, 2000, http://www.metrotimes.com/editorial/story/ap?id=725.

181. *See* Kara Baker, "Is Justice for Sale in Ohio? An Examination of Ohio Judicial Elections and Suggestions for Reform," 35 *Akron L. Rev.* 159 (2001). Randy Ludlow, "Big Business Goal: Oust Ohio Justice," *Cincinnati Post*, September 9, 2000, at A1.

182. *See* John D. Echevveria, "Changing the Rules by Changing the Players: The Environmental Issue in State Judicial Elections," 9 *N.Y.U. Envtl. L.J.* 217, 238–54 (2001).

183. *Ward v. Village of Monroeville*, 409 U.S. 57, 62 (1972).

184. Alexander Tabarrok and Eric Helland, "Court Politics: The Political Economy of Tort Awards," 42 *J. L. & Econ.* 157 (1999).

185. Stephen J. Ware, "Money, Politics, and Judicial Decisions: A Case Study of Arbitration Law In Alabama," 15 *J. L. & Pol.* 645, 684 (1999).

186. John D. Echevveria, "Changing the Rules by Changing the Players: The Environmental Issue in State Judicial Elections," 9 *N.Y.U. Envtl. L.J.* 217, 220 (2001).

187. Anthony Champagne, "Interest Groups and Judicial Elections," 34 *Loy. L.A. L. Rev.* 1391, 1407–8 (2001).

188. *Southern Christian Leadership Conf. v. Sup. Ct. of La.*, 61 F. Supp.2d 499, 513 (E.D. La. 1999), *aff'd.*, 252 F.3d 781 (5th Cir.), *cert. denied*, 122 S. Ct. 484 (2001). For a brief commentary on the case, *see* Mark Kozlowski, "The Soul of an Elected Judge," *Legal Times*, August 9, 1999, at 15.

189. Lou Cannon, "One Tough Cop," *New York Times Magazine*, October1, 2000, 62.

190. Quoted in Paul Redinger, "The Politics of Judging," *ABA Journal*, April 1987, 58.

191. Gerald F. Uelmen, "The Fattest Crocodile," *Criminal Justice*, Spring 1998, 4.

192. "Note: State Judicial Elections and Procedural Due Process," 31 *Harv. C.R.C.L. L. Rev.* 187, 199 (1996). For a comprehensive treatment of the politics of the death penalty in judicial elections, *see* Stephen B. Bright, "Political Attacks on the Judiciary: Can Justice Be Done amid Efforts to Intimidate and Remove Judges from Office for Unpopular Decisions?" 72 *N.Y.U. L. Rev.* 308 (1997).

193. 1 *Democracy in America* 269 (Anchor ed. 1969).

NOTES TO CONCLUSION

Note: I freely admit to stealing the title of this chapter from an excellent lecture on the value of judicial independence that was delivered to the Association of the Bar of the City of New York. *See* Anthony Lewis, "Why the Courts," 22 *Cardozo L. Rev.* 133 (2000).

1. Fed 22 at 150.

2. Grant Gilmore, *The Ages of American Law*, 91–92 (1977).

3. *Id.* at 92.

4. Lino Graglia, "It's Not Constitutionalism, It's Judicial Activism," 19 *Harv. J. Law & Pub. Pol'y* 293, 294 (1996).

5. Robert A. Dahl, *A Preface to Democratic Theory*, 4 (1956). More recently, Professor Dahl has drawn attention to what is clearly the greatest ongoing affront within our constitutional order to the principle of majority rule: the United States Senate. The fact that each state is afforded two senators regardless of its population "is a profound violation of the democratic idea of political equality among all citizens. . . . In the extreme case, the ratio of over-representation of the least populated state, Wyoming, to the most populous state, California, is just under 70 to 1." Robert A. Dahl, *How Democratic Is the American Constitution?*, 49–50 (2001). What is more, the Senate's rule of representation almost certainly cannot be amended. First, the number of state legislatures required to propose or affirm such an amendment makes it unlikely that a sufficient number of states that benefit from the current inequality will give their consent. Even more potently, Article V of the Constitution provides that "no State, without its Consent, shall be deprived of its equal Suffrage in the Senate." *Id.* at 144–45.

A reviewer of Professor Dahl's book has provided further figures of interest: "[H]alf the U.S. population sends 18 senators to Washington while the other half sends 82. Twenty senators represent 54 percent of the population; another 20 represent less than 3 percent. California gets two senators; the 20 least populous states, which combined have roughly the same number of people as California, get 40 senators." George Scialabba, "Democracy Proof," *American Prospect*, July 1,

2002, 34. Two political scientists have recently written a comprehensive study of the manner in which the Senate's offense against majority rule prevents policy outcomes that would likely result if Senate seats were apportioned on the basis of a state's population. *See* Frances E. Lee and Bruce I. Oppenheimer, *Sizing Up the Senate* (1999). Perhaps what we really need is an Imperial Senate thesis.

6. Gordon Wood, *The Creation of the American Republic, 1776–1789,* 502 (1969).

7. Oliver Wendell Holmes, "The Gas-Stokers' Strike," in Richard A. Posner, ed., *The Essential Holmes,* 122 (1992).

8. Much of the rest of the world certainly seems to agree: "Prior to 1920, only a few other nations, nearly all in Latin America, had adopted judicial review. . . . Since 1945, however, constitutional practice has changed, and judicial review has spread worldwide." William E. Nelson, *"Marbury v. Madison: The Origins and Legacy of Judicial Review,* 104, 106 (2000). Of course, exceptions remain, such as the People's Republic of China: "Judicial officers are still subject to political education to 'arm them with the correct theory,' in the words of Xiao Yang, the chief judge of the Supreme People's Court. And any judge who strays from the party line on sensitive political issues such as the Falun Gong, the outlawed spiritual movement, will immediately be removed from office and stripped of all privileges." Richard McGregor, "Legal Evolution with Strings Attached," *Financial Times,* May 2, 2001, at 14. In other words, it is not the courts that practice "moral intimidation" in China.

9. Benjamin Cardozo, *The Nature of the Judicial Process,* 167–68 (1921).

Index

abortion, 150–51; irreconcilability of debate, 151–58, 261n. 20, 262n. 33; movement to liberalize, 158–64. See also *Roe v. Wade*

Adair, Douglass, on *Federalist* 10, 173

Adair (U.S. v.), 250n. 166

Adams, John: on judicial independence, 54; on republicanism, 170

Administrative Procedure Act, 182–83

administrative state, 179–86

Age Discrimination in Employment Act, 272n. 48

Amar, Akhil Reed: on Fourteenth Amendment, 32; on *Miranda* rights, 142

amendment process, as means of overturning court rulings, 191

American Civil Liberties Union, legal victories of, 226n. 67

Anti-Federalists: opposition to judicial review, 67–69; on statutory interpretation, 76–77, 85

Arkes, Hadley, on *Cohen*, 129

Ashcroft, John, attack on judiciary, 7

Bailyn, Bernard, 57, 80

Baker v. Carr, See redistricting cases

Baker v. State, 123–24, 253n. 33

Barr, Robert: attack on judiciary, 8; on homosexual marriage, 124

Bell, David, 83

Berea College v. Kentucky, 248n. 118

Berger, Raoul: on *Brown*, 35–36; on *Cruikshank*, 108; on judicial review, 76, 81; and originalism, 31–33, 34–36, 229n. 98, 241n. 112; on rule of law in America, 145; on *Slaughterhouse*, 103–4, 249n. 127

Berns, Walter: on Fourteenth Amendment, 32; on need to restrain majorities, 108

Bill of Rights, Federalist opposition to, 77–80

Black, Charles L.: on Ninth Amendment, 79; on *Slaughterhouse*, 103

Blackstone, William: on judicial independence, 52–53; on liability, 93; on warmaking powers, 207

Bolick, Clint: on campaign finance reform, 175; on Clinton judges, 194

Boot, Max: attacks on judiciary, 5, 86, 108; on *Brown*, 276n. 127; on rights of criminal defendants, 140; on rights revolution, 118

Bork, Robert, 4, 5; on *Baker*, 235n. 200; on *Brown*, 36–37; on *Cohen*, 129; on First Amendment, 131–33, 255n. 77; on foreign affairs, 208–9; on impeachment of federal judges, 242n. 145; on judicial cultural bias, 29–30, 114n. 67, 229n. 86; on judicial usurpation of politics, 49–59, 118–19; on Ninth Amendment, 79; nomination to Supreme Court, 162, 193–94, 265n. 63; and originalism, 30, 33–35, 48–49, 241n. 112; on redistricting cases, 126; on *Roe v. Wade*, 150, 230n. 112; on *Slaughterhouse*, 108, 249n. 127

Brennan, William: on state court protection of rights, 122; on welfare rights, 135–36, 137

Breyer, Stephen: on abortion, 158; on Federal Sentencing Guidelines, 209; on *Goldberg v. Kelly*, 136; nomination to Supreme Court, 162, 194–95

Brody, David, on labor law, 182

Brown v. Board of Education: implementation of, 195–96, 200–202; and originalism, 31–32, 35–37, 232n. 137

Buckley, James L.: attacks on judiciary, 86, 236n. 201; on *Roe v. Wade*, 160

Buckley, William F., on *Roe v. Wade*, 86

Buckley v. Valeo, 150–51, 164–66, 169, 252n. 20. *See also* campaign finance reform

Burger Court, 17, 21

Burke, Edmund, on judicial independence, 53–54

Burnham, Walter Dean, on Supreme Court in American politics, 197

Bush v. Gore, 223n. 26

Bussiere, Elizabeth, on welfare rights, 257n. 109

Calabresi, Guido: on administrative agency power, 181, 182; on judicial lawmaking, 88

Caldwell, Christopher, on abortion, 164, 261n. 20

California Democratic Party v. Jones, 268n. 127

campaign finance reform, 150–51, 164–66; and originalism, 166–75, 296n. 128

Cardozo, Benjamin: on freedom of speech, 45; on judicial discretion, 187, 219–20; on spending power, 240n. 109

Carrington, Paul, on judicial elections, 213–14

Cary v. Daniels, 90

Casey v. Planned Parenthood of Southeastern Pennsylvania, 19, 21, 151–52, 162–63

Champagne, Anthony, on judicial elections, 213, 215

Charles River Bridge v. Warren Bridge, 95–96, 245n. 56

Chayes, Abram, on role of judge in complex litigation, 203

Chevron U.S.A., Inc. v. Natural Resources Defense Counsel, 183

China, judiciary of, 283n. 8

Chisholm v. Georgia, overturned by Eleventh Amendment, 191, 202

Civil Rights Act of 1964: judicial interpretation of, 187–90, 272n. 54; and school desegregation, 202

Civil Rights Act of 1991, 189–90

Civil Rights Cases, 105, 248n. 107

Clean Air Act, 184–86, 271n. 43

Clinton, William, selection of judges by, 194–95, 274n. 88

Cockburn, Alexander, on redistricting cases, 254n. 50

Cohen v. California, 129

Cole, David: on legal representation of the poor, 146, 260n. 149; on prison population, 138–39

Colgrove v. Green, 127

Coppage v. Kansas, 250n. 166

Corfeild v. Coryell, 38–39, 102

Cox, Archibald: on libel, 130; on redistricting cases, 126–27; on Warren Court, 15–16

criminal defendants, rights of, 138–48

Croly, Herbert, attack on judiciary, 115

Cruikshank (U.S. v.), 104

Cumming v. County Bd. of Ed., 106–7

Currie, David, on Revolutionary state constitutions, 54

Curtis, Michael Kent: on First Amendment, 32; on Fourteenth Amendment, 44–45; on *Slaughterhouse*, 102–3

Dahl, Robert: on "Madisonian democracy," 218; on U.S. Senate, 282n. 5

Dandridge v. Williams, 136–37

Davis, Martha, on RU-486, 157

Debs, Eugene V.: imprisonment for opposition to World War I, 45; and Pullman Strike, 112–13

DeLay, Tom: on campaign finance reform, 175; on impeachment of federal judges, 81, 192

DeShaney v. Winnebago County Dept. of Social Services, 120–21

Dickerson v. U.S., 142

Dole, Robert, attack on judiciary, 118

Douglas, Davison, on busing, 199

Douglass, Frederick, on failure of Reconstruction, 108

Dowell (Oklahoma City Public Schools v.), 199

Dred Scott v. Sandford: comparisons to *Roe v. Wade*, 86–87, 160, 243n. 7; overturned by Civil War amendments, 191

DuBois, W. E. B., on racial violence in American South, 104

Dunn, John, on conflicts of rights, 154

Dworkin, Ronald, purported influence on judiciary, 27, 227nn. 71, 72

Easterbrook, Gregg, on abortion, 156

Eastland, Terry: attacks on judiciary, 18–19; on impeachment of federal judges, 192

Edsall, Thomas Byrne, on busing, 197

Eisenhower, Dwight D.: and implementation of *Brown*, 201; selection of judges by, 193

Eleventh Amendment, Scalia on, 232n. 148

Ellsworth, Oliver: on constitutional language, 69; on judicial review, 66

Elshtain, Jean Bethke, on abortion, 152

Ely, John Hart: on Ninth Amendment, 79–80; on redistricting cases, 128; on warmaking powers, 207

"End of Democracy? The" (*First Things*), 22–23

Epstein, Richard, on *Griggs*, 189

Eskridge, William, on statutory interpretation, 76–77

Estrich, Susan, on *Roe v. Wade*, 264n. 54

exclusionary rule, 133–34, 144–45, 256n. 90

Farwell v. Boston & Worcester R.R. Co., 94–95

FDA v. Brown & Williamson Tobacco Co., 183–84

Feder, Don: attacks on judiciary, 5, 19, 222n. 12; on *Baker v. State*, 253n. 33

Federal Election Comm'n. v. Colorado Republican Fed. Campaign Comm., 267n. 107

Federal Sentencing Guidelines, 209–11

Federalist 10. *See* Madison, James

Feeley, Malcolm, and Rubin, Edward, on prison reform, 203–5

Fein, Bruce: attacks on judiciary, 18, 19; on *Roe v. Wade*, 161; on *Weber*, 189

Fifteenth Amendment, 98–99, 107, 191

First Amendment, judicial expansion of, 44–47. *See also* campaign finance reform; libel, and Warren Court

Fiss, Owen, on *Swann*, 196

Foner, Eric: on Civil War Amendments, 98–99; on *Cruikshank*, 104

Forbath, William: on courts and labor movement, 110–13; on welfare rights, 138

foreign affairs, and courts, 205–9, 279n. 151

Fourth Amendment, 43–44. *See also* exclusionary rule

Fourteenth Amendment: early judicial interpretation of, 98–107, 247nn. 90, 96, 97, 248n. 107; and incorporation, 229n. 99, 231n. 114; and originalism, 31–33, 35–39

Frankfurter, Felix: on labor injunction, 111; on rights of poor, 121

Freeman, Joanne, on early American politics, 169

Freeman v. Pitts, 199–200

Fried, Charles, on *Roe v. Wade*, 150

Friedman, Barry, on resistance to Supreme Court decisions, 202

Friedman, Lawrence, 97; on judicial elections, 212; on 19th-century criminal law, 140, 259n. 137; on 19th-century tort law, 93

Frum, David, attacks on judiciary, 5, 27, 227n. 72

funding of courts, Congressional control over, 191–92

Gallagher, Maggie, attacks on judiciary, 3–4, 28

Gandhi, Indira, and rule of law, 230n. 106

Garnett, Richard, on *Troxel*, 41, 233n. 153

Garrow, David: on abortion, 153, 158, 163; on Bork nomination, 162

George, Robert P., on Berger, 35

Gideon v. Wainright, 145–48

Gigot, Paul, attack on judiciary, 3

Giles v. Harris, 107

Gillman, Howard, on *Lochner*, 110

Gilmore, Grant, 9, 88; on administrative state, 217–18; on 19th-century contract law, 92–93

Ginsburg, Ruth Bader, nomination to Supreme Court, 162, 194–95

Glazer, Nathan: on affirmative action, 228n. 78; "Towards an Imperial Judiciary?," 16–18, 86, 87, 197

Glendon, Mary Ann: on abortion, 152, 155–56; on judicial usurpation of politics, 20–23, 108; on legal academics, 228n. 76; on rights revolution, 119–20, 121

Goldberg v. Kelly, 135–37

Goldman v. Weinberger, 206

Gompers v. Buck's Stove & Range Co., 111

Gompers, Samuel, on courts and labor movement, 114

Graber, Mark: on statutory interpretation by Marshall Court, 77, 242n. 137; on welfare rights, 257n. 92

Graglia, Lino: attacks on judiciary 5, 12–13, 218; on busing, 197; on judicial cultural bias, 26–27, 130

Green v. New Kent County, 195–96, 200–201, 202, 276n. 113

Griggs v. Duke Power Co., 188–90

Gross, Robert, on politics in colonial America, 167–68

Guinier, Lani, on redistricting cases, 254n. 50

Gutmann, Amy, on abortion, 158

Hall, Kermit: on *Lochner*, 109–10; on state constitutions, 123; on Warren Court, 224nn. 15, 25

Hall (U.S. v.), 99–100, 104

Hamilton, Alexander: on bills of rights, 78; and constitutional debates of 1790s, 73–75, 240n. 104; on constitutional language, 70–72, 239n. 88; on impeachment of federal judges, 81; on judicial independence, 52, 62–63; on judicial elections, 212–13; on judicial review, 65–66, 75, 80–81; on judiciary as "least dangerous branch," 6–8, 84–85; on need to restrain majorities, 60, 84; on political relations between social classes, 172; on republics, 170; on Revolutionary state constitutions, 56; on statutory interpretation, 76–77, 217, 241n. 116; on war-making powers, 207

Harris v. McRae, 122

Harris v. New York, 142

Henry, Patrick, on judicial review, 67

Hill v. Colorado, 46–47

Hitler, Adolph, and rule of law, 230n. 106

Hofstadter, Richard: on framers' view of political parties, 174–75; "paranoid style" thesis, 29, 49

Holmes, Oliver Wendell, 107, 113; on social solidarity, 219

homosexuals, rights of. See *Baker v. State*; *Romer v. Evans*

Horwitz, Morton: on Bork nomination, 265n. 63; on 19th-century contract law, 92; on 19th-century property law, 89–90, 91–92; on redistricting cases, 254n. 45; on Warren Court, 14, 273n. 66

Houppert, Karen, on abortion, 156

Hovenkamp, Herbert, on courts and labor movement, 111

Howard, Philip K., on rights revolution, 118

Howe, Daniel Walker, on *Federalist* 10, 174

Huntington, Samuel P., on *Federalist* 10, 83

Hurst, J. W.: on judicial lawmaking, 88–89; on 19th-century contract law, 92; on 19th-century property law, 92

impeachment, of federal judges, 81–82, 192, 242nn. 145–46, 274n. 73

Jefferson, Thomas: attacks on judiciary, 64, 213

judges, federal: and life tenure, 63–64, power of judicial review, 65; selection of, 192–200, 225n. 36, 274nn. 79, 88. *See also* impeachment, of federal judges; jurisdiction, of federal courts; statutory interpretation

judges, state: independence of, 64–65; in 19th-century America, 87–98; election of, 98, 211–16; and protection of rights, 122–25; judicial review by, 244n.10

judicial independence, 230n. 106; emergence of concept during American Revolution, 52–56; framers' view of need for, 61–63

judicial review: framers' view of, 65–72, 84, 239n. 72; international spread of, 235n. 199, 283n. 8

judiciary: cultural bias of, 24–30, 118–19; in 2000 presidential election, 1–4; as usurper of democratic politics, 20–24, 49, 50. *See also* judges, federal; judges, state; judicial independence; judicial review; statutory interpretation

jurisdiction, of federal courts, 190–91

Kannar, George, on exclusionary rule, 145

Kaus, Otto, on elected judges, 216

Kekes, John, on Dworkin, 27

Kennedy, Anthony: conservative criticisms of, 19, 26; nomination to Supreme Court, 162, 265n. 63

Keyes v. District No. 1, Denver, Colorado, 196

Kristol, William, attack on judiciary, 1–2

Kulturkrampf, 226n. 63

Kurland, Philip, on Warren Court, 14–15

Kyllo v. U.S., 43–44

labor movement: and administrative state, 182; judicial opposition to, 109–15, 250nn. 157, 166

LaFollette, Robert, attack on judicial power, 115

Laslett, Peter, on Locke, 52, 236n. 5

Leo, John, on judicial cultural bias, 27

Leon (U.S. v.), 144–45

Levy, Leonard, 64

Lewis, Anthony: on libel, 130, 132; on redistricting cases, 127

Lexington & Ohio Rail Road Co. v. Applegate, 90–91

libel, and Warren Court, 129–33, 267n. 109

Lincoln, Abraham, and *Dred Scott,* 243n. 7

Lochner v. New York, 109–10

Locke, John, on judicial independence, 52

Loffredo, Stephen, on welfare rights, 134–35

Losee v. Buchanan, 91

Luban, David, on Warren Court, 133–34

Luker, Kristin, on abortion, 154, 158

MacKinnon, Catharine, purported influence on judiciary, 27, 227n. 72

Madison, James: on amendment process, 191; on bills of rights, 77; and constitutional debates of 1790s, 73–75; on constitutional language, 69–72; on electioneering, 168; *Federalist* 10, 83, 173–75; on judicial independence, 61–62; on judicial review, 84; on life tenure of federal judges, 64; on need to restrain majorities, 58–61; on Revolutionary state constitutions, 54, 55–57; on Sedition Act, 171–72; on separation of powers, 190; on statutory interpretation, 76–77; on warmaking powers, 208

Maltz, Earl: on *Brown,* 36; on *Troxel,* 233n. 154

Mapp v. Ohio. See exclusionary rule

Marshall, John: on judicial review, 66; and statutory interpretation, 77

Marx, Karl, on judicial elections, 280n. 172

McConnell, Michael: on abortion, 262n. 33; on *Brown,* 35–36

McConnell, Mitch, on campaign finance reform, 175, 270n. 130

McCoy, Drew, 59

McCullough v. Maryland, 34–35

McDonald, Forrest, attack on judiciary, 6–7

McDowell, Gary: on *Dred Scott*, 86–87, 243n. 7; on legal academics, 27, 29; on originalism, 47–48

McGinnis, John O., on campaign finance reform, 269n. 128

McIntyre v. Ohio Elections Comm'n., 42

Meese, Edwin, and originalism, 30–31

Mencken, H. L., on First Amendment, 45

Meritor Savings Bank v. Vinson, 188, 273n. 54

Michelman, Frank, on welfare rights, 134

Mill, John Stuart, on American government, 179

Milliken v. Bradley, 198–99

Miranda v. Arizona, 142–44, 259nn. 125, 131

Missouri v. Jenkins, 200

Montesquieu: on judging, 77; on judicial independence, 52

Montgomery, David, on labor injunctions, 113

Morgan, Richard E., on *Weber*, 189

Morrison (U.S. v.), 248n. 107

National Labor Relations Act, 115, 182

Neely, Richard: on judicial elections, 211–12; on rights of criminal defendants, 140–41

Nelson, William: on international spread of judicial review, 283n. 8; on 19th-century contract law, 92–93; on *Slaughterhouse* 104; on state court judicial review, 244n. 10

Neuborne, Burt, on *Buckley*, 166

Neuhaus, Richard John, on American culture, 82–83

Newsome, Kevin Christopher, on *Slaughterhouse*, 247n. 90

New York Times Co. v. Sullivan. See libel, and Warren Court

Ninth Amendment, 39–41, 79–80

Nixon, Richard: opposition to busing, 198; opposition to Warren Court, 14, 30

Nixon v. Shrink Missouri Government PAC, 171–75

O'Connor, Sandra Day: conservative criticisms of, 19, 26; nomination to Supreme Court, 274n. 79

Ohio v. Akron Center for Reproductive Health, 152

Ollman v. Evans, 130–33

Oregon v. Mitchell, overturned by Twenty-Sixth Amendment, 191

Orfield, Gary, on school desegregation, 200

originalism, 30–49, 234n. 187; and abortion, 151; and campaign finance reform, 166–76, 269n. 128; and early judicial interpretations of Fourteenth Amendment, 99–107, 249n. 127; and First Amendment, 255n. 77, 267n. 109; and impeachment of federal judges, 242n. 145; and political parties, 268n. 127

O'Rourke, Timothy, on redistricting cases, 127–28

Orren, Karen, on codification movement, 97

parole, right to, 258n. 115

Parshall, Janet, on RU-486, 157

Peretti, Terri Jennings, on judicial selection, 200

Pilon, Roger, attack on judiciary, 4

Plato, on Nocturnal Council, 177–78

Plessy v. Ferguson, 105–6

Pollack v. Farmers' Loan and Trust Co., overturned by Sixteenth Amendment, 191

Pollitt, Katha, on abortion, 156

Ponnuru, Ramesh, attack on judiciary, 2–3

poor, constitutional rights of, 134–38, 257n. 109

Posner, Richard, on rights revolution, 120

Powe, Lucas: on implementation of *Brown*, 201; on Warren Court, 14

Powell, Jefferson, on originalism, 72–73, 76, 80

Prison Legal Reform Act, 204–5, 278nn.139, 141–42

prisons: population of, 138–40; reform of, 203–5

Pullman Strike, judicial suppression of, 112–13

Rabkin, Jeremy, on judicial cultural bias, 27–28, 228n. 74
Rakove, Jack, 65, 179, 237n. 33
Rauch, Jonathan, on abortion, 152–53
Reagan, Ronald: opposition to busing, 199; on *Roe v. Wade*, 161; selection of judges by, 193–94, 274n. 79
redistricting cases, 125–28, 254n. 50
Reese (U.S. v.), 107
Rehnquist Court, 18
Rehnquist, William: on First Amendment, 45; on Fourteenth Amendment, 247n. 96
Reich, Robert, on welfare reform, 137–38
Reinhardt, Steven, on Clinton judges, 194
Reynolds v. Sims. See redistricting cases
Rhodes (U.S. v.), 99
rights: American limits upon, 120–25, 252n. 18; conservative critiques of, 20–21, 117–20; statutory rights revolution, 186
Roberts, Paul Craig: attack on judiciary, 33; on *Brown*, 276n. 127
Roe v. Wade, 18, 150–53, 158–64, 263nn. 50, 52, 264n. 54; comparisons to *Dred Scott*, 86–87, 160, 243n. 7; feminist criticisms of, 264n. 54
Romer v. Evans, 24–26
Rosen, Jeffrey, on *Brown*, 196
Rosenberg, Gerald: on implementation of *Brown*, 201; on *Roe v. Wade*, 263n. 52
RU-486, 156–57. *See also* abortion

Saenz v. Roe, 38–39
Sante Fe Independent School District v. Doe, 202–3, 277n. 132
Saporta, Vicki, on RU-486, 157
Scalia, Antonin: on abortion, 22, 152; on Eleventh Amendment, 232n. 148; on First Amendment, 44–47; on Fourth Amendment, 43–44; on judicial cultural bias, 24–26; on "living Constitution," 46–47; on *Miranda* rights, 142; on Ninth

Amendment, 40–41; originalism of, 39, 42, 48; on political parties, 268n. 127; on Revolutionary state legislatures, 61
Schneckloth v. Bustamonte, 143
school desegregation, 196–200
Schroedel, Jean Reith, on abortion, 156–57, 160
Schuck, Peter, on *Roe v. Wade*, 263n. 52
Schwartz, Herman, on Clinton judges, 194
Sedition Act, 171–72, 267n. 109
Sellers, Charles, on judicial power in 19th-century America, 98
Shapiro, Robert, and state court protection of rights, 122–23, 124
Shapiro v. Thompson, 257n. 109
Shea, Dennis, on impeachment of federal judges, 192
Skowronek, Stephen, on power of courts in 19th-century America, 88, 95
Slaughterhouse Cases, 100–104, 247n. 90
Smith, Bradley: on *Buckley*, 270n. 129; on early American politics, 168–69
Solzhenitsyn, Alexander, on rights, 117–18
Souter, David: conservative criticisms of, 19, 26; nomination to Supreme Court, 162
Sowell, Thomas, attacks on judiciary, 24, 26
Starr, Kenneth, on libel, 131
statutory interpretation: of administrative agency charter statutes, 182–86; of civil rights legislation, 186–90; framers' view of, 76–77
Stevens, John Paul, on judicial elections, 212
Stimson, Shannon, on judicial independence, 62–63
Stith, Kate, and Cabranes, Jose, on Federal Sentencing Guidelines, 209–10
Strauss, David, on First Amendment, 45
Strickland v. Washington, 146–47
Sunstein, Cass: on Civil Rights Act of 1964, 187–88; on Rehnquist Court, 28–29; on rights revolution, 45, 186
Swann v. Charlotte-Mecklenburg Bd. of Ed., 196

Talbot, Margaret, on RU-486, 157

Tenth Amendment, 240n. 99

Terry v. Ohio, 144

Thirteenth Amendment, 98–99, 191, 246n. 71

Thomas, Clarence: on campaign finance reform, 171–75; on Fourteenth Amendment, 38–39, 40, 42, 48; nomination to Supreme Court, 162; on right of privacy, 162; on rights of criminal defendants, 141

Tocqueville, Alexis de: on judicial power in America, 8–9, 87; on judicial elections, 216

Tomlins, Christopher, on codification movement, 97

Tribe, Laurence: on abortion, 158, 159, 262n. 33; purported influence upon judiciary, 27, 227n. 72; on Scalia, 47; on warmaking powers, 208

Troy, Gil, on early American politics, 168

Troxel v. Granville, 39–42, 233nn. 153–54

Truax v. Corrigan, 113

Turley, Jonathan, on *Miranda* rights, 143–44

Tushnet, Mark: attack on judicial power, 11–13; on Bork, 235n. 196; on First Amendment, 133

Uelmen, Gerald, on state judges, 216

United Steel Workers of America v. Weber, 188

Varadarajan, Tunku, attacks on judicial power, 4, 178

Veronia School Dist. 47J v. Acton, 43

Vile, M. J. C., on Revolutionary state constitutions, 54, 61

War Powers Act, 279n. 158

Wards Cove Packing Co. v. Antonio, overturned by Civil Rights Act of 1991, 189

warmaking powers. *See* foreign affairs

Warren Court, 125, 148–49, 224n. 15; conservative criticisms of, 13–15, 18–19, 21, 33; liberal criticisms of, 11–13, 14–15

Washington Legal Foundation: on Clean Air Act, 185; legal victories of, 226n. 67

Webster v. Reproductive Health Services, 162

Weeks (U.S. v.), 256n. 90

welfare, 135, 137–38

Wesberry v. Sanders. See redistricting cases

White, G. Edward: on Fourteenth Amendment, 109; on Rehnquist Court, 18; on Warren Court, 119

Whittington, Keith, on originalism, 47

Will, George F.: attacks on judiciary, 3, 7, 41–42, 44; on *Brown*, 276n. 127; on campaign finance reform, 175

Williams v. Mississippi, 107

Williams v. Taylor, 147–48

Willis, Ellen, on *Roe v. Wade*, 264n. 54

Wilson, James: on bills of rights, 78; on impeachment of judges, 82; on judicial independence, 62, 64; on judicial review, 66–67; on need to restrain legislatures, 57, 237n. 30; on warmaking powers, 208

Wood, Gordon, 51; on need to restrain majorities, 218; on republicanism, 169–70, 267n. 104; on Revolutionary state constitutions, 54–55, 59–60

Young, Robert, on state judges, 115–16

Zeppos, Nicholas, on administrative agencies, 180

About the Author

Mark Kozlowski is Associate Counsel at the Brennan Center for Justice at the New York University School of Law. He holds a doctorate in political science from Columbia University and is a graduate of Harvard Law School.